**Advances
in COMPUTERS
VOLUME 15**

Contributors to This Volume

Alan W. Biermann
Donald Bitzer
David J. Kuck
Larry H. Reeker
John R. Rice

Advances in
COMPUTERS

EDITED BY

MORRIS RUBINOFF

Moore School of Electrical Engineering
University of Pennsylvania
and
Pennsylvania Research Associates, Inc.
Philadelphia, Pennsylvania

AND

MARSHALL C. YOVITS

Department of Computer and Information
   Science
Ohio State University
Columbus, Ohio

VOLUME 15

ACADEMIC PRESS ∎ New York ∎ San Francisco ∎ London—1976
A Subsidiary of Harcourt Brace Jovanovich, Publishers

COPYRIGHT © 1976, BY ACADEMIC PRESS, INC.
ALL RIGHTS RESERVED.
NO PART OF THIS PUBLICATION MAY BE REPRODUCED OR
TRANSMITTED IN ANY FORM OR BY ANY MEANS, ELECTRONIC
OR MECHANICAL, INCLUDING PHOTOCOPY, RECORDING, OR ANY
INFORMATION STORAGE AND RETRIEVAL SYSTEM, WITHOUT
PERMISSION IN WRITING FROM THE PUBLISHER.

ACADEMIC PRESS, INC.
111 Fifth Avenue, New York, New York 10003

United Kingdom Edition published by
ACADEMIC PRESS, INC. (LONDON) LTD.
24/28 Oval Road, London NW1

LIBRARY OF CONGRESS CATALOG CARD NUMBER: 59-15761

ISBN 0-12-012115-8

PRINTED IN THE UNITED STATES OF AMERICA

Contents

CONTRIBUTORS ix
PREFACE xi

Approaches to Automatic Programming

Alan W. Biermann

1. Introduction 1
2. Extensions to Traditional Automatic Programming Methods . 3
3. Program Synthesis from Examples 16
4. Synthesis from Formal Input–Output Specifications . . . 29
5. Translation of Natural Language Commands 40
6. Heuristic Knowledge-Based Algorithm Synthesis . . . 46
7. Comments 58
   References 59

The Algorithm Selection Problem

John R. Rice

1. Introduction 65
2. Abstract Models 67
3. Concrete Application—The Selection of Quadrature Algorithms . 77
4. Concrete Application—The Selection of Operating System Schedulers 82
5. Discussion of the Two Concrete Applications 90
6. Approximation Theory Machinery 91
   References 117

Parallel Processing of Ordinary Programs

David J. Kuck

1. Introduction 119
2. Theoretical Fundamentals 127
3. Program Analysis 141
4. Machine Considerations 158
5. Conclusions 174
   References 176

The Computational Study of Language Acquisition

Larry H. Reeker

1. The Problem. 181
2. Modeling Language Acquisition 191
3. The Problem-Solving Theory 196
4. Conclusion 223
5. Appendix: Grammar Representation 224
   References 235

The Wide World of Computer-Based Education

Donald Bitzer

1. Introduction 239
2. The PLATO System 243
3. System Configuration 254
4. Teaching Strategies 256
5. Computational Applications 266
6. A Word about TUTOR 269
7. Evaluation 272

8. Cost of Services	276
9. Conclusion	281
References	281

AUTHOR INDEX	285
SUBJECT INDEX	289
CONTENTS OF PREVIOUS VOLUMES	297

Contributors to Volume 15

Numbers in parentheses indicate the pages on which the authors' contributions begin.

ALAN W. BIERMANN, *Department of Computer Science, Duke University, Durham, North Carolina* (1)

DONALD BITZER, *Computer-Based Education Research Laboratory, University of Illinois at Urbana-Champaign, Urbana, Illinois* (239)

DAVID J. KUCK, *Department of Computer Science, University of Illinois at Urbana-Champaign, Urbana, Illinois* (119)

LARRY H. REEKER, *Department of Computer Science, University of Arizona, Tucson, Arizona* (181)

JOHN R. RICE, *Department of Computer Science, Purdue University, West Lafayette, Indiana* (65)

Preface

Volume 15 of *Advances in Computers* treats a number of important and significant areas in computer science of particular current interest. I am pleased that we have been able to obtain contributions for this volume from highly regarded authors with established reputations in their fields. The current volume of these advances, I believe, accurately reflects the present growth of computer science and its applications.

In his article on automatic programming, Alan Biermann of Duke University treats an important current topic which should have considerable practical application. He indicates that automatic programming is the natural evolution of what began as hand coding in machine language and which led to assembly language programming and then to the development of high level languages. He covers many of the various approaches to automatic programming, some of which he indicates seem to have much promise for the future. He points out that this field, however, is still in its very early stages of development. Biermann suggests that research in automatic programming involves the relationship between human languages and machine languages and the process of translating between the two. He states that the main task in automatic programming is the discovery of the nature of these languages and the implementation required to perform the translation between them.

The chapter by John Rice of Purdue University on algorithm selection is concerned with the problem of selecting an effective or even a good algorithm for use in a wide variety of situations. He is concerned with the common features of the selection process, and the purpose of his chapter is to formulate models appropriate for selecting good algorithms. He points out that these models will clarify the consideration of the selection problem and shows that some approaches used in the past have been based on incorrect and naïve assumptions. As part of this chapter, Rice lists 15 specific open problems and questions yet to be answered before algorithms can be selected. This chapter was based on a presentation by Professor Rice given as the George E. Forsythe Memorial Lecture at the Computer Science Conference in Washington, D.C., in February 1975.

David Kuck of the University of Illinois discusses parallel processing. He considers the problem of integrating users' problems into the design procedure. He looks first at the programs users run with the primary design goal being the fast execution of programs. He concludes that parallelism in machine organization has been widely exploited but that compilers for parallel machines have been difficult to write. He gives two important reasons for this: it has been difficult to discover operations that can be executed simultaneously, and the organization of these machines has made it difficult to implement parallel operations efficiently. In his chapter, he discusses both of these problems and possible solutions to them.

The chapter on "The Computational Study of Language Acquisition" by Larry Reeker of the University of Arizona addresses itself to the general problem of how to supply to a computer program a set of utterances in some language and then have the program produce as output a grammar that can generate the remainder of the language as well as the initial utterances themselves. The language he discusses specifically is English. Reeker hopes that his program also models the way that children acquire language. He explores a number of the different approaches to the language acquisition problem and discusses the success of each. He points out that one of the major problems of computational linguistics is the task of language simulation. He is also concerned about the general learning problem as well. Reeker points out that learning a natural language is a major accomplishment of humans, and understanding how this learning develops provides an important area of research with many potential applications.

The final chapter in the volume has to do with one of the most important applications of computers, namely their use in education. Donald Bitzer, head of the Computer-Based Research Laboratory at the University of Illinois, points out that over $60 billion are spent in the United States each year on education with little significant increase in its productivity over the years. Bitzer points out that the use of a digital computer for delivering education could be the first major innovation in education since the development of the printing press. He discusses a number of the projects that have been undertaken in the field of computer-assisted instruction and then goes on to describe in detail the University of Illinois PLATO system which represents the advanced state of the art. It also represents the longest continuous work in the field. Bitzer points out that future potential uses of computer-based education are almost unlimited and indicates that plans are already underway to develop a large educational system which may have as many as a million terminals by the early 1980s. He believes that such widescale computer services will probably touch the lives of nearly all people, many of whom will have to redefine their roles in the light of new technology.

PREFACE

I wish to thank the contributors to this volume, who have given extensively of their time and energy to make this a significant and important publication in the field of computer and information science. Editing this volume has been a most rewarding experience.

Marshall C. Yovits

Approaches to Automatic Programming

ALAN W. BIERMANN

Department of Computer Science
Duke University
Durham, North Carolina

1. Introduction 1
2. Extensions to Traditional Automatic Programming Methods . . . 3
   2.1 Introduction 3
   2.2 Higher Level Languages 4
   2.3 Special Purpose Program Generators 10
   2.4 Summary 15
3. Program Synthesis from Examples 16
   3.1 Introduction 16
   3.2 The Method 18
   3.3 Program Synthesis from Example Computations 20
   3.4 Features of an Autoprogrammer 24
   3.5 Synthesis of LISP Programs 25
   3.6 Discussion 29
4. Synthesis from Formal Input–Output Specifications 29
   4.1 Introduction 29
   4.2 Synthesizing Branching and Looping Structures 31
   4.3 Problem Reduction Methods 37
   4.4 Discussion 40
5. Translation of Natural Language Commands 40
   5.1 Introduction 40
   5.2 Syntactic Analysis 41
   5.3 Generating PLANNER Code 42
   5.4 Discussion 46
6. Heuristic Knowledge-Based Algorithm Synthesis 46
   6.1 Introduction 46
   6.2 The Major Phases of Processing 48
   6.3 Actors, Beings, Frames, and Others 50
   6.4 On the Development of Knowledge about Knowledge . . . 53
   6.5 Summary 57
7. Comments 58
   References 59

1. Introduction

Ever since the early days of electronic computers, man has been using his ingenuity to save himself from the chores of programming. Hand coding in machine language gave way to assembly language programming, which was replaced for most users by compiled languages. Today the evolution continues as many higher level languages come into existence and as a number of research efforts move toward more exotic systems. This chapter surveys recent developments in the broad area of computer science known as "automatic programming."

The order of coverage of the material is from the most conservative approaches to the most futuristic. Section 2 discusses extensions to traditional automatic programming methods, higher level languages, and special purpose languages. Sections 3–6 describe the major current efforts to break away from the more traditional approaches: program synthesis from examples, synthesis from formal input–output specifications, synthesis by translation of natural language, and heuristic synthesis from a knowledge base. All of these approaches are active new areas of research, which hold much promise for the future but are still in the very early stages of development.

The coverage of each of the approaches is by example. Rather than to include a superficial mention of large numbers of research contributions, it was decided to include a more detailed discussion of a few representative systems of each type. Many examples are worked out to expose the mechanisms that enable each approach to work. In some cases, details have been omitted or even modified for the sake of clarity and understandability in the discussion. The reader is always encouraged to return to the original sources for more complete and precise descriptions. If, on the other hand, the reader finds too many details included about a particular system, he should skip to the next discussion, since the sequential sections do not build on one another and can be read independently. There are some other overview papers on automatic programming that might be of interest, for example, Balzer (1972, 1973), Feldman (1972a), Leavenworth and Sammet (1974), and Perlis (1972).

We begin our discussions at the bottom of the hierarchy with machine language. The earliest coding had to be in terms of numerical operation codes and absolute addresses, and programmers had complete control over almost every atomic operation within the machine. Programmers, however, were burdened with too much control, many operation codes to remember, hand calculation of addresses, and much hand bookkeeping. The emphasis from the beginning was to restyle the language in terms that would be more natural for humans to use, to automate the mundane portions of the task, and to improve the ability of the programmer to write correct code. The goals that motivate current work in automatic programming are the same as those which produced the early assembly languages. Figure 1 shows an IBM/370 machine language program for adding a col-

```
41400004              LA   4,4
1B55                  SR   5,5
1B66                  SR   6,6
5870C020              L    7,N
5A65C028         LAB  A    6,A(5)
1A54                  AR   5,4
4670C00C              BCT  7,LAB
5060C024              ST   6,SUM

     (a)                  (b)
```

FIG. 1. Adding a column of numbers. (a) IBM/370 machine language. (b) IBM assembly language.

umn of integers and its assembly language equivalent. Hexadecimal coding has been replaced in the assembly language version by symbolic addresses and mnemonic operation codes for a huge net improvement in readability.

The next major step, of course, was to high level languages that could be compiled or interpreted, and Fig. 2 shows the same example written in such a language. In fact, this particular example of adding a column of numbers will be continued throughout this chapter to show how each approach can be used for its synthesis. Compilers and interpreters have helped tremendously to give the user's input to the machine some resemblance to languages that humans use anyway: arithmetic expressions, boolean expressions, and a few words from natural language. The programmer was taken one step farther from the machine, with consequent advantages in readability, debugability, and ease of use. Associated with this improvement in convenience was a loss in efficiency in the object code, which system designers up to the present day have been working to remedy. The long history of developments in programming languages has led to an impressive array of high level languages and sets the stage for the research to be discussed in this chapter.

2. Extensions to Traditional Automatic Programming Methods

2.1 Introduction

A little study of typical programs using traditional compiled languages shows that the same patterns seem to appear again and again in the code.

```
SUM=0;
do I=1 to N;
   SUM=SUM + A(I);
end;
```

FIG. 2. Adding a column of numbers with a compiled language.

The development of higher level languages has largely been involved with discovering these patterns and designing constructs that implement them automatically. In the following section, we will examine three kinds of patterns and languages that save the user from having to code them by hand. The three chosen examples will be:

(1) DO-loops (or FOR-loops) and their implicit implementation in APL,

(2) searching with automatic backtracking and its inclusion in PLANNER, and

(3) the representation and handling of certain mathematical entities such as sets and relations in some higher level languages.

The examples given here were chosen very arbitrarily, and a whole world of other important languages and features awaits the interested reader. Thus one might study APL (Iverson, 1962), CONNIVER (Sussman and McDermott, 1972), PLANNER (Sussman et al., 1971), POPCORN (Hardy, 1973), QA4 (Rulifson et al., 1972), SAIL (Feldman et al., 1972), SETL (Schwartz, 1974), VERS2 (Earley, 1974), and others (Leavenworth and Sammet, 1974; Bobrow and Raphael, 1974).

Section 2.3 examines some special purpose program generators. Such systems have been developed in some practical situations when it was desired to produce a number of programs with strong resemblances to each other. The program synthesizer is capable of generating any of a whole class of similar programs, and the user needs only to input special information related to his particular application. On the basis of this input, the system outputs reasonably standard code adapted appropriately for the user's task. Examples of such systems are compiler–compilers or certain program generators for industrial applications such as scheduling, inventory management, or payroll. This section will discuss some of these extensions to traditional automatic programming methods.

2.2 Higher Level Languages

One of the most common patterns in standard programming languages is the DO-loop or FOR-loop and a reasonable goal for a language designer might be to collapse those several lines of code into just one or two symbols. The language APL by Iverson (1962) gives us a superb example of just how well this can be done. For example, the program of Fig. 1 that adds the column A can be written in APL as simply $+/A$. If A were a two-dimensional array, we could add the columns (along dimension 1) with the code $+/[1]A$ or the rows (along dimension 2) with the code $+/[2]A$. Adding the scalar 2 to every element of array A is done with the code

2+A, and adding two arrays A and B of identical dimensions element by element is done with A+B.

We will examine several APL constructs and then show how they can be combined into a program. Consider the predicate = operating on two scalars, U=V. If U equals V, then U=V evaluates to 1; otherwise it evaluates to 0. If the rightmost argument is an array A, then U=A yields an array of ones and zeros indicating which elements of A equal U. Thus if A=(4 2 1 2 3), then 2=A yields (0 1 0 1 0).

The compression operator / allows one to select out a sequence of elements from an array. For example, (0 1 1 0 1)/A for the above A yields (2 1 3). We can represent the linear array of length N with entries 1, 2, 3, ..., N with the notation ⍳N. That is ⍳N=(1 2 3 ... N). Thus (0 1 1 0 1)/⍳5 yields (2 3 5).

We can combine every element of a linear array with every element of another linear array using outer product. For example, (4 7 2)∘.+A yields

$$\begin{matrix} 8 & 6 & 5 & 6 & 7 \\ 11 & 9 & 8 & 9 & 10 \\ 6 & 4 & 3 & 4 & 5 \end{matrix}$$

where the i,jth entry in the result is obtained by adding the ith element of the first argument to the jth element of the second argument. The | operator yields the remainder of the second argument after division by the first; thus 3 | 7 yields 1 and 3 | 8 yields 2. The analogous outer product ∘.| similarly combines every element of the first argument with every element of the second. Thus (⍳5)∘.|⍳5 yields

$$\begin{matrix} 0 & 0 & 0 & 0 & 0 \\ 1 & 0 & 1 & 0 & 1 \\ 1 & 2 & 0 & 1 & 2 \\ 1 & 2 & 3 & 0 & 1 \\ 1 & 2 & 3 & 4 & 0 \end{matrix}$$

This matrix is useful in computing prime numbers since a positive integer is prime if and only if it is divisible by itself and 1. That is, i is prime if and only if the ith column in the matrix has exactly two zeros.

Using this insight, a program for generating prime numbers can be written as given in Abrams (1970, p. 176):

PRIMES N   (2=+/[1]0=(⍳N)∘.|⍳N)/⍳N

The code (⍳N)∘.|⍳N generates the matrix that has two zeros in the ith column if i is prime. The code 0= changes all zeros to 1 and everything else to 0 in that matrix. +/[1] adds the columns in that matrix to produce a linear array that gives the number of zeros in each column of the original matrix. Then 2= converts each 2 to 1 and leaves everything else zero. The resulting linear array is applied with the compression operator to actually pick out the primes, (0 1 1 0 1 ...)/(1 2 3 4 5 ...). Thus PRIMES 12 yields (2 3 5 7 11).

This brief excursion gives some of the flavor of the APL language. The ubiquitous DO-loops of traditional languages are gone and are replaced by concise operators. If the operations available have some resemblance to the user's concept of his task, rather elegant, simple, and reliable programs can be constructed. The reader should consult an APL manual (for example, Wiedmann, 1974) to see how many other common mathematical operators have been concisely represented. The use of a higher level language typically produces some inefficiencies in both space and CPU time but the savings in human effort is often worth the expense. APL has been especially popular because it has been implemented in a high quality interactive programming system.

Another higher level language worth discussing is PLANNER, as described in Sussman *et al.* (1971). A typical program in an artificial intelligence environment will do considerable searching with backtracking whenever the search fails. It is not surprising, therefore, that artificial intelligence researchers have developed languages with a built-in search and backtrack mechanism. PLANNER is such a language and a few of its constructs will be examined here.

We will study primarily the THGOAL statement, which asks the system to try to prove an assertion. The system may do this by examining the data base and determining whether the assertion is already true or by proving the assertion using an assemblage of available facts and theorems. THGOAL either succeeds and returns the proven assertion or it fails and backup is initiated. An example program segment follows, which describes a typical artificial intelligence task: Find a red pyramid that is supported by a green block:

(1) (THGOAL (#IS $?X1 #PYRAMID))
(2) (THGOAL (#COLOR $?X1 $RED))
(3) (THGOAL (#IS $?X2 #BLOCK))
(4) (THGOAL (#COLOR $?X2 #GREEN))
(5) (THGOAL (#SUPPORT $?X2 $?X1))

Assume this program is executed with the following data base:

(#IS :B1 #BLOCK)
(#IS :B2 #BLOCK)

(#IS :B3 #PYRAMID)
(#IS :B4 #PYRAMID)
(#COLOR :B1 #GREEN)
(#COLOR :B2 #GREEN)
(#COLOR :B3 #GREEN)
(#COLOR :B4 #RED)
(#SUPPORT :B2 :B4)

This data base indicates that there is a block called :B1 that is green, a block called :B2 that is also green, and so forth. Then the system begins executing statement (1) by looking for a $?X1 such that (#IS $?X1 #PYRAMID) is in the data base. It succeeds with $?X1 = :B3 and so proceeds to statement (2). Now that $?X1 is bound, statement (2) will search for the pattern (#COLOR :B3 #RED) but will fail. At this point, the PLANNER automatic backup feature works and statement (1) is executed again. However, statement (1) is executed with the knowledge that $?X1 = :B3 has failed, and so some new instantiation of $?X1 is tried. This time $?X1 = :B4 is tried, and when control passes to (2) it succeeds, allowing control to pass to (3). The computation proceeds as follows, with success being finally achieved with $?X1 = :B4 and $?X2 = :B2:

Statement number	Event
(1)	$?X1←:B3
(2)	fail
(1)	$?X1←:B4
(2)	succeed
(3)	$?X2←:B1
(4)	succeed
(5)	fail
(3)	$?X2←:B2
(4)	succeed
(5)	succeed

The point is that a great deal of computation is going on and yet the programmer did not have to trouble himself with the details. Since the PLANNER mechanism embodies the appropriate kind of processing capability, the user can concentrate his attentions on higher level, more important problems.

THGOAL may not always find the result in the data base as indicated above and may be required to deduce the assertion from known theorems that are in the data base. Also, THGOAL may not have to do a blind search as indicated and can be told specifically which theorems to try. For example, the code (THGOAL (#SUPPORT $?X1 $?X2) (THUSE T1 T2

T3)) means "attempt to prove (#SUPPORT $?X1 $?X2) using theorems T1, T2, and T3." The PLANNER language, of course, includes many other features such as branching and looping constructs, but none of them need to be considered further here.

Mathematicians prefer to think in terms of sets, relations, n-tuples, sequences, and other abstract structures that are not typically available on computers, and a number of efforts by Adam (1975), Earley (1974), Feldman and Rovner (1969), Morris (1973), Rulifson et al. (1972), Schwartz (1974), and others have been directed toward incorporating them into higher level languages. Thus one might be interested in representing a set of objects S and then referring, perhaps, to the set of objects in S that satisfy property P : $\{X \in S \mid P(X)\}$. One might wish to assign the set a name $T \leftarrow \{X \in S \mid P(X)\}$, do manipulations on sets $S \cup T$, $S - T$, $S \cap T$, ..., build predicates with sets that can be used in conditional statements $Y \in T$ (is Y in T?), $\exists Y \in T \mid P(Y)$ [is there a $Y \in T$ such that $P(Y)$?], etc., or index through a set DO FOR EACH $Y \in T$.... Such languages can have an ability to represent finite sequences [, , ..., ,] or n-tuples $\langle , , ..., \rangle$ of objects. Often a pattern-matching facility is part of such a language, so that the user can perhaps test for a match of sequence V with another sequence, say an arbitrary sequence ARB1, followed by a given sequence X, followed by another arbitrary one ARB2: IF V MATCH [ARB1,X,ARB2] THEN .... Or one might index through each possible such match: DO FOR EACH ARB1,ARB2|V MATCH [ARB1,X,ARB2]....

Using these constructs, it is easy to write programs that otherwise might require considerable effort. The following example does not follow the syntax of any specific language, but gives the flavor of several of them. Suppose that strings of symbols in a formal language are represented as sequences and a grammatical production X→Y in the language is represented as a 2-tuple $\langle X,Y \rangle$, where X and Y are sequences. Then a program that generates the set of all successors of string V using grammatical rule X→Y is

    gen(V, $\langle X,Y \rangle$);
    begin;
    S←{ };
    do for each ARB1,ARB2|V match [ARB1,X,ARB2];
        S←S ∪ [ARB1,Y,ARB2];
        end;
    return S;
    end;.

Then if a grammar G is represented as a set of productions and if a routine

TERMINAL is written to check whether a string is terminal or not, the following program will print out all terminal strings that can be generated in N steps or less by G starting with string W:

```
enum(G,N,W);
begin;
  S←{W};
  do I = 1 to N;
    do for each V ∈ S;
      do for each R ∈ G;
        S←S U gen(V,R);
      end;
    end;
  end;
  print {V ∈ S | TERMINAL(V)};
end;.¹
```

Efficient compilation of such code can be extremely difficult because the constructs of the language differ so greatly from the hardware capabilities of the machine. For example, sets can be represented as linear linked lists, binary trees, bit strings, hash tables, fixed length arrays, and others, and the choice of data structure greatly affects the efficiency of the program. A test for membership in a set of size N requires about one or two operations for a hash table representation or about log N operations for a binary tree. Set intersection or union can be done in one operation using a bit string representation on many machines, while it can require N or more operations using some of the other representations. Ordinarily these decisions concerning representation would be made by the programmer, who knows the nature of his data and how they should be ordered and accessed. The higher level language compiler must either make arbitrary decisions at the risk of terrible performance or gather information about the usage of each data structure and attempt to make optimum decisions. Low (1974) and Schwartz (1974) discuss methods for making such choices on the basis of an automatic analysis of the source program and from information provided by the user. Low (1974) has written a compiler for a subset of SAIL (Feldman *et al.*, 1972) that also makes use of statement execution counts obtained by running the program.

In summary, higher level languages take the user one step farther away from the machine, enabling him to write programs more quickly, more con-

---

[1] This routine assumes that on entry to the second "do" a copy of S is saved for V to index through. Thus modifications of S within the loop will not affect the sequence of values taken on by V.

cisely, and more reliably. Higher level languages will probably be successful to the extent that they embody the structure and processing that fit the user's problems and the user's concept of his problems. These languages usually are considerably less computationally efficient than more traditional languages because their processors are not able to utilize completely special domain-dependent information in the way that a human coder could.

2.3 Special Purpose Program Generators

If a large number of fairly similar programs are to be written, it is sometimes possible to segment the synthesis task into two parts, routine portions that are common to all programs in the class and task-dependent portions that must be different for each new program. A special purpose program generator is a program that automatically executes the more routine portions of the program synthesis task and enables the user conveniently to input the task-dependent information so that the desired program can be created.

Consider, for example, the tasks of writing a compiler for some kind of a manipulative machine and writing one for standard numerical computation. In the first case, a typical source statement might be

$$\text{move right 2 feet}$$

which might translate to

```
L       R,XPOS
A       R,=24
ST      R,XPOS
MOVETO  XPOS,YPOS,ZPOS.
```

That is, the x coordinate is to be loaded into register R, incremented by 24, stored again, and the manipulative device is to move to the new position. In the case of a numerical computation, a typical source statement might be

$$A = B + C + D$$

which might translate to

```
L    R,B
A    R,C
A    R,D
ST   R,A
```

The authors of these two compilers might feel that they are doing uniquely different tasks, and yet as has been known for many years (Feldman and

Syntactic rules	Semantic rules
S→ACT DES	c(S) = c(DES)c(ACT)
DES→DIR DIST	$c(DES) = \begin{cases} L & R, w(DIR) \\ y(DIR) & R, = v(DIST) \\ ST & R, w(DIR) \end{cases}$
DIST→NUM UNIT	v(DIST) = v(NUM)*v(UNIT)
ACT→move	c(ACT) = MOVETO XPOS,YPOS,ZPOS
DIR→right	y(DIR) = A
	w(DIR) = XPOS
NUM→i i = nonnegative integer	v(NUM) = i
UNIT→feet	v(UNIT) = 12

Semantic function definitions

c yields a segment of generated code
v yields a value (amount of movement)
w yields the direction of movement (XPOS, YPOS, or ZPOS)
y yields A or S, add or subtract

FIG. 3. A partial grammar for a manipulative language.

Gries, 1968; Gries, 1971; Knuth, 1968; McKeeman *et al.*, 1970), the two tasks are expressible in similar terms. Specifically, each source language may be expressible in terms of a formal grammar with semantics. Then if a program (compiler–compiler) could exist that would translate such a formal grammar into a compiler, both of the desired compilers could be generated automatically from their respective grammars.

A formal grammar is given in Fig. 3 for the manipulative machine example. Associated with each syntactic rule on the left is a set of semantic rules that assign values to attributes (Knuth, 1968). The meaning of any statement in the source language is found by finding its parse using the syntactic rules and then applying the associated semantic functions. The meaning of the statement is the semantic valuation given to the start symbol S after all semantic functions have been evaluated. Figure 4 shows a complete parse of the given statement "move right 2 feet" with all semantic functions evaluated. Similarly one can produce a partial grammar for numerical computations as shown in Fig. 5.

Thus, a translator from such grammars into compilers is a good example of a special purpose program generator. The grammar serves as a high level language that the user can employ to define the desired program. The compiler–compiler attends to the many programming details that the user would prefer to ignore. Ideally, the user might actually know nothing about compiler writing and still be able to produce perfectly acceptable compilers with the system.

More recently there have been some efforts to produce automatic pro-

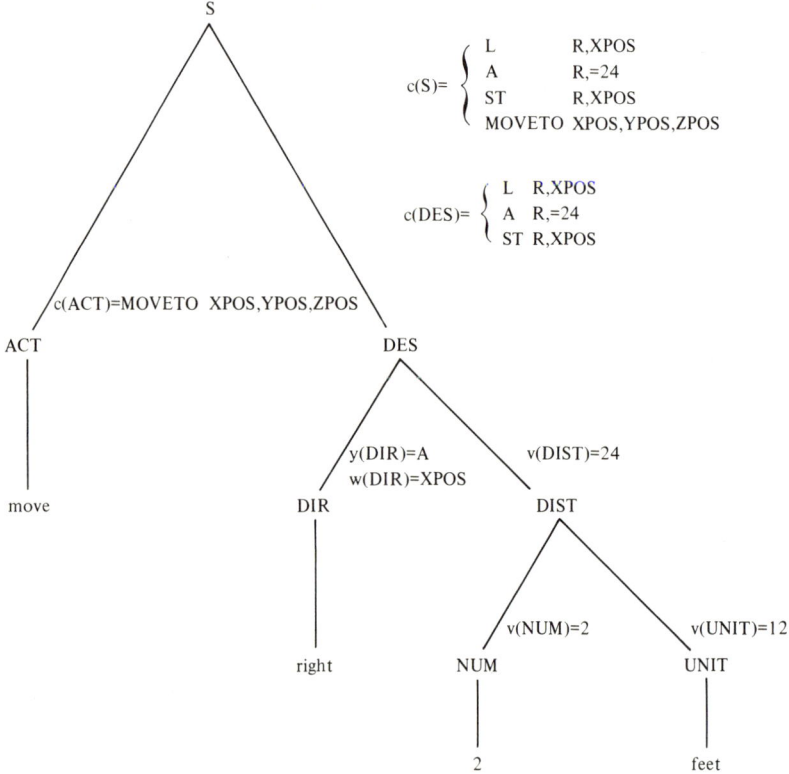

FIG. 4. Parse of the statement "move right 2 feet."

gram generators for business applications. These efforts are aimed at giving the businessman with no traditional programming expertise an ability to generate useful programs while working with familiar terms. The Business Definition Language (BDL) system being developed at IBM (Goldberg, 1975a; Hammer et al., 1974) and PROTOSYSTEM I (Martin et al., 1974) at MIT are examples of such systems.

The BDL system models a business as a set of information processing units that are connected by communications paths. The processing units convert incoming information to the appropriate output form and then send it on to other processing units. The communication paths leading into a processing unit are queues that collect information waiting to be processed. Any one processor does nothing until appropriate incoming information appears, at which time it immediately begins its computational task without external prompting.

$S \to L = P$ $\quad\quad\quad\quad c(S) = \begin{cases} c(P) \\ ST \quad R, u(L) \end{cases}$

$P_1 \to P_2 + E$ $\quad\quad\quad c(P_1) = \begin{cases} c(P_2) \\ A \quad R, u(E) \end{cases}$

$E \to$ (identifier) $\quad\quad u(E) =$ (identifier)
$P \to$ (identifier) $\quad\quad c(P) = L \quad R,$ (identifier)
$L \to$ (identifier) $\quad\quad u(L) =$ (identifier)

FIG. 5. A partial grammar for numerical computations. P_1 and P_2 denote separate occurrences of variable P.

The user of the BDL system creates the flow chart at an interactive graphics display terminal. An example of such a flow chart appears in Fig. 6. It should be emphasized that such diagrams are not simply descriptive of the program being created; they *are* the program or at least they are part of it. Furthermore, any individual processing center may itself be described in terms of another such flow chart, so that a whole hierarchy of levels of processing can be modeled.

At the lowest level of the flow chart hierarchy, each output stream must be specified in terms of available input information. This is done with a tabular language in which the user specifies the fields that are to appear on the output file and what the contents of those fields are to be. A greatly simplified example of such a table appears in Fig. 7, where the invoice output is being specified in terms of the available inputs. The tabular specification facilities of BDL actually differ considerably from the example

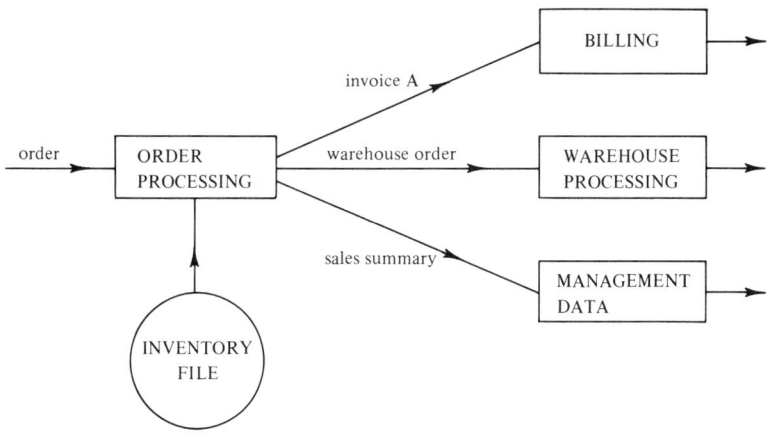

FIG. 6. A flow chart specification of order proceessing.

FIELD	SOURCE
INVOICE	
CUSTOMER NAME	ORDER: CUSTOMER NAME
CUSTOMER ADDR	ORDER: CUSTOMER ADDR
ITEM GROUP	
ITEM QUANTITY	ORDER: ITEM QUANTITY
ITEM NAME	ORDER: ITEM NAME
ITEM NUMBER	ORDER: ITEM NUMBER
ITEM UNIT COST	INVENTORY FILE (ITEM NAME,NUMBER): COST
ITEM TOTAL COST	ITEM QUANTITY * ITEM UNIT COST
TOTAL	SUM (ITEM TOTAL COST)

FIG. 7. A tabular specification of the invoice output A from ORDER PROCESSING.

shown here, but the nature of the approach should be clear. The invoice is to include the customer name and address, which are obtained from the order. Also it is to contain a "group" of entries, one for each ordered item, giving each item quantity, name, number, and cost. Notice that each item unit cost is taken from the INVENTORY FILE and the item total cost is obtained by multiplying together two other fields, ITEM QUANTITY and ITEM UNIT COST. The TOTAL field is filled in with the sum of all item total costs.

The above two classes of programming, flow charts and tabular output specifications, are enough to define the computation to be done. Notice that this is truly a higher level language in that all decisions concerning the representation of data and the sequencing of events are made by the system without the knowledge or concern of the user. The user presumably can be a businessman without programming knowledge, and the system is designed to enable him to specify his program in a convenient form using terminology that is familiar to him. BDL clearly has an extremely specialized form and would not be a pleasant language to use for general scientific computing. However, if its constructs successfully model the user's view of his problem domain, it should be a superbly convenient language to use.

The BDL language is a *data flow* type of language, in that the user's specifications are in terms of the data and their movement through a series of processes. This is in contrast to most traditional languages, which are formulated in terms of *control flow* and the sequences of operations that are to be performed. One of the reasons for moving toward the data flow model comes from a series of interesting psychological experiments recently done at IBM (Goldberg, 1975b). In these experiments, persons without programming experience were asked to specify methods for completing certain tasks using whatever instructions seemed appropriate. Goldberg (1975b) writes:

> There were several interesting results of this study. First, in almost all cases, where there was a choice between element-by-element processing and the processing of entire aggregates, the latter was chosen. Second, transfer of control was largely left unspecified. Another characteristic was the disregard for exceptional conditions, such as unused data. Thus one would see sets of instructions of the following sort:
>
> (1) See if the person is over 50;
> (2) Write his name down on a list.
>
> This little example illustrates another characteristic of these natural language protocols, namely the preference for qualified rather than conditional statements. Thus one would more likely see
> "Put the red things in the box."
> than
> "If the thing is red, put it in the box."
> Finally, it goes without saying that in the body of the protocol there were no references to declarations, datatypes, or other programming notions (p. 3).

These results clearly make traditional language constructs appear inappropriate for inexperienced programmers and have led to the data flow concept in programming. Goldberg describes these experiments in more detail and indicates how they affected the design of BDL.

The BDL effort is only a part of a larger program at IBM, which emphasizes the study of every aspect of automatic programming from psychological studies to the optimization of object code. Although no overview of this work exists, additional information can be found in the abovementioned papers as well as Mikelsons (1975) and Howe et al. (1975).

2.4 Summary

Extensions to traditional automatic programming methods have attempted to automate the coding process further. Repetitious coding tasks can be eliminated by implementing languages with special operators and form designed for particular types of computation. These higher level languages are meant to embody constructs that are adapted for particular applications and that are natural for conceptualizations in the problem domain. Such languages usually allow the programs to be quite concise, but they typically result in computational inefficiency (measured in CPU time and memory space) even though their designers may invest considerable effort into making them efficient.

Such languages enable the user to think, code, and debug at a higher level, leaving the system to handle all lower level implementation decisions.

They may improve the ability of the user to produce correct and reliable programs because many of the causes of errors, low level coding mistakes, can be avoided by a (presumably debugged) automatic system. Such languages are designed to reduce greatly the amount of human effort required to obtain a correct and executable program.

3. Program Synthesis from Examples

3.1 Introduction

Many a programmer has wished for a system that would read in a few examples of the desired program behavior and automatically create that program. Thus, such a system might be given the input–output pairs (1, 2), (2, 3), (3, 5), (4, 7), (5, 11) and be expected to print out a program that reads an integer i and prints the ith prime number. It is quite possible that the program to be constructed would be adequately defined by a relatively few such examples, so that the user of such a synthesizer would have an easy job. But the synthesis task itself from such weak input information is incredibly difficult. [See Amarel (1962) for a discussion of this problem.]

As an example, suppose the program is to be created using the following set of instructions:

```
start
halt
move    op 1   op 2
+       op 1   op 2
-       op 1   op 2
*       op 1   op 2
/       op 1   op 2
if (predicate) then go to (label)
```

Here "move op 1 op 2" means move the contents of location op 1 to the location op 2, "+ op 1 op 2" means add the contents of op 1 to op 2, and so forth. Further suppose that it is desired to create the program that adds a column of numbers:

```
        start
        move   1      I
        move   X(1)   Y
LOOP    +      1      I
        +      X(I)   Y
        if I≠#X then go to LOOP
        halt
```

The symbol #X stands for the number of elements in array X. Then the program synthesis system would be given a set of input–output pairs such as ((9 4 7), (20)), ((5 7 6 5), (23)), and ((16 11), (27)) and asked to create this program.

The program synthesizer could attempt to do its job by enumerating the set of all possible programs in the language in order of increasing length, testing each one to see if it is capable of the desired behavior. When it finds such a program, it prints it out as its answer and halts. We know that the correct answer will exist somewhere in the enumeration so that it will be found eventually. But this strategy has a severe pitfall because it is not possible to tell for an arbitrary program whether or not it can produce the desired behavior. That is, since the halting problem for an arbitrary program on given data is undecidable, one cannot tell what the program might print out, since one cannot tell whether it will even halt (Hopcroft and Ullman, 1969). This problem cannot, in general, be avoided, so that we have a theorem: The programs for the partial recursive functions cannot be generated from samples of input–output behavior. The only way this strategy can be made to work is to enumerate a subset of the partial recursive functions for which the halting problem is solvable or to allow for a partial solution to the halting problem by limiting the number of steps a program may complete before it halts. These theoretical issues and others are discussed at length in Biermann and Feldman (1972), Barzdin and Freivald (1972), Blum and Blum (1975), Feldman (1972b), Gold (1967), and Solomonoff (1964).

Suppose the solution by enumeration method can be made to work by one of the above techniques. It is still possible that the system might produce a wrong answer because some program that precedes the correct answer in the enumeration might be able to complete the given examples. In the current case, the system would probably print the following wrong answer:

```
start
move   16      SUM
 +     A(2)    SUM
halt
```

If this happens, the user only needs to add one or two more example input–output pairs to cause the enumeration to continue on toward the target. It appears that for most practical problems, the number of input–output pairs required to define the desired program is not large.

The severest difficulty with the solution by enumeration is the extreme cost of the enumeration. The target program in the current example would be beyond the billionth program in most enumerations, meaning that a great amount of time might pass before even this trivial program could be found.

Therefore, the task of program synthesis from examples is essentially intractable unless these problems can be avoided. This section will discuss two methods for making the approach feasible. One is to limit the class of synthesizable programs, and the other is to include intermediate information about how each output is obtained from its corresponding input. Section 3.2 discusses a general approach to the problem of program synthesis from examples, and Sections 3.3 and 3.4 describe the design of the "autoprogrammer" that implements part of this approach. Section 3.5 describes the synthesis of LISP programs from input–output pairs, and Section 3.6 makes some summary comments.

3.2 The Method[2]

A reasonable technique for generating programs from examples of their behavior executes the following two steps:

(I) For each example input X_i and its associated output Y_i, determine the sequence S_i of operations required to convert X_i to Y_i.

(II) Find a program that executes each required sequence of operations S_i when given its associated input X_i.

As an illustration of the method, suppose that the input $X = (9\ 4\ 7)$ is known to yield an output $Y = (20)$ and that the program to be created is made up of instructions of the type given in Section 3.1. Further suppose that it is known that in these instructions op 1 always refers to a location in X and op 2 to a location in Y. Then step I would start looking for the desired sequence S of instructions that convert $X = (9\ 4\ 7)$ to $Y = (20)$. Step I might actually begin enumerating the set of all possible such sequences:

start, halt
start, move $X(1)\ Y(1)$, halt
start, move $X(2)\ Y(1)$, halt
$\vdots$
start, move $X(1)\ Y(1)$, $+ X(2)\ Y(1)$, $+ X(3)\ Y(1)$, halt

The last such sequence given does successfully convert the example X to Y completing Step I. Step II then constructs a program that when given the example input $X = (9\ 4\ 7)$ executes the instructions start, move $X(1)$

---

[2] Sections 3.2, 3.3, and 3.4 are adapted from Sections 2 and 3 of "The Use of Examples in Program Construction and Debugging," by A. W. Biermann, *ACM 1975 Annual Conference Proceedings*, October 1975, pp. 242–247. Copyright 1975, Association for Computing Machinery, Inc., adapted by permission.

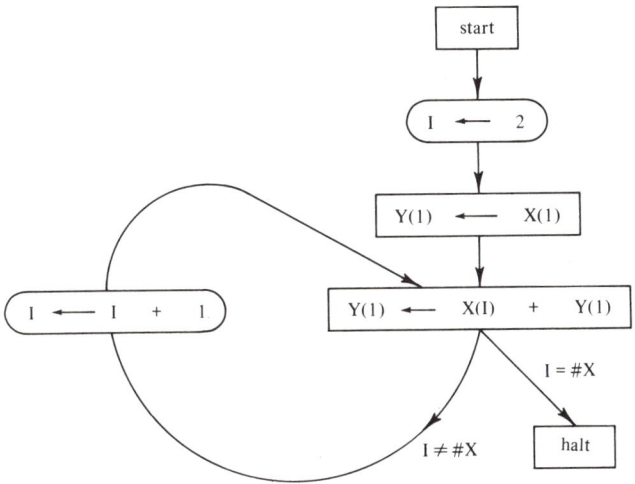

FIG. 8. The program for adding a column. The symbol #X stands for the number of entries in X.

$Y(1)$, $+ X(2) Y(1)$, $+ X(3) Y(1)$, halt. Step II would probably realize that an index should be created to advance through array X and construct the program of Fig. 8. The next section explains this process in much more detail.

The satisfactory completion of Step I involves considerable difficulties, which continue to be a subject for research. First of all, the discovery of acceptable sequences S_i can involve an astronomical amount of enumeration. Also, there may be many sequences S_i that convert X_i to Y_i and a method must be found for discovering which sequence to use for each i. The large amount of enumeration can be reduced by discovering pruning techniques applicable to the specific problem domain and by limiting the class of programs that may be synthesized. Thus, in the above illustration only the class of programs are synthesizable that use the given instructions with op 1 restricted to locations in X and op 2 to locations in Y.

Step II, on the other hand, has been studied considerably, and reasonably effective techniques exist for constructing programs of practical size and complexity (Biermann, 1972, 1975; Biermann and Krishnaswamy, 1974; Biermann *et al.*, 1975; Petry, 1975). This has led to the following approach to automatic programming: Let the user actually work through the example showing the sequence S_i of steps required to produce the output. Then automatically synthesize the program from the S_i's using known techniques. The very difficult Step I can be avoided and the user, after all, usually knows how he wants the computation to be performed. In fact, a

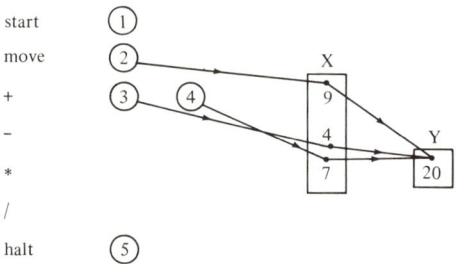

FIG. 9. The five required instructions to add a column by hand.

programming system can be built around a computer display system that enables the user conveniently to work through example computations in a scratch-pad fashion and have programs automatically generated that can do the examples. Figure 9 shows how such a scratch-pad calculation can be done on such a system. The user declares the data structures he needs, and they are displayed on the screen with example data. Then the user executes the example with a lightpen or touch-sensitive screen using available commands, which are also displayed. This method for program synthesis is called *autoprogramming* and is described further in the next sections.

3.3 Program Synthesis from Example Computations

The 11 graphic hits shown in Fig. 9 result in the execution of five autoprogrammer instructions:

```
start
move    X(1)    Y(1)
 +      X(2)    Y(1)
 +      X(3)    Y(1)
halt
```

The task of the program synthesizer is to find the shortest program, not counting indexing instructions, that can execute this computaiton *trace*. The synthesis method is to move down the trace sequentially and for each executed instruction either

(1) create an instruction in the program to do that execution, or
(2) find a previously created instruction in the program to do that execution and add transitions properly to guarantee that the instruction execution will be performed properly.

Beginning with the first two instructions of the trace, the construction of the program starts as shown in Fig. 10a. The third instruction in the trace (+ X(2) Y(1)) is examined to see whether any program instruction

APPROACHES TO AUTOMATIC PROGRAMMING

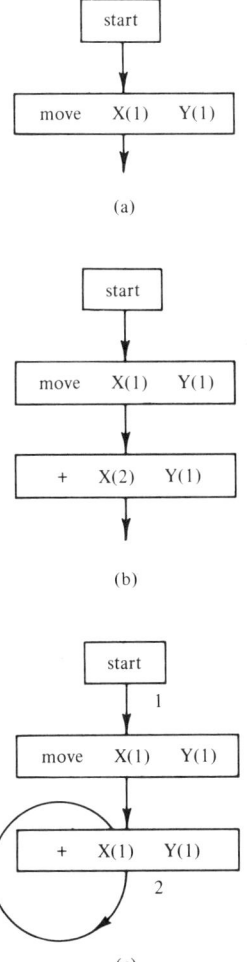

FIG. 10. Constructing the example program.

could have done this task and finds that none could. So another program instruction is created (see Fig. 10b). Comparison of the fourth instruction in the trace with the already created instructions in the program indicates that the instruction (+ X(2) Y(1)) in the program might also be able to perform the current calculation (+ X(3) Y(1)). The goal is thus to *merge* these two instructions, which can be done by inserting proper indexing instructions.

Automatically inserted indexing instructions are thought of as being attached to already existing instruction-to-instruction transitions in the program. So the problem of adding indexing instructions is formulated in these three statements:

(a) Which transitions should have associated indexing instructions?

(b) Which allowed indexing form should be attached to the chosen transitions, I ← C or I ← I+C?[3]

(c) What should be the values of the newly created constants C?

Concerning (a), it can be shown that without loss of generality no transition need have an associated indexing instruction unless the instruction initiating the transition either

(1) has more than one transition entering it,
(2) has more than one transition leaving it,
(3) has references to an index, or
(4) is the start instruction.

Suppose m transitions have been found with property (1), (2), (3), or (4); then there are 2^m ways of possibly assigning to these transitions their associated indexing forms, I ← C or I ← I + C. Each of these possible feasible assignments is tried until one is found such that there is a solution to the problem of determining the values of the constants. (Any assignment that increments I, I ← I + C, before initializing I, I ← C, is considered not feasible.)

Because the possible indexing instructions are so simple, the set of unknown constants can be determined by linear algebra. Returning to the above example, the proposed program now has three instructions and three transitions (see Fig. 10c). The two transitions marked 1 and 2 satisfy the criteria (4) and (3) above, respectively, and so may have indexing instructions attached. If we attach the form I ← C_1 to transition 1 and I ← I + C_2 to transition 2, two equations may be derived from the original trace:

$$2 = C_1, \quad 3 = C_2 + 2$$

There exists a solution to these equations and so the associated indexing instructions can be added to the program as shown in Fig. 11.

Given this program, we would expect the fifth instruction in the trace to be + X(4) Y(1), the sixth to be + X(5) Y(1), and so forth. But, in fact, the fifth instruction is halt, so either a way must be found to break out of the loop or it must be concluded that the partial program is incorrect

---

[3] The newly created index is named I in this case and the C's will be constants that must be determined later. More complicated forms of indexing instructions could be allowed such as I ← I ∗ C + C' at the cost of considerably more computation in the synthesis process.

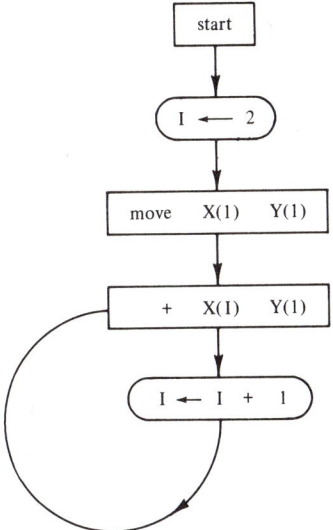

Fig. 11. The partial program with indexing instructions inserted.

and should be changed. However, the system notes the contradiction and tries to find a test that will enable the addition of a new transition out of the instruction $+$ X(I) Y(1). It checks whether the index I equals any important variable like an array dimension, sees that I = #X, and so completes the synthesis shown in Fig. 8.

This example gives the flavor of this approach to program synthesis without introducing the considerable complexities that arise when the process is attempted in the most general case. The reader can find a great deal of additional detail in Biermann (1972), Biermann and Krishnaswamy (1974), and Biermann et al. (1975), and will find the automatic indexing problem discussed in Biermann (1975). For the purposes of this chapter, it is sufficient to say that this process is enumerative so that one can guarantee that if there is a program that can execute the given trace, the system will find that program (or one equivalent to it). The trace may have indexing instructions missing as in the above example, and all of these missing instructions and tests on indexes will be found and properly constructed if they are of a type handled by the synthesizer. A moderately elaborate synthesis system with such capabilities has been implemented and tested as described in Biermann (1975).

Bauer (1975) has discussed a modification of the autoprogrammer approach where the example calculations are input with a subset of English. A translator converts the natural language specification to traces similar to the ones described above and then the synthesis proceeds.

3.4 Features of an Autoprogrammer

Working examples by hand on an autoprogramming system can be tiresome because of the repetitive nature of some calculations, so it is desirable to have features that will lessen the work. As an illustration, the example of the previous section would have been significantly more bothersome to complete if the array to be added had had twenty entries rather than just three. There are various ways to add the twenty entries properly without having to execute by hand nineteen identical add instructions in sequence.

One technique involves the use of dynamic program synthesis and the *continue* feature. The autoprogrammer dynamically maintains a partial program at all times during execution of the example calculation, which is able to execute the portion of the trace that has been seen up to that time. This means that the sequence of partial programs of Section 3.3 is constructed as the calculation proceeds, so that after the third item in X is added the partial program of Fig. 11 exists in the machine. Interestingly enough, this partial program is capable of adding the other seventeen entries in the array without further intervention from the user. So if at any time the system constructs a program such that the instruction just executed by the user is followed by a valid transition, it flashes the word "continue" on the screen. If the user wishes to allow the constructed partial program to continue the calculation rather than doing the instructions by hand, he can simply hit the newly available continue command repeatedly and watch the calculation proceed. If the internal program comes to an instruction with no valid next transition, the word continue disappears from the screen and the user is forced to proceed by hand. If while using the continue feature, the user observes the partial program making an error, he may use the *backup* command to undo mistakes just made, and then he can insert the correct instructions by hand. In any case, he can use the continue feature to hurry through all repetitive parts of any example and save himself considerable trouble.

Once the continue feature is built into the system, the testing of a newly constructed program is straightforward. One simply loads the data structures with test data and uses the continue feature to advance the calculation through the program from the initial start instruction. If an error is observed in the test program's behavior, it is necessary to change the synthesized program using the *override* feature.

The override feature assumes that earlier traces do not correctly express the current desires of the programmer. Either the programmer has made an error in previous example calculations or he has changed his mind about what the program should do. Whatever the situation, this feature can be called while advancing through an example using the continue feature. If the test program begins some action that does not agree with the user's desire, he calls backup to undo the undesired action, then he calls override and inserts by hand whatever instructions he prefers, and finally, if appropriate, he can return to the use of continue to finish the calculation. Override assumes that the transition that was about to be executed is incorrect. Furthermore, it assumes that all previous traces are incorrect at the point where they imply the offending transition. Therefore, it deletes the incorrect transition both from the synthesized program and from all previous traces.

3.5 Synthesis of LISP Programs

The synthesis of LISP programs from input–output examples provides an attractive problem for research partly because the "trace" of the calculation is often easy to obtain. Thus if the input X = (A B C) yields output Y = (C B A), one suspects that the output was obtained by placing the leftmost element of X into the rightmost location of Y, the second element of X into the second location of Y, and the rightmost element of X into the first position of Y. In the LISP language, this is written

$$Y = \text{cons}(\text{caddr}(X); \text{cons}(\text{cadr}(X); \text{cons}(\text{car}(X); \text{nil})))$$

Thus the trace of the calculation can be found immediately and step I of Section 3.2 is solved. So the synthesizer can proceed directly to step II, program construction. The synthesis of LISP functions from such input–output pairs has been studied by Shaw *et al.* (1975), Hardy (1974), and Summers (1975a,b). We will first examine the method of Summers.

The Summers system builds programs using the LISP primitives car, cdr, cons, and atom:

car(X) yields the first element of list X. Thus if X = (A B C) then car(X) = A.

cdr(X) yields the list X with the first element removed. Using the same example X, cdr(x) = (B C).

cons(Z;X) yields list X with element Z added to the first location so that cons(D,X) would yield (D A B C) for the example list X.

atom(X) is a predicate that is true if X is an atom or a list of length zero (which is written "nil").

Since the car and cdr functions are often nested deeply, an abbreviation for such nestings is often used. As an illustration, car(cdr(cdr(X))) is written caddr(X). Using the same example X,

$$\text{cadr}(X) = B, \quad \text{caddr}(X) = C$$

The Summers approach can be illustrated by synthesizing a program that always returns the rightmost element of a list. Thus the example input–output pairs are

$$\begin{array}{ll} X & Y \\ (\,) & \text{nil} \\ (A) & A \\ (A\ B) & B \\ (A\ B\ C) & C \end{array}$$

For each of the examples, the function required to produce the ith output from its associated input will be denoted f_i:

$$\begin{aligned} f_1(X) &= \text{nil} \\ f_2(X) &= \text{car}(X) \\ f_3(X) &= \text{cadr}(X) \\ f_4(X) &= \text{caddr}(X) \end{aligned}$$

Thus the following trivial program can be constructed for handling these four examples:

$$\begin{aligned} F(X) = (\text{cond } &(p_1(X) \to f_1(X)) \\ &(p_2(X) \to f_2(X)) \\ &(p_3(X) \to f_3(X)) \\ &(T \to f_4(X))) \end{aligned}$$

The conditional cond operates as follows: $p_1(X), p_2(X), \ldots$ are tested sequentially until one is found to be true. If $p_i(X)$ is the first predicate found to be true then its associated $f_i(X)$ is returned as the function result. If $p_1, p_2,$ and p_3 all yield false then $f_4(X)$ is returned. For this example, the required predicates are

$$\begin{aligned} p_1(X) &= \text{atom}(X) \\ p_2(X) &= \text{atom}(\text{cdr}(X)) \\ p_3(X) &= \text{atom}(\text{cddr}(X)) \end{aligned}$$

The general form of the desired program is a recursive function discovered through a process that Summers calls *differencing*. Each function f_i is written in terms of earlier functions f_j, where $j < i$:

$$\begin{aligned} f_1(X) &= \text{nil} \\ f_2(X) &= \text{car}(X) \\ f_3(X) &= f_2(\text{cdr}(X)) \\ f_4(X) &= f_3(\text{cdr}(X)) \end{aligned}$$

Here we see a pattern $f_i(X) = f_{i-1}(\text{cdr}(X))$ for $i > 2$. So the desired program becomes

$$F(X) = (\text{cond } (\text{atom}(X) \to \text{nil})$$
$$(\text{atom}(\text{cdr}(X))) \to \text{car}(X))$$
$$(T \to F(\text{cdr}(X)))))$$

That is, functions f_i and f_{i-1} are merged in much the same manner as trace instructions in Section 3.3 except that the mechanism of recursion is used instead of looping.

This technique is quite adequate for the construction of many programs, but it sometimes fails. For example, if it is necessary to create auxiliary variables to hold temporary results during a calculation, a mechanism must exist for creating such variables. Summers has developed a fascinating method for creating additional variables, which we will demonstrate by examining one of his examples.

Specifically, Summers (1975b) shows how a program for reversing a list can be constructed. Suppose the input–output pairs are as follows:

X	Y
( )	( )
(A)	(A)
(A B)	(B A)
(A B C)	(C B A)

Then the associated functions are

$f_1(X) = \text{nil}$
$f_2(X) = \text{cons}(\text{car}(X);\text{nil})$
$f_3(X) = \text{cons}(\text{cadr}(X);\text{cons}(\text{car}(X);\text{nil}))$
$f_4(X) = \text{cons}(\text{caddr}(X);\text{cons}(\text{cadr}(X);\text{cons}(\text{car}(X);\text{nil})))$

Then if the idea of differencing is attempted, we obtain

$$f_2(X) = \text{cons}(\text{car}(X);f_1(X))$$
$$f_3(X) = \text{cons}(\text{cadr}(X);f_2(X))$$
$$f_4(X) = \text{cons}(\text{caddr}(X);f_3(X))$$

It is not immediately clear how to convert this to a recursive program and so Summers resorts to what Siklóssy (1974) has called the "insane heuristic." Upon finding difficulty in solving one problem, he resorts to attacking a more general one (see also Boyer and Moore, 1975). Specifically, he attempts to construct a function $g(X,Z)$ such that if Z is properly instantiated, say $Z = a$, then $g(X,a) = f(X)$. Examining the functions f_1, f_2, f_3, and f_4 above, the only common subexpression found is nil, so g is constructed such that $g(X,\text{nil}) = f(X)$:

$g_1(X,Z) = Z$
$g_2(X,Z) = \text{cons}(\text{car}(X);Z)$
$g_3(X,Z) = \text{cons}(\text{cadr}(X);\text{cons}(\text{car}(X);Z))$
$g_4(X,Z) = \text{cons}(\text{caddr}(X);\text{cons}(\text{cadr}(X);\text{cons}(\text{car}(X);Z)))$

Then differencing is done resulting in two possible explanations for each g_i:

$g_2(X,Z) = \{\text{cons}(\text{car}(X);g_1(X,Z)),g_1(v;\text{cons}(\text{car}(X);Z))\}$
       $v = \text{anything}$
$g_3(X,Z) = \{\text{cons}(\text{cadr}(X);g_2(X,Z)),g_2(\text{cdr}(X);\text{cons}(\text{car}(X);Z))\}$
$g_4(X,Z) = \{\text{cons}(\text{caddr}(X);g_3(X,Z)),g_3(\text{cdr}(X);\text{cons}(\text{car}(X);Z))\}$

Astonishingly enough, the second of the given differences yields a general form for the computation. So the desired program is $F(X) = G(X,\text{nil})$, where

$G(X,Z) = (\text{cond } (\text{atom}(X) \to Z$
         $(T \to G(\text{cdr}(X),\text{cons}(\text{car}(X);Z))))$

This short discussion thus gives two of the central contributions of Summers' work: (1) the idea of differencing separate traces in order to obtain a recursive schema for doing a computation and (2) the method for creating additional internal variables.

One might suspect that instead of requiring the user to input a number of input–output pairs that can be differenced as shown above, it might be possible to create many programs of interest from just one example. Thus it would seem that the information that (A B C D) results in output (D C B A) might be enough to indicate to a system that the reversal program is desired. The efforts of Shaw et al. (1975) and Hardy (1974) address this more difficult problem of synthesis. Because of the reduction in available information, such a system cannot use as simple a mechanism as described by Summers and must include many more heuristics (as defined in Section 6).

For example, Shaw et al. (1975) discuss the problem of creating a program that yields (A B A C A D B C B D C D) from the input (A B C D). This program uses heuristics to find a change in pattern in the output so that it can be separated into a *head* and a *recurrate*. In this example, the head is the portion A B A C A D and the recurrate is the rest of the output B C B D C D. The generated program computes the head and then produces the recurrate with recursive calls. In this example, the computation of the head is specified as a subgoal: From inputs A, (B C D) produce (A B A C A D). A routine is created to compute this head function (see COMB2.AUX1 below) and that routine is used in the top level program to complete the calculation. The Shaw et al. (1975) system creates the following program:

COMB2(X) = (cond ((null X) nil)
                (T (append(COMB2.AUX1(car X) (cdr X))
                (COMB2(cdr X)))))
COMB2.AUX1(U V) = (cond ((null V) nil)
                   (T (cons(list U (car V))
                   (COMB2.AUX1 U cdr V))))

3.6 Discussion

Program synthesis from examples, which was thought to be a totally intractable problem a few years ago, is slowly becoming possible using techniques described in this section. Program construction processes have been speeded up sufficiently through the use of enumeration pruning, limiting assumptions on the class of programs being synthesized, and user-specified example calculations so that programs of practical size can be created automatically. An autoprogramming system of the type described here has been constructed by Biermann and Krishnaswamy (1974) although not all of the features described were implemented. The system has been used to create a large number of programs including a few examples as complex as a small compiler. The approach has the following advantages:

(1) The user has no need to learn traditional language syntax.
(2) The user has direct visual contact with his data structures and can manipulate them in an extremely natural manner with his hands.

Major disadvantages of the approach are that display terminals are not large enough to display easily large or multidimensional data structures, and the correctness of automatically generated programs is not always easy to determine.

The efforts to synthesize LISP programs have also been quite successful. The "trace" of the computation can be efficiently constructed for large classes of functions from the structures of the input and output lists. Furthermore, the programs can be built from the traces almost algorithmically with little or no searching. A number of theoretical results have been developed, including a technique for creating and properly utilizing extra variables.

4. Synthesis from Formal Input–Output Specifications

4.1 Introduction

Rather than giving examples of the desired program behavior, it may be preferable to specify precisely the required input–output characteristics and have the program automatically generated from these. For example, in the case of the program that computes the ith prime number, the input would be specified as a positive integer by the predicate

$$P(x) = \begin{cases} \text{true} & \text{if } x \text{ is an integer and } x > 0 \\ \text{false} & \text{otherwise} \end{cases}$$

and the output would be specified by the predicate

$$R(x,z) = \begin{cases} \text{true} & \text{if } z \text{ is the } x\text{th positive integer with the property that its only divisors are 1 and itself} \\ \text{false} & \text{otherwise} \end{cases}$$

The program can be generated by proving the theorem

$$(\forall x)[P(x) \supset (\exists z) R(x, z)].$$

This theorem states that for all x, the truth of $P(x)$ implies that there exists a z such that $R(x, z)$ is true. Proving the theorem requires that a method be discovered for finding the required z for each such x, and this method is indeed the desired program. Many times there is no restriction $P(x)$ on the input, in which case the theorem to be proven is $\forall x \exists z\, R(x, z)$.

The complete process can be illustrated by synthesizing a program to compute $f(x) = x^2 + 1$. Assume that f_1 and f_2 are primitive computing operations that, respectively, square and increment their arguments:

$$f_1(x) = x^2, \qquad f_2(x) = x + 1$$

Let R_1 and R_2 be predicates for the square and increment operations:

$$R_1(x,z) = \begin{cases} \text{true} & \text{if } z = x^2 \\ \text{false} & \text{otherwise} \end{cases}$$

$$R_2(x,z) = \begin{cases} \text{true} & \text{if } z = x + 1 \\ \text{false} & \text{otherwise} \end{cases}$$

Then $(\forall x) R_1(x, f_1(x))$ and $(\forall x) R_2(x, f_2(x))$ are true. Suppose that there are no input specifications $P(x)$ and that the output specification is $\exists y(R_1(x, y) \land R_2(y, z))$, there exists a y such that $R_1(x, y)$ and $R_2(y, z)$ are true. Then the following theorem must be proved:

$$\forall x\, \exists z\, \exists y\, (R_1(x, y) \land R_2(y, z))$$

The theorem prover might attempt many different transformations on this theorem, but one reasonable possibility would be to propose $y = f_1(x)$.

Then the following theorem must be proven:

$$\forall x\, \exists z\, [R_1(x, f_1(x)) \wedge R_2(f_1(x), z)]$$

Here the theorem prover might substitute $z = f_2(f_1(x))$, leaving the following theorem to be proven:

$$\forall x\, [R_1(x, f_1(x)) \wedge R_2(f_1(x), (f_2(f_1(x))))]$$

But this follows from the above assertions $(\forall x) R_1(x, f_1(x))$ and $(\forall x) R_2(x, f_2(x))$ completing the proof of the original theorem. Notice that the instantiation of z required to prove the theorem is exactly the desired program, $z = f_2(f_1(x))$.

This approach to automatic program synthesis thus assumes that the synthesizer has a large amount of information available about programming and about the domain within which programs are to be written. This information is coded in the form of formal axioms and rules of inference and a powerful theorem prover is needed to find the necessary proofs. Techniques similar to the one described in the previous paragraph have been developed to generate straight line programs (i.e., a sequence of operations) that can convert an input to an output meeting certain formally stated specifications. Methods have been developed for synthesizing branching and looping constructions as described in the next section. The reader interested in a more complete coverage of this approach should consult Dershowitz and Manna (1975), Duran (1975), Green (1969a,b,c), Green and Raphael (1968), Lee *et al.* (1974), Manna and Waldinger (1971), Waldinger (1969), and Waldinger and Lee (1969). A synthesis method that combines goal reduction techniques and logic is described in Section 4.3 as developed by Buchanan (1974) and Buchanan and Luckham (1974). Section 4.4 will summarize and discuss this work.

4.2 Synthesizing Branching and Looping Structures

Modern systems that function by proving theorems in formal logic usually use "resolution" as the rule of inference (Robinson, 1965). A short, somewhat oversimplified discussion of resolution theorem proving will be included here and the reader is referred to Chang and Lee (1973), Nilsson (1971), and Slagle (1971) for additional details. In resolution theorem proving, all axioms and theorems are converted to *clause* form, a set of predicates in disjunctive form with all universal and existential quantifiers removed. That is, any well-formed formula can be converted to a set of clauses of the form $P_1 \vee P_2 \vee P_3 \vee \cdots \vee P_n$, where each P_i is a (possibly negated) predicate symbol with zero or more arguments, which may or may not be instantiated. The conversion process of an arbitrary

$$P \lor R_1 \lor R_2 \lor \cdots \lor R_n \qquad \neg P \lor Q_1 \lor Q_2 \lor \cdots \lor Q_m$$

$$R_1 \lor R_2 \lor \cdots \lor R_n \lor Q_1 \lor Q_2 \lor \cdots \lor Q_m$$

FIG. 12. Resolving two clauses.

formula to its clause form is complicated and will not be discussed here. As an example, the well-formed formula $\exists x_1 \forall x_2 \exists x_3 \, (P(x_1, x_2) \lor Q(x_3))$ has clause form $P(a, x) \lor Q(g(x))$, where a denotes the item asserted to exist ($\exists x_1$), x is a variable that is universally quantified since all variables in clause form are so quantified, and $g(x)$ denotes the x_3 asserted to exist for each possible x_2: ($\forall x_2 \exists x_3$).

Two clauses can be *resolved* if one of them contains a predicated P such that an identically instantiated negation of P is in the other clause. Thus $P \lor R_1 \lor R_2 \lor \cdots \lor R_n$ and $\neg P \lor Q_1 \lor Q_2 \lor \cdots \lor Q_m$ can be resolved to yield $R_1 \lor R_2 \lor \cdots \lor R_n \lor Q_1 \lor Q_2 \lor \cdots \lor Q_m$. The result of this resolution is the disjunction of all elements in the two clauses except for P and $\neg P$ and is a logical result of the two clauses. Such a resolution is often denoted graphically as shown in Fig. 12. As mentioned above, the predicate P being resolved out must be identically instantiated in each clause. Thus before resolving $P(x, y) \lor Q(y)$ and $\neg P(z, b) \lor R(z)$, a substitution must be made (z for x and b for y) before the result is formed (see Fig. 13).

With this amount of mechanism it is possible to explain the method of Lee *et al.* (1974) for automatically synthesizing branching code. Suppose it is desired to build a piece of code that checks the contents of x and then prints POS, NEG, or ZERO depending on whether x is positive, negative, or zero. Then the theorem prover is given the following information:

Assertion	Clause form
If x is positive, then the result is POS	$\neg P(x) \lor R(x, \text{POS})$
If x is negative, then the result is NEG	$\neg N(x) \lor R(x, \text{NEG})$
If x is neither positive nor negative, then the result is ZERO	$P(x) \lor N(x) \lor R(x, \text{ZERO})$

The method of Lee *et al.* (1974) requires that one other clause be input to the theorem prover, $\neg R(x, z) \lor \text{Ans}(z)$, which may be interpreted as saying that if z results for input x, then z is an answer to the problem. These clauses give the input–output specifications for the desired program and are the basis from which it is constructed.

The method first calls the theorem prover to deduce a clause that contains only the Ans predicate. For this example, the required series of resolu-

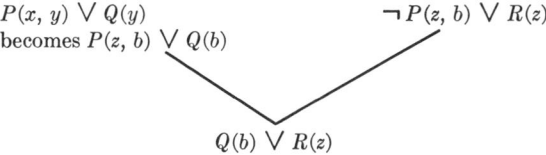

FIG. 13. An example resolution with substitutions.

tions appears in Fig. 14. The tree of Fig. 14 is then manipulated as follows: If clause $C = P \vee R_1 \vee \cdots \vee R_n$ is resolved with another clause to eliminate P, then P instantiated (by the most general unifier) for the resolution is placed on the arc below C. All substitutions made during the resolution are also placed on the arc below C as shown in Fig. 15. Then all nodes on the tree that have no Ans predicate are deleted and the start and halt nodes are labeled as shown in Fig. 16. This completes the construction of the desired program: If x is negative, then $z \leftarrow$ NEG else if x is positive, then $z \leftarrow$ POS else $z \leftarrow$ ZERO.

The Lee et al. (1974) paper precisely defines this synthesis algorithm and proves its correctness. The answer predicate technique was originally developed for general question answering and problem solving systems, and more information is available in Green (1969a,b,c), including some of the first examples of automatic program synthesis using formal methods.

The process of building looping constructions using theorem proving techniques has been studied by Manna and Waldinger (1971) as well as others. The Manna and Waldinger approach requires that the theorem prover be able to execute a proof by induction and then it builds a program loop for each such induction.

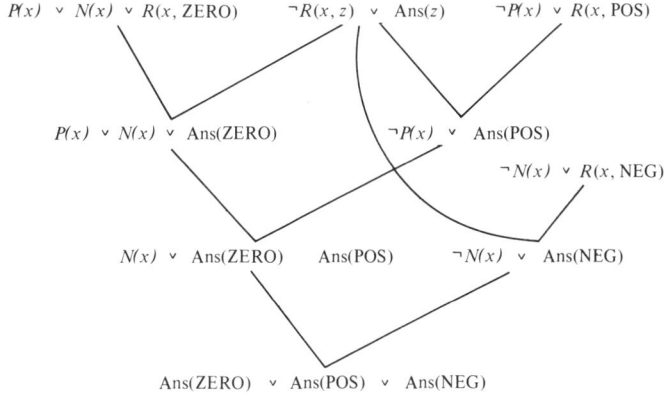

FIG. 14. Resolving to obtain the clause with only the Ans predicate.

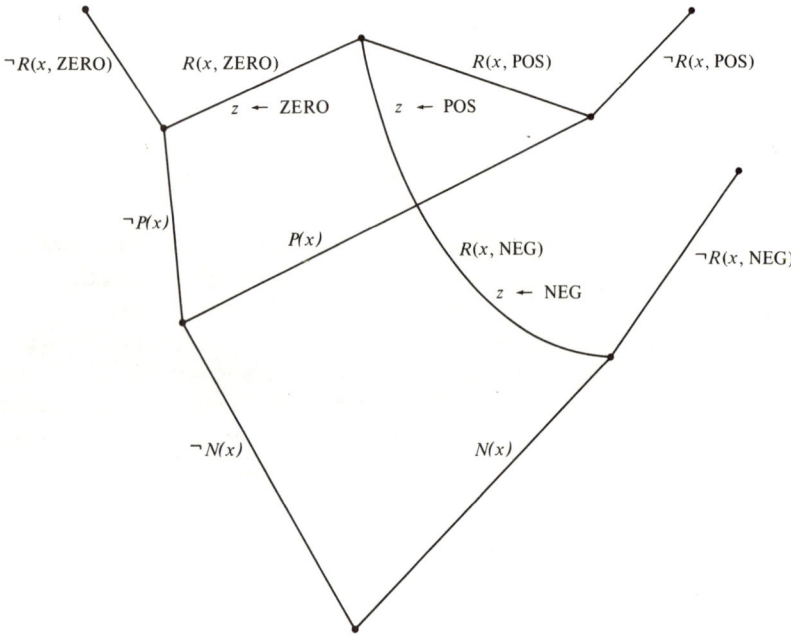

Fig. 15. The resolved predicates and the substitutions made.

Rules of inference in the following discussion will be written

$$\frac{H_1, H_2, \ldots, H_k}{K}$$

meaning that if statements $H_1, H_2, \ldots, H_k$ are all known to be true, then K (the conclusion) is also known to be true. The induction principle may thus be written

$$\frac{P(0), \forall y_1\,(P(y_1) \supset P(y_1 + 1))}{\forall x\, P(x)}$$

The premises above the line specify the basis and induction arguments that must be made, and the conclusion is given below the line. In the case of program synthesis, the theorem to be proved is $\forall x\, \exists z\, R(x, z)$ so the proper form of the induction rule is

$$\frac{\exists y_2 R(0, y_2),\ \forall y_1\,(\exists y_2\, R(y_1, y_2) \supset \exists y_3\, R(y_1 + 1, y_3))}{\forall x\, \exists z\, R(x, z)}$$

Associated with this induction rule is the program of Fig. 17, which includes the desired loop. That is, if the premises of the induction rule can be proven, this program is guaranteed to compute the z asserted to exist in the conclusion of the induction rule. The unknown quantities a and g in the program are discovered in the process of proving the premises.

This technique can be illustrated by showing how it may be used to create the program that adds a column of numbers. The inputs to the program are the array A and its dimension N and the output is SUM. Thus it is necessary to prove that $\forall A \ \forall N \ \exists SUM \ R(A,N,SUM)$, where

$$R(u,x,z) = \begin{cases} \text{true} & \text{if } z = \sum_{i=1}^{x} u(i) \\ \text{false} & \text{otherwise} \end{cases}$$

Since u will not change during the computation, it can be removed as an argument, and we will write $R_u(x, z)$ instead of $R(u, x, z)$. Certain knowledge must be available to the theorem prover before the proof can be done. Among other things, the theorem prover must have the facts $R_u(0, 0)$ and $\forall x \ \forall y \ (R_u(x, y) \supset R_u(x + 1, u(x + 1) + y))$. Then the proof of the basis argument $\exists y_2 \ R_u(0, y_2)$ yields $a = 0$ and the proof of the induction step $\forall y_1 \ (\exists y_2 \ R_u(y_1, y_2) \supset \exists y_3 \ R_u(y_1 + 1, y_3))$ yields $g(y_1, y_2) = u(y_1 + 1) + y_2$. So the synthesized program is as shown in Fig. 18.

Manna and Waldinger (1971) give other forms of the induction rule and show how they lead to other iterative constructions or to recursive programs. The reader should refer to the original paper for additional details.

This section has thus shown approximately how straight line, branching,

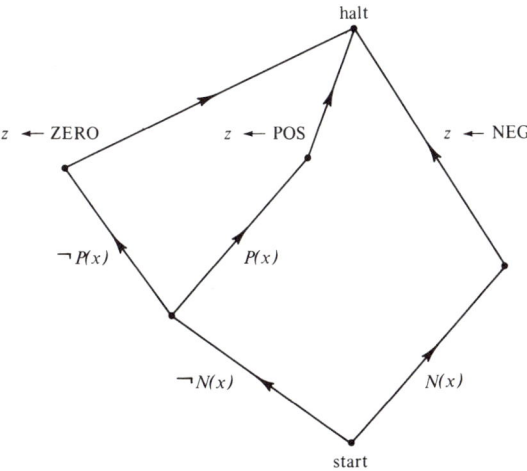

FIG. 16. The program constructed by modifying the resolution tree.

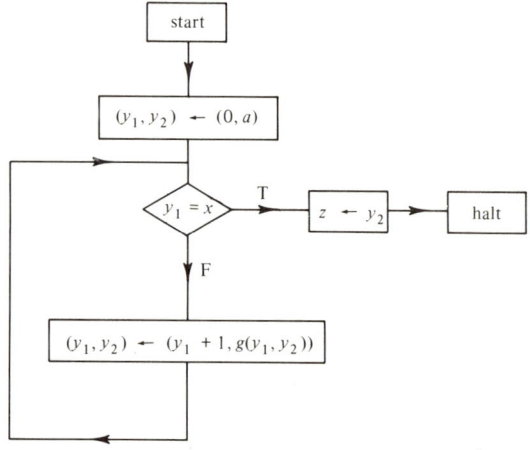

FIG. 17. Looping program associated with the inductive argument (from Manna and Waldinger, 1971).

and looping constructions can be built from proofs of theorems. A combination of these abilities leads to a totally general programming ability. Some of the original papers describe the synthesis of complicated programs that involve all of these constructions. The next section will describe a different type of formalism for program synthesis, which uses formal logic techniques.

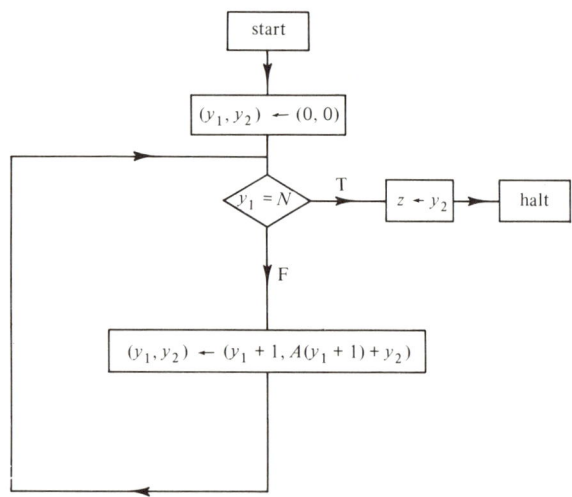

FIG. 18. The column sum routine.

4.3 Problem Reduction Methods

Nilsson (1971) has discussed problem reduction methods as an approach to problem solving in artificial intelligence. The task is broken down into subtasks, which are further broken down in a hierarchy until at the lowest level all subtasks are trivially solvable. The solution to the highest level task is a composite of the solutions at the lower levels. In the program synthesis domain, we will use the notation P{A}Q to mean that if assertions P are true and program A is executed to a halt, then Q will be true. The program synthesis problem then can be stated: Given input specifications I and output specifications G, find A such that I{A}G. A typical reduction step would be to divide A into two segments A_1 and A_2 and attempt to construct A_1 and A_2 separately (see Fig. 19). A set of intermediate specifications Q are determined and the two problems I{A_1}Q and Q{A_2}G are attacked separately.

Buchanan (1974) and Buchanan and Luckham (1974) have built a program synthesis system using the problem reduction approach. Their system has many resemblances to the STRIPS system described in Fikes and Nilsson (1971). The Buchanan and Luckham approach assumes that the system has a large amount of programming knowledge in the form of inference rules such as those shown in Fig. 20. If the conclusion of such a rule resembles the problem to be solved, the rule is applied backwards and all of its premises become subgoals to be solved. Thus in the example above, the problem I{A_1;A_2}G is broken into two subgoals using rule R2. The problem decomposition continues until trivial subproblems are obtained and then the solution is constructed.

Besides having general programming knowledge, the system needs domain specific information, which Buchanan and Luckham call *frame* information. Frame rules may be in the form of inference rules like R1, R2, ..., R5, or they may be in the form shown in Fig. 20, particular code segments and their associated input-output specifications.

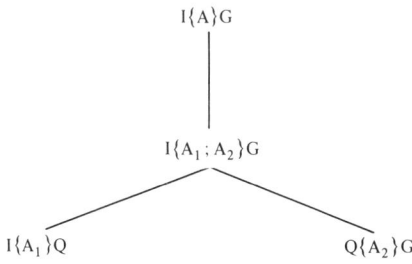

FIG. 19. Reducing the problem I{A}G to two simpler problems.

General rules

R1. Rules of consequence: $\dfrac{P\supset Q,\ Q\{A\}R}{P\{A\}R}$, $\dfrac{P\{A\}Q,\ Q\supset R}{P\{A\}R}$

R2. Rule of composition: $\dfrac{P\{A\}Q,\ Q\{B\}R}{P\{A;B\}R}$

R3. Rule of invariance: $\dfrac{P\{A\}Q,\ A \text{ does not affect } R}{P \wedge R\{A\}Q \wedge R}$

R4. Rule of iteration: $\dfrac{Q \wedge L\{A\}R,\ R\{B\}Q,\ Q \wedge \neg L \supset G}{Q\{\text{while } L \text{ do } (A;B)\}G}$

R5. Conditional rule: $\dfrac{P \wedge Q\{A\}R,\ P \wedge \neg Q\{B\}R}{P\{\text{if } Q \text{ then } A \text{ else } B\}R}$

Frame rules

F1. $(N1 = x \wedge N2 = y)\{N1 \leftarrow N1+N2\}(N1 = x+y, N2 = y)$
F2. $(\text{null})\{N1 \leftarrow \text{constant}\}(N1 = \text{constant})$

FIG. 20. Programming knowledge for program synthesis.

We will again return to our canonical example to illustrate this method. In this case, the input specification will be I: $A(i)$ is an integer for $i = 1, 2, 3, \ldots, N$, and $N > 0$. The output specification will be G: $\sum_{i=1}^{N} A(i) = \text{SUM}$. The problem is to find B such that I$\{B\}$G and after some searching the system will find (hopefully) the goal reduction tree of Fig. 21. Each subgoal is found using rules or transformations available to the system and the subgoals at the bottom of the tree are achieved using frame information and/or the theorem prover. The predicates referred to in the figure are defined as follows:

Predicate	Meaning
G	$\sum_{i=1}^{N} A(i) = \text{SUM}$
I	$A(i)$ is an integer for $i = 1, 2, \cdots, N$, and $N > 0$
I'	$I \wedge (J = 1)$
I''	$I \wedge (J = 1) \wedge (\text{SUM} = 0)$
L	$J \leq N$
T	$\sum_{i=1}^{J-1} A(i) = \text{SUM}$ and $1 \leq J \leq N+1$
T'	$\sum_{i=1}^{J} A(i) = \text{SUM}$ and $1 \leq J \leq N$

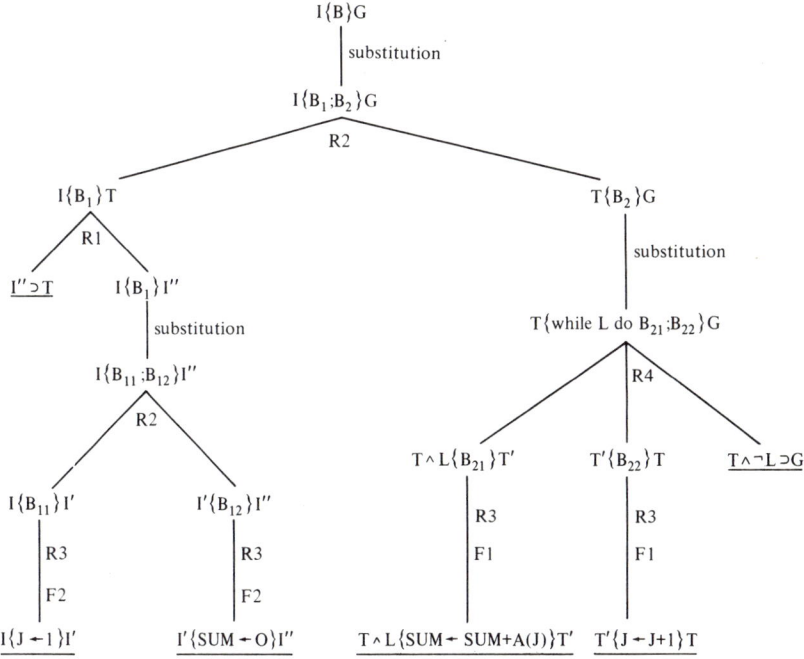

Fig. 21. The problem reduction tree for the synthesis of the column sum program.

Thus the synthesized program is

$$B = B_{11}; B_{12}; \text{ while } L \text{ do } (B_{21}; B_{22};)$$

or

$J \leftarrow 1;$
$SUM \leftarrow 0;$
while $J \leq N$ do
$\quad SUM \leftarrow SUM + A(J);$
$\quad J \leftarrow J + 1;$

Notice that the intermediate specifications I', I'', L, T, and T' are key to the problem solution and require considerable intelligence to derive. Ideally, an artificially intelligent system would construct these automatically and the whole synthesis process would occur without human intervention. Actually these assertions are usually inserted manually by the user either as a part of the frame rules or in some other kind of interaction. The Buchanan–Luckham system that has been implemented does include interactive capabilities, which help the user guide the system to a solution. This system has been used to solve a number of nontrivial problems such as the generation of a program to convert arithmetic expressions from infix to Polish notation. A specialization of this system has been used by Gerritsen (1973) to generate programs for information retrieval.

4.4 Discussion

The program synthesis methods of this section have the advantage that they are well founded in formal logic, a much studied area of mathematics. The program synthesis capability is completely general and each constructed program comes with a proof of its correctness. Probably the greatest contribution of this research is its illumination of the chain of steps that link a program with its input–output specifications. Other work that concentrates on this subject is the literature on the correctness of programs (see, for example, Boyer and Moore, 1975; Dahl *et al.*, 1972; Elspas *et al.*, 1972; Floyd, 1967; Gerhart, 1972; Good *et al.*, 1975; Hoare, 1969; London, 1970).

Progress toward making these systems practical is somewhat impeded by the lack of adequate theorem proving mechanisms. Such systems in their current form are also not necessarily easy to use because formal logic notation is not particularly easy or natural for humans. However, if a system is ever to exist that constructs programs on the basis of behavioral specifications rather than program structural specifications, one might suspect that it will be based on techniques like these.

5. Translation of Natural Language Commands

5.1 Introduction

One of the ultimate conveniences one could hope for in an automatic programming system would be the ability to converse with it in natural language. If this were possible, then all the facilities of giant machines would be available to nonspecialists in computer science, such as doctors, lawyers, businessmen, children, and teachers. The processing of natural languages has been studied by large numbers of individuals such as Bobrow (1968), Coles (1968), Heidorn (1974), Shank (1972), Simmons *et al.* (1968), Winograd (1972), and Woods (1970). It is important that at least one of these works be discussed here, and the work of Winograd seems appropriate for the purpose of this chapter.

Section 5.2 gives a brief discussion of Winograd's approach to syntactic analysis and Section 5.3 attempts to show approximately how PLANNER code can be generated from an English language input.

5.2 Syntactic Analysis

Winograd's syntactic analysis of English is based upon *systemic grammars* as developed by Halliday (1967, 1970). Systemic grammars hierarchically decompose utterances into three basic classes: clauses, groups, and words. Each sentence is broken down into one or more clauses, clauses are primarily made up of groups, and groups are primarily composed of words. Clauses may be *major* as in

> *The boy ran down the street.*

or *secondary* as in

> The boy *who loved chocolate* ran down the street.

Major clauses can be imperative, declarative, or question.

There are four types of groups: noun, verb, preposition, and adjective. Some example noun groups are "the boy" in the first sentence above and "the boy who loved chocolate" in the second sentence. In the latter example, "who loved chocolate" is considered part of the noun group that modifies or classifies the main noun. An example verb group from the above sentences is the simple word "ran," and an example preposition group is "down the street." An example adjective group is in the sentence

> The boy *more athletic than the others* ran down the street.

Words, the lowest level in the hierarchy, are classified as noun, verb, adjective, and so forth, and can have features depending on their classification. Thus verbs can have the features auxiliary, imperative, infinitive, transitive, intransitive, modal, and/or others. The complete parse of one of the example sentences in terms of these three levels appears in Fig. 22.

Winograd's system completes a syntactic analysis of a sentence and then semantic routines create a PLANNER program, which is an interpretation of the meaning of the sentence. The system then responds to the sentence by executing the PLANNER program and generating an appropriate output in English. Although the sequence of processing is approximately as given (syntax, semantics, execution, response), Winograd emphasizes the complex interrelationships between all of these phases. Thus, as an illustration, the syntactic analysis may not be possible to complete until certain semantic processing is done. For example,

> Moving cars can bother the men.

will be parsed in distinctly different ways depending on whether the world model shows men in the driver seats of automobiles or working in the street.

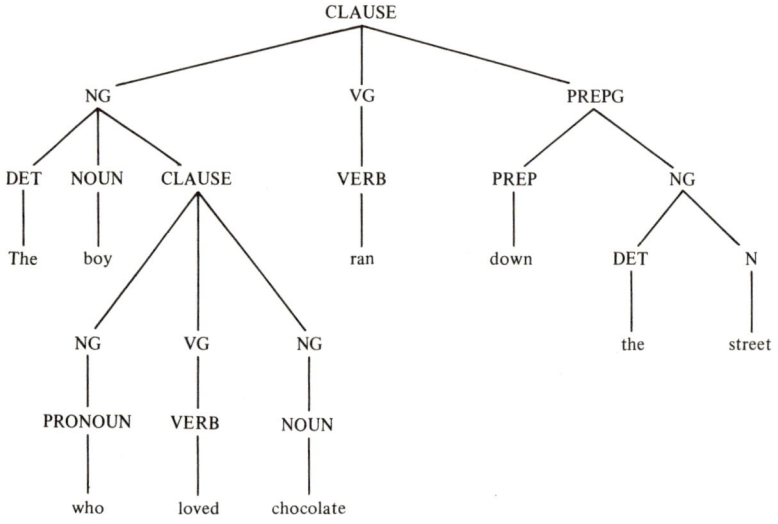

Fig. 22. A parse of a sentence using systemic grammar.

We cannot be sure how Winograd's system might process our ongoing example of adding a column of numbers, but the analysis given here is probably a reasonable approximation. Suppose we input the sentence

Add up the numbers in array A.

The resulting syntactic analysis might be as given in Fig. 23. This forms the basis for the semantic processing described in the next section.

5.3 Generating PLANNER Code

Associated with each word in the vocabulary of the machine is a dictionary entry that gives the meaning of the word in terms of some features and some PLANNER-like code. As an example, Winograd gives the following as the meaning of "block":

(BLOCK((NOUN(NMEANS ((#MANIP #RECTANGULAR)
((#IS *** #BLOCK))))))

"Block" is a noun with features #MANIP and #RECTANGULAR, which is defined by the PLANNER-like statement (#IS *** #BLOCK). Words, of course, may have several meanings, all of which can be included in the dictionary entry. "Block" could thus also be listed as a verb with another meaning, and the particular meaning used in any given situation would depend on the output from the syntax analyzer.

The task of the semantic routines is to build a program using the word meanings in conjunction with the syntactic analysis and to execute that program to achieve the desired result. Consider the sentence

Pick up a red pyramid which is supported by a green block.

Here the semantic routines would construct for the major noun group this code:

(THGOAL (#IS $?X1 #PYRAMID))
(THGOAL (#COLOR $?X1 #RED))
(THGOAL (#IS $?X2 #BLOCK))
(THGOAL (#COLOR $?X2 #GREEN))
(THGOAL (#SUPPORT $?X2 $?X1))

These routines have discovered that there are two objects that have been named $?X1 and $?X2 and that are associated by the relationship #SUPPORT. Furthermore, they have looked up the meaning of each word associated with each object and constructed the descriptions shown. The execution of this code to obtain proper instantiations of $?X1 and $?X2 was discussed in Section 2.2.

The interpretation of the imperative "pick up" in this sentence would first involve executing the above code imbedded in the PLANNER function THFIND ALL $?X1. That is, it would run the above code until it has found all possible such $?X1. Then it would be clever enough to examine each such $?X1 to discover which one would be nearest at hand and easiest to pick up (i.e., not covered up by other objects). Having chosen a particular object, say :OBJ, it would then execute the statement

(THGOAL (#PICKUP :OBJ)(THUSE TC-PICKUP)).

Sentence segment	Analysis
Add up the numbers in array A	CLAUSE, MAJOR, IMPERATIVE, PARTICLE, TRANSITIVE
Add up	VERB GROUP, IMPERATIVE
Add	VERB, IMPERATIVE, TRANSITIVE
up	PARTICLE
the numbers in array A	NOUN GROUP, DIRECT OBJECT, DETERMINED, DEFINITE, PLURAL
the	DETERMINER, DEFINITE
numbers	NOUN, PLURAL
in array A	PREPOSITION GROUP, QUALIFIER
in	PREPOSITION
array	NOUN, CLASSIFIER
A	NOUN, PREP OBJECT, PROPER, SINGULAR

FIG. 23. A parse of the sentence "Add up the numbers in array A."

The TC-PICKUP routine would check to see whether any objects cover :OBJ, remove them if necessary, and finally pick up :OBJ.

In the column sum example, the world model might be described by the following assertions:

(#NUMBER 3)
(#NUMBER 4)
(#NUMBER 7)
(#NUMBER 9)
(#IN :A 4)
(#IN :A 9)
(#IN :A 7)
(#IN :N 3)
(#TYPE :A #ARRAY)

That is, 3, 4, 7, and 9 are numbers, 4, 9, and 7 are in array A, 3 is in N, and A is an array. Then working on the example sentence as analyzed in Fig. 23, the semantic routines would construct a series of PLANNER statements and execute them within a THFIND statement as described above:

(THFIND ALL $?X1 ($?X1)
 (THGOAL (#TYPE :A #ARRAY))
 (THGOAL (#IN :A $?X1))
 (THGOAL (#NUMBER $?X1)))

The resulting set in this case would be {4, 9, 7}, and this would be turned over to the interpretation routine for "add," which would yield 20. Finally, the answer generation program would probably create the response from a template:

OK, THE ANSWER IS *TWENTY*.

Notice that the THFIND program given is an excellent implementation for the noun group "the numbers in array A." First, it checks to be sure that A is indeed an array and returns nothing if the test fails. If A is not an array, one would expect an intelligent system to object to the command rather than proceeding forward to add up whatever could be found. Second, the routine checks that each item returned is actually a number. If there happen to be any umbrellas or apples in array A, they will wisely be ignored in the computation. The system will, in fact, correctly carry out the command: "Add up the numbers in array A."

Besides executing imperatives as described above, the Winograd system can answer questions. Thus the user could ask

Which red pyramid is supported by a green block?

and the system would execute the THFIND ALL code describe above. If it finds such a red pyramid, its language response system must construct a description of that pyramid and print it out. If it finds none or several such pyramids, it must produce appropriate answers. The user might ask

> How many red pyramids are supported by green blocks?

and again the same THFIND ALL code would be used. This time the cardinality of the resulting set would be given as the answer.

The user might ask the question

> When was a red pyramid supported by a green block?

or

> Why was a red pyramid supported by a green block?

Here the system must reference an event list that is maintained throughout the dialogue, giving the major events that have occurred and the reasons associated with them. When questions are asked about past events or their reasons, it deduces answers and prints them out in English. Thus, after the system had solved a block-stacking problem, Winograd was able to carry it through the following sequence:

- U. Why did you do that?
- A. TO CLEAN OFF THE RED CUBE.
- U. Why did you clean off that cube?
- A. TO PUT IT ON A LARGE GREEN CUBE.
- U. Why did you do that?
- A. TO STACK UP THE RED CUBE, A LARGE RED BLOCK, AND A LARGE GREEN ONE.
- U. Why did you do that?
- A. BECAUSE YOU ASKED ME TO.
- U. How did you do it?
- A. BY PUTTING A LARGE RED BLOCK ON THE TABLE; THEN LETTING GO OF IT; THEN PUTTING....

Finally, Winograd's system can accept some kinds of declarative information. Such sentences result in new theorems or facts being stored into the system's knowledge base as illustrated by the following sequence:

- U. A "steeple" is a stack that contains two green cubes and a pyramid.
- A. I UNDERSTAND.
- U. Are there any steeples now?
- A. NO.
- U. Build one.
- A. OK.

5.4 Discussion

Clearly such brief coverage of any system that claims to process a portion of the English language cannot begin to explain the immense complexities involved. However, it is hoped that the reader can at least partially understand the nature of the mechanisms that make it work. The reader is encouraged to return to the original source for considerably more detail.

No general natural language processing capability exists today and so it is not possible to generate arbitrary programs from an English input. However, a very limited natural language ability can be built into a system if the domain of discourse is sufficiently small. The reader might wish to examine Heidorn (1974) as another interesting example.

6. Heuristic Knowledge-Based Algorithm Synthesis

6.1 Introduction

Most traditional approaches to program synthesis are called *uniform* or *algorithmic*. That is, these methods can be proven to be both "sound" and "complete" in the following senses: A program synthesis system is said to be *sound* if the program produced is guaranteed to meet the specifications input to the system (as given by a higher level language, example computations, or a formal logic description); a system is said to be *complete* if it is capable of producing every possible program over the domain of interest (usually the partial recursive functions). While it is very satisfying to base the design of a system on such firm mathematical foundations, the actual performance obtainable is frequently somewhat disappointing. In using typical programming systems, we are often bothered by how "dumb" they seem to be. A piece of code that would be perfectly clear to any reader is rejected because of the most microscopic imperfections. The most obvious facts imaginable about a program and its execution are completely beyond the "understanding" of a typical system. Artificial intelligence research is aimed at overcoming some of these weaknesses and giving machines a measure of common sense. Some artificial intelligence researchers even dare to hope that computers might someday have a deep thinking ability.

Whatever the case, the goal of the efforts described in this section is to build a knowledge-handling capability into the machine so that it can in some sense "understand" what it is doing. It is desired that the system should have

(1) programming knowledge such as how to declare data structures, build loops and branches, and so forth,

(2) problem domain knowledge such as what are the significant variables and how are they related,

(3) debugging knowledge such as how to discover and remove the cause of a discrepancy between program performance and specifications, and

(4) knowledge of the user such as what information to expect from him, what information to send him, and how to converse with him in his own language.

It is desired that the system be able to acquire, manipulate, and dispense particularly the first two kinds of knowledge and to function as a programming robot for a human user. Some researchers (Balzer, 1973; Goldberg, 1975a,b; Green et al., 1974; Heidorn, 1974) would like the robot to write programs for computer users who may know nothing about programming: doctors, lawyers, businessmen, engineers, and so forth. Others (Hewitt and Smith, 1975) are interested in developing a skilled assistant for the professional programmer. Some individuals (such as Sussman, 1973) would expect the robot to simulate in some ways the process a human being goes through in thinking and in writing code: making guesses as to how to do something, trying out ideas, criticizing, modifying, debugging, learning, and using hunch, analogy, and intuition.

In contrast to an algorithmic program, a *heuristic* program will be defined for the purposes of this chapter as a program whose input–output characteristics are not easily specified (except perhaps by paraphrasing the program itself). Since the input–output specifications of a heuristic program cannot practically be made precise, a proof of correctness (soundness and completeness) is out of the question. It is, of course, always desirable to have an algorithmic program but not always possible. Thus if one is to write a checker-playing program, the ideal strategy would be to have it search the game tree to the end and always play an optimal game. This would be an algorithmic program because optimality in this case is well defined. However, a complete search is not possible, so that any practical such program must make each next move on the basis of whatever strategy its designer can invent. This is a heuristic program. Its next move may be optimal; it may be terrible. The only way to specify what it will do is to point to the code and say that the program will do that. An example of a high quality heuristic program is the checker-playing program by Samuel (1959, 1967).

It appears that most nontrivial intellectual tasks such as playing checkers, writing creative programs, or understanding natural language must involve heuristic processing. We do not know how to state for these tasks precise input–output characteristics that can be practically achieved. Thus, in writing programs to do these tasks, we must write the best code we can in each case and hope that it will do reasonably well most of the time. Humans seem to handle these tasks quite well and there is much evidence that they do not use uniform search algorithms in the process. It is this observation, along with the desire to increase greatly the intelligence of programming systems, that motivates artificial intelligence researchers to turn to heuristic methods. While the program synthesizer using heuristics might produce false starts, try various ideas, modify partial solutions, and erase and begin again, it is hoped that it can slowly converge to a reasonable solution, particularly if it can work continuously in an interaction with a human being.

The reader should consult the following references for a detailed coverage of this work: Balzer (1972, 1973, 1975), Goldstein (1975), Green *et al.* (1974), Green and Barstow (1975b), Heidorn (1974), Hewitt and Smith (1975), Lenat (1975), Manna and Waldinger (1975), Martin *et al.* (1974), Siklóssy (1973, 1974), Simon (1972), Srinivasan (1973), Sussman (1973), and Winograd (1973).

The next sections give an overview of this approach to automatic programming, outline some new ideas in system organization that have been growing up in recent years, and discuss current thinking about knowledge and its application to program synthesis.

6.2 The Major Phases of Processing

Balzer (1972, 1973, 1975) has described the automatic programming process as being divided into four major phases:

(1) problem acquisition when the system interacts with the user to build a model of the problem domain and the problem to be solved,

(2) process transformation when the problem-relevant portions of the model are sifted out to obtain an efficient representation for problem solution,

(3) model verification when testing and debugging are done to check whether the abstracted model is correct, and

(4) automatic coding when the program is actually generated.

A system that exemplifies three of these phases is the one described by Heidorn (1974), which will be briefly described here.

The Heidorn system is capable of carrying on an English dialogue on the subject of queuing problems. During the conversation the system builds a model of the particular queuing problem and then verifies the model by returning an English language description of it. If the user finds the description acceptable, the system translates the model into a GPSS simulation program.

The system views a queuing problem as a set of physical entities moving through a system of stations where they are serviced in some manner. Internally the entities, the stations, the actions performed, and the interrelationships between them are stored in a set of records with attribute lists and pointers back and forth. The automatic programming system is composed of a set of translators into and out of this internal representation. The initial dialogue through a sequence of exchanges causes the model to be slowly built up. A translator from internal representation into English sends a description of the model back to the user, and a translator from internal representation into the GPSS language creates the desired program.

Heidorn includes an example of his system's performance. The dialogue carries the system through Balzer's first phase, problem acquisition:

(1) When a vehicle arrives at a station, it leaves there immediately if the length of the line at a pump in the station is not less than 2.
(2) 75% of the vehicles are cars and 25% are trucks.
(3) There is just one pump.
(4) A simulation run time of 8 hours is desired.
(5) Ask questions for further info.
(6) HOW OFTEN DO THE VEHICLES ARRIVE AT THE STATION?
(7) The arrivals of vehicles are normally distributed with a mean of 8 minutes.
(8) WHAT IS THE STANDARD DEVIATION OF THE NORMAL DISTRIBUTION? ETC.

Balzer's phase 2, process transformation, is largely omitted because the coding of the problem description for this system is immediately usable by the later processes. In the 30th statement of the dialogue, the user asks for a verification of the model (Balzer's phase 3), and the English generation mechanism takes over. The internal representation is slowly scanned with the English sentences being generated along the way:

THE VEHICLES ARRIVE AT THE STATION. THE TIME BETWEEN ARRIVALS OF THE VEHICLES AT THE STATION IS NORMALLY DISTRIBUTED, WITH A MEAN OF 8 MINUTES...

Being satisfied with this description, the user asks for a generated program and receives about one page of GPSS code.

Other efforts along these same lines are described by Balzer (1972, 1973, 1975), Green et al. (1974), Green and Barstow (1975a,b), and Lenat (1975). In each case a reasonably narrow problem domain was defined so that the representation problem could be worked out and so that the number of facts required for nontrivial behavior could be kept within bounds. Balzer (1975) describes a program for a message distribution system, which their system is to generate when it is complete. Green et al. (1974) and

Green and Barstow (1975a,b) are working on a system that can generate large numbers of sorting routines, and Lenat (1975) has developed a system that can generate certain inductive inference programs. Of course, all of these efforts attempt to be general enough to solve problems in other domains if the proper knowledge is made available.

The next section will introduce some ideas in information processing that may become important in the development of these systems over the years.

6.3 Actors, Beings, Frames, and Others

Within several of the artificial intelligence projects in recent years have been growing up some ideas about modularity. These ideas have taken on many forms but this chapter will discuss two kinds of modularity: modules of knowledge and modules of programming. We will examine these concepts, why they seem important, and how they are related.

Modules of knowledge seem to become extremely important when humans carry on a conversation in natural language. For example, if a room is mentioned in a sentence, a whole spectrum of information comes into the human consciousness and any of that information can be referenced. The concept of a room probably includes the concepts of a ceiling, a floor, four walls, rectangularity, and perhaps doors, windows, colors, woodwork, and even furnishings. A person can mention a room in one sentence and perhaps the color of the ceiling or the number of windows in the next sentence without any confusion on the part of the hearer. The hearer does not need to be told that the room has a ceiling or that the ceiling has a color because rooms usually have ceilings and ceilings usually have color. This is what is known as "common sense." Natural language conversation is greatly facilitated if the participants have similar such templates of knowledge that can be called up at will and referenced back and forth. Huge numbers of facts are available to each individual, which never need be mentioned in the conversation even though these facts are essential to the understanding of the interchange.

In the automatic programming domain, if we mention a fact to the system, we would like it similarly to reference such a body of information. If we say

Array A will be an argument

we would like the system to know that arrays have dimensions, they may have a type, a declaration may be required in the program, arrays are sometimes initialized at the beginning of a program, they are scanned using nested FOR loops, and many other facts. If the system has such information it can give an intelligent response. Thus, it might return

WHAT ARE THE DIMENSIONS OF ARRAY A?

It is, of course, desirable for the system to have domain-dependent information also, so that, for example, in an airline scheduling problem, it is not necessary to say that when a plane flies from Atlanta to Birmingham its passengers also go from Atlanta to Birmingham.

Modules of knowledge must necessarily have default values. That is, many facts that do not come up in the conversation about a thing are automatically assumed to be true. This is what enables such modules to help people economize on the length of the interaction. But in a particular situation it must be possible to override almost any of the details in any given module without destroying its usefulness. Thus we would like to be able to talk about a room with five or six walls and perhaps no specifiable color at all, and still use the myriad of facts from the information template on rooms. The hearer would still assume that the room has a floor, a ceiling, and other characteristics of typical rooms. Such modules must have much information but must also be very flexible to be useful.

A particular kind of modularity in programming has also been receiving much attention recently from artificial intelligence researchers. The programming modules are thought of as being relatively independent entities, which activate themselves and which send and receive information without prompting. Thus the control structure of a traditional large program with its well-defined hierarchy of subroutines is being abandoned and being replaced by a kind of democracy of routines. Each routine has knowledge about what it can do, what it needs to know, when it can function, how much work it may have to do, what other routines may be able to help it, and other things. Lenat (1975) speaks of a "community of experts," and if a problem is made available to them, each one comes forth to contribute knowledge and help if he is able. Thus the control structure of a set of such routines is very ill-defined and widely distributed throughout the system.

The kinds of messages that might pass between such routines are also not conventional. Instead of an individual routine receiving x and sending back a value $f(x)$, the whole group of routines might receive the request: Does anyone know anything about "adding"? Several routines might respond, one that knows about adding numbers, another that knows about adding data structures, and a third that can add passengers to a scheduled airplane. The request may have to be followed with more information until one routine sees its own applicability and takes control. If that routine is being asked to add an array, it may have to call for information about arrays and see what it can find out. So the messages being passed around pertain to relevant knowledge. They may be fragmentary; they may be requests, guesses, suggestions, helps, complaints, or criticisms. They will hopefully enable the set of individual modules to put together the needed bits of information from many sources to come to a solution to the problem.

The attractions of this type of programming are many. It enables the programmer to delay decisions about the control structure until knowledge modules are being constructed and to base control decisions on the contents of these individual modules. It makes it possible to design individual modules without as much concern for their effect on the rest of the system. It enables the programmer to add routines and thus capabilities to the system and to hope that previously debugged code will still continue to function properly. The problem with such code, of course, is that upon being given a task to do, the group of routines may be contented to sit there and send messages back and forth without ever making any progress.

These ideas of modules of knowledge and of programming have come together in various ways to form *actors* (Hewitt *et al.*, 1973; Hewitt and Smith, 1975), *beings* (Green *et al.*, 1974; Lenat, 1975), *frames* (Minsky, 1974, 1975; Hewitt, 1975), and other such entities. That is, the community-of-experts approach to programming becomes an implementation of the above described modules-of-knowledge view of the world. The concept of actors seems to place more emphasis on aspects of programming; the concept of frames places more emphasis on modularity of knowledge. Beings stress both. The remainder of this section will show how a set of beings might be constructed that can write a program to sum an array.

This hypothetical system will have three data structures, which will act like a blackboard that all beings can see:

CURRENT SENTENCE. This holds the most recent input from the user. After the sentence is processed it is erased.

REQUESTS. The natural language processor translates inputs into special format requests, which appear in this list. As processing proceeds to satisfy these requests, they are marked "satisfied."

PROGRAM. The requests are translated into a program, which appears here.

All beings continuously observe these data structures, and if any one sees that it is applicable, it activates itself and does its work. There are five beings, as shown in Fig. 24. Each being has three parts, which give, respectively, its name, the criteria that must be satisfied before it will go into action, and the processing that it will perform.

This system, if implemented, can complete the following interaction with

APPROACHES TO AUTOMATIC PROGRAMMING

a user (the internal result of each exchange is indicated):

Dialogue	Result
System: WHAT CAN I DO FOR YOU?	
User: Write a program for me that adds.	Requests PROGRAM, ADD
System: WHAT IS THE NAME OF YOUR PROGRAM?	
User: COLSUM.	NAME = COLSUM first line of code is generated PROGRAM request is satisfied
System: WHAT IS TO BE ADDED?	
User: The array A.	OP 1 = A
System: WHAT IS A TO BE ADDED TO?	
User: No, you don't understand. The elements of A are to be totaled up.	(TO BE TOTALED)
System: WHERE IS THE RESULT TO BE PLACED?	
User: In SUM.	OP 3 = SUM summing routine is produced ADD request is satisfied terminate code with END

System: I HAVE GENERATED A PROGRAM.
HOW IS THIS?
PROCEDURE COLSUM;
SUM = 0;
FOR I = 1 TO #A;
 SUM = SUM + A(I);
 END;
END;

The REQUESTS data structure at the end of the exchange would look like this:

REQUESTS
 PROGRAM NAME = COLSUM (SATISFIED)
 ADD OP1 = A (TO BE TOTALED) OP3 = SUM
 (SATISFIED)

This example is, of course, very simple. Any system that performs nontrivial tasks must necessarily have many more beings and much more complexity within each being. Lenat (1975) has implemented a system that uses about 100 beings each of which has 29 parts.

6.4 On the Development of Knowledge about Knowledge

Thus far the emphasis of the heuristic programming efforts has been on the study of knowledge: how it is represented, how it is acquired, manipu-

name: ADDER
application: if request is ADD, AND, PLUS, SUM
processing:
   if OP 1, OP 2, OP 3 are known, produce code, mark request satisfied, exit
   if OP 1 and OP 3 are known and OP 1 is to be totaled, produce code, mark request satisfied, exit
   if OP 1 is not known
      output WHAT IS TO BE ADDED?, exit
   if OP 2 is not known and OP1 is not to be totaled
      output WHAT IS (OP 1) TO BE ADDED TO?, exit
   if OP 3 is not known
      output WHERE IS THE RESULT TO BE PLACED?, exit

name: INITIALIZER
application: if no requests have been made
processing:
   output WHAT CAN I DO FOR YOU?, exit

name: NAMER
application: if request is PROGRAM
processing:
   if NAME is not known
      output WHAT IS THE NAME OF YOUR PROGRAM?, exit
   if NAME is known, produce code, mark request satisfied, exit

name: TERMINATER
application: if all requests are satisfied
processing:
   add END to generated program
   output I HAVE GENERATED A PROGRAM. HOW IS THIS?
   output the program
   exit

name: TRANSLATOR
application: if current sentence is nonblank
processing:
   translate current sentence into request format
   erase current sentence
   exit

FIG. 24. Five beings.

lated, and accessed, and how it is used to create programs. It is perhaps worthwhile to indicate briefly some of the ideas about knowledge that are currently developing.

The most important problem to be addressed is the representation problem: How is knowledge to be represented? Facts could be stored in the machine in terms of tables, property lists, semantic nets, formal logic axioms, executable programs, and many other forms. The reader should examine Minsky (1968) for discussions of various ideas developed during the 1960s. Most current thinking, as indicated in the previous discussion, is that knowledge must be represented "procedurally." That is, knowledge has been found to be so dynamic, so unpredictable in form, and so lacking in uniformity that no simple method for representation seems adequate. The full power of a programming language has been required to store the facts necessary to do most nontrivial artificial intelligence tasks. Thus the procedural representation of knowledge as described by Winograd and the modules of programming approach discussed above are the embodiment of current theories on the representation problem.

Second, one might ask how much knowledge is required to do a particular task, and the studies of Green et al. (1974) address this particular question. For example, Green and Barstow (1975a) give a long hypothetical dialogue between a man and a machine, which exhibits the knowledge required to create a simple sorting routine. The required amount of knowledge could be measured in terms of numbers of facts or perhaps numbers of beings. Thus Lenat (1975) states that 87 "experts" were required to create his concept formation program, 70 of which dealt with programming and 17 of which were problem specific. Green et al. (1974) estimate that "a few-thousand 'facts' could enable a program to understand simple list-processing programs." As these efforts approach more maturity, more specific such information will become available.

A major concern, of course, is the usefulness of these facts or beings in the creation of many different kinds of programs. Thus Lenat (1975) reports that 46 of the 70 available general programming beings were used in creating a grammatical inference program.

Another recent interest is the study of approximate knowledge and its use and modification. Sussman (1973), for example, has his system propose a program to solve a problem, even though the program may not be at all correct. Then his system modifies the first approximation until it converges on a solution. Balzer (1975) discusses "imprecise program specification" and the problem of creating code on the basis of input from an unsophisticated user. Many of the other references listed above attempt to deal with approximate knowledge of one kind or another.

How is knowledge about knowledge to be obtained? The answer from the artificial intelligence community seems to be unanimous: One should study examples. Thus in the program synthesis domain, one should very carefully study how one example program might be created. Then one should look sequentially at how several similar programs might be produced, how a class of related programs might be produced, and eventually how the synthesis capability might be extended to other classes of programs. The philosophy is not totally unlike that of Section 3. If one has a program that can do one or several examples, the chances are that one is not too far away from having a program that can do many examples.

In conclusion, we will examine one simple program synthesis from the literature and the nature of the required knowledge. In this case, we will study the creation of a set union program as described by Manna and Waldinger (1975). Some primitives that are available in the programming language are

head (s) = first element in an ordered set s
tail (s) = set s with the first element omitted
add $(x\ s)$ = set s with x added as an additional element
empty (s) = true if set s is empty, false otherwise

The system is then assumed to have the following knowledge about sets:

(1) $x \in s$ is false if empty (s) is true.
(2) $x \in s$ is equivalent to ($x =$ head (s) or $x \in$ tail (s)) if empty (s) is false.
(3) $\{x \mid x \in s\}$ is equal to s.
(4) $\{x \mid x = a$ or $Q(x)\}$ is equal to add $(a\{x \mid Q(x)\})$.

It is desired to create a program to compute

union $(s\ t) = \{x \mid x \in s$ or $x \in t\}$.

In addition to problem domain knowledge, there is programming knowledge in the system. Heuristic rules that might resemble those of a human programmer are associated with each type of programming construct. Thus the

if p then q else r

construct is used if knowledge of the fact p helps in writing the program. Manna and Waldinger call this "world splitting;" instead of writing a program with uncertainty about p, q can be written knowing p is true and r can be written knowing p is false. Each is, hopefully, a simpler task than the original one. In the case of the union program, the application of rules (1) and (3) yields a very simple program for union. That is, if it is known that empty (s) is true then

$$\begin{aligned} \text{union } (s\ t) &= \{x \mid x \in s \text{ or } x \in t\} \\ &= \{x \mid \text{false or } x \in t\} \\ &= \{x \mid x \in t\} \\ &= t \end{aligned}$$

So the Manna and Waldinger heuristic mechanism proposes the partial program

$$\text{union } (s\ t) = \text{if empty } (s) \text{ then } t \text{ else} \ldots$$

A recursive subroutine call is another programming construct that is discussed in this work. Such a call is made if a subgoal is generated that is identical in form to the top level goal associated with the program. In the case of the union program, the "else" portion of the code must be created [knowing that empty (s) is false]. Here rules (2) and (4) are applicable, giving the following transformations:

$$\begin{aligned}
\text{union } (s\ t) &= \{x \mid x \in s \text{ or } x \in t\} \\
&= \{x \mid x = \text{head } (s) \text{ or } x \in \text{tail } (s) \text{ or } x \in t\} \\
&= \text{add } (\text{head } (s)\ \{x \mid x \in \text{tail } (s) \text{ or } x \in t\})
\end{aligned}$$

But $\{x \mid x \in \text{tail } (s) \text{ or } x \in t\}$ can be recognized to be of the same form as the top level goal, so that a recursive call can be generated and the complete program becomes

$$\text{union } (s\ t) = \text{if empty } (s) \text{ then } t \text{ else add } (\text{head } (s)$$
$$\text{union } (\text{tail } (s)\ t)).$$

The original source and Waldinger (1975) discuss other problems in program synthesis and give many additional examples.

6.5 Summary

This section has discussed a number of research efforts directed toward building knowledge-handling facilities into programming systems. It is desired that these systems have some common sense and perhaps even a thinking ability, which can be called on to help the user create a correct program. The goals of the designers of these systems are ambitious: to build in a natural language understanding and generation ability, to incorporate a model-building function and nontrivial problem-solving abilities, to include learning and inductive abilities, and much more.

Attacking these problems seems to require the use of heuristic methods, and new concepts in program organization are developing for writing these programs. These new concepts involve distribution of control functions throughout the program, a new kind of program modularity, collection together of related knowledge and the procedural representation of that knowledge, and many kinds of internal communications.

The research described here is still in its initial stages of development and some years will pass before it will have a chance to reach fruition.

7. Comments

We might conclude this survey by asking what fundamental mechanisms are available for creating programs. An examination of the literature discussed here seems to indicate that there are exactly three basic processes that a system can use in obtaining the desired program.

(1) The system can be directly given the program or information from which the program can be directly built. Thus the program might be typed in by the user in a language that can be directly converted to the target program, or the target program may already exist in a library.

(2) The system may have to enumerate from the set of all possible programs, from the set of all possible proofs, or from some other space until an acceptable answer is found.

(3) The system may be able to build the desired program by modifying and combining known programs.

It appears that every algorithm available today came to us through combinations of these processes and that all future algorithms will be constructed from them. A study of the approaches discussed in this chapter reveals that they all seem to use all three processes. For example, when a very high level language compiler produces some object code, it is partially being given the algorithm by the high level specification, it may search through a number of possible representations before it chooses the data structures, and it usually produces code with a macroexpansionlike technique that is a form of modifying and combining previously known algorithms. One can examine the other approaches and see all three mechanisms at work in each case.

Research in automatic programming involves a study of the languages of the human mind, the languages of machines, and the process of translating between the two. This author views the main task in automatic programming to be the discovery of the nature of these languages and the clever implementation of the three given processes to do the translation. The literature surveyed by this chapter represents the efforts of a large number of researchers in this direction.

Acknowledgments

The author would like to thank, first of all, Professor Susan L. Gerhart for innumerable suggestions and contributions during the preparation of this chapter. I am also very grateful to a number of other individuals who have read the first draft and made comments that have helped me improve the paper's accuracy, completeness, and readability: Drs. Patricia Goldberg, Cordell Green, and Richard Waldinger, Messrs.

David Barstow, John Fairfield, Douglas Lenat, and Douglas Smith. Finally, I would like to thank Mrs. Sharon Christensen for her invaluable help in preparing the manuscript.

The research reported in Section 3 is supported by National Science Foundation Grant Number DCR74-14445.

References

Abrams, P. (1970). "An APL Machine," Rep. No. 114. Stanford Linear Accelerator, Stanford, California.

Adam, A. (1975). GADGET—un programme de génération automatique de programs sur les graphes et les ensembles. Ph. D. Thesis, University of Paris VI, Paris.

Amarel, S. (1962). On the automatic formation of a computer program which represents a theory. *In* "Self-Organizing Systems—1962" (M. Yovits, G. T. Jacobi, and A. D. Goldstein, eds.), pp. 107–175. Spartan Books, Washington, D.C.

Balzer, R. M. (1972). "Automatic Programming," Tech. Rep. No. 1. Information Sciences Institute, University of Southern California, Marina Del Rey.

Balzer, R. M. (1973). A global view of automatic programming. *Proc. J. Conf. Artif. Intell., 3rd, 1973* p. 494.

Balzer, R. M. (1975). Imprecise program specification. *Proc. Consiglio Nazl. Ric. Ist. Elaborazione Inf., 1975*.

Barzdin, J., and Freivald, R. V. (1972). On the prediction of general recursive functions. *Sov. Math. (Engl. Transl.)* **13**, No. 5, 1224–1228.

Bauer, M. (1975). Ph.D. Thesis, Department of Computer Science, University of Toronto, Toronto (forthcoming).

Biermann, A. W. (1972). On the inference of turing machines from sample computations. *Artif. Intell.* **3**, No. 3, 181–198.

Biermann, A. W. (1975). "Automatic Indexing in Program Synthesis Processes," Tech. Rep. Computer Science Department, Duke University, Durham, North Carolina.

Biermann, A. W., and Feldman, J. A. (1972). A survey of results in grammatical inference. *In* "Frontiers of Pattern Recognition" (S. Watanabe, ed.), p. 31. Academic Press, New York.

Biermann, A. W., and Krishnaswamy, R. (1974). "Constructing Programs from Example Computations," Tech. Rep. OSU-CISRC-TR-74-5. Ohio State University Computer and Information Science Research Center, Columbus (to appear in *IEEE Trans. Software Eng.*).

Biermann, A. W., Baum, R. I., and Petry, F. E. (1975). Speeding up the synthesis of programs from traces. *IEEE Trans. Comput.* **C24**, No. 2, 122–136.

Blum, L., and Blum, M. (1975). Toward a mathematical theory of inductive inference. *Inf. Control* **28**, 125–155.

Bobrow, D. G. (1968). Natural language input for a computer problem solving system. *In* "Semantic Information Processing" (M. Minsky, ed.), pp. 217–252. MIT Press, Cambridge, Massachusetts.

Bobrow, D. G., and Raphael, B. (1974). New programming languages for artificial intelligence research. *Comput. Surv.* **6**, No. 3, 153–174.

Boyer, R. S., and Moore, J. S. (1975). Proving theorems about LISP programs. *J. Assoc. Comput. Mach.* **22**, 129–144.

Buchanan, J. R. (1974). "A Study in Automatic Programming," Tech. Rep. Computer Science Department, Carnegie-Mellon University, Pittsburgh, Pennsylvania.

Buchanan, J. R., and Luckham, D. C. (1974). "On Automating the Construction of Programs," Tech. Rep., Stanford Artificial Intelligence Project, Stanford, California.

Chang, C.-L., and Lee, R. C.-T. (1973). "Symbolic Logic and Mechanical Theorem Proving." Academic Press, New York.

Coles, L. S. (1968). An on-line question-answering system with natural language and pictorial input. *Proc. Conf. Assoc. Comput. Mach., 23rd, 1968* pp. 157–167.

Dahl, O.-J., Dijkstra, E. W., and Hoare, C. A. R. (1972). "Structured Programming." Academic Press, New York.

Dershowitz, N., and Manna, Z. (1975). On automating structured programming. *Proc. Int. Symp. Proving Improving Programs, 1975.*

Duran, J. W. (1975). "A Study of Loop Invariants and Automatic Program Synthesis," Rep. SESLTR-12. Department of Computer Science, University of Texas, Austin.

Earley, J. (1974). High level operations in automatic programming. *Proc. Symp. Very High Level Lang., 1974* pp. 34–42.

Elspas, B., Levitt, K. N., Waldinger, R. J., and Waksman, A. (1972). An assessment of techniques for proving program correctness. *ACM Comput. Surv.* **4,** No. 2, 97–147.

Feldman, J. A. (1972a). "Automatic Programming," Rep. CS-255. Department of Computer Science, Stanford University, Stanford.

Feldman, J. A. (1972b). Some decidability results on grammatical inference and complexity. *Inf. Control* **20,** No. 3, 244–262.

Feldman, J. A., and Gries, D. (1968). Translator writing systems. *Commun. ACM* **11,** No. 2, 77–113.

Feldman, J. A., and Royner, P. (1969). An Algol-based associative language. *Commun. ACM* **12,** No. 8, 439–449.

Feldman, J. A., Low, J., Swinehart, D., and Taylor, R. (1972). Recent developments in SAIL—an Algol-based language for artificial intelligence. *Proc. Fall Jt. Comput. Conf., 1972* pp. 1193–1202.

Fikes, R. E., and Nilsson, N. J. (1971). STRIPS: A new approach to the application of theorem proving to problem solving. *Artif. Intell.* **2,** No. 3/4, 189–208.

Floyd, R. W. (1967). Assigning meanings to programs. *Proc. Symp. Appl. Math.* **19,** 19–32.

Gerhart, S. L. (1972). Verification of APL programs. Ph.D. Thesis. Department of Computer Science, Carnegie-Mellon University, Pittsburgh, Pennsylvania.

Gerritsen, R. (1973). "Automatically Generated Programs for Information Retrieval," Tech. Rep., Graduate School of Industrial Administration, Carnegie-Mellon University, Pittsburgh, Pennsylvania.

Gold, M. (1967). Language identification in the limit. *Inf. Control* **10,** No. 5, 447–474.

Goldberg, P. C. (1975a). Automatic programming. *In* "Programming Methodology" (G. Goos and J. Hartmanis, eds.), Lect. Notes Comput. Sci., Vol. 23, p. 347. Springer-Verlag, Berlin and New York.

Goldberg, P. C. (1975b). "Structured Programming for Non-Programmers," Rep. No. RC-5318. IBM Research, Yorktown Heights, New York.

Goldstein, I. P. (1975). Summary of MYCROFT: A system for understanding simple picture programs. *Artif. Intell.* **6,** No. 3, 249–288.

Good, D. I., London, R. L., and Bledsoe, W. W. (1975). An interactive program verification system. *IEEE Trans. Software Eng.,* **sel,** No. 1, 59–67.

Green, C. C. (1969a). Theorem proving by resolution as a basis for question answering systems. *In* "Machine Intelligence 4" (B. Meltzer and D. Michie, eds.), pp. 183–205. Edinburgh Univ. Press, Edinburgh.

Green, C. C. (1969b). Application of theorem proving to problem solving. *Proc. Int. Jt. Conf. Artif. Intel., 1st, 1969* pp. 219–239.

Green, C. C. (1969c). The application of theorem proving to question answering systems. Ph.D. Thesis. Artificial Intelligence Laboratory Rep. STAN-CS-69-138. Computer Science Department, Stanford University, Stanford, California.

Green, C., and Barstow, D. (1975a). "A Hypothetical Dialogue Exhibiting a Knowledge Base for a Program-Understanding System," Rep. AIM-258. Stanford Artificial Intelligence Laboratory, Stanford, California.

Green, C., and Barstow, D. (1975b). Some rules for the automatic synthesis of programs. *Proc Int. Jt. Conf. Artif. Intel., 4th, 1975* pp. 232–239.

Green, C. C., and Raphael, B. (1968). The use of theorem proving techniques in question answering systems. *Proc. ACM Natl. Conf., 23rd, 1968* pp. 169–181.

Green, C. C., Waldinger, R. J., Barstow, D. R., Elschlager, R., Lenat, D. B., McCune, B. P., Shaw, D. E., and Steinberg, L. I. (1974). "Progress Report on Program-Understanding Systems," Memo AIM-240. Stanford Artificial Intelligence Laboratory, Stanford, California.

Gries, D. (1971). "Compiler Construction for Digital Computers." Wiley, New York.

Halliday, M. A. K. (1967). Notes on transitivity and theme in English. *J. Ling.* **3**, 37–81; **4**, 179–215.

Halliday, M. A. K. (1970). Functional diversity in language as seen from a consideration of modality and mood in English. *Found. Lang.* **6**, 322–361.

Hammer, M. M., Howe, W. G., and Wladawsky, I. (1974). An interactive business definition system. *Proc. Symp. Very High Level Lang., 1974* pp. 25–33.

Hardy, S. (1973). "The POPCORN Reference Manual," Rep. CSM-1. Essex University.

Hardy, S. (1974). Automatic induction of LISP functions. *AISB Summer Conf., 1974* pp. 50–62.

Heidorn, G. E. (1974). English as a very high level language for simulation programming. *Proc. Symp. Very High Level Lang., 1974* p. 91.

Hewitt, C. E. (1975). STEREOTYPES as an ACTOR approach towards solving the problem of procedural attachment in FRAME theories. *Proc. Interdiscip. Workshop Comput. Linguistics, Psychol., Linguistics, Artif. Intell., 1975* pp. 94–103.

Hewitt, C. E., and Smith, B. (1975). Towards a programming apprentice. *IEEE Trans. Software Eng.*, **se1**, No. 1, 26–45.

Hewitt, C. E., Bishop, P., and Steiger, R. (1973). A universal modular ACTOR formalism for artificial intelligence. *Proc. Int. Jt. Conf. Artif. Intel., 3rd, 1973* pp. 235–245.

Hoare, C. A. R. (1969). An axiomatic basis for computer programming. *Commun. ACM* **12**, 576–583.

Hopcroft, J. E., and Ullman, J. D. (1969). "Formal Languages and Their Relation to Automata." Addison-Wesley, Reading, Massachusetts.

Howe, G. W., Kruskal, V. J., and Wladawsky, I. (1975). "A New Approach for Customizing Business Applications," Rep. No. RC 5474 (#23258). IBM Research, Yorktown Heights, New York.

Iverson, K. E. (1972). "A Programming Language." Wiley, New York.

Knuth, D. E. (1968). Semantics of context-free languages. *In* "Mathematical Systems Theory 2," No. 2, pp. 127–145. Springer-Verlag, Berlin and New York.

Leavenworth, B. M., and Sammet, J. E. (1974). An overview of nonprocedural languages. *Proc. Symp. Very High Level Lang., 1974* pp. 1–12.

Lee, R. C. T., Chang, C. L., and Waldinger, R. J. (1974). An improved program-synthesizing algorithm and its correctness. *Commun. ACM* **17**, No. 4, 211–217.

Lenat, D. B. (1975). BEINGS: Knowledge as interacting experts. *Proc. Int. Jt. Conf. Artif. Intel., 4th, 1975* p. 126.

London, R. L. (1970). Bibliography on proving the correctness of programs. In "Machine Intelligence" (B. Meltzer and D. Michie, eds.), Vol. 5, pp. 569–580. New York.

Low, J. R. (1974). "Automatic Coding: Choice of Data Structures," Tech. Rep. No. 1. Department of Computer Science, University of Rochester, Rochester, New York.

McKeeman, W. M., Horning, J. J., and Wortman, D. B. (1970). "A Compiler Generator." Prentice-Hall, Englewood Cliffs, New Jersey.

Manna, Z., and Waldinger, R. J. (1971). Toward automatic program synthesis. *Commun. ACM* **14**, No. 3, 151–164.

Manna, Z., and Waldinger, R. J. (1975). Knowledge and reasoning in program synthesis. *Artif. Intell.* **6**, No. 2, 175–208.

Martin, W. A., Ginzberg, M. J., Krumland, R., Mark, B., Morgenstern, M., Niamir, B., and Sunguroff, A. (1974). Internal memos. Automatic Programming Group, Massachusetts Institute of Technology, Cambridge.

Mikelsons, M. (1975). Computer assisted application definition. "Conference Record of the Second Symposium on Principles of Programming Languages," pp. 233–242. Palo Alto, California.

Minsky, M. (1968). "Semantic Information Processing." MIT Press, Cambridge, Massachusetts.

Minsky, M. (1974). "A Framework for Representing Knowledge," AI Rep. 306. Massachusetts Institute of Technology, Cambridge.

Minsky, M. (1975). Frame system theory. *Proc. Interdiscip. Workshop Comput. Linguistics, Psychol., Linguistics, Artif. Intel., 1975* pp. 104–115.

Morris, J. B. (1973). "A Comparison of MADCAP and SETL." Los Alamos Sci. Lab., University of California, Los Alamos, New Mexico.

Nilsson, N. J. (1971). "Problem Solving Methods in Artificial Intelligence." McGraw-Hill, New York.

Perlis, A. J. (1972). Automatic programming. *Q. Appl. Math.* **30**, 85–90.

Petry, F. E. (1975). "Program Inference from Example Computations Represented by Memory Snapshot Traces," Tech. Rep. OSU-CISRC-TR-75-1. Ohio State University Computer and Information Science Research Center, Columbus.

Robinson, J. (1965). A machine oriented logic based on the resolution principle. *J. Assoc. Comput. Mach.* **12**, 23–41.

Rulifson, J. F., Derksen, J. A., and Waldinger, R. J. (1972). "QA4: A Procedural Calculus for Intuitive Reasoning," Tech. Rep. No. 73. Stanford Research Institute, Menlo Park, California.

Samuel, A. (1959). Some studies in machine learning using the game of checkers. *IBM J. Res. Dev.* **3**, 210–229.

Samuel, A. (1967). Some studies in machine learning using the game of checkers. II. *IBM J. Res. Dev.* **11**, 601–617.

Schwartz, J. T. (1974). Automatic and semiautomatic optimization of SETL. *Proc. Symp. Very High Level Lang., 1974* pp. 43–49.

Shank, R. (1972). Conceptual dependency: A theory of natural language understanding. *Cognitive Psychol.* **3**, No. 4, 552–631.

Shaw, D. E., Swartout, W. R., and Green, C. C. (1975). Inferring LISP programs from examples. *Proc. Int. Jt. Conf. Artif. Intel., 4th, 1975* pp. 260–267.

Siklóssy, L. (1973). The case for, and some experience with, automated consultants. *Proc. Tex. Conf. Comput. Syst., 2nd, 1973*.

Siklóssy, L. (1974). The synthesis of programs from their properties, and the insane heuristic. *Proc. Tex. Conf. Comput. Syst., 3rd, 1974* p. 23-1.

Simmons, R. F., Burger, J. F., and Schwarcz, R. A. (1968). A computational model of verbal understanding. *Proc. Fall Jt. Comput. Conf., 1968* pp. 441–456.

Simon, H. A. (1972). The Heuristic compiler. *In* "Representation and Meaning" (H. Simon and L. Siklóssy, eds.), pp. 9–43. Prentice-Hall, Englewood Cliffs, New Jersey.

Slagle, J. R. (1971). "Artificial Intelligence: The Heuristic Programming Approach." McGraw-Hill, New York.

Solomonoff, R. (1964). A formal theory of inductive inference. *Inf. Control* pp. 1–22, 224–254.

Srinivasan, C. V. (1973). "Programming Over a Knowledge Base: The Basis for Automatic Programming," Rep. SOSAP-TM-4. Dept. of Computer Science, Rutgers University, New Brunswick, New Jersey.

Summers, P. (1975a). Program construction from examples. Ph.D. Thesis, Yale University, New Haven, Connecticut.

Summers, P. D. (1975b). A methodology for LISP program construction from examples. *Proc. ACM Sym. Prin. Prog. Lang., 3rd, 1975* p. 68.

Sussman, G. J. (1973). "A Computational Model of Skill Acquisition," Rep. AI-TR-297. Artificial Intelligence Laboratory, Massachusetts Institute of Technology, Cambridge.

Sussman, G. J., and McDermott, D. V. (1972). From PLANNER to CONNIVER— a genetic approach. *Proc. Fall Jt. Comput. Conf., 1972* Vol. 41.

Sussman, G. J., Winograd, T., and Charniak, E. (1971). "Micro Planner Reference Manual," Artif. Intell. Memo No. 203A. Artificial Intelligence Laboratory, Massachusetts Institute of Technology, Cambridge.

Waldinger, R. J. (1969). Constructing programs automatically using theorem proving. Doctoral Thesis, Carnegie-Mellon University, Pittsburgh, Pennsylvania.

Waldinger, R. J. (1975). "Achieving Several Goals Simultaneously," Artif. Intell. Cent. Tech. Note No. 107. Stanford Research Institute, Menlo Park, California.

Waldinger, R. J., and Lee, R. C. T. (1969). PROW: A step towards automatic program writing. *Proc. Int. Jt. Conf. Artif. Intel., 1st, 1969* pp. 241–252.

Wiedmann, C. (1974). "Handbook of APL Programming." Petrocelli Books, New York.

Winograd, T. (1972). "Understanding Natural Language." Academic Press, New York.

Winograd, T. (1973). Breaking the complexity barrier again. *Proc. ACM SIGPLAN-SIGIR Interface Meet., 1973* pp. 13–22.

Woods, W. A. (1970). Transition network grammars for natural language analysis. *Commun. ACM* **13**, No. 10, 591–606.

The Algorithm Selection Problem[*]

JOHN R. RICE

Department of Computer Science
Purdue University
West Lafayette, Indiana

1. Introduction 65
2. Abstract Models 67
   2.1 The Basic Model and Associated Problems 67
   2.2 The Model with Selection Based on Features 70
   2.3 Alternate Definitions of Best for the Models 73
   2.4 The Model with Variable Performance Criteria 75
3. Concrete Application—The Selection of Quadrature Algorithms . . 77
   3.1 The Components in the Abstract Model 77
   3.2 Review of Previous Work on Quadrature Algorithm Evaluation . 79
   3.3 A Systematic Evaluation and Selection Approach 81
4. Concrete Application—The Selection of Operating System Schedulers . 82
   4.1 The Components in the Abstract Model 82
   4.2 An Actual Scheduling Algorithm 84
   4.3 An Approach to the Selection of the "Best" Scheduler . . . 85
5. Discussion of the Two Concrete Applications 90
6. Approximation Theory Machinery 91
   6.1 Formulation and Structure of the Approximation Problem . . 91
   6.2 Norms and Approximation Forms 91
   6.3 Classification of Problems, Degree of Convergence, Complexity, and Robustness 95
   6.4 Brief Survey of Approximation Form Attributes 101
   6.5 An Error to Avoid 108
   6.6 The Mathematical Theory Questions 109
   6.7 Conclusions, Open Questions, and Problems 115
   References 117

1. Introduction

The problem of selecting an effective or good or best algorithm arises in a wide variety of situations. The context of these situations often obscures

[*] This work was partially supported by the National Science Foundation through Grant GP-32940X. This chapter was presented as the George E. Forsythe Memorial Lecture at the Computer Science Conference, February 19, 1975, Washington, D. C.

the common features of this selection problem, and the primary purpose of this chapter is to formulate abstract models appropriate for considering it. Within the framework established by these models we present a variety of questions that can (and usually should) be asked in any specific application.

It should be made clear that we do not believe that these models will lead directly (by simple specialization) to superior selection procedures. This will always require exploitation of the specific nature of the situation at hand. Even so, we do believe that these models will clarify the consideration of this problem and, in particular, show that some approaches used are based on naive assumptions about the selection process.

Three concrete examples follow, which the reader can use to interpret the abstractions in this chapter.

(a) **Quadrature** One is given a function $f(x)$, an interval $[a,b]$, and a tolerance $\epsilon > 0$. One is to select an algorithm to estimate

$$\int_a^b f(x)\, dx$$

which is efficient [uses few evaluations of $f(x)$] and reliable (produces an estimate within the specified tolerance).

(b) **Operating Systems** One is given an environment for a large computer operation. Information known includes the mix of jobs between batch, interactive and semi-interactive, some basic characteristics of these classes of jobs, and the characteristics of the computer operation. One is to select an algorithm to schedule the execution of these jobs that produces (1) high batch throughput, (2) good response to interactive jobs, (3) good service to semi-interactive jobs, and (4) high priority fidelity.

(c) **Artificial Intelligence** One is given a description of the game Tic-Tac-Toe. One is to select an algorithm to play the game that is effective, i.e., never loses and wins whenever an opponent's mistake allows it.

A selection procedure is invariably obtained by assigning values to parameters in general "form." More precisely, the selection procedure itself is an algorithm and a specific class of algorithms is chosen with free parameters, which are then chosen so as to satisfy (as well as they can) the objectives of the selection problem. Classical forms include polynomials (with coefficients as parameters) and linear mappings (with matrix coefficients or weights as parameters). Other relevant forms are decision trees (with size, shape, and individual decision elements as parameters) and programs (with various program elements as parameters).

The models presented here are primarily aimed at algorithm selection problems with the following three characteristics:

(d) Problem Space The set of problems involved is very large and quite diverse. This set is of high dimension in the sense that there are a number of independent characteristics of the problems that are important for the algorithm selection and performance. There is usually considerable uncertainty about these characteristics and their influences.

(e) Algorithm Space The set of algorithms that needs to be considered is large and diverse. Ideally there may be millions of algorithms, and practically there may be dozens of them. In counting algorithms we do not distinguish between two that are identical except for the value of some numeric parameter. Again this set is of high dimensions and there is uncertainty about the influence of algorithm characteristics.

(f) Performance Measure The criteria to measure the performance of a particular algorithm for a particular problem are complex and hard to compare (e.g., one wants fast execution, high accuracy, and simplicity). Again there is considerable uncertainty in assigning and interpreting these measures.

2. Abstract Models

2.1 The Basic Model and Associated Problems

We describe the basic abstract model by the diagram in Fig. 1. The items in this model are defined below in detail so as to make the nature of the model completely clear:

- $\mathcal{P}$ problem space or collection
- x member of $\mathcal{P}$, problem to be solved
- $\mathcal{A}$ algorithm space or collection

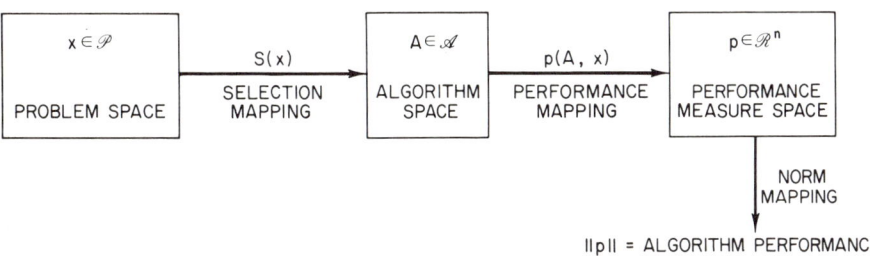

FIG. 1. Schematic diagram of the basic model for the algorithm selection problem. The objective is to determine $S(x)$ so as to have high algorithm performance.

A member of $\mathcal{A}$, algorithm applicable to problems from $\mathcal{P}$
S mapping from $\mathcal{P}$ to $\mathcal{A}$
$\mathcal{R}^n$ n-dimensional real vector space of performance measures
p mapping from $\mathcal{A} \times \mathcal{P}$ to $\mathcal{R}^n$ determining performance measures
$\| \|$ norm on $\mathcal{R}^n$ providing one number to evaluate an algorithm's performance on a particular problem

For completeness we now state the:

(a) Algorithm Selection Problem   Given all the other items in the above model, determine the selection mapping $S(x)$.

There must, of course, be some criteria for this selection and we present four primary ones:

(A) *Best selection.* Choose that selection mapping $B(x)$ which gives maximum performance for each problem:

$$\| p(B(x),x) \| \geq \| p(A,x) \| \quad \text{for all} \quad A \in \mathcal{A}$$

(B) *Best selection for a subclass of problems.* One is to choose just one algorithm to apply to every member of a subclass $\mathcal{P}_0 \subset \mathcal{P}$. Choose that selection mapping $S(x) = A_0$ which minimizes the performance degradation for members of $\mathcal{P}_0$ [compared to choosing $B(x)$]:

$$\max_{x \in \mathcal{P}_0} [\| p(B(x),x) \| - \| p(A_0,x) \|]$$
$$\leq \max_{x \in \mathcal{P}_0} [\| p(B(x),x) \| - \| p(A,x) \|] \quad \text{for all} \quad A \in \mathcal{A}$$

(C) *Best selection from a subclass of mappings.* One is to restrict the mapping $S(x)$ to be of a certain form or from a certain subclass $\mathcal{S}_0$ of all mappings from $\mathcal{P}$ to $\mathcal{A}$. Choose that selection mapping $S^*(x)$ from $\mathcal{S}_0$ which minimizes the performance degradation for all members of $\mathcal{P}$:

$$\max_{x \in \mathcal{P}} [\| p(B(x),x) \| - \| p(S^*(x),x) \|]$$
$$\leq \max_{x \in \mathcal{P}} [\| p(B(x),x) \| - \| p(S(x),x) \|] \quad \text{for all} \quad S \in \mathcal{S}_0$$

(D) *Best selection from a subclass of mappings and problems.* One is to choose just one algorithm from a subclass $\mathcal{S}_0$ to apply every member of a subclass $\mathcal{P}_0 \subset \mathcal{P}$. Choose that selection mapping $S^*(x)$ from $\mathcal{S}_0$ which minimizes the performance degradation for all members of $\mathcal{P}_0$:

$$\max_{x \in \mathcal{P}_0} [\| p(B(x),x) \| - \| p(S^*(x),x) \|]$$
$$\leq \min_{S \in \mathcal{S}_0} \max_{x \in \mathcal{P}_0} [\| p(B(x),x) \| - \| p(S(x),x) \|]$$

These four criteria do not exhaust the meaningful criteria but they do illustrate the principal ideas. There are five main steps to the analysis and solution of the algorithm selection problem:

Step 1 (Formulation). Determination of the subclasses of problems and mappings to be used.
Step 2 (Existence). Does a best selection mapping exist?
Step 3 (Uniqueness). Is there a unique best selection mapping?
Step 4 (Characterization). What properties characterize the best selection mapping and serve to identify it?
Step 5 (Computation). What methods can be used actually to obtain the best selection mapping?

The reader familiar with the theory of approximation of functions will recognize this framework, within which we may put that classical theory. The space $\mathcal{P}$ is a function space and the algorithm space $\mathcal{A}$ may be identified with a subspace of $\mathcal{P}$. The algorithm enters as the means of evaluating elements of $\mathcal{A}$. The performance mapping is

$$p(A,x) = ||\, x(t) - A(t)\,||_\mathcal{P}$$

where the norm is taken on $\mathcal{P}$. Thus the performance measure space is $\mathcal{R}^1$ and the norm mapping is trivial.

There are two remarks needed about this observation. First, the body of significant material in approximation theory is large. It would require, no doubt, from 2000 to 4000 pages to present a reasonably complete and concise exposition of the results currently known. This implies that there is a very rich body of material waiting to be applied to the algorithm selection problem, either directly or by analogy. Second, and more important, the algorithm selection problem is an essential extension and generalization of approximation theory. We will see concrete examples of this problem where the current theory of approximation has nothing relevant to apply except by the faintest analogies.

Two concrete examples of the model are discussed in detail in Sections 3 and 4 of this chapter. We present a third, simpler one from the area of artificial intelligence.

(b) Example: A Game-Playing Problem We are to devise an algorithm for playing Tic-Tac-Toe. The problem space is the set of partial games of Tic-Tac-Toe. While this number is large, there are in fact only 28 distinct reasonable games if one eliminates blunders, symmetries, and board rotations. The space $\mathcal{A}$ may be represented as a space of large tables of responses for each situation. However, we restrict our selection to a decision tree that involves only the existence of immediate winning positions and

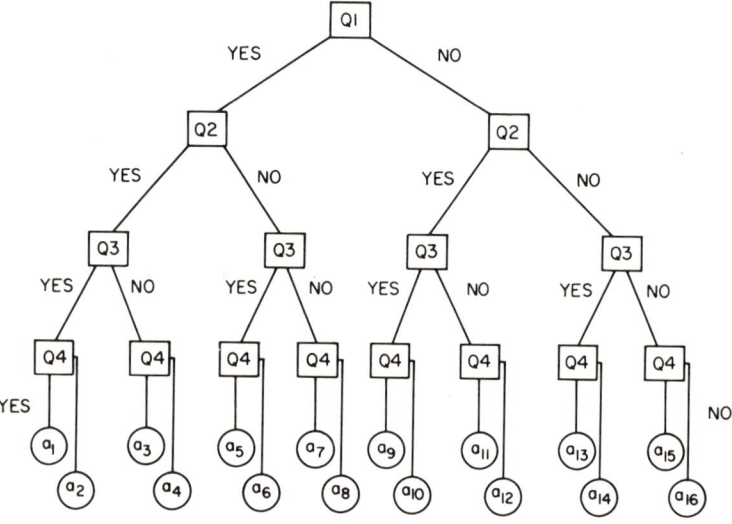

FIG. 2. The form of the selection mapping for the Tic-Tac-Toe example. Each a_i is one of five moves. Q1: Do I have a winning position? Q2: Does opponent have a winning position? Q3: Is the center free? Q4: Is a corner free?

vacant position types. The algorithm form may then be represented as shown in Fig. 2. There are 16 parameters a_i, which take on one of the following five values:

(1) Play the winning move.
(2) Block the opponent's win.
(3) Play in the center square.
(4) Play in a corner (first free one clockwise from upper right).
(5) Play in a side (first free one clockwise from right).

This example is so simple that one can make immediate assignments of certain of the values of the a_i. Experiments have shown that a variety of crude schemes for computing values of the a_i (selecting the best algorithm) work very quickly. Nevertheless, it is still of interest to reflect upon how one would compute this if one had no *a priori* information about the game.

2.2 The Model with Selection Based on Features

An examination of various instances of the algorithm selection problem shows that there is another ingredient almost always present. It is sometimes explicit and sometimes not and we call this selection based on features of the problem. This model is described by the diagram in Fig. 3.

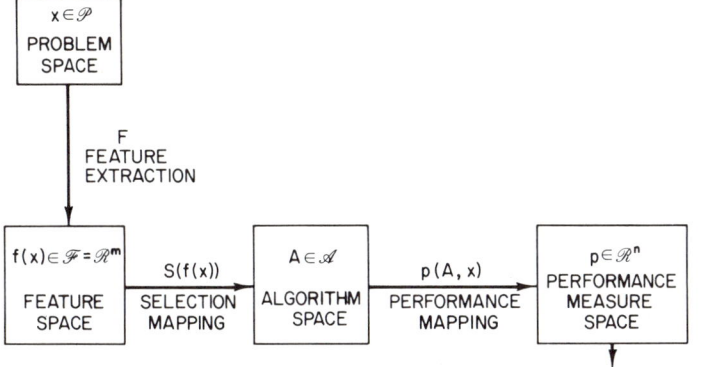

FIG. 3. Schematic diagram of the model with selection based on features of the problem. The selection mapping depends only on the features $f(x)$, yet the performance mapped still depends on the problem x.

The additional definitions for this model are $\mathcal{F}$, feature space identified with $\mathcal{R}^m$ here to suggest it is simpler and of lower dimension than $\mathcal{P}$, and F, mapping from $\mathcal{P}$ to $\mathcal{F}$ that associates features with problems. Note that the selection mapping now depends only on the features $f(x)$, yet the performance mapping still depends on the problem x. The introduction of features may be viewed as a way to systematize the introduction of problem subclasses in the basic model.

The previous statement of the algorithm selection problem and the criteria for selection are still valid for this new model as well as the five steps in the analysis and solution of the problem. The determination of the features to be used is frequently part of the selection process, often one of the most important parts. One may view the features as an attempt to introduce an approximate coordinate system in $\mathcal{P}$. Ideally, those problems with the same features would have the same performance for any algorithm being considered. Since this ideal is rarely achieved, we may pose several specific questions about the determination of features.

(E) *Best features for a particular algorithm.* Given an algorithm A and the dimension m of $\mathcal{F}$, what m features are the best for the prediction of the performance of A? Let $\mathcal{E}(f)$ denote the equivalence class of all those problems $x,y \in \mathcal{P}$ so that $F(x) = F(y) = f$. We then wish to determine the mapping F^* and associated equivalence classes $\mathcal{E}^*(f)$ so that

$$d_m^*(A) = \max_{f \in \mathcal{F}} \max_{x,y \in \mathcal{E}^*(f)} \| p(A,x) - p(A,y) \|$$

$$\leq \max_{f \in \mathcal{F}} \max_{x,y \in \mathcal{E}(f)} \| p(A,x) - p(A,y) \|$$

The selection of best features corresponds to the selection of best approximating subspaces in approximation theory and leads one to ideas of n-widths and entropy of the problem space $\mathcal{P}$. Roughly speaking, if d_m^* is large, then the effective dimension of $\mathcal{P}$ (for the problem at hand) is probably much larger than m and, conversely, if d_m^* is small, then the effective dimension of $\mathcal{P}$ is close to m.

(F) *Best features for a class of algorithms.* Given a set $\mathcal{A}_0 \subset \mathcal{A}$ and the dimension m of $\mathcal{F}$, what m features are the best for prediction of the performance of algorithm $A \in \mathcal{A}_0$? With the previous notation we wish to determine F^* and $\mathcal{E}^*(f)$ so that

$$d_m^*(\mathcal{A}_0) = \max_{f \in \mathcal{F}} \max_{A \in \mathcal{A}_0} \max_{x,y \in \mathcal{E}^*(f)} \| p(A,x) - p(A,y) \|$$

$$\leq \max_{f \in \mathcal{F}} \max_{A \in \mathcal{A}_0} \max_{x,y \in \mathcal{E}(f)} \| p(A,x) - p(A,y) \|$$

(G) *Best features for a subclass of selection mappings.* Given a subclass $\mathcal{S}_0$ of selection mappings from $\mathcal{F}$ to $\mathcal{A}$, what m features are the best for prediction of the performance of algorithms? With the previous notation we wish to determine F^* and $\mathcal{E}^*(f)$ so that

$$d_m^*(\mathcal{S}_0) = \max_{f \in \mathcal{F}} \max_{S \in \mathcal{S}_0} \max_{x,y \in \mathcal{E}^*(f)} \| p(S(f),x) - p(S(f),y) \|$$

$$\leq \max_{f \in \mathcal{F}} \max_{S \in \mathcal{S}_0} \max_{x,y \in \mathcal{E}(f)} \| p(S(f),x) - p(S(f),y) \|$$

The determination of the best (or even good) features is one of the most important, yet nebulous, aspects of the algorithm selection problem. Many problem spaces $\mathcal{P}$ are known only in vague terms and hence an experimental approach is often used to evaluate the performance of algorithms over $\mathcal{P}$. That is, one chooses a sample from $\mathcal{P}$ and restricts considerations to this sample. An appropriate sample is obviously crucial to this approach and if one has a good set of features for $\mathcal{P}$, then one can at least force the sample to be representative with respect to these features. Note that the definition of best features is such that they are the items of information most relevant to the performance of algorithms for the problem at hand.

In some well-understood areas of computation there is a generally agreed upon (if not explicitly stated) set of features. For example, consider the problem of solving a linear system $Ax = b$ of equations. The features include descriptors like small order, sparse, band, diagonally dominant, positive definite, and ill conditioned. Given values for these features, an experienced numerical analyst can select an appropriate algorithm for this problem with considerable confidence. The selection problem for quadrature is already much more difficult and the solution of simultaneous systems of nonlinear equations is very poorly understood. If this situation exists for problems that have been studied for one or two centuries then one should not be surprised by the difficulties and uncertainties for problems that have just appeared in the past one or two decades.

2.3 Alternate Definitions of Best for the Models

In the preceding sections we have uniformly taken a minimax approach to the definition of best or optimum selection. That is, we have minimized the effect of the worst case. It is reasonable to ignore the performance for the worst case and instead consider optimizing some sort of average behavior. In this section we exhibit the resulting mathematical problems corresponding to using a least squares or least deviation approach (these correspond to L_2 and L_1 optimization in mathematical terms). We have identified seven problems labeled A through G. Problem A is unaffected by these considerations so let us consider problem B (best selection for a subclass of problems). We use the notation introduced with the original mathematical statement of this problem, which is:

Minimax approach

$$\max_{x \in \mathcal{P}_0} [|| p(B(x),x) || - || p(A^*,x) ||]$$

$$\leq \max_{x \in \mathcal{P}_0} [|| p(B(x),x) || - || p(A,x) ||] \qquad \text{for all} \quad A \in \mathcal{A}$$

The corresponding mathematical statements for the least squares and least deviation approach are

Least squares approach

$$\int_{\mathcal{P}_0} [|| p(B(x),x) || - || p(A^*,x) ||]^2 \, dx$$

$$\leq \int_{\mathcal{P}_0} [|| p(B(x),x) || - || p(A,x) ||]^2 \, dx \qquad \text{for all} \quad A \in \mathcal{A}$$

Least deviations approach

$$\int_{\mathcal{P}_0} | \, || p(B(x),x) || - || p(A^*,x) || \, | \, dx$$

$$\leq \int_{\mathcal{P}_0} | \, || p(B(x),x) || - || p(A,x) || \, | \, dx \qquad \text{for all} \quad A \in \mathcal{A}$$

The use of integrals in these formulations implies that a topology has been introduced in the problem space $\mathcal{P}$. Many common examples for $\mathcal{P}$ are discrete in nature and in these cases the topology introduced reduces the integrals to sums. This technicality is unlikely to cause real difficulties and we continue to use integrals, as this gives the neatest formulations. Note that the only difference between the two new formulations is the exponent (2 or 1) in the integrand. Thus we may avoid repeating these formulations twice by making this a variable, say r, which has values 1 or 2. Note that in approximation theory it is shown that minimax is the limiting case as $r \to \infty$ so that all three approaches can be expressed in one formulation with r as a parameter.

We recall that problem C is the best selection from a subclass of mappings. The alternative mathematical formulation of this problem is

$$\int_{\mathcal{P}} |\,||p(B(x),x)|| - ||p(S_0(x),x)||\,|^r\,dx$$

$$\leq \int_{\mathcal{P}} |\,||p(B(x),x)|| - ||p(S(x),x)||\,|^r\,dx \qquad \text{for all} \quad S \in \mathcal{S}_0$$

The alternative formulation for problem D is identical to this except that the problem subclass $\mathcal{P}_0$ replaces $\mathcal{P}$ as the domain of integration.

The next three problems involve features and we choose to use a consistent approach for the reformulations. That is, if we use least squares on the problem space we also use it on the feature space $\mathcal{F}$ and the algorithm space $\mathcal{A}$. If we set

$$d_m{}^r(A,\mathcal{E}) = \int_{f \in \mathcal{F}} \left[\int_{x,y \in \mathcal{E}(f)} \int ||p(A,x) - p(A,y)||^r \right]^{1/r}$$

then for problem E (best feature for a particular algorithm), the objective is to find the feature mapping F^* and associated equivalence classes $\mathcal{E}^*(f)$ that minimize $d_m{}^r(A,\mathcal{E})$, i.e.,

$$d_m{}^r(A) = d_m{}^r(A,\mathcal{E}^*) = \min_{\mathcal{E}} d_m{}^r(A,\mathcal{E})$$

For problem F we introduce

$$d_m{}^r(\mathcal{A}_0,\mathcal{E}) = \int_{f \in \mathcal{F}} \left[\int_{A \in \mathcal{A}_0} \int_{x,y \in \mathcal{E}(f)} \int ||p(A,x) - p(A,y)||^r \right]^{1/r}$$

and then the objective is to determine F^* and associated $\mathcal{E}^*(f)$ so that

$$d_m{}^r(\mathcal{A}_0) = d_m{}^r(\mathcal{A}_0,\mathcal{E}^*) = \min_{\mathcal{E}} d_m{}^r(\mathcal{A}_0,\mathcal{E})$$

A similar approach to problem G yields a similar expression except that the integral over $\mathcal{A}_0$ is replaced by an integral over $\mathcal{S}_0$.

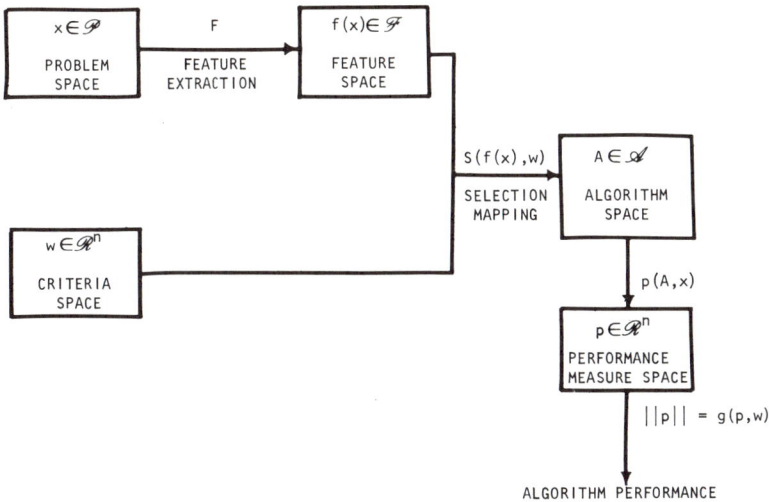

Fig. 4. Schematic diagram of the model with selection based on problem features and variable performance criteria.

In many practical problems there is little to guide one in the choice of a particular formulation of the mathematical optimization problem, i.e., should we choose $r = 1, 2,$ or ∞? These choices might not be particularly significant in the larger context, but they are very significant in determining the difficulty of the resulting mathematical optimization problem. A lesson learned from practical approximation theory might be applicable in this larger context. *This lesson is, roughly, that the crucial ingredients for success are proper choices of the subclasses $\mathcal{P}_0$, $\mathcal{A}_0$, and $\mathcal{S}_0$.* Once these are made properly then the mathematical optimization should be made for that value of r which gives the least difficulty. If the problem is completely linear then $r = 2$ (least squares) almost always results in the least mathematical difficulty. The situation is more variable for nonlinear problems. Note that there are practical approximation problems where the choice of r is crucial and no doubt there are similar cases for the algorithm selection problem. We are saying that the choice of r is important only in a small number of instances.

2.4 The Model with Variable Performance Criteria

We have assumed so far that there is a fixed way to measure the performance of a particular algorithm for a particular problem. There are, however, many situations where it is reasonable to view the performance criteria as input to the selection problem. Consider, for example, the selection of a program to solve ordinary differential equations and the criteria of speed, accuracy, reliability, and ease of use. In different situations the weight given to each of these might vary from almost zero to almost 100%. A model for this version of the selection problem is shown in Fig. 4.

The additional definition for this model is g, norm function from $\mathcal{R}^n \times \mathcal{R}^n$ to R^1, which measures the algorithm performance $p(A,x)$ with the criterion w. Some of the mappings have now changed domains, but their nature is the same. The choice of $\mathcal{R}^n$ for the criteria space is clearly arbitrary (and perhaps unnecessarily restrictive) but it is natural for the most common choice of the norm function $g(p,w) = p \cdot w$.

We can at this point formulate new versions of the algorithm selection problem involving the criteria space. The variables of these formulations are

Problem subclasses:	$\mathcal{P}_0$
Algorithm subclasses:	$\mathcal{A}_0$
Selection mapping subclasses:	$\mathcal{S}_0$
Feature space:	$\mathcal{F}$
Norm mapping:	g

The number of interesting combinations is now quite large and we refrain from formulating all of them. Some of the more important problems are as follows.

(H) *Best selection for a given criterion.* We assume that $g(p,w)$ is known, that $\mathcal{F} = \mathcal{P}$ (and F is the identity), and that w is given. The problem then is to determine that selection mapping $B(x,w)$ which gives maximum performance:

$$g(p(B(x,w),x)w) \geq g(p(A,x),w) \quad \text{for all} \quad A \in \mathcal{A}$$

(I) *Best selection from a subclass of mappings for a given criterion and feature space.* We restrict S to a subclass $\mathcal{S}_0$ of all mappings from $\mathcal{F} \times \mathcal{R}^n$ to A and, for a particular specified value of w and problem x, we wish to determine the best mapping $S^*(x,w)$ so that

$$g(p(S^*(f(x),w),x),w) \geq g(p(S(f(x),w),x),w) \quad \text{for all} \quad S \in \mathcal{S}_0$$

(J) *Best selection from a subclass of mappings, problems, and algorithms for a given criterion and feature space.* This is a model of perhaps the most realistic situation. We have the feature space $\mathcal{F}$ and norm function g specified. We restrict ourselves to subclasses $\mathcal{S}_0$, $\mathcal{P}_0$, and $\mathcal{A}_0$ of selection mappings, problems, and algorithms, respectively. Note we have $\mathcal{S}_0: \mathcal{F} \times \mathcal{R}^n \rightarrow$

$\mathcal{A}_0$. Within this framework we wish to select that mapping S^* so that

$$\max_{w \in \mathbb{R}^n} \max_{x \in \mathcal{P}_0} g(p(B(x,w),x),w) - g(p(S^*(f(x),w),x),w)$$

$$\leq \max_{w \in \mathbb{R}^n} \max_{x \in \mathcal{P}_0} g(p(B(x,w),x),w) - g(p(S(f(x),w),x),w)$$

for all $S \in \mathcal{S}_0$. Note that $g(p(B(x,w),x),w)$ is the best possible performance and the other g terms are the performances of the algorithms actually selected.

We note that the abstract model presented in this section could be elaborated upon considerably. The study of the theoretical questions of the existence, uniqueness, and characterization of best selection mappings and features can be expanded to fill a thick monograph. Those familiar with the mathematician's ability to develop theoretical structures from simple models can visualize how this would be done. However, the crucial point of a model is not its theoretical structure but its relevance to underlying real world problems. In other words, does this model allow us to develop better insight, understanding, and analysis of real algorithm selection problems? This question is addressed in the next two sections.

3. Concrete Application—The Selection of Quadrature Algorithms

3.1 The Components in the Abstract Model

The next two sections are independent of one another and each has the following format:

Formulation of the general problem and definition of the relevant spaces,
Examination of concrete cases,
Formulation of a specific and simpler selection problem,
Discussion of the simpler problem and the computations required to solve it.

The general case of the quadrature algorithm selection problem may be expressed in one of the two following ways:

(A) Given a collection of functions (with reasonably well-known attributes), which one of the 15–25 well-known quadrature algorithms should be selected so as to give the best performance?

(B) Given that a program library for a computing center should contain a small (1–4) number of quadrature algorithms, which ones should be selected?

A thorough analysis of these two questions is a formidable task. We will formulate this problem (version B) more precisely and summarize the rather extensive amount of information bearing on the question. Then we formulate a somewhat simpler and more concrete problem and discuss its solution. This general problem is modeled as in Section 2.4, which involves spaces for the problems, the features, the criteria, the algorithms, and the performance measures. These spaces are described as follows:

(a) Problem Space This space consists of a rather broad class of functions of one variable. While the population characteristics are not well known, it is likely that the bulk of the functions are simple, smooth, and well behaved, and yet a small but still significant proportion of the functions have properties that cause real difficulty in quadrature. The possible properties are illustrated by the feature space.

(b) Feature Space The features of these problems that should be included are indicated by a key word followed by a short explanation:

Smoothness: either mathematical or intuitive.

Jumps: jump discontinuities of various sizes are present (or absent).

Singularities: local behavior of the form t^α, $-1 < \alpha < 1$ or $\alpha > 1$ and not integer; $\log t$, etc.

Peaks: small subintervals where the function makes a radical change in size; may be actual peaks or "smoothed" jump discontinuities.

Oscillations: oscillatory behavior of various amplitudes, frequencies, and extent.

Round-off: the presence of significant random uncertainty in the value of the function.

Symbolic: some attributes may be obtained by a cursory examination of the function's description.

Accuracy: the desired accuracy of the quadrature estimate.

Domain: the interval of integration (might be infinite).

No doubt there are other significant problem features that have been overlooked in this list.

(c) Algorithm Space There are about 15 or 20 quadrature algorithms that have been completely defined and studied to a certain extent in the literature. In addition, there are a number of very classical algorithms (e.g., Simpson's rule) that must be considered even though they are not standardized (i.e., they really are classes of algorithms). Note that this small number is from a *very large population* of many millions (see Rice, 1975). The actual algorithms one might consider are mentioned in the various references, and many of them are named later.

(d) Performance Measures The most commonly considered measures of performance are *work* (measured in number of function evaluations) and *reliability* (1 if the requested accuracy is achieved). Other important algorithm characteristics are *ease of use*, *understandability* (for possible modification), *memory* requirements (both for the algorithm and problem data generated), and ease of *analysis*.

(e) Criteria Space This consists of some numbers designed to weight the relative importance of the performance measures. The measures in this case are not very compatible and it is difficult to find a completely satisfactory method of comparing the various measures. Scaling all the measures from zero to one and then applying simple weights is a naive approach with considerable appeal. Comparisons that involve step functions are more realistic but less tractable to use or describe to users.

3.2 Review of Previous Work on Quadrature Algorithm Evaluation

A substantial number of experimental tests have been made and reported in the literature. The functions involved have primarily been chosen from one of the following three *test function sets* (samples from the problem space):

(A) Casaletto *et al.* (1969): a set of 50 functions,
(B) Kahaner (1971): a set of 21 functions,
(C) de Boor (1971): three performance profiles.

There is a small overlap among these sets and some authors have used various subsets, occasionally with a few additions.

There have been ten substantial testing efforts reported, which are listed below in chronological order. We indicate the test functions used (by A, B, or C), the requested accuracies (by ϵ values), and the algorithms involved. The algorithms are named and described, but for detailed references one must refer to the test reports.

(1) Casaletto *et al.* (1969). Complete details not reported. Test set A with $\epsilon = 10^{-1}, 10^{-2}, \ldots, 10^{-8}$. Algorithms: QUAD (adaptive Simpson rule), QUADS4 (adaptive 4-point Gauss quadrature), QUADS6 (adaptive 6-point Gauss quadrature), SIMP (adaptive Simpson rule; almost identical with SIMPSN), SIMPSN (adaptive Simpson rule), SQUANK (improved version of SIMPSN), ROMBRG (adaptive Romberg integration), RIEMAN (adaptive Riemann sums).

(2) Kahaner (1971). Extensive tables of detailed results. Test set B with $\epsilon = 10^{-3}, 10^{-6}, 10^{-9}$. Algorithms: SIMPSN, SQUANK, GAUSS (adaptive Gauss using 5- and 7-point rules), G96 (96-point Gauss rule),

HAVIE (improved version of ROMB), QABS (combination Romberg and Curtis–Clenshaw), QNC7 (adaptive 7-point Newton–Cotes rule), QUAD (adaptive 10-point Newton–Cotes rule), RBUN (adaptive Romberg), ROMB (standard Romberg), SHNK (Romberg type using Wynn's ϵ-algorithm for extrapolation).

(3) de Boor (1971). Results compatible with Kahaner plus graphs. Test set B with $\epsilon = 10^{-3}$, 10^{-6}, 10^{-9} plus test set C. Algorithm: CADRE (adaptive Romberg with cautious extrapolation).

(4) Gentleman (1972). Considerable detail. Test set A with $\epsilon = 10^{-1}$, 10^{-2}, ..., 10^{-8}. Algorithm: CCQUAD (Curtis–Clenshaw quadrature).

(5) Patterson (1973). Partial results reported involving CADRE and QSUBA. Test set selected from A and B plus three others; total of 13 functions. Algorithms: CADRE, SQUANK, QSUB (iterated Gauss–Kronrod rules up to 255 points), QSUBA (adaptive version of QSUB).

(6) Piessens (1973a). Complete details not reported. Test set A with $\epsilon = 10^{-2}$, 10^{-3}, ..., 10^{-13}. Algorithms: CCQUAD, SQUANK, AIND (adaptive Gauss–Kronrod rules up to 21 points), HRVINT (improved version of HAVIE, (adaptive Romberg).

(7) Piessens (1973b). Considerable detail given, some round-off effects studied. Test set A with $\epsilon = 10^{-5}$, 10^{-7} (with noise), 0. Algorithms: AIND, CADRE, SQUANK.

(8) Einarsson (1974). Complete detail for selected cases only. Test set A with $\epsilon = 10^{-1}$, 10^{-2}, ..., 10^{-6}. Algorithms: CCQUAD, DRMBIU (IMSL version of Romberg quadrature; two versions), QATR (IBM-SSP version of Romberg quadrature), QAR (IBM-SL-MATH version of Romberg quadrature), ROMINT (Romberg quadrature; algorithm 351 of *Comm. ACM*).

(9) Blue (1975). Considerable detail for a large number of cases plus numerous performance profiles for his own algorithm. Test set B with $\epsilon = 10^{-3}, 10^{-6}, 10^{-9}$. Algorithms: CADRE, QABS, QNC7, QSUBA, QUAD, RBUN, ROMB, SIMPSN, SQUANK, DQUAD (adaptive Romberg with cautious extrapolation).

(10) Krogh and Snyder (1975). Extensive tables of detailed results. Test set of combined nature and several hitherto unused integrands, $\epsilon = 10, 1, \ldots, 10^{-7}$. Algorithms: AIND, CADRE, QNC7, QSUBA, RBUN, GAUS8 (adaptive 8-point Gauss algorithm), SINT (extensive revision of QSUBA).

Also see Lyness and Kaganove (1976) for further discussion on the nature of this problem. This testing has provided much useful information and served to identify some poor algorithms. However, it has not been well enough organized to allow definitive conclusions and there is still considerable doubt about the relative merits of the better algorithms. We note that a much better experiment can be performed.

3.3 A Systematic Evaluation and Selection Approach

We assume the quadrature problem is $\int_0^1 h(t)\, dt$. We choose a feature space with four dimensions:

Feature name	Values assumed	Remarks
Smoothness	0, ½, 1	0 is smooth, 1 is not
Singularity	[−1, 2]	Value is exponent of singularity
Peak	[0, 100]	Strength = $\dfrac{[\text{average size of } h(t) - \text{ave. peak}]}{(\text{peak base})*(\text{ave. size of peak})}$
Oscillation	[0, 100]	Maximum frequency of oscillation

We choose four one-parameter families of functions that represent each of the features (the performance profiles) and then each coordinate axis of $\mathfrak{F}$ is discretized and families introduced with characteristics of each of the remaining features. Such families can be easily constructed by addition or multiplication (e.g., $|t^2-0.25|^\alpha$ has a singularity, $\sin[N(t^2+1)]$ is oscillatory, and both $|t^2-0.25|^\alpha + \sin[N(t^2+1)]$ and $|t^2-0.25|^\alpha \sin[N(t^2+1)]$ are oscillatory with a singularity). This process gives a test set that produces a grid over the entire feature space. This test set can be combined with accuracy values of $\epsilon = 10^{-2}, 10^{-4}, 10^{-8}, 10^{-12}$, to permit a much more precise measurement of algorithm performance.

There are about a dozen existing algorithms that merit inclusion in this experiment and a little estimation shows that a rather substantial computation is required for this experiment. An important result of the systematic nature of this approach is that one can consider probability distributions in the problem space that induce a probability distribution on the feature space and algorithm performances can be compared (over this problem subdomain) without repeating the experiment.

This suggested experiment is far from the most general of interest and is clearly biased against certain well-known algorithms. For example, SQUANK takes considerable care in handling round-off effects (a feature omitted here) and explicitly ignores oscillations (a feature included here). Thus one would not expect SQUANK to compare favorably with some other algorithms on the basis of this experiment.

We consider two criteria of performance: *efficiency* and *reliability*. These two variables are scaled to the interval [0,1] as follows:

(a) Efficiency Let N_x be the minimum number of integrand evaluations required to solve problem x (this must be estimated for each problem) and

N_A the actual number used by a particular algorithm A. Then the value of the efficiency is $N_x/N_A = p_1(A,x)$ for algorithm A and problem x.

(b) Reliability Let ϵ_x be the requested accuracy and ϵ_A the accuracy actually achieved. The value of reliability is then taken to be

$$p_2(A,x) = \begin{cases} 1 - (1 - \epsilon_x/\epsilon_A)^2 & \epsilon_A > \epsilon_x \\ 1/(1 + 0.1(\log \epsilon_A/\epsilon_x)^2) & \epsilon_A < \epsilon_x \end{cases}$$

This places a severe penalty on failing to achieve ϵ_x, and a mild penalty on achieving much more accuracy than ϵ_x. These conventions allow us to find the performance vector $(p_1(A,x), p_2(A,x))$. We introduce a criteria unit vector (w_1, w_2) and the norm of $p(A,x)$ is then

$$\| p(A,x) \| = w_1 p_1(A,x) + w_2 p_2(A,x)$$

4. Concrete Application—The Selection of Operating System Schedulers

4.1 The Components in the Abstract Model

The general case of this problem may be expressed as follows: Consider a computing installation with a fixed configuration and a work load with reasonably well-known attributes. How should jobs be scheduled in order to give the best service?

A thorough analysis of this problem requires many hundreds of pages and is beyond the scope of this chapter. We will formulate this problem more precisely within the framework provided by the abstract models. This formulation is oriented toward the specific case of the operation in the Purdue University Computing Center, which is a typical example of large-scale, complex operation. Then we describe a simplified version of the current scheduling algorithm and, in turn, formulate a much more specific algorithm selection problem. A discussion is then given of how one could attempt to solve this problem in terms of the information that is known or obtainable.

The abstract model involves spaces for the problems, the features, the criteria, the algorithms, and the performance measures. These spaces are described as follows:

(a) Problem Space This space consists of configurations of computer runs, which are mixtures of batch, remote batch, time-shared, and interactive jobs. These configurations are very dynamic in nature and normally only general average values are known for the population characteristics (and most of these values are not known accurately). In addition to very rapid and substantial changes in the problem characteristics, there are often well-identified long-term variations in the average values of the problem characteristics.

(b) Feature Space The features of a configuration of computer runs are a combination of the features of the individual jobs. The features of individual jobs that should be considered are indicated by a keyword plus a short explanation:

Priority: value given by user and computing center.

CPU time: value estimated for job by user.

Memory: value estimated for job by user and observed by operating system; both core and auxiliary memory values may be considered.

I/O requirements: values estimated by user for use of standard devices (printers, punches, disk channels, etc.).

Special facilities: indications of use of less common facilities (e.g., tape units, plotters, graphics consoles).

Program locality and stability: indication of the likelihood of page requests or job roll-outs.

In addition, features of the total problem configuration should be considered as follows:

Batch load: length of the input queue plus average values for some of the job features.

On-line load: number of terminal users plus average values features for the stream of jobs they create.

Interactive load: number of users and nature of system being used.

I/O load: length of queues at the various I/O devices.

No doubt there are other significant problem features not included in this list.

(c) Algorithm Space A fair variety of scheduling algorithms have been proposed and analyzed to a certain extent (Coffman and Denning, 1974; Wilkes, 1973). An essential characteristic of successful algorithms is that they are fast to execute (otherwise the system devotes an excessive amount of its resources to scheduling instead of production). This favors some very simple schemes (e.g., round-robin, first-come first-served, simple priority) but one must realize that rather complex algorithms can be fast to execute.

(d) Performance Measures The performance of an operating system depends on one's viewpoint—each user wants instant service and the computing center director wants zero angry or dissatisfied customers. Neither of these desires is very realistic, but efforts to measure the progress made toward satisfying them usually involve throughput and response time. These measures are applied to different classes of jobs as follows:

Batch: small job response; median and maximum turnaround for jobs with small resource requirements.

Batch: large job response; median and maximum turnaround for all batch jobs other than small ones (or special runs).

On-line response: median and maximum response time for common service functions (e.g., fetching a file, editing a line, submitting a batch job).

Interactive response: median and maximum response times for standard short requests.

Throughput: total number of jobs processed per unit time, number of CPU hours billed per day, etc.

(e) Criteria Space This consists of numbers to weight the relative importance of the performance measures. Values of some of these measures can be improved only by making others worse and it is difficult to compare them. Scaling the measures to a standard interval (say 0 to 1) and then applying weights (which sum to unity) is simple, but often satisfactory.

4.2 An Actual Scheduling Algorithm

We present a version of the scheduling algorithm used on the CDC 6500 system at Purdue University (see Abell, 1973). This algorithm has been simplified by omitting features for preventing deadlock, "first pass" priority given initially to all jobs, and job origin priority. Jobs are scheduled according to priority, i.e., if a waiting job has queue priority QP_1 larger than an executing job with queue priority QP_2 and if the central memory CM_2 used by the executing job is large enough for the waiting job (which requires CM_1 in memory) then the executing job is terminated and rolled out and the waiting job is rolled in and placed into execution. In summary, if $QP_1 > QP_2$ and $CM_1 \leq CM_2$ than job 2 is rolled out and replaced by job 1.

The queue priority QP is a function of six priority parameters $\mathbf{r} = (r_1, r_2, r_3, r_4, r_5, r_6)$ as follows:

- r_1 job card priority parameter
- r_2 central memory (current requirement)
- r_3 time remaining on CPU time estimate
- r_4 I/O units remaining on I/O transfer unit estimate
- r_5 number of tape units in use
- r_6 number of rollouts experienced so far

The value of QP is then a linear combination

$$QP = \sum_{i=1}^{5} R_i(r_i)$$

where

$$R_1(r_1) = 2^6 * r_1$$

$$R_2(r_2) = |r_2 - 150,100|/128$$

$$R_5(r_5) = \begin{cases} 0 & \text{if } r_5 = 0 \\ 300 + 128 |r_5 - 1| & \text{if } r_5 \geq 1 \end{cases}$$

$$R_6(r_6) = r_6$$

and R_3 and R_4 are shown in Fig. 5. This function QP involves about 22 coefficients.

4.3 An Approach to the Selection of the "Best" Scheduler

We now consider algorithms that involve three features of the configuration of computer runs:

- f_1 number of short jobs (with 30 seconds or less CPU time estimate)
- f_2 remaining number of jobs
- f_3 number of active terminals (which may be used in a variety of modes)

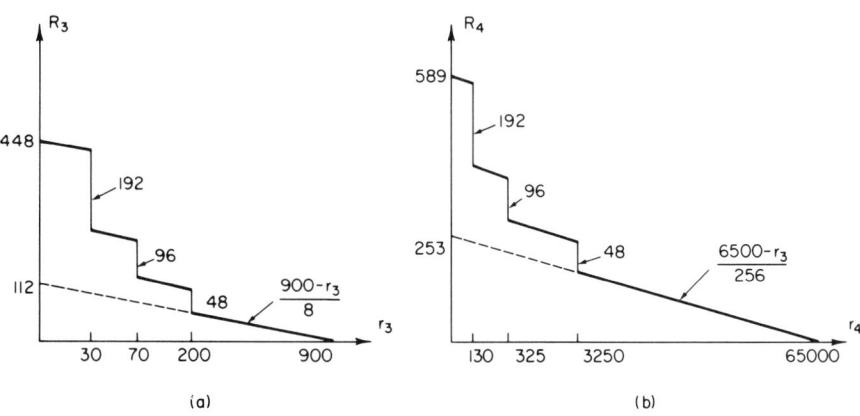

FIG. 5. Graphs of the function $R_3(r_3)$ and $R_4(r_4)$. The horizontal axes are not drawn to scale. Each function is linear plus three step functions. (a) Priority contribution for CPU time; (b) priority contribution for I/O units.

In addition, we use the six-job parameters **r** given above and compute queue priority as

$$QP = \sum_{i=1}^{6} R_i(r_i)$$

where

$R_1(r_1) = a_1 * r_1$

$R_2(r_2) = a_2 * (150{,}100 - r_2)$

$R_3(r_3) = a_3 * \max(a_4 - r_3, 0) + a_5 * \mid a_6 - r_3 \mid_+^0 + a_7 * \mid a_8 - r_3 \mid_+^0$

$R_4(r_4) = a_9 * \max(a_{10} - r_4, 0) + a_{11} * \mid a_{12} - r_4 \mid_+^0 + a_{13} * \mid a_{14} - r_4 \mid_+^0$

$R_5(r_5) = a_{15} * \mid r_5 - a_{16} \mid_+^0 + a_{17} * \mid a_{18} - r_5 \mid_+^0$

$R_6(r_6) = a_{19} * r_6$

Recall the notation

$$\mid x - c \mid_+^n = \begin{cases} (x-c)^n & \text{if } x \geq c \\ 0 & \text{if } x \leq c \end{cases}$$

This queue priority function is a slightly modified and simplified version of the actual one above.

We choose a three-dimensional performance measure space with $\mathbf{p} = (p_1, p_2, p_3)$, where

p_1 (mean internal processing time for short batch jobs)/1000
p_2 (mean internal processing time for other batch jobs)/4000
p_3 (mean response time for standard short on-line tasks)/10

The scaling implies that $\mathbf{p} = (1,1,1)$ corresponds to approximately a 15-minute average processing time for short batch jobs, a 1-hour average processing time for other jobs, and a 10-second response time on-line. The algorithm performance is then measured by

$$\| \mathbf{p} \| = w_1 p_1 + w_2 p_2 + w_3 p_3$$

where **w** is from the three-dimensional criteria space with $w_i \geq 0$ and $w_1 + w_2 + w_3 = 1$.

The situation for determining the coefficients of the scheduling algorithm is as follows:

1. The computer operator selects a criteria vector **w**.
2. The operating system measures the configuration features f_1, f_2, f_3.
3. The appropriate best coefficients **a** are used for these values of w_i and f_i.

Thus we see that the 19 coefficients are, in fact, functions of six other independent variables. One could, for example, attempt to determine coefficients α_{ij} so that

$$a_i = \alpha_{i0} + \sum_{j=1}^{3} (\alpha_{ij}f_j + \alpha_{i,j+3}w_j)$$

There is no *a priori* reason to assume this linear relationship is appropriate, but it might be and it is simple. It leads then to 133 coefficients α_{ij}, $i = 1$ to 19, $j = 0$ to 6, for the algorithm selection problem.

It is appropriate to question the validity of this form of the scheduling algorithm from the point of view of the intrinsic complexity of the problem. Such a consideration is entirely subjective at this point because no one has made a thorough analysis of this problem. It seems intuitively plausible that the complexity of this scheduling algorithm form is somewhat high. That is, considering the number of variables involved and the desired precision of the scheduling, it is likely that an adequate form exists with perhaps 40–70 independent coefficients. A crucial point is that (at this time) not enough is known about the effect of scheduling algorithms on system performance for one to identify the really concise, yet adequately precise, forms for scheduling algorithms.

We now consider how to find the best scheduler of this form. To set the context, let us outline how the computation might go in an ideal world. The basic building block would be the computation of best a_i for given w_j and f_j. This block is designated by the function OPT, i.e., OPT$(\mathbf{w},\mathbf{f})$ is the set of 19 best coefficients. Note that this does not involve any assumption about the form of the relationship between the a_i and the variables w_j and f_j, i.e., the α_{ij} are not involved. We would then select an appropriate set of values for the variables w_j and f_j, say w_{jl}, $l = 1$ to m_w, and f_{jk}, $k = 1$ to m_f, and execute the algorithm

For $l = 1$ to m_w, $k = 1$ to m_f do $a_i(l,k) = \text{OPT}(\mathbf{w}_l, \mathbf{f}_k)$

At this point we now have a tabulation of the coefficients a_i as a function of the w_j and f_j. The final step is to do a linear least squares fit to obtain the final coefficients α_{ij}.

Let us consider ways that this simple-minded computational approach may go wrong. We list some obvious ways (no doubt there are others waiting if one actually tries the approach):

(1) The function OPT is too difficult to compute. We would say that 50–200 evaluations of functions (that is, **p** as a function of **a**) should be considered reasonable. More than 500 or 1000 indicates real difficulties and less than 50 real luck.

(2) The form chosen for QP as a function of **a** is inadequate. This is not likely since the form is the one in current use.

(3) The linear form for the **a** as a function of the w_j and f_j is inadequate.

(4) One is unable to vary f_1, f_2, and f_3 over the range of values as indicated in the system, and thus they are dynamically varying and uncontrollable. To create configurations with known features is probably a very substantial task.

(5) The measurement of $\|\mathbf{p}\|$ is uncertain due to the dynamic nature of the process. That is, in the 15 minutes that it takes for a batch job to go through the system there may have been wide variations in the values of **f** (due to the changing job configuration) and the values of **a** (due to changes made by OPT).

We note that difficulties 2 and 3 are from the problem formulation and not the computation, so we ignore them here. The difficulty with OPT might be very real, but one can be optimistic that a good minimization polyalgorithm will handle this part of the computation—especially after some experience is obtained so that good initial guesses are available. This leaves difficulties 4 and 5, which are very interesting and somewhat unusual in standard optimization problems.

It seems plausible that one can obtain values of $\|\mathbf{p}\|$ that are fairly tightly associated with values of **w**, **f**, and **a**. This means that it is, in principle, feasible to carry out the optimization problem. A simplified example of the situation is shown in Fig. 6, where we assume there is one variable for **a**, and one variable for **w** and **f**.

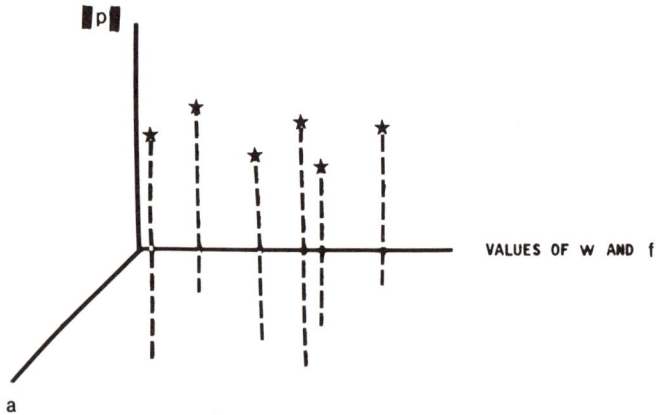

Fig. 6. Function values of $\|\mathbf{p}\|$ obtained when there is no direct control over some of the arguments (**f** in this case).

In order to compensate for the irregular nature of the values obtained, one should use an integral form of the minimization problem and then introduce quadrature rules to accommodate the irregularity. Standard quadrature rules for this situation are not available. Reasonable accuracy can be achieved by using ordinary Reimann sums with areas determined from a space-filling curve map. That is, one maps the high-dimensional domain onto $[0,1]$, then one assigns weights to the points according to the length their images span in $[0,1]$. Note that certain values of **f** might be very uncommon and hence the optimization obtained there might be unreliable. Fortunately, the rarity of these values of **f** means that the reliability of the scheduling algorithm in that domain is not so crucial. In summary, it appears that adequate methods probably can be found to carry out the computational approach outlined earlier.

As a final note, we consider the time that might be required for a complete determination of the "best" scheduling algorithm. Given a fairly constant job configuration, we assume that we can obtain values for $\|\mathbf{p}\|$ and all other quantities within a 10-minute time interval. This corresponds to one function evaluation. Thus we are led to assume that one evaluation of OPT takes from $\frac{1}{2}$ to 1 day of system time. The inefficiency due to the lack of control over setting parameters will probably double this time, say to $1\frac{1}{2}$ days. The number of evaluations of OPT needed to obtain semi-reasonable reliability in the α_{ij} computations is probably of the order of 50 or 100. This implies about 3 to 6 months to select the best scheduling algorithm.

Note how this approach differs from the common theoretical approach. There one assumes some model for the computer operation and then analytically obtains a good (or optimum) scheduling algorithm for that model. Here there is no explicit model of the computer operation; one tries to obtain a good scheduling algorithm by observing the systems behavior directly rather than through the intermediary of a mathematical model. It is, or course, yet to be seen just how feasible or effective this direct approach will be.

It is obvious that the determination of the best scheduler by this means involves a substantial investment of effort. One has very little feel for the possible payoff from obtaining the best scheduler. It might be nil if the system efficiency is determined by bottlenecks located elsewhere. It might be very large if the scheduler is one of the bottlenecks. One way to estimate the possible gain would be to make a system simulation and perform the optimization there. This would still be a substantial project and would only give an estimate of the possible gain in optimizing the scheduler. Nevertheless, it appears that it might be wise to do this simulation before attempting to involve a running computer system. Finally, we note that the algorithm selection approach described here can be applied to the other resource scheduling tasks (disk access, communications controllers, etc.) in the same way.

5. Discussion of the Two Concrete Applications

The purpose of the preceding two sections was to examine concrete problems within the framework of the abstract models developed. Our main objective is to examine these two problems and not to solve them. We do, however, given an outline of how a realistic selection might proceed. These concrete examples show the diversity of real problems that fit into the abstract models. We might have also included an examination of a function evaluation problem [e.g., $SQRT(X)$ or $SIN(X)$], but that seems rather dull since such selection problems have been analyzed in great detail by others.

The two problems considered here have some characteristics in common:

(1) They are real problems subject to active research.

(2) The problem space for the algorithms is of high dimension and the overall nature of the problem is not too well understood. One concludes that the selection problem is essentially complicated by this high dimensionality.

(3) Performance criteria are somewhat subjective and vary considerably from context to context.

(4) The algorithms involve familiar mathematical functions and the algorithm selection problem can be formulated as a more or less standard (though complicated) mathematical approximation problem.

There are also some large differences in the characteristics of these two problems:

(5) There is a substantial body of relevant data available for the quadrature problem, but nothing for the scheduling problem. The data for the quadrature problem have not been collected systematically and are thus less useful than one might hope.

(6) The scheduling algorithm involves a complex dynamic process in such a way that:
- (a) some independent parameters cannot be varied at will;
- (b) reproducibility of results is unlikely since one rarely has the same element of the problem space twice;
- (c) large amounts of calendar time are required for the selection of "best" algorithms.

6. Approximation Theory Machinery

6.1 Formulation and Structure of the Approximation Problem

The purpose of this section is to analyze the algorithm selection problem within the framework of approximation theory. We will see that the principal questions of this problem can be formulated within the traditional framework of approximation theory. Even so, the answers to many of the questions require the development of very novel techniques and theories of approximation. More specifically then, our purpose is systematically to examine these questions, to indicate what light can be shed on them from the existing theory of approximation, and to point out the new problems in approximation theory that are raised by the algorithm selection problem. Needless to say, we do not propose to solve these new problems here. The principle questions are divided into four groups:

(1) norms and approximation forms,
(2) degree of convergence, complexity, and robustness,
(3) existence, uniqueness, and characterization,
(4) computation.

The question of computation is not considered in this chapter since it would seem to involve half the known methods of computation.

6.2 Norms and Approximation Forms

The question of norms enters in the final step from the algorithm performance space $\Re^n$ to the single number that represents the algorithm performance. Since we have a norm on a standard n-dimensional vector space, the possibilities are well known. The most common are of the form

$$\| p \| = \left[\sum_{i=1}^{N} w_i p_i^r \right]^{1/r}$$

with typical values of r being 1, 2, or ∞ (for the Tchebycheff or minimax norm). However, the nature of the selection problem is such that we can anticipate using nonstandard norms. The reason is that the performance measures tend to include essentially incomparable variables, e.g.,

p_1 computer time used (measured in seconds)

p_2 computer memory used (measured in words)

p_3 complexity of setting up the computer run (measured in hours required by the programmer)

A plausible norm to use in such a context might be

$$\| p \| = p_1 + \alpha(p_2) p_2 + \beta(p_3) p_3$$

where

$$\alpha(p_2) = \begin{cases} 0 & \text{for} \quad p_2 \leq 10{,}000 \\ 10^{-5} & \text{for} \quad 10{,}000 \leq p_2 \leq 20{,}000 \\ 2*10^{-5} & \text{for} \quad 20{,}000 \leq p_2 \leq 30{,}000 \\ 7p_2*10^{-9} & \text{for} \quad p_2 \geq 30{,}000 \end{cases}$$

$$\beta(p_3) = \begin{cases} 0 & \text{for} \quad p_3 \leq 0.5 \\ 2 & \text{for} \quad 0.5 \leq p_3 \leq 2 \\ p_3 & \text{for} \quad p_3 \geq 2 \end{cases}$$

There are two observations, one positive and one negative, about such complicated norms that can be made based on current experience in approximation. The negative one is that they do complicate the theory sometimes and more often make the computations substantially more difficult. The positive one is that the choice of norm is normally a secondary effect compared to the choice of approximation form. That is, if one has a good choice of approximation form, one obtains a good approximation for any reasonable norm. This implies that one can, within reason, modify the norm used so as to simplify the analysis or computations. A significant corollary to this last observation is that one cannot compensate for a poor choice of approximation form by computing power or technical skill in analysis.

We now turn to the crucial question of approximation forms, which we group into five classes: (a) discrete, (b) linear, (c) piecewise, (d) general nonlinear: standard mathematical, separable, abstract, and (e) tree and algorithm forms.

In order to discuss these choices, we need to formulate more precisely the standard idea of approximation form as it currently exists in approximation theory. The form is to be used for the selection mapping $S(f(x))$: $\mathfrak{F} \to \mathfrak{A}$ and we visualize a parameter (or coefficient) space $\mathfrak{C}$ plus a particular form of the mapping. To show explicitly the dependence of S on the coefficients, we may write $S(f(x),c)$ at times. Specific examples of the five classes of approximation forms are given below:

(a) *Discrete*

$$S(f(x),1) = \text{computer program 1}$$
$$S(f(x),2) = \text{computer program 2}$$
$$S(f(x),3) = \text{computer program 3}$$

(b) *Linear*

$$S(f(x),c) = c_1 + c_2 f_1 + c_3 f_1^2 + c_4 (f_1 f_2)^2 + c_5 (f_2 - f_3)^3 + c_6/f_3$$

Note that linear refers to the dependence on the coefficients c_i and not the features f_j.

(c) *Piecewise linear*

$$S(f(x),c) = \begin{cases} c_1+c_2f_1+c_3f_2+c_4f_1f_2+c_5/f_2 \\ \qquad\qquad\text{for}\quad |f_1+f_2| \geq 2 \\ \\ c_6+c_7f_1+c_8f_2+c_9f_1f_2+c_{10}f_1^2 \\ \qquad\qquad\text{for}\quad |f_1+f_2| \leq 2\quad\text{and}\quad f_1 \leq f_2 \\ \\ c_{11}+c_{12}f_1+c_{13}f_2+c_{14}\dfrac{f_1-f_2}{1+f_1+f_2} \\ \qquad\qquad\text{for}\quad |f_1+f_2| \leq 2\quad\text{and}\quad f_1 \geq f_2 \end{cases}$$

We see that the feature space is subdivided into pieces and $S(f(x),c)$ is defined linearly on each of the pieces.

(d) *Nonlinear, standard forms*

$$S(f(x),c) = \begin{cases} \dfrac{c_1+c_2f_1+c_3f_2}{c_4+c_5(f_1+f_2)^2} \quad \text{(rational)} \\ \\ c_1e^{-c_2f_1}+c_3e^{-c_4f_2}+c_5e^{-c_6(f+1f_2)^2} \quad \text{(exponential)} \\ \\ c_1+c_2f_1+c_3f_2+c_5(f_1-c_4)_++c_7(f_2-c_6)_+ \quad \text{(spline)} \\ \qquad\text{where}\quad (f-c)_+ = \begin{cases} 0 & \text{for}\quad f \leq c \\ f-c & \text{for}\quad f \geq c \end{cases} \\ \\ g_1(f_1,c_1,c_2)+g_2(f_2,c_3,c_4)+g_3(f_3,c_5,c_6) \\ \qquad\qquad\qquad\qquad\text{(nonlinear, separable)} \end{cases}$$

The spline example has variable pieces. If c_4 and c_6 were constants, then this would be piecewise linear. For the nonlinear separable case the effects of the different features (and their associated coefficients) are completely independent of one another. The exponential example given just above is also of this form.

The abstract nonlinear form is an arbitrary function of the features $f(x)$ and the coefficients c.

(e) *Tree and algorithm forms:*

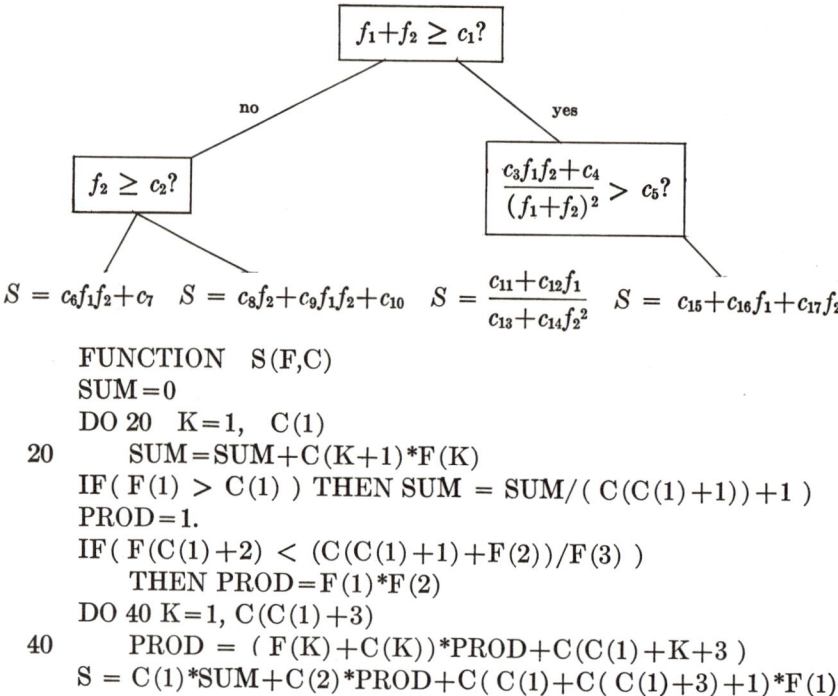

```
        FUNCTION   S(F,C)
        SUM=0
        DO 20   K=1,  C(1)
   20       SUM=SUM+C(K+1)*F(K)
        IF( F(1) > C(1) ) THEN SUM = SUM/( C(C(1)+1))+1 )
        PROD=1.
        IF( F(C(1)+2) < (C(C(1)+1)+F(2))/F(3) )
            THEN PROD=F(1)*F(2)
        DO 40 K=1, C(C(1)+3)
   40       PROD = ( F(K)+C(K))*PROD+C(C(1)+K+3 )
        S = C(1)*SUM+C(2)*PROD+C( C(1)+C( C(1)+3)+1)*F(1)
```

The main thrust of approximation theory is for the case where the coefficients c are used to parameterize a relatively simple form (i.e., such as the linear, piecewise linear, and nonlinear forms). The distinguishing characteristic of these cases is that the set of approximation forms can (at least locally) be identified with a manifold in some ordinary finite-dimensional space. The approximation theory machinery is then used to obtain the best coefficients or parameters (again, at least locally) from this manifold.

One thus may conclude that there are three distinct situations as far as the applicability of approximation theory machinery. The first and most favorable situation is for the linear, piecewise linear, and nonlinear approximation forms. Here the machinery may be applied essentially as it currently exists. This does not mean that all of these cases are already solved and all one has to do is to "copy" the solutions from somewhere. Rather, it means that these are the kinds of problems the machinery is supposed to handle and, if it is currently inadequate in some specific instance, it needs to be extended in the direction it is already headed.

The second situation is for the tree and algorithm forms. Here it seems that a major change in emphasis is required. The exact nature of the new machinery is certainly unclear and no doubt there are hidden difficulties not apparent from a casual inspection. However, it seems plausible that the general spirit of the approach and techniques may well be similar to that already existing. For example, the piecewise linear forms may be visualized as one of the simplest of the tree forms. The development and analysis for the piecewise forms (even for variable pieces) has progressed fairly smoothly over the past 10 years and the resulting body of results has very much of the flavor of the previously established linear and specialized nonlinear theories. There were (and still are), of course, some difficult questions for the piecewise linear, but the prospects do not appear to be too bad for developing a useful body of approximation theory machinery for the tree and algorithm forms.

The third and least favorable situation is for the discrete forms. The standard mathematical approach results in stating that the problem is trivial in this case. One ascertains the best selection mapping by a finite enumeration. Unfortunately, the enumeration may well be over very large sets. Even 1000 elements (algorithms) are completely unmanageable in most instances and it is easy to find problems where there are millions of algorithms to be considered (at least in some abstract sense). It is not at all clear how algorithm selection procedures are to evolve in this situation and the development of such procedures is one of the foremost open questions in this entire area of study.

We close this section by repeating a fundamental observation: *The most important single part of the successful solution of an approximation problem is the appropriate choice of the approximation form.* Approximation theory machinery comes into play *after* this choice is made. Thus it is essential to have insight into both the problem and algorithm spaces and into the possible forms one might choose for the selection mappings.

6.3 Classification of Problems, Degree of Convergence, Complexity, and Robustness

This section has two distinct parts. First, we introduce the concept of classifying problems, and second, we introduce three other concepts that are intimately related to ways of classifying problems. These three concepts—degree of convergence, complexity, and robustness—are important for evaluating the overall value of various approximation forms for the algorithm selection problem.

6.3.1 Classification of Problems

An important approach to obtaining insight into the nature of the problem space is to partition it into particular classes of problems. Ideally there is a representative member or property of each class that is especially relevant to the selection of algorithms. The exact nature of the classification depends, of course, essentially on the specific problem space. Some typical examples include the following.

(a) Numerical quadrature: Compute $If = \int_a^b f(x)\,dx$.
Class 1: Those $f(x)$ which have continuous curvature.
Class 2: Those $f(x)$ which have five or fewer oscillations in $[a,b]$.
Class 3: Those $f(x)$ which are analytic.

Mathematics has a highly developed classification system for functions [integrands $f(x)$], which provides literally dozens of classes relevant to numerical integration algorithms.

(b) Scheduling a CPU in an operating system.
Class 1: Batch processing multiprogramming, one CPU, two I/O channels, and one disk.
Class 2: Time sharing, two CPU's, 50 terminals.
Class 3: Time sharing with a batch processing background, two CPU's, 50 terminals, saturation loading.

We see that the problem classification has many independent variables giving a high-dimensional problem space.

(c) Scene analysis.
Class 1: One connected object, a line drawing with 50 or fewer lines.
Class 2: Up to 10 objects, each composed of from 1 to 10 rectangles, triangles, or circular arcs.
Class 3: Unknown number of separated objects of one of four types; distinguishing properties are color, texture, size, position, and orientation.

It is easy to visualize thousands of particular types of scenes to analyze.

The idea of problem classification is simple, but important. Most algorithms are developed for a particular class of problems even though the class is never explicitly defined. Thus the performance of algorithms is unlikely to be understood without some idea of the problem class associated with their development.

It is particularly common to attempt a classification system that goes from easy to hard. Thus one visualizes a nested set of problems where the innermost set consists of very easy problems and the largest set consists of very hard ones. Unfortunately, it is not always easy to make such a classification (at least in a reasonable way) for complex problem spaces. One is lacking the insight to know in all circumstances just what makes a problem hard or easy.

6.3.2 Degree of Convergence

The idea of degree of convergence comes from considering a sequence of approximation forms and asking: How much better do these forms do as one goes further out in the sequence? A standard example would be for computing log x by polynomials of degree $0, 1, 2, 3, \ldots, N, \ldots$. We assume that for each approximation from the sequence we have the best coefficients possible.

In the present context, our ultimate objective is to choose the best algorithm for every problem. If we let $A^*(x)$ be the best algorithm for problem x and $A_N(x)$ the algorithm chosen by the best coefficients for the Nth approximation form, then the question is: *How does*

$$\epsilon_N(x) = ||\,p(A^*(x))\,|| - ||\,p(A_N(x))\,||$$

behave as N gets big? Does it go to zero for every x? Suppose we set

$$\epsilon_N = \max_{x \in \mathcal{P}} \epsilon_N(x)$$

Does ϵ_N go to zero fast, slowly, or at all? The answer to these questions is called the *degree of convergence* for the problem space $\mathcal{P}$ and the sequence of approximation forms.

In standard mathematical situations this idea is well developed and the degree of convergence is known for many cases. In the standard case the problem is to evaluate a function $f(x)$ and the best algorithm $A^*(x)$ is taken to be the exact value of $f(x)$. The measure of performance of an algorithm A that produces an approximation $a(x)$ is taken to be $|f(x) - a(x)|$. Thus, for computing $\sin(x)$ for $x \in \mathcal{P} = [0, \pi/2]$ we know that polynomial forms give $\epsilon_N \sim KN^{-N}$ for some constant K. In this case, ϵ_N goes to zero extremely fast. If one replaces $\sin(x)$ by $\text{ABS}(X-1)$, then $\epsilon_N \sim KN^{-1}$, which is not very fast at all.

The analogy with approximately evaluating a function can be carried further, but theoretical information about the degree of convergence is limited to "mathematical" functions, that is, functions defined in a mathematical context where one knows a variety of properties. We can say, however, that really fast convergence using simple forms (i.e., polynomials and similar linear forms) *requires* that the function involved be very well behaved. By well behaved we mean smooth (no jumps or discontinuities any kind, including in derivatives) and of a consistent global nature (i.e., if it oscillates one place, it oscillates everywhere, if it is flat one place, it is flat everywhere). A large proportion (at least 50%) of the "functions" that arise naturally in the real world are *not* well behaved in this sense.

6.3.3 Complexity

A fashionable idea related to degree of convergence is complexity. Thus the complexity of a function is some intrinsic measure of how hard it is to compute the function. The idea extends directly to solving problems by noting that solving a problem is equivalent to computing the value of the function that gives the solution of the problem.

In actually measuring complexity, one does several things:

A. Introduce some measure of the work involved in a computation. Typical examples are number of arithmetic operations, number of multiplies, execution time of a real program on a particular real computer, length of FORTRAN program needed, number of steps in a Turing machine computation.

B. Assume that one considers the most efficient scheme. There is no limit on how badly one can evaluate a function; complexity is measured with methods of optimal efficiency.

C. Restrict the kinds of steps in the algorithms used for the computation. For example, polynomial approximation excludes division, so $1/x$ may be difficult to compute, but if division were allowed then this would be a very easy function. Similarly $|x-0.5|$ is very easy if ABS is allowed or if a test and branch operation is allowed.

A uniform way to impose the above conditions on the complexity question is to say that the function is to be evaluated by a particular machine or, essentially equivalent, by one of a particular class of programs for a general purpose machine. We illustrate this approach for polynomials in Fig. 7.

The advantage of the idea of complexity over that of the degree of convergence is that much greater generality is achieved. Degree of convergence can be normally interpreted as complexity using a very specialized machine. For example, a machine that can only add and multiply but that can be programmed to do this in more or less arbitrary sequence and with arbitrary operands is considerably more versatile than the polynomial evaluation machine shown in Fig. 7. It could, for example, evaluate the function X^{1024} in 10 operations rather than the 1024 required for the strictly limited polynomial evaluation machine. This added generality also makes it possible to place the standard mathematical approximation forms into the same framework as the piecewise forms and the tree or algorithm forms. One merely adds or changes a piece of "hardware" on the machine.

The disadvantage of the idea of complexity is that its generality makes it very difficult to obtain specific results. Current research is very intensive and yet concentrated on rather simple problems as seen in Table I. These

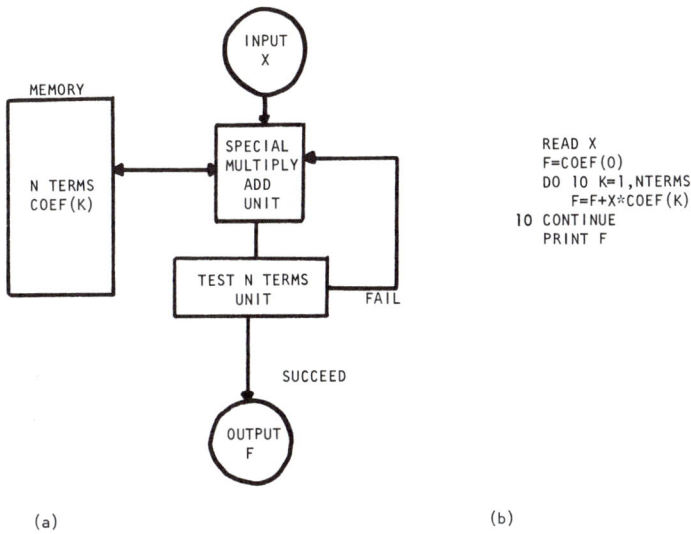

Fig. 7. Polynomial evaluation via (a) machine or (b) program. The special MULTIPLY/ADD unit and TEST unit of the machine are such that they can only (and automatically do) execute the program on the right.

problems are orders of magnitude simpler than the typical situation that arises in the algorithm selection problem. Thus there is little hope for the near future that we will obtain optimal algorithms for most of these problems (except possibly from *very* limited subclasses of algorithms).

In spite of the low probability of obtaining precise results about complexity in the algorithm selection problem, there are three good reasons to consider the idea. First, it provides the proper framework within which to

TABLE I

SUMMARY OF COMPLEXITY RESULTS FOR SOME COMMON COMPUTATIONS

Computation	Work or complexity of		
	Standard method	Optimal	Best known
Add two N-digit integers	N	N	N
Multiply two N-digit integers	N^2	?	$N \log^2 N$
Evaluate polynomial of degree N	N multiplies	?	$[N/2] + 2$ multiplies
Median of list of length N	$N \log N$	N	N
Multiply two $N \times N$ matrices	N^3	?	$N^{2.7}\ldots$

contemplate the problem. Second, the results for simple problems show that the standard ways of doing things are often not optimal or even anywhere close to best. Third, the high degree of complexity in "real" problems indicates that simple-minded approaches are unlikely to do well and even sophisticated approaches will often fall very short of optimal. Indeed, it is likely that further theoretical developments in the area will indicate that it is essentially impossible to obtain the optimal algorithms for many real problems.

6.3.4 Robustness

Robustness is a technically precise term in statistics that relates the quality of statistical estimates in extreme situations. Thus an estimation procedure is robust if its quality degrades gracefully as the situation becomes more and more extreme. We do not attempt to define this concept precisely here but it is quite useful in considering the selection of algorithms. It is a common phenomena for algorithms to do very well on a certain class of "easy" problems and to do increasingly worse as one moves away from these easy problems. A robust algorithm, then, is one whose performance degrades slowly as one moves away from the problems for which it was designed. Since the problem space is so large and so poorly understood in many real situations, this quality can be extremely important. There is a reasonable probability that one will face a problem with a completely unforeseen combination of attributes, which invalidate some of the "working assumptions" used in the development of the algorithm. The worst situation is, of course, an algorithm that fails completely and quietly as soon as one moves away from the ideal problems.

Consider the simple example of estimating the wealth of the "typical" student in a classroom. One has three candidate algorithms for the estimate: the average wealth, the medium wealth, and the midrange wealth. In a "normal" situation, these algorithms produce similar estimates, any one of which is satisfactory. A difficulty occurs with the presence of Hughes Hunt III (wealth of $625 million) or John D. Mellon V (wealth of $398 million) in the class. The midrange now produces ridiculous estimates like $200 or $300 million and the average is not much better with estimates like $20 or $30 million. The median estimate is, however, essentially unaffected by the presence of such a wealthy person and thus is a very robust algorithm for this problem. While the average is more robust than the midrange, it is not very satisfactory in extreme situations.

Finally, we note that robustness is frequently difficult to identify or measure. In some situations one can achieve robustness with very simple algorithms. In others it seems that robustness requires a complex algorithm that has numerous tests for special situations and cases.

6.4 Brief Survey of Approximation Form Attributes

This section presents a survey of the general attributes of five important types of approximation forms. Of necessity we speak in generalities, and thus there is a real danger that a casual reader will be misled. The statements we make about attributes apply "usually" or "commonly." Realistic specific situations exist that exhibit behaviors exactly opposite to the usual one. We have already noted that the most crucial decision in the algorithm selection problem is that of the approximation form. Ideally, this process goes as follows: One is intimately familiar with the problem space and with a large variety of approximation forms. One weighs the various advantages and disadvantages of the forms as they interact with the special features of the problem space. Perhaps some simple experimentation is made. Finally, a choice of form for the algorithm selection mapping is made that achieves a good balance with the overall objectives.

Thus one can visualize this section as a primer on the choice of approximation forms. Unfortunately, it is only an elementary primer and there is no substitute for detailed experience with a variety of real situations.

6.4.1 Discrete Forms

One might tend to dismiss this case as "degenerate." After all, if one is merely to select the best one of three or 11 algorithms, there seems to be little need for any elaborate machinery about approximation forms. We do not imply that identification of the best will be easy; rather we say that concepts like complexity, degree of convergence, etc., do not play a role. This reaction is appropriate in many cases. However, sometimes there are some very interesting and challenging features of these forms.

The principal feature is that the finite number of algorithm is either in fact or in concept a *very large* set. Even though we may have selected just three algorithms, we often visualize that these are representative samples from a very much larger set. Recall from the discussion of the numerical quadrature problem that there may well be tens of millions of algorithms of even a rather restricted nature. Thus in the mind's eye there is almost a continuum of algorithms, even though we may in fact be examining only three of them. One of the major weaknesses of modern mathematical machinery is in its ability to handle problems involving very large finite sets. The emphasis has been on developing tools to handle problems with infinite sets (e.g., the continuum) and one frequently draws a complete blank when faced with a finite set of, say, 10^{123} elements.

We are really saying that the proper way to consider discrete forms is as a discretization of a continuum. One then applies some intuitive ideas about continuous forms (such as presented later in this section) and hopefully obtains satisfactory results.

Unfortunately, we cannot continue a meaningful discussion here along these lines because we have no knowledge of the possible continuum behind the discrete set.

We conclude by recalling that robustness is a property of individual algorithms and thus immediately relevant to discrete forms. It could be evaluated for each algorithm in the discrete set. However, if the set is large, then this is impractical. In this latter case, one probably must attempt to transfer information about robustness from some underlying continuum.

6.4.2 Linear Forms

There are so many obviously nice things about linear forms that we might tend to concentrate too much on what is bad about them, or we might tend to ignore anything bad about them. Some of these nice things are

They are simple and efficient to use.
They are the easiest to analyze (by far).
They are easy to understand and visualize intuitively.
They are often extremely successful in achieving good approximation.

These observations imply that we should give these forms first consideration and that we should try other things only after we are fairly sure that some linear form does not suffice.

The bad thing about these forms comes from the following experimentally observed fact: *Many real world processes are not linear or anywhere close to being linear.* In particular, we would like to emphasize: *Most of the world processes are not a linear combination of simple, standard mathematical entities.* Since these facts are experimental rather than theoretical, we cannot prove them here. Indeed, certain theoretical results (e.g., the Weierstrass theorem) are frequently used to support just the opposite conclusion (e.g., one can use polynomials for everything).

Let us illustrate the situation by a trivial example: Our problem space $\mathcal{P}$ has just one attribute of consequence and we call it x (which identifies the problem with a real number that measure this attribute). Our algorithm space $\mathcal{A}$ is likewise simple with one attribute, which we call A. Suppose that x and A range between 0 and 1 and suppose the best algorithm

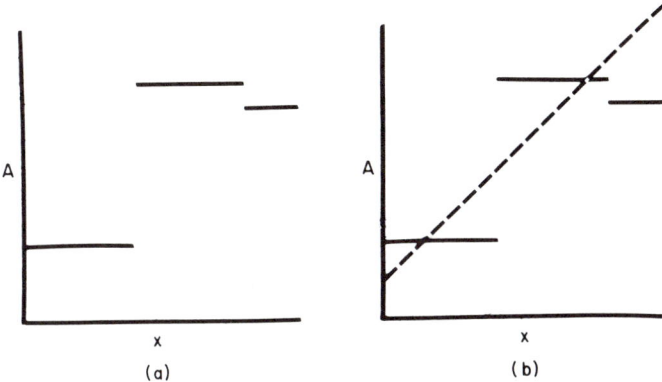

FIG. 8. (a) Graphical representation of the optimal algorithm selection mapping for a simplified example. (b) The optimal plus the best linear algorithm selection mapping.

is for $A = 0.27$ if $x < 0.41$, $A = 0.82$ if $0.41 \leq x \leq 0.8$, and $A = 0.73$ if $x > 0.8$. The best or optimal algorithm selection mapping is then as shown in Fig. 8a. If we attempt a linear form then we would have $A = \alpha + \beta x$, where α and β are coefficients to be determined. The optimal values α^* and β^* for these coefficients give a mapping shown as the dashed line in Fig. 8b. This mapping is clearly not very close to being optimal.

Once this completely linear form is recognized as inadequate, one then tends to proceed on to something more flexible. A natural idea is to use polynomials, e.g.,

$$A = \alpha_1 + \alpha_2 x + \alpha_3 x^2 + \alpha_4 x^3 + \cdots + \alpha_N x^{N-1}$$

If one carries this out for $N = 4$ (cubic polynomials) and $N = 20$, one can expect results such as shown in Fig. 9 (provided one has been careful in the computations). It is hard to argue that either one of these selection mappings is a good approximation to the optimal one. Note that in both cases that the polynomials are truncated at either $A = 0$ or at $A = 1$ in order to avoid obtaining nonexistent algorithms for some values of x.

Can one hope to do much better by choosing something besides polynomials? One frequently sees Fourier series (sines and cosines), exponentials, Bessel functions, etc. None of these give noticeably better approximations. There is, of course, a way to obtain excellent results by a linear form, $A = \alpha + \beta \omega(x)$. By merely choosing $\omega(x)$ to be the optimal selection mapping, then we find $\alpha^* = 0$ and $\beta^* = 1$ gives a perfect approximation.

This last observation shows the impossibility of making universal judgments about linear forms. If one chooses linear combinations of the right things, then the linear forms can do very well indeed. In practice though, one is usually limited to just a few possibilities and one has very little in-

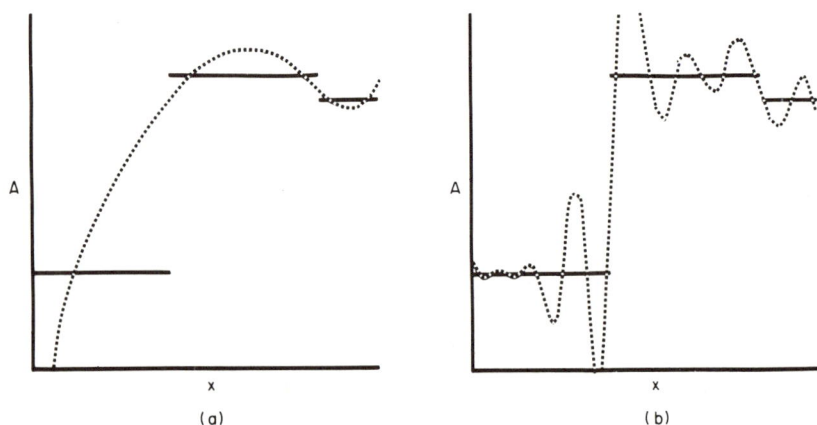

Fig. 9. Graphical representation of the optimal plus the best cubic (a) and best 20th degree (b) polynomial selection mappings.

formation about the optimal mapping. Note that a typical real problem has 5 to 15 dimensions in each of x and A variables. One is not likely to hit upon the optimal mapping as one of the things to include in the linear mapping.

We now attempt to motivate the above conclusions from the point of view of degree of convergence and complexity. For standard mathematical situations there are numerous results about how the errors of polynomial and similar functions behave as the number of terms increases. The phenomenon of Fig. 9 shows very slow convergence, or poor degree of convergence. Of course, if the optimal selection mapping has a jump as seen Fig. 8, there will always be a large error at that jump. We also see that the large error at the jump induces large errors everywhere.

If the optimal mapping is continuous but has breaks in the slope, then it is known that the degree of convergence for N-terms is like $1/N$. That means that if one term gives a unit error, then ten terms give a 0.1 error, 100 terms give 0.01 error, etc. This is a very bad situation even for the simplest case of a one-dimensional problem space. Higher dimensions compound this difficulty enormously. Thus if several of these breaks occur in a K-dimensional problem space, then the error behaves like $1/N^{1/k}$, where N is again the number of terms. For $K = 5$, if 1 term gives a unit error, then we would expect to need about 32 terms for $\frac{1}{2}$ unit error, 1000 terms for $\frac{1}{4}$ unit error, and 100,000 for 0.1 error. For $K = 10$, the corresponding numbers are 1000, 1,000,000, and 10^{10}, respectively, for errors of $\frac{1}{2}$, $\frac{1}{4}$, and 0.1. Clearly polynomials and related functions are hopeless in such situations except for the crudest of approximations to the optimal selection mapping.

ALGORITHM SELECTION PROBLEM

How often can one expect the problem space to produce selection mappings with these troublesome properties? Experimental evidence with phenomena from physics and engineering problems indicates that more than 50% of these functions are unsuitable for polynomials and other standard linear mathematical forms. This includes Fourier series, which are currently widely used in engineering situations where they cannot possibly give accurate results. There is an intuitive reason why one should expect this. Many physical phenomena have several domains where different factors completely dominate the behavior. As one goes from one domain to another there is a kind of discontinuity in behavior even if there is no sharp break in the slope. These discontinuities affect the degree of convergence directly and, expecially for low accuracies, lead to a very excessive number of turns being required. Recall that polynomials, Fourier series, etc., have the property that their global behavior is completely determined by their behavior on an arbitrarily small domain. This property is not present in many real world situations and is another intuitive reason for doubting the general applicability of the standard mathematical forms.

One must admit that the above arguments are taken from simplified and specialized situations. The extrapolation to all kinds of algorithm selection problems is very tenuous indeed. Yet, we conjecture that things get worse rather than better as one gets away from these situations into a broad range of real world problems.

6.4.3 Piecewise Linear Forms

In simple terms, we break up the problem domain into pieces and use separate linear forms on each piece. The motivation is to circumvent the difficulties described in the preceding discussion. In many cases the most crucial step is to determine the appropriate pieces, and yet these forms assume that they are fixed and given by some *a priori* process. In these cases we have, in fact, a two-stage process: first, an intuitive, hopefully realistic, partition of the problem domain into separate pieces, and second, the application of mathematical techniques to obtain the best coefficients for each of the linear pieces. Note that there are often some interconnections between the pieces (for example, broken lines are piecewise linear functions of one variable that join up continuously) that give rise to mathematical problems that are nonstandard but still linear (and hence usually tractable.

It is difficult to draw general conclusions about this approach because of the vagueness of the process for determining the pieces. Indeed if the pieces are poorly chosen or too big, then one can have all the difficulties mentioned with the traditional linear forms. On the other hand, there are the following hopeful facts about this approach:

(1) Sometimes one does have good enough intuition to determine the pieces so that a very significant improvement is made. Sometimes only a very few pieces are required for this improvement to happen.

(2) Sometimes the problem domain is small enough that one can break it up into more or less equal pieces that are small enough to obtain good results and yet still not obtain an intractable number of pieces.

(3) There are theoretical results (admittedly again from the narrow context of approximating functions of one variable) that indicate that if the best selection of pieces is made, then there are fantastic improvements possible, that is, so that the degree of convergence may change from something like $1/N^{1/2}$ to $1/N^3$, where N is the number of coefficients involved. If one piece gives accuracy 1, then these convergence rates indicate that about 10,000 or 5 coefficients, respectively, are needed to give an accuracy of 0.01 in the determination of the best selection mapping. Such an improvement obviously changes the entire nature of the problem.

We conclude that piecewise linear forms merit separate consideration for three reasons:

(1) They are nonstandard in mathematical/scientific analysis and might be overlooked if lumped into a larger class.

(2) Once the difficult determination of pieces is made, then more or less standard machinery can be used in further analysis and computation.

(3) They have been very useful in a variety of difficult situations and, while they are not a panacea, there is reason to believe that they will continue to be very useful.

6.4.4 General Nonlinear Forms

It is not very profitable to discuss such forms in the abstract. These forms include everything, including the best possible selection mapping, and thus one can do perfectly with them. Therefore, we must really be concerned with various specific classes of nonlinear forms. The literature on approximation theory contains a considerable development of a variety of such classes. A partial list of these with simple examples is as follows.

Rational functions:

$$\frac{c_1 + c_2 x + c_3 x^2}{c_4 + c_5 x}$$

Exponential/trigonometric functions:

$$c_1 e^{c_2 x} + c_3 e^{c_4 x} + c_5 \cos(c_6 x)$$

Piecewise polynomials:

$$\begin{cases} c_1 + c_2 x + c_3 x^2 & \text{for} \quad -\infty < x \leq c_4 \\ c_5 + c_6 x + c_7 x^2 + c_8 x^3 & \text{for} \quad c_4 \leq x \leq c_9 \\ c_{10} + c_{11} x + c_{12} x^2 & \text{for} \quad c_9 \leq x < \infty \end{cases}$$

Unisolvent functions: The set of all conic sections in the place.

Varisolvent functions: A general class of nonlinear forms, which includes the rationals, exponentials, etc.

There are several general statements that one can make about these forms:

(1) A considerable (or even very extensive) amount of analysis has been made of the theory of approximation.

(2) In those cases where degree of convergence results are available (e.g., piecewise polynomials and rationals), they imply that these special forms are much more capable of approximating a wide variety of behaviors. For example, both rationals and piecewise polynomials can do very well at approximating a jump discontinuity or a behavior like $x^{1/2}$ or $1/x^{1/2}$.

(3) The computational effort required to obtain best (or even very good) coefficients of these forms can be substantial. The development of computational methods is more difficult than for linear forms. However, it is practical to carry out these computations in a variety of cases.

Thus one expects (and observes) these forms to be useful in a variety of situations. The key to success is to analyze one's particular situation sufficiently to obtain general knowledge of the required behavior of the selection mapping. One then chooses that nonlinear form which possesses this behavior and for which one can handle the analytical and computational difficulties.

In conclusion, the determination of the proper nonlinear form is still somewhat of an art and there is no algorithm for making the choice. On the other hand, the degree of convergence and complexity results for rational functions and piecewise polynomials show that they have great flexibility and are likely to do well in most situations. Doing well might not be good enough. In real problems the dimensionalities are high, and needing five coefficients per dimension implies that 5^n coefficients are required for an n-dimensional feature (or problem) space. With $n = 2$ this is a modest 25 coefficients, but $n = 10$ would then require almost 10 million coefficients. This 10 million may be considered doing well compared to the 6 decillion coefficients of another approach, but in either case one cannot use the forms.

6.4.5 Tree and Algorithm Forms

These forms are most intriguing because they promise so much and have the mystery of the unknown. Perhaps it is a case of the grass being greener on the other side of the fence. These forms may have difficulties and disadvantages that are not apparent now but that may limit their usefulness much more than one hopes.

The primary basis for their promise is their flexibility and potential for complexity. They certainly should complement the more traditional mathematical forms. Their flexibility and complexity might be the limitation on their application. Computational methods for good coefficients of traditional forms have taken many years to develop and even now can be quite demanding. It may well be that the computation of good coefficients will severely restrict the usefulness of these forms for many years.

The piecewise linear forms are an example of a simple tree form and their success bodes well for other cases. Computational techniques and theoretical analysis for these forms are progressing steadily and we can look for them to enter into the "standard and routine" category before long. This development should serve as a useful guide for other simple tree and algorithmic forms. Still, we are very far removed from the time when we can select as our approximation form a 72-line FORTRAN program and then compute the best "coefficient values" (FORTRAN statements) for a particular application.

In summary, we have very little hard information about these forms, but they appear to hold great promise and to provide a great challenge for theoreticians and practitioners.

6.5 An Error to Avoid

Occasionally one observes the following situation develop:

(1) A real world problem is considered.
(2) A crude model is made of it. This model perhaps has some undetermined coefficients or is to be manipulated to obtain predictions about the real world problem's solution.
(3) A huge effort is spent in obtaining accurate coefficients or predictions based on the model.

In the specific instance at hand, the real world problem is the algorithm selection mapping, the model is the approximation form selected, and the effort is in determining the coefficients of this form. The error that one can make is in believing that finding the best coefficients of the selection mapping will result in good selections. In many cases *there is no reason to believe that the best coefficients will give good selections.* One is particularly susceptible to making this error when using simple linear forms for the selection mapping. One may refer to Fig. 8 for an illustration of this situation.

6.6 The Mathematical Theory Questions

This section presents an intuitive summary of the three principal topics of approximation theory. The algorithm selection problem presents some new open questions in these topics, some of which are indicated. There is more emphasis on summarizing the theory of approximations than on the implications for the algorithm selection problem.

6.6.1 The Existence Question

In concrete situations one rarely worries about the existence of best selection algorithms (even though one continually worries about the existence of good ones). Yet, from time to time this question sheds important light on practical questions. Parameterization plays an important role here: one is continually identifying algorithms by means of a set of coefficients or parameters. The question of existence of a best algorithm then becomes a question of the existence of a best set of coefficients. In the simplest cases (e.g., linear forms) the coefficients are just sets of real numbers and the question is readily reduced to a problem about sets of real numbers. One then attempts to show that (a) infinite coefficients cannot be best, and (b) the algorithms depend continuously on the coefficients. It then follows from standard mathematical arguments that a best set of coefficients exists.

This line of reasoning may fail at various points for nonlinear approximation forms. The failure is usually because of some weakness in the parameterization. A key point to remember is to *distinguish carefully between an approximation form and the particular set of coefficients used to parameterize it*. Consider the two simple examples

$$S(f,c) = c_1 + f/c_2, \qquad S(f,c) = c_1 + e^{-c_2 f}$$

In both of these cases $c_2 = +\infty$ corresponds to a constant and hence a perfectly reasonable function. In the first example this is due to a silly parameterization; one should have $c_1 + c_2 f$ instead. It is sometimes not so easy to see such silliness in more complex examples. The second example presents a more delicate situation, as there is no familiar mathematical way to rewrite this form so that the difficulty disappears. One can, however, obtain a perfectly satisfactory parameterization by taking c_1 and c_2 to be the values of $S(f,c)$ at $f = 0$ and $f = 1$, respectively. However, there is now no nice way to express $S(f,c)$ explicitly in terms of c_1 and c_2.

True nonexistence is fairly common for nonlinear forms and discrete sets. The standard example is

$$S(f,c) = c_1/(1+c_2 f^2) \quad \text{for } f \in \{-1,0,1\}$$

Thus the feature f can take on only one of three possible values and we choose to give S the form of the reciprocal of a quadratic polynomial. Suppose now that the best selection (of all possible forms and problems) is 1 if $f = 0$ and 0 if $f \neq 1$. Consider the case where $c_1 = 1$; we have

$$S(0,c) = 1/(1+0*f^2) = 1$$

$$S(-1,c) = S(+1,c) = 1/(1+c_2)$$

We can make $S(\pm 1, c)$ as close to zero as we want by making c_2 large; however, if we set $c_2 = \infty$, then $S(0,c)$ is ruined. The difficulty in this example is an essential one. There is no way to reparameterize $S(f,c)$ so as to obtain the best selection; yet we can come as close to it as we please.

Study of the existence question occasionally leads one to realize that the approximation form chosen must be extended in some way. A simple mathematical example of this occurs for the two-exponential form

$$S(f,c) = c_1 e^{c_2 f} + c_3 e^{c_4 f}$$

Let $c_2 = (1 + \epsilon)c_4$ and expand the first term in a Taylor series after factoring out $c_1 e^{c_4 f}$ to obtain

$$c_1 e^{c_4 f}\left[1 + \epsilon c_4 f + \frac{(\epsilon c_4 f)^2}{2!} + \frac{(\epsilon c_4 f)^3}{3!} + \cdots\right] + c_3 e^{c_4 f}$$

This may be rewritten as

$$e^{c_4 f}[c_1 + c_3 + c_1 \epsilon c_4 f + c_1(\epsilon c_4 f)^2/2 + \cdots]$$

Now let $c_1 = -c_3$, $c_1 = \alpha/\epsilon$, and then let ϵ go to zero. The result is $\alpha f e^{c_4 f}$ and we see that this form with two exponentials also contains a function of completely different mathematical form. However, the plot of fe^f and neighboring curves in Fig. 10 shows that there is nothing exceptional about $S(f,c)$ near this curve. Even so, the coefficients are $c_1 = +\infty$, $c_3 = -\infty$, $c_2 = c_4$, with

$$(c_4 - c_2)*c_1 = \alpha$$

There is a singularity in the parameterization near this curve, much as there is a singularity at the north and south poles for the geographic coordinates parameterization of the globe.

A variation of this phenomenon occurs with the piecewise forms. Consider piecewise linear forms (broken lines) with variable break points.

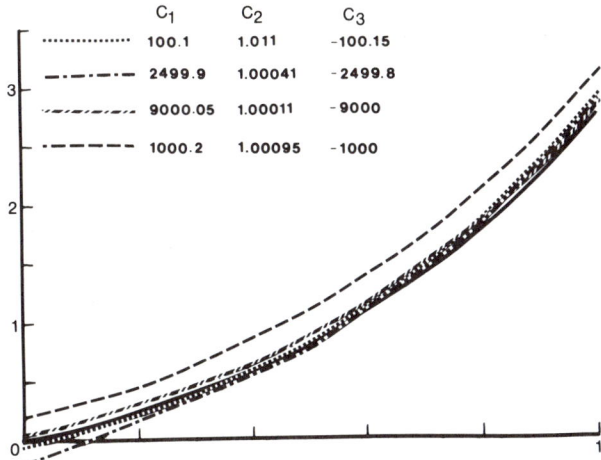

FIG. 10. The curve fe^t and nearby curves of the form $c_1 e^{c_2 t} + c_3 e^t$ with various values of c_1, c_2, and c_3.

Figure 11 shows two things that can happen when the break points come together. In Fig. 11a we see that two of them can converge, so that the result is a step function with a jump discontinuity. In Fig. 11b we see that four break points can converge, so that an isolated peak (a "delta" function) of arbitrarily small base and large height is obtained.

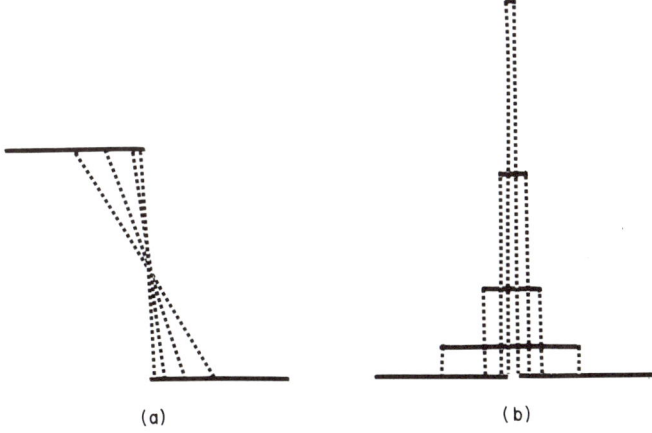

FIG. 11. Two ways that nonlinear break points in a broken line form can introduce new forms: (a) a jump discontinuity and (b) a "delta" function.

Study of the existence question can have implications for computations in the following way. If either nonexistence or the need for extending the definition are discovered, then one can expect computational difficulties. For example, if one is using the two-exponential form $c_1 e^{c_2 t} + c_3 e^{c_4 t}$ and the best approximation is $f e^t$ (or nearly so), then the computations become extremely ill conditioned and normally collapse in a blizzard of highly magnified round-off errors.

So far we have discussed only classical mathematical forms, and we expect the same phenomena to occur for the tree and algorithm forms. A very interesting open question is whether other phenomena may occur.

6.6.2 The Uniqueness Question

One is usually not interested in this question *per se*; any best (or good) approximation will do. However, its study, like that of existence, can give insight into computational difficulties that may arise.

Global uniqueness is a rare property except for linear problems. This fact is intuitively illustrated by the simple problem of finding the closest point on a curve (a class of algorithms) from a given point (the optimal algorithm). This is illustrated in Fig. 12.

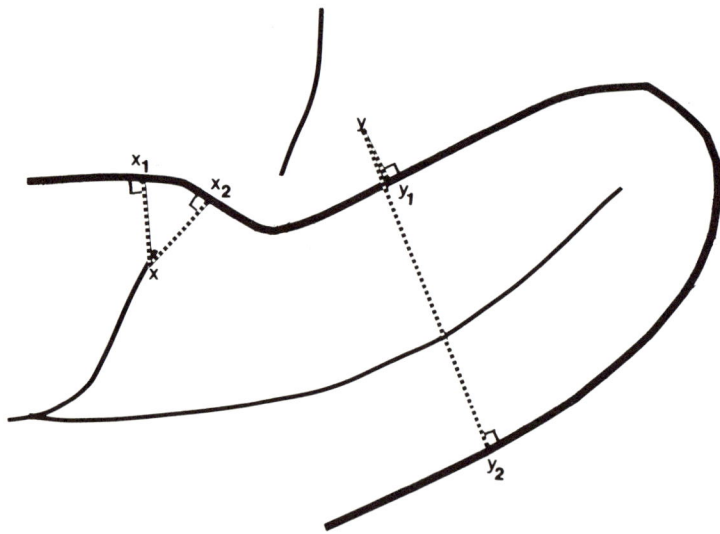

FIG. 12. Illustration of nonuniqueness of best approximation for a nonlinear problem. In a linear problem, the curve would be a straight line and every point would have a unique closest point on the line. The heavy line represents algorithms obtained by the mapping S. The light line represents problems where more than one algorithm is best.

Two other properties of the uniqueness question are illustrated by Fig. 12. First, almost all points have a unique best approximation even if a few do not. Second, we see that when there is more than one best approximation, they tend to be reasonably separated from one another. The point x, for example, has best approximations x_1 and x_2. Finally, the point y illustrates the most difficult situation where even though the closest point (y_1) is uniquely determined, there is another point (y_2) much further away, which is locally best and unique. That is to say, there is no point close to y_2 that is closer to y than y_2 is.

There are enormous computational implications of the phenomena illustrated in Fig. 12. First, and somewhat less important, one can expect trouble at those points where two or more closest points are close together. This occurs near the three ends of the "lines of nonuniqueness" in Fig. 12. More important is the fact that computational schemes are almost always local in nature and thus might well locate y_2 as the closest point to y. Further, such schemes usually give no inkling that there might be a point much closer to y. Note that this unfortunate situation occurs when we find a bad approximation (y_2 is far from y), and our limited experience in these matters does support the hope that "good" locally best approximations are likely to be global best approximations.

6.6.3 The Characterization Question

A characterization theorem gives some property of a best approximation, which characterizes it, i.e., which allows us to distinguish it from other approximations. An elementary approach to the question goes as follows: If we have a best approximation $S(F,C^*)$ with best coefficients C^*, then we have minimized something, namely, our measure of performance $\|p(S(F,C),F)\|$. At minima we have derivatives equal to zero. Therefore, a characteristic property comes from the equations that result from evaluating the derivative of the measure of performance and setting it equal to zero.

The application of this approach is straightforward in many instances, for example, the derivation of the normal equations for least squares approximations. In other instances, the characteristic conditions might appear to be completely unrelated to this approach. However, there usually is a direct relationship. For example, the conditions for optimality in linear programming problems is obtained this way modulo the changes necessary to include "differentiation" at the corners of multidimensional polyhedra. As an example, we derive the classical alternation theorem of minimax approximation using this elementary approach. Assume we want to approximate $f(x)$ by $S(c,t)$ with coefficients $c = c_1, c_2, \ldots, c_n$, so that

$$\max_t |f(t) - S(c,t)| = \text{minimum}$$

Then we want

$$\frac{\partial}{\partial c_j} \max_t |f(t) - S(c,t)| = 0 \quad \text{for } j = 1, 2, \ldots, n$$

Now, the maximum only occurs at the extrema of $|f - S|$ and if we denote them by t_i^*, $i = 1, 2, 3, \ldots$, we have

$$\frac{\partial}{\partial c_j} |f(t) - S(c,t)| _{\text{at } t_i^*} = 0 \quad \text{for } j = 1, 2, \ldots, n, \quad i = 1, 2, 3, \ldots$$

We now differentiate off the absolute value sign to get

$$\text{sign} |f - S|_{\text{at } t_i^*} \frac{\partial}{\partial c_j} S(c,t)_{\text{at } t_i^*} = 0$$

$$\text{for } j = 1, 2, \ldots, n, \quad i = 1, 2, 3, \ldots$$

If $S(c,t)$ is linear, i.e., $S(c,t) = \sum_{j=1}^n c_j \phi_j(t)$, then we have

$$\text{sign} |f - S| \phi_j(t)_{\text{at } t_i^*} = 0 \quad \text{for } j = 1, 2, \ldots, n, \quad i = 1, 2, 3, \ldots \tag{1}$$

That this is a variation of the alternation theorem is seen as follows [for the case of polynomial approximation, $\phi_j(t) = t^{j-1}$]. First note that there must be at least n extrema t_i^* because otherwise we could find a polynomial $S(d,t)$ of degree $n-1$ so that

$$S(d,t_i^*) = \text{sign} |f(t_i^*) - S(c,t_i^*)| \quad \text{for } i = 1, 2, 3, \ldots, k \leq n \tag{2}$$

which contradicts the preceding relationship (1). More generally, the extrema t_i^* must occur with a combination of signs so that it is impossible to achieve (2) with any choice of coefficients d. Thus, using elementary properties of polynomials, one finds that there must be a set of extrema t_i^* so that

$$\text{sign} |f - S|_{\text{at } t_i^*} = (-1)^i \text{ or } (-1)^{i+1} \quad \text{for } i = 1, 2, \ldots, n+1$$

This is the classical alternation property that characterizes best minimax approximations.

The main point made is that almost all characterization conditions come from setting derivatives equal to zero, even though in some cases it may look much different because of special situations or because the conditions have been manipulated after equating the derivatives to zero.

The implication for computation is that they also are based on finding coefficients where the derivative is zero. In many situations the key to an effective computational procedure is to find a proper interpretation of the derivative in the problem at hand. These procedures are generally iterative in nature (unless one is lucky) and share many of the computational properties of similar methods of elementary numerical analysis (e.g., Newton's method, secant method, bisection, fixed point iteration). Unfortunately, these shared properties are not that attractive in high-dimensional problems. That is, some of them are slow to converge, computationally expensive, or difficult to initialize for convergence. Some methods may have all three of these unattractive properties in certain cases.

6.7 Conclusions, Open Questions, and Problems

One objective of this section is to explore the applicability of approximation theory to the algorithm selection problem. We conclude that there is an intimate relationship here and that approximation theory forms an appropriate base upon which to develop a theory of algorithm selection methods. We also conclude that approximation theory currently lacks much of the necessary machinery for the algorithm selection problem. There is a need to develop new results for and apply known techniques to these new circumstances. The final pages of this chapter form a sort of appendix, which lists 15 specific open problems and questions in this area.

We note that there is a close relationship between the algorithm selection problem and general optimization theory. This is not surprising since the approximation problem is a special form of the optimization problem. We have not attempted to detail this relationship here, but one may refer to Rice (1970), where the relationship between nonlinear approximation and optimization is explored.

We conclude that most realistic algorithm selection problems are of moderate to high dimensionality and thus one should expect them to be quite complex. One consequence of this is that most straightforward approaches (even well-conceived ones) are likely to lead to enormous computations for the best selection. Indeed, the results of Rabin (1974) suggest that this complexity precludes the determination of the best selection in many important cases.

Finally, we reiterate the observation that the single most important part of the solution of a selection problem is the appropriate choice of the form for the selection mapping. It is here that theories give the least guidance and that the art of problem solving is most crucial.

We list 15 questions that are given or suggested by the developments of this chapter.

(1) What is the relationship between tree forms and piecewise linear forms? Can all tree forms be made equivalent to some piecewise form, linear or nonlinear?

(2) What are the algorithm forms for the standard mathematical forms? Do they suggest useful simple classes of algorithm forms? See Hart et al. (1968, Chapter 4) for algorithm forms for some polynomial and rational forms.

(3) Determine specific classes of tree forms where the current machinery of nonlinear approximation is applicable.

(4) Develop some general approaches (or methods) to classifying problems within a problem space. This is related to the next problem.

(5) Develop an abstract machinery for analyzing optimal features. Such a machinery might well combine the theoretical ideas of n-widths and/or entropy (see Lorentz, 1966) with the intuitive ideas of performance profiles (see Lyness and Kaganove, 1976).

(6) What is the nature of the dependence of the degree of convergence on the dimensionality of the problem? Some results are known for polynomial approximation to multivariate functions. Are these typical of what one should expect in general?

(7) What is the nature of the dependence of complexity on the dimensionality of the problem? Can results of (6) be translated directly into statements about complexity?

(8) Obtain more precise information about the nature of real world functions. The generalities used in this report were obtained by selecting a large number of empirically determined functions from the "Handbook of Chemistry and Physics" (1960) and then observing how effective polynomial approximation is. Are the results of this experiment representative of other contexts? Can more precise information about the properties of such classes be obtained?

(9) Determine the computational complexity of the following specific problems. For simplicity, one may use one evaluation of $f(x)$ as the unit of computation and ignore all other work.

  (a) Approximation to $f(x)$ via interpolation by polynomials. Assume various kinds of smoothness for $f(x)$.
  (b) Least squares approximation to $f(x)$ on $[0,1]$ by polynomials. Assume various kinds of smoothness for $f(x)$.
  (c) Evaluation of $\int_0^1 f(x)\,dx$. This is closely related to the least squares problem.

(10) Formulate a more precise and general concept of robustness.

(11) Develop useful mechanisms to embed certain classes of discrete forms into continuous ones. This is particularly relevant for nonstandard mathematical forms.

(12) Develop techniques to partition high-dimensional problem sets into subsets where good linear approximations are possible. A particular instance would be to develop adaptive algorithms for piecewise linear (no continuity) approximations in high dimensions. See Pavlidis (1973) for some work in one dimension.

(13) Develop existence theorems for various classes of tree form approximations. Do the difficulties of coalesced knots that occur in spline approximation have an analogy in general tree forms?

(14) What are the relationships between best algorithm selection and the results in automata theory about computability and computational complexity?

(15) Is there any way to "differentiate" the tree form so as to obtain a local characterization theorem?

REFERENCES

Abell, V. (1973). "Queue Priorities in the Purdue MACE Operating Systems," PUCC Publ. ZO QP-1. Purdue University, West Lafayette, Ind.

Blue, J. L. (1975). "Automatic Numerical Quadrature—DQUAD," Comput. Sci. Tech. Rep. No. 25. Bell Telephone Labs, Murray Hill, N.J.

Casaletto, J., Picket, M., and Rice, J. (1969). A comparison of some numerical integration programs. *SIGNUM Newslett.* **4**, 30–40.

Coffman, E. G., and Denning, P. J. (1974). "Operating Systems Theory," Chapters 3 and 4. Prentice-Hall, Englewood Cliffs, New Jersey.

de Boor, C. (1971). CADRE—an algorithm for numerical quadrature. *In* "Mathematical Software" (J. Rice, ed.), pp. 417–449. Academic Press, New York.

Einarsson, B. (1974). Testing and evaluation of some subroutines for numerical quadrature. *In* "Software for Numerical Mathematics" (D. J. Evans, ed.), pp. 149–157. Academic Press, New York.

Gentleman, M. W. (1972). Algorithm 424, Clenshaw-Curtis quadrature. *Commun. ACM* **14**, 337–342 and 353–355.

"Handbook of Chemistry and Physics." (1960). Handbook Publishers Inc., Sandusky, Ohio.

Hart, J. F. *et al.* (1968). "Computer Approximations." Wiley, New York.

Kahaner, D. K. (1971). Comparison of numerical quadrature formulas. *In* "Mathematical Software" (J. Rice, ed.), pp. 229–259. Academic Press, New York.

Krogh, F. T., and Snyder, M. V. (1975). "Preliminary Results with a New Quadrature Subroutine," Comput. Memo. No. 363, Sect. 914. Jet Propulsion Laboratory, Pasadena, Calif.

Lorentz, G. G. (1966). "Approximation of Functions." Holt, New York.

Lyness, J. N., and Kaganove, J. J. (1976). Comments on the nature of automatic quadrature routines. *ACM Trans. Math. Software* **2**, 65–81.

Patterson, T. N. L. (1973). Algorithm 468, algorithm for automatic numerical integration over a finite interval. *Commun. ACM* **16**, 694–699.

Pavlidis, T. (1973). Waveform segmentation through functional approximation. *IEEE Trans. Comput.* **c-22**, 689–697.

Piessens, R. (1973a). An algorithm for automatic integration. *Angew. Inf.* **9**, 399–401.

Piessens, R. (1973b). "A Quadrature Routine with Round-off Error Guard," Rep. TW17. Appl. Math. Prog. Div., Katholicke Universiteit, Leuven.

Rabin, M. O. (1974). Theoretical impediments to artificial intelligence. *Proc. IFIP, 1974* pp. 615–619.

Rice, J. R. (1970). Minimization and techniques in nonlinear approximation. *Stud. Numer. Anal.* **2,** 80–98.

Rice, J. R. (1975). A metalgorithm for adaptive quadrature. *J. Assoc. Comput. Mach.* **22,** 61–82.

Wilkes, M. (1973). Dynamics of paging. *Comput. J.* **16,** 4–9.

Parallel Processing of Ordinary Programs*

DAVID J. KUCK

Department of Computer Science
University of Illinois at Urbana-Champaign
Urbana, Illinois

1. Introduction 119
   1.1 Speed Limits 122
   1.2 Logic Design and Compiler Uniformity 123
2. Theoretical Fundamentals 127
   2.1 Arithmetic-Expression Tree-Height Reduction 128
   2.2 Recurrence Relations 134
   2.3 Column Sweep Algorithm 136
   2.4 Product Form Recurrence Method 137
   2.5 Constant-Coefficient Recurrences 139
3. Program Analysis 141
   3.1 Wave Front Method 145
   3.2 Loop Speedup Hierarchy 146
   3.3 Loop Distribution 148
   3.4 Loop Distribution Algorithm 149
   3.5 IFs in Loops 152
4. Machine Considerations 158
   4.1 Control Units 163
   4.2 Parallel Memory Access 165
   4.3 Array Access 165
   4.4 Parallel Random Access 168
   4.5 Alignment Networks 170
   4.6 A Cost Effectiveness Measure 172
5. Conclusions 174
   References 176

1. Introduction

In the decade 1965–75 we have seen a number of changes in computer technology and computer use. Integrated circuits have arrived and with

---

* This work was supported in part by the National Science Foundation under Grant No. US NSF DCR73-07980 A02.

them have come large, fast semiconductor memories; microprocessors that can be used as components; and the potential for a variety of new system architectures. Users of computers in this period have become quite concerned about the reliability of their hardware and software. They have also come to expect computer services to fit their needs, whether this be through a personal minicomputer, a supercomputer at the other end of a network, or a special purpose computer in their computer center.

In the mid-1960s there were many debates about which direction computer organization would go. Stacks versus registers, binary versus hexadecimal, time sharing versus batch processing versus remote batch were all being discussed. Whether fast computers should be organized as multiprocessors, array processors, pipeline processors, or associative processors was widely discussed. The discussions were often mainly emotional, with no substantive arguments to back them up. Not surprisingly, everybody won in many of these contests. Indeed, computers are wonderfully flexible devices and can be twisted into many forms with great success.

This is not to say that every new computer organization is a good idea and will survive. In fact, in this decade the entire computer divisions of several major companies have failed. Nor is it to say that we lack ideas of universal applicability. As examples, hierarchies of virtual memory and microprogrammed control units have at last been adopted, if not *discovered*, by just about everybody.

In the mid-1970s one can still hear a number of debates. Some of them have not changed from the mid-1960s. There are also new ones about how to make reliable hardware and software, how to bring computer services to ordinary people, and how to exploit ever higher levels of integrated circuit technology. The latter subject obviously provides one of the cornerstones of the whole subject of computer design and use.

While circuit speeds have improved in the past decade, their costs have improved even more. Thus designers can afford to use more and more gates in computer systems. But some of the traditional design considerations have changed. At the present time, printed circuit board and wire delays often dominate gate delays in system design. Thus computer organization itself would now seem to be a more important question than circuit type and gate count minimization at the hardware level of computer design.

It is also clear that by properly organizing a machine, various software features can be more easily supported. Stacks, extra bits, special registers, and instructions are examples of this. And the availability of low-cost integrated circuits makes all of these feasible, even in low-cost machines.

Besides these hardware and software considerations, a computer designer must worry about what applications are to be served by his machine. In the days of truly general purpose computers, "Any color you want as long

PARALLEL PROCESSING OF ORDINARY PROGRAMS   121

at it's black," was sufficient. But general purpose machines, in this sense, have disappeared. Even the IBM 360 series provided specialization in terms of size and speed. And the list of specialization improvements over that series is very long, ranging from minis to supers, from scientific to banking, and from real time to background specializations.

Some people would argue that software design is a much more important question than computer system design. As support they would offer the skyrocketing costs of software and the sharply dropping hardware costs. However, these observations probably support the converse position even more. In view of decreasing hardware costs, how can we better organize machines so that software and applications are better and less expensively handled? Indeed, software is not an end in itself.

One of the main points of confusion and disagreement over the design of better hardware and software has always been in deciding on goals. People of one background or another tend to have biases of one kind or another. And an entire computer and software system has so much complexity that it is difficult for one person to think about all the interrelating details. Even if a "perfect" system could be conceptualized by one person, he could not build it by himself. Many people must be involved. Indeed, this has been the downfall of many systems, the first such having been Charles Babbage's analytical engine.

The above remarks are well understood by any serious hardware or software designer. A point that is not so well understood, or at least it is widely ignored, is that a good system's main goal is to serve its end users well. Many computers and many software systems are designed from beginning to end with only a nod to the ultimate users, the main design goals being whatever "improvements" the designers can make over their previous designs. Such "improvements" are often intrinsic to the hardware or software and may or may not be reflected in what the end user sees.

The standard way to design any big system—hardware, software, highway, or bridge—is to break it up into hierarchies and subparts. When parts that are analytically tractable are found, the proper analysis provides a solution for those parts. Other parts are solved using the best intuition the designer has.

A key question in improving the system design procedure would seem to be the following: How can we integrate users' problems into the design procedure? The answer to this is not obvious. Usually, users do not know exactly what they want. They often know what was wrong with their previous system. But solving these problems is often similar to making improvements of an intrinsic hardware or software nature as mentioned above. They do not lead to a global, system improvement.

A partial answer to what the user wants may be found in looking at the programs he runs. While these may not reflect exactly the algorithms he wishes to run, they at least provide an objective measure of what he is doing. If a system could handle these programs well, then at least for a short while, the user would be happy.

In this chapter we will consider several aspects of the problem of integrating the analysis of users' programs with the design of computer systems. To tackle the problem in a concrete way, it is reasonable to restrict our initial study. We will first deal with FORTRAN programs because there are many of them in existence and because the language is quite simple. Our primary design goal will be the fast execution of programs. This goal is indeed probably the primary objective of "users" ranging from computer center managers who want high system throughput to individual programmers who want fast turnaround. Of course, reliability, ease of use, quality of results, and so on are also important, but we will deal with one problem at a time. The ideas we will discuss are applicable to programs in languages other than FORTRAN—we use it because it is popular and of relatively low level—as we shall mention in Section 5.

1.1 Speed Limits

What are the factors that limit the speed of machine computation? Or, to sharpen the question a bit: Given a set of programs, what determines how fast they can be executed? Basically, there are two aspects to the answer. One aspect concerns the physics of the hardware being used. The other aspect concerns the logic of the machine organization and the program organization.

The physical limits on computer speed are rather widely understood. Gates can switch in some fixed time, and we must pay for the sum of a number of gate delays to perform various computer operations. Additionally, signals must propagate along printed circuit boards and on wires between boards, and these delays are often larger than gate delays. We shall not concern ourselves with these questions. Rather, we shall assume that circuit speeds are fixed and consider the logical problems involved.

The logic of machine organization has been studied for many years. Greater machine speed through simultaneity or parallelism has been a subject of much study. Parallelism has been used at many levels, between bits, between words, between functions, and so on. Shortly we shall give more details of this.

The relations between the organization of a machine and the organization of a program to be executed on that machine have not been studied much. Of course, the compilation of a FORTRAN program for execution on a serial computer is a special case of this. But compiler theory has mainly been developed with respect to languages. The semantic or machine-related aspects of compilation are usually handled in *ad hoc* ways.

Beyond this, we are really concerned with the syntactic transformation of algorithms given in the form of programs into forms that exhibit high amounts of parallelism. At the same time, we are interested in clarifying what kinds of machine organizations correspond to the parallel forms of programs. Thus we seek program transformations and machine organizations that together allow for high speed and efficient execution of any given serial programs.

A properly developed theory will have a number of benefits. For one thing, it will allow us to see what the logical limits of computation speed are (in contrast to the physical limits) and to see how close to them we are operating. It will also give us constructive procedures for designing machines and compilers for those machines. Another benefit, which we discuss below, is that we can obtain a unified approach to logic design and compiler design since, abstractly, many of the problems are identical.

Our analysis of FORTRAN-like programs can be carried out at several levels. First, we can consider the elementary statements in the language, e.g., assignment, IF, DO, etc. Then we can consider whole programs and see how these statements fit together. This can be done at an abstract level and also by studying real programs using the abstract theory. The chapter also contains several discussions of algorithms in other programming languages, but we will not develop these points at much length here.

With a good understanding of the structure of programs behind us, it is proper to consider machine organizations. In this chapter we will mainly discuss processor, switch, and primary-memory design. Control units and memory hierarchies are being studied in a similar way but these areas are not as well developed at this point.

Our long-term objective is to develop methods for the rational design of computer systems that are well matched to the classes of programs they are to execute. By developing our ideas theoretically, we can see what our ultimate objectives in terms of bounds might be. We can also observe that several dissimilar aspects of computer system design consist of ideas that are identical at a theoretical level. Thus a coherent body of theoretical material can be used at the logic design level and also at the compiler design level.

1.2 Logic Design and Compiler Uniformity

To give an intuitive overview of our ideas, let us begin with a few simple examples. The basic question is, How fast can we carry out certain functions?

First, consider the problem of performing logical operations on two n-bit computer words $a = (a_1 \cdots a_n)$ and $b = (b_1 \cdots b_n)$. If we have $a = (101101)$ and $b = (011001)$, then the result of a logical OR defined as $(a_i + b_i)$ is $c = (111101)$, and the result of a logical AND defined as $(a_i \cdot b_i)$ is $d = (001001)$. Note that either the AND or the OR function is performed on pairs of bits of a and b, independently of all other bits in the words. Hence it is obvious that either of these functions can be computed in a time (say, one gate delay) that is independent of the number of bits involved. This assumes that we can use as many gates as we need; in this case the number of AND and OR gates will be proportional to n.

Now let us turn our attention to arithmetic operations rather than logical operations. Again consider $a = (a_1, \ldots, a_n)$ and $b = (b_1, \ldots, b_n)$, but now let the a_i and b_i be full computer words each representing a number. If we have $a = (3,5,2,1,0,7)$ and $b = (1,2,3,4,5,6)$, then the result of a vector add is $c = (4,7,5,5,5,13)$ and the result of a vector multiply is $d = (3,10,6,4,0,42)$. Just as in the logical case, we can perform all of the above arithmetic operations independently of one another. Thus, regardless of n, the dimension of the vectors, we can form c in one add time or d in one multiply time. This assumes that we have n adders or n multipliers available.

Next, let us consider some more difficult problems at the bit and arithmetic level.

Suppose we have one computer word $a = (a_1 \cdots a_n)$ in which bit a_i corresponds to the occurrence of some event. In other words, let $a_i = 1$ if event e_i has occurred and $a_i = 0$ otherwise. Further, let b and c be one-bit indicators defined as follows. If any of events $e_1, \ldots, e_n$ have occurred, we want b to be 1, otherwise $b = 0$. And if all of events $e_1, \ldots, e_n$ have occurred, we want c to be 1, otherwise $c = 0$.

What are the fastest possible designs for logical circuits that compute b and c? It is intuitively clear that these problems are more difficult than those we discussed above, namely, the pairwise logical AND and OR problems. Here, all bits in the word a are involved in the computation of b and c. A simple way to solve this, which also turns out to be the fastest, is the following. To form b, we compute $a_1 + a_2, a_3 + a_4, \ldots, a_{n-1} + a_n$, simultaneously using $n/2$ OR gates (assuming $n = 2^k$). Then we compute $(a_1 + a_2) + (a_3 + a_4)$ and so on, fanning in the result to a single result bit b, as shown in Fig. 1. If we replace the logical OR by a logical AND in the above discussion we form the result c.

It is not difficult to prove that for such problems this kind of fan-in approach yields the best possible result. The technique is useful in many logic design problems.

Now we consider the arithmetic problems corresponding to the above logic design questions. If $a = (a_1, \ldots, a_n)$ is a vector of n numbers stored

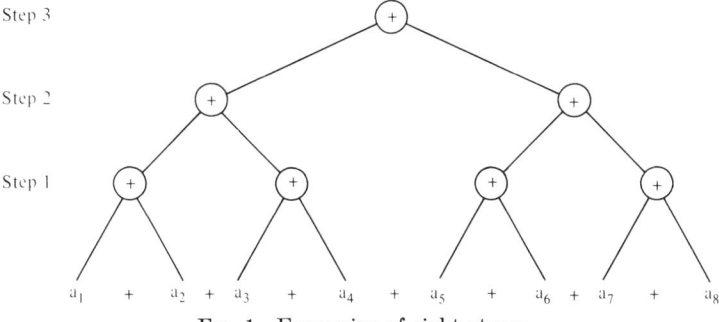
Fig. 1. Expression of eight atoms.

in a computer, suppose we want to compute the sum and product

$$b = \sum_{i=1}^{n} a_i, \quad c = \prod_{i=1}^{n} a_i$$

Instead of dealing with gates, we must now consider adders or multipliers as our basic building blocks. Again, the best solutions to these problems are obtained by simply fanning in the arguments. The tree of Fig. 1 illustrates this. If we now interpret the + as an arithmetic addition, the result is b, and similarly for c.

We see from the above discussion that for a class of computations that require the interaction of more than two data elements, more time is required than was needed by our first type of computation. In particular, for these calculations, if n arguments are involved then we need $\lceil \log_2 n \rceil$ operation times to compute the result. An operation time may be a logical OR or AND, or it may be an arithmetic add or multiply.

Finally, let us consider an even messier kind of computation. Suppose we have two n-bit words $a = (a_1 \cdots a_n)$ and $b = (b_1 \cdots b_n)$ and we want to compute

$$c_i = \begin{cases} 0 & \text{if} \quad i = 0 \\ a_i + b_i c_{i-1} & \text{if} \quad 1 \leq i \leq n \end{cases}$$

This may seem to be a strange logic design problem. It is not very unusual, however, since it forms the heart of the design of a binary adder. In particular, this recurrence relation accounts for carry generation, which is the main time delay in an adder circuit. How much time is required to compute the vector of carry bits c?

The solution of this problem is not as obvious as were the solutions of our earlier problems. Before discussing how to solve it, let us consider an analogous arithmetic problem that frequently occurs in the numerical computation for evaluating a polynomial

$$p(x) = a_n + a_{n-1}x + a_{n-2}x^2 + \cdots + a_0 x^n$$

Traditionally, we are told to do this using Horner's rule,

$$h(x) = a_n + x(a_{n-1} + x(a_{n-2} + \cdots + x(a_1 + xa_0)\cdots)) \qquad (1)$$

since it requires only $O(n)$ operations. This can be restated as a program of the form

```
P = A(0)
FOR I = 1 TO N
P = A(I) + X * P
```

which computes the expression $h(x)$ from inside out in N iterations.

It is clear that both problems share an important property. Both are recurrences in which step i depends on the result that was computed during step $i-1$. This may initially give us the sinking feeling that no speedup is possible here. To show that $O(n)$ steps are not required to compute such linear recurrence functions is in general a nontrivial problem that has been studied in many forms. We will give more attention to this at the program level later. At the logic design level, it is discussed in Chen and Kuck (1975a), where algorithms are given for transforming any linear sequential circuit specification into a fast combinational circuit. Time and component bounds are given for such circuits as adders, multipliers, and one's position counters, which compare favorably with those derived by traditional methods.

We can derive two important theoretical problems from the above. One is tree-height reduction for arithmetic expression parse trees or for combinational logic expressions. The other is the fast solution of linear recurrences derived either from programs or from logic design problems. If we have fast, efficient procedures for solving both types of problems in a parallel way, we will have a good understanding of important theoretical aspects of compiler writing and logic design automation, respectively.

In Section 2, we will discuss some details of these problems. It can, in fact, be shown that any arithmetic expression or simple linear recurrence containing $O(n)$ arguments can be solved in $O(\log n)$ time steps. The width of the tree (number of processors) needed is just $O(n)$ in either case. Thus for any of these calculations, which require $O(n)$ time steps if performed serially, we can speed them up by a factor of $O(n/\log n)$, using just $O(n)$ processors. As we saw above, some computations can be speeded up even more [e.g., by $O(n)$]. And as we shall see in Section 2, the best known speedups for some computations are much less than this.

Using this theoretical background, we will turn our attention to the analysis of whole programs in Section 3. We will consider transformations of blocks of assignment statements, loops, conditional statements, and program graphs. Algorithms for such transformations, as well as resulting time and processor bounds, will be discussed. Such algorithms can serve as the basis for program measurement to aid in the design of effective machines. They can also be used as a model of a compiler for parallel or pipeline computers. Above the bit level of logic design, these are our primary motivations, but we can also interpret our work in several other ways. Since we are really engaged in a study of the structure of programs, our results seem useful in the contexts of structured programming (e.g., since we remove GOTOs) and also memory hierarchy management (e.g., since we can reduce program page space–time products).

In Section 4, we discuss some aspects of real computers, including the assessing, aligning, and processing of data. We also sketch some results from our analysis of a number of real FORTRAN programs. To relate parallel machine organizations to algorithm organizations, we give a cost/effectiveness measure and a number of examples of its use.

2. Theoretical Fundamentals

The two basic building blocks of any numerical programs are arithmetic expressions and linear recurrences. In this section we will give upper bounds on the time and number of processors needed for the fast parallel evaluation of both of these. In order to keep our discussion simple, we will (in this section) ignore memory and data alignment times as well as control unit activity. Although we will bound the number, we assume as many processors as needed are available.

We will assume that each arithmetic operation takes one unit of time. Our recurrence methods allow all processors to perform the same operation at the same time. This SIMD [single-instruction, multiple-data (Flynn, 1972)] operation is the simplest for a parallel or pipeline machine organization to perform. Our arithmetic expression bounds assume that different processors can perform different operations at the same time. This MIMD [multiple-instruction, multiple-data (Flynn, 1972)] behavior assumes a more complex control unit. However, it is obvious that the bounds need be adjusted by only a small constant to allow them to be used for SIMD machines. In the worst case, we can assume a machine that simply cycles through each of the four arithmetic operations on each "macrostep," although more delicate schemes are easy to devise. In any case, most of our speedup in most programs comes from the speedup of linear recurrences.

Subscripted arithmetic expressions (which are not recurrences) inside loops can simply be handled as trees of arrays, so SIMD operation holds.

We will give a number of results about tree-height reduction first. This theory has been well developed and we will give more results than are justified for practical compilation. But we will indulge ourselves a bit, since the material is interesting in an abstract sense, at least.

If T_p is the number of unit time steps required to perform some calculation using $p \geq 1$ processors, we define the *speedup* of the p processor calculation over a uniprocessor as

$$S_p = T_1/T_p \geq 1$$

and we define the efficiency of the calculation as

$$E_p = S_p/p \leq 1$$

which may be regarded as actual speedup divided by the maximum possible speedup using p processors. For various computations we will discuss the maximum possible speedup known according to some algorithm and in such cases we use P to denote the minimum number of processors known to achieve this maximum speedup. In such cases we will use the notation T_P, S_P, and E_P to denote the corresponding time, speedup, and efficiency, respectively.

Time and processor bounds for some computation A will be expressed as $T_P[A]$ and $P[A]$ in the minimum time cases and $T_p[A]$ in the restricted processor $(p < P)$ case. When no ambiguity can result, we will write $T[A]$ or just T in place of $T_P[A]$ and P in place of $P[A]$, for simplicity. We write $\log x$ to denote $\log_2 x$ and $\lceil x \rceil$ for the ceiling of x.

2.1 Arithmetic-Expression Tree-Height Reduction

Now we consider time and processor bounds for arithmetic expression evaluation. We restrict our attention to transforming expressions using associativity, commutativity, and distributivity, which leads us to speedups of $O(n/\log n)$ at efficiencies of $O(1/\log n)$. Since this is asymptotic to the best possible speedup, more complex transformations (e.g., factoring, partial fraction expansion) seem unnecessary.

Definition 1 An *arithmetic expression* is any well-formed string composed of the four arithmetic operations $(+,-,*,/)$, left and right parentheses, and *atoms*, which are constants or variables. We denote an arithmetic expression E of n distinct atoms by $E\langle n \rangle$.

If we use one processor, then the evaluation of an expression containing n operands requires $n - 1$ units of time. But suppose we may use as many processors as we wish. Then it is obvious that some expressions $E\langle n \rangle$ may be evaluated in $\log_2 n$ units of time as illustrated in Fig. 1. In fact, we can establish, by a simple fan-in argument, the following lower bound:

Lemma 1 Given any arithmetic expression $E\langle n\rangle$,

$$T[E\langle n\rangle] \geq \lceil \log n \rceil$$

On the other hand, it is easy to construct expressions $E\langle n\rangle$ whose evaluation appears to require $O(n)$ time units regardless of the number of processors available. Consider the evaluation of a polynomial by Horner's rule as in Section 1. A strict sequential order is imposed by the parentheses in Eq. (1) and more processors than one are of no use in speeding up this expression's evaluation.

However, we are not restricted to dealing with arithmetic expressions as they are presented to us. For example, the associative, commutative, and distributive laws of arithmetic operations may be used to transform a given expression into a form that is numerically equivalent to the original but may be evaluated more quickly. We now consider examples of each of these.

Figure 2a shows the only parse tree possible (except for isomorphic images) for the expression $(((a + b) + c) + d)$. This tree requires three steps for its evaluation and we refer to this as a tree height of three. However, by using the associative law for addition we may rearrange the parentheses and transform this to the expression $(a + b) + (c + d)$, which may be evaluated as shown in Fig. 2b with a tree height of two. It should be noted that in both cases, three addition operations are performed.

Figure 3a shows a parse tree for the expression $a + bc + d$; again we have a tree of height three. In this case the tree is not unique, but it is obvious that no lower height tree can be found for the expression by use

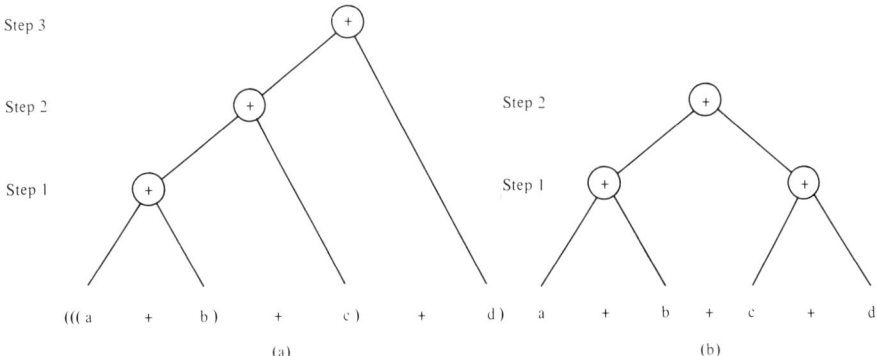

FIG. 2. Tree-height reduction by associativity (a) $T_1 = 3$. (b) $T_2 = 2$, $S_2 = \frac{3}{2}$, $E_2 = \frac{3}{4}$.

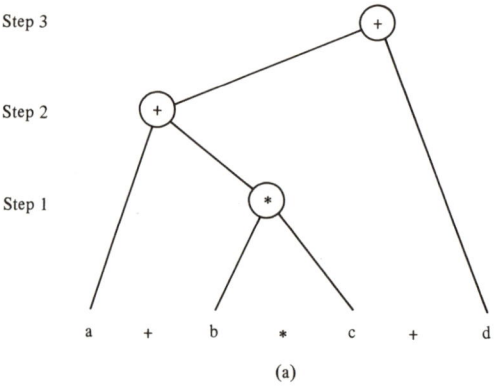

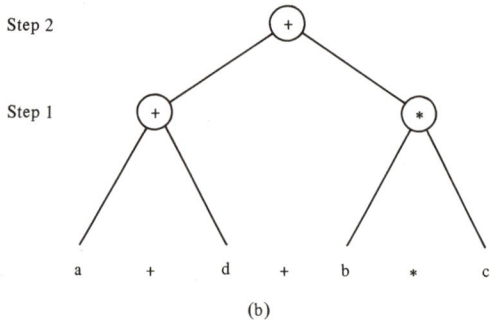

FIG. 3. Tree-height reduction by commutativity (a) $T_1 = 3$. (b) $T_2 = 2, S_2 = \frac{3}{2}, E_2 = \frac{3}{4}$.

of associativity. But by use of the commutative law for addition, we obtain the expression $a + d + bc$ and the tree of Fig. 3b, whose height is just two. Again we remark that both trees contain three operations.

Now consider the expression $a(bcd + e)$ and the tree for it given in Fig. 4a. This tree has height four and contains four operations. By use of associativity and commutativity, no lower height tree can be found. But using the arithmetic law for the distribution of multiplication over addition, we obtain the expression $abcd + ae$, which has a tree of minimum height three, as shown in Fig. 4b. However, unlike the two previous transformations, distribution has introduced an extra operation; the tree of Fig. 4b has five operations compared to the four operations of the undistributed form.

Having seen a few examples of arithmetic-expression tree-height reduction, we are naturally led to ask a number of questions. For any arithmetic

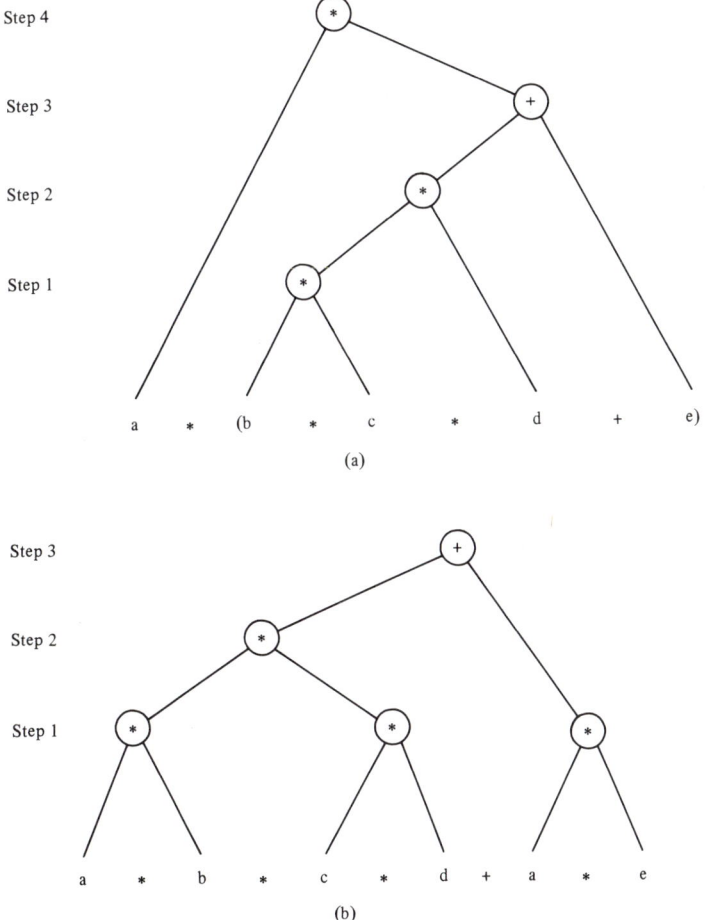

FIG. 4. Tree-height reduction by distributivity. (a) $T_1 = 4$. (b) $T_3 = 3, S_3 = \frac{4}{3}, E_3 = \frac{4}{9}$.

expression, how much tree-height reduction can be achieved? Can general bounds and algorithms for tree-height reduction be given? How many processors are needed?

To answer these questions, we present a brief survey of results concerning the evaluation of arithmetic expressions. Details and further references may be found in the papers cited. Assuming that only associativity and commutativity are used to transform expressions, Baer and Bovet (1968) gave a comprehensive tree-height reduction algorithm based on a number of earlier papers. Beatty (1972) showed the optimality of this method. An upper bound on the reduced tree height assuming only associativity and commutativity are used, given by Kuck and Muraoka (1974), is the following.

Theorem 1 Let $E\langle n \mid d \rangle$ be any arithmetic expression with depth d of parenthesis nesting. By the use of associativity and commutativity only, $E\langle n \mid d \rangle$ can be transformed such that

$$T_P[E\langle n \mid d \rangle] \leq \lceil \log n \rceil + 2d + 1$$

with $P \leq \lceil \tfrac{1}{2}n - d \rceil$.

Note that if the depth of parenthesis nesting d is small, then this bound is quite close to the lower bound of $\lceil \log n \rceil$. The complexity of this algorithm has been studied in Brent and Towle (1975), where it is shown that in addition to the standard parsing time, tree-height reduction can be performed in $O(n)$ steps. Unfortunately, there are classes of expressions, e.g., Horner's rule polynomials or continued fractions, for which no speed increase can be achieved by using only associativity and commutativity.

Muraoka (1971) studied the use of distributivity as well as associativity and commutativity for tree-height reduction and developed comprehensive tree-height reduction algorithms using all three transformations. An algorithm that considers operations that take different amounts of time is presented by Kraska (1972).

Bounds using associativity, commutativity, and distributivity have been given by a number of people (Brent, 1974; Kuck and Maruyama, 1975; Muller and Preparata, 1975). In Brent (1974) the following theorem is proved.

Theorem 2 Given any expression $E\langle n \rangle$, by the use of associativity, commutativity, and distributivity, $E\langle n \rangle$ can be transformed such that

$$T_P[E\langle n \rangle] \leq \lceil 4 \log n \rceil$$

with $P \leq 3n$.

The complexity of the algorithm of Brent (1974) has been studied in Brent and Towle (1975), where it is shown that tree-height reduction can be done using $O(n \log n)$ steps in addition to normal parsing. Also if the number of processors is allowed to grow beyond $O(n)$, the time coefficient of Theorem 2 has been reduced to 2.88 by Muller and Preparata (1975).

A number of other results are available for arithmetic expressions of special forms or for general expressions if more information is known about them. In Kuck and Maruyama (1975), expressions without division, continued fractions, general expressions with a known number of parenthesis pairs or division operations, and other such cases are considered. Polynomials are discussed in this paper and earlier by Maruyama (1973).

One other case should be mentioned here. For programming languages with array operators, other compilation techniques may be of interest. For example, Muraoka and Kuck (1973) solves the problem of minimizing the time to evaluate the product of a sequence of conformable arrays on a parallel machine. In Kuck and Maruyama (1975) it is shown that any matrix expression including addition, subtraction, multiplication, and matrix inversion can be handled as follows. If any of these four operations takes one matrix operation time step, then any matrix expression of n arrays can be evaluated in $6 \log n$ matrix operation steps. The coefficient is the sum of three addition times, two multiplication times, and one inversion time. Matrix addition and multiplication are straightforward, but the time required to invert a matrix measured in standard arithmetic operations varies, depending on the method used (cf. Sameh and Kuck, 1975a,b).

Most arithmetic expressions appearing in real programs have a rather small number of atoms. If the atoms are subscripted, then the arrays may be quite large, but it is usually advisable to evaluate these as a tree of arrays, one array operation at a time. If tree-height reduction techniques are used on such expressions, there are two possibly bad consequences. One is the passing from SIMD to MIMD operation as discussed earlier. The other is that redundant operations are generally introduced, making the overall computation less efficient. However, for expressions outside loops, for unsubscripted expressions inside loops, or for expressions of small arrays inside loops, tree-height reduction can be of value.

The number of processors required to evaluate such expressions is usually less than required for recurrence solving, as we shall see later. However, there may be cases where tree-height reduction is desirable, but the number of available processors is very small. The following results cover this case and are theoretically interesting.

Corollary 1 Given any expression $E\langle n \rangle$ and p processors for its evaluation, by the use of associativity, commutativity, and distributivity, $E\langle n \rangle$ can be transformed such that

$$Tp[E\langle n \rangle] \leq 4 \log n + 10(n-1)/p$$

This is a corollary of Theorem 2 and was proved by Brent (1974). This result has been improved by Winograd (1975), who shows that if p processors are available, we can evaluate any $E\langle n \rangle$ in $5n/2p + O(\log^2 n)$ steps. For small p, this result is an improvement on Corollary 1.

We have given a number of different upper bounds on time and processors for arithmetic expression evaluation. While the only lower bound (Lemma 1) is naive, the upper bounds are close enough to it for practical purposes. It is clear that the theory is quite well developed and improvements on these results will be quite difficult to obtain. We conclude that any arithmetic expression $E\langle n \rangle$ can be evaluated in $O(\log n)$ steps at an efficiency of $O(1/\log n)$.

2.2 Recurrence Relations

Linear recurrences share with arithmetic expressions a role of central importance in computer design and use, but they are somewhat more difficult to deal with. While an expression specifies a static computational scheme for a scalar result, a recurrence specifies a dynamic procedure for computing a scalar or an array of results. Linear recurrences are found in computer design, numerical analysis, and program analysis, so it is important to find fast, efficient ways to solve them.

Recurrences arise in any logic design problem that is expressed as a sequential machine. Also, almost every practical program that has an iterative loop contains a recurrence. While not all recurrences are linear, the vast majority found in practice are, and we shall concentrate first on linear recurrences.

We shall begin with several examples. First, consider the problem of computing an inner product of vectors $a = (a_1, \ldots, a_n)$ and $b = (b_1, \ldots, b_n)$. This can be written as a linear recurrence of the form

$$x = x + a_i b_i, \quad 1 \leq i \leq n \qquad (2)$$

where x is initially set to zero and finally set to the value of the inner product of a and b.

As another example of a linear recurrence that produces a scalar result, the evaluation of a degree n polynomial $p_n(x)$ in Horner's rule form can be expressed as

$$p = a_i + xp, \quad 2 \leq i \leq n \qquad (3)$$

where p is initially set to a_1 and finally set to the value of $p_n(x)$.

Techniques to handle both of these recurrences should be familiar from our discussion of expression evaluation. Note that Eq. (2) can be expanded by substituting the right-hand side into itself (statement substitution) as follows:

$$x = a_1 b_1$$
$$x = a_1 b_1 + a_2 b_2$$
$$x = a_1 b_1 + a_2 b_2 + a_3 b_3$$
$$\vdots$$

After n iterations we have an expression that can be mapped onto a tree similar to that of Fig. 1.

Earlier, we also discussed polynomial evaluation. Thus, by carrying out a procedure similar to the above, we could obtain an expression that could be handled by tree-height reduction, and we would expect that these and similar recurrences could be solved in $T_P = O(\log n)$ time steps using $P = O(n)$ processors.

But there are other, more difficult looking linear recurrences. For example, a Fibonacci sequence can be generated by

$$f_i = f_{i-1} + f_{i-2}, \quad 3 \leq i \leq n \qquad (4)$$

where $f_1 = f_2 = 1$. As another example, consider the addition of two n-bit binary numbers $a = a_n \ldots a_1$ and $b = b_n \ldots b_1$. The propagation of the carry across the sum can be described by

$$c_i = y_i + x_i \cdot c_{i-1}, \quad 1 \leq i \leq n \qquad (5)$$

where $c_0 = 0$, $x_i = a_i + b_i$, and $y_i = a_i \cdot b_i$. Here we use $+$ to denote logical OR and $\cdot$ to denote logical AND. This is an example of a bit level linear recurrence, in contrast to our previous examples whose arguments were assumed to be real numbers.

In both Eqs. (4) and (5) we are required to generate a vector result because of the subscripted left-hand side. This is in contrast to the scalar results of Eqs. (2) and (3). Because of this, we can expect a good deal more difficulty in trying to obtain a fast, efficient solution to these recurrences. With the above as an introduction, we now turn to a formalization of the general problem. We will then give bounds for the solution of the general problem and several important special cases.

Definition 2 An *mth-order linear recurrence system* of n equations $R\langle n,m \rangle$ is defined for $m \leq n$ by

$$x_i = \begin{cases} 0 & \text{for } i \leq 0 \\ c_i + \sum_{j=i-m}^{i-1} a_{ij} x_j & \text{for } 1 \leq i \leq n \end{cases}$$

If $m = n - 1$, we call the system a *general linear recurrence system* and denote it $R\langle n \rangle$.

Note that we can express any linear recurrence system in matrix terms as $x = c + Ax$, where

$$c = (c_1, \ldots, c_n)^t, \quad x = (x_1, \ldots, x_n)^t$$

and A is a strictly lower triangular (banded if $m < n - 1$) matrix with

$a_{ij} = 0$ for $i \leq j$ or $i - j > m$. We refer to A as the coefficient matrix, c as the constant vector, and x as the solution vector.

It should be observed that the constant vector and coefficient matrix generally contain values that can be computed before the recurrence evaluation begins. Thus, the x_i and y_i values of Eq. (5) would be precomputed from the a_i and b_i. We will assume that the elements of c and A are precomputed (if necessary) in all cases so that our bounds on recurrence evaluation can be simply stated, and that m and n are powers of 2.

How can we solve an $R\langle n \rangle$ system in a fast, efficient way using many simultaneous operations? The following is a straightforward way, which uses $O(n)$ processors to solve the system in $O(n)$ steps.

2.3 Column Sweep Algorithm

Given any $R\langle n \rangle$ system, we initially know the value of x_1. On step 1 we broadcast this value, c_1, to all other equations, multiply by a_{j1}, and add the result to c_j. Since we now know the value of x_2, this leads to an $R\langle n-1 \rangle$ system, which can be treated in exactly the same way. Thus after $n - 1$ steps, each of which consists of a broadcast, a multiply, and an add, and each of which generates another x_i, we have the solution vector x. The method requires $n - 1$ processors on step 1 and fewer thereafter, so $T_P = 2(n - 1)$ with $P = n - 1$.

What speedup and efficiency have we achieved by this method? The time required to solve this system using a single processor that might sweep the array by rows or columns would be

$$T_1 = 2[1 + 2 + \cdots + (n - 1)] = 2\left[\frac{n(n - 1)}{2}\right] = n(n - 1)$$

Hence the above method achieves a speedup of

$$S_P = n(n-1)/2(n-1) = n/2$$

with an efficiency of

$$E_P = S_P/P = n/2(n - 1) > \tfrac{1}{2}$$

Thus we can conclude that the column sweep algorithm is a reasonable method of solving an $R\langle n \rangle$ system. But how does it perform in the $R\langle n,m \rangle$ case for $m \ll n$?

It can be seen that the column sweep algorithm will achieve $S_P = O(m)$ for an $R\langle n,m \rangle$ system. So if m is very small, the method performs poorly, particularly if we have a large number of processors available. It should be noted that the $m \ll n$ case occurs very often in practice. Note that all of our examples [Eqs. (2)–(5)] had $m \leq 2$.

What are our prospects for finding a faster algorithm? First, we observe that the total number of initial data values in an $R\langle n,m \rangle$ system is $O(mn)$. This is the total of the constant vector c and the coefficient matrix A. Assuming that these numbers all interact in obtaining a solution, a fan-in argument (cf. Lemma 1) indicates that we need at least $O(\log mn)$ steps to solve an $R\langle n,m \rangle$ system, since $m \leq n$, $O(\log mn) = O(\log n)$. The column sweep algorithm required $O(n)$ steps, so we still have a big gap in time.

2.4 Product Form Recurrence Method

The next theorem is based on an algorithm for the fastest known method of evaluating an $R\langle n,m \rangle$ system. For large m, the number of processors required is rather large, but for small m, the number of processors is quite reasonable. We also give bounds for the case of a small number of processors; Corollary 4 is particularly important in the case of $m < p < P$. This theorem's proof can easily be stated in terms of the product form of the inverse of the coefficient matrix A (Chen and Sameh, 1975; Sameh and Brent, 1975). It is also proved in Chen (1975) and Chen and Kuck (1975b).

Theorem 3 Any $R\langle n,m \rangle$ can be computed in

$$T_P \leq (2 + \log m) \log n - \tfrac{1}{2}(\log^2 m + \log m)$$

with

$$P \leq \begin{cases} m^2 n/2 + O(mn) & \text{for } m \ll n \\ n^3/68 + O(n^2) & \text{for } m \leq n \end{cases}$$

The details of transforming a system to meet this bound are fairly straightforward (Chen, 1975). We will give a simple example here as a basis for some intuition about how the technique of Theorem 3 works. Consider an $R\langle 4,2 \rangle$ system. This method would generate the following expressions for the evaluation of the x_i:

$$x_1 = c_1$$
$$x_2 = (c_2 + a_{21}c_1)$$
$$x_3 = (c_3 + a_{31}c_1) + a_{32}(c_2 + a_{21}c_1)$$
$$x_4 = c_4 + (a_{42} + a_{43}a_{32})(c_2 + a_{21}c_1) + a_{43}(c_3 + a_{31}c_1)$$

Note that all of the parenthetical expressions can be computed simultaneously in two steps (there are just three distinct ones). Then x_4, the largest calculation, can be completed in three more steps for

$$T_P = (2 + \log 2)(\log 4) - \tfrac{1}{2}(\log^2 2 + \log 2) = 5$$

This time bound may be achieved using just three processors in this case. But as n grows larger, the number of processors required becomes very large as shown in the tables of Chen and Kuck (1975b).

In practice, we may have a machine with a limited number of processors $p < P$, so that Theorem 3 cannot be used directly. Several schemes are available for mapping a computation onto a smaller set of processors and generally increasing the efficiency of the computation as well. While the techniques described below may be applied to arithmetic expressions as derived from Theorem 1 or 2, the expressions found in typical programs usually do not require enough processors to warrant such reductions (Knuth, 1970).

First, we describe a *folding scheme*, which reduces the number of processors at a much faster rate than the computation time increases. The P-processor computation for $R\langle n,m \rangle$ resulting from Theorem 3 contains log n stages, each consisting of many independent tree computations of height (log $m + 1$) resulting from inner products of two m-vectors. Such a tree of height t will contain $2^t - 1$ operation nodes and its evaluation requires 2^{t-1} processors. P is the maximum of the total number of processors used at each stage. It is easy to show that given such a tree its height increases only one step by halving the number of processors (called one *fold*), and after f folds ($f \leq t - 2$) are performed, the tree height is $(t + 2^{f+1} - f - 2)$, while the number of processors is reduced to $2^{t-1}/2^f$. If all trees at the same stage are folded uniformly, then this folding scheme can provide us T_p as stated below.

Corollary 2 Let $R\langle n,m \rangle$ and P be as in Theorem 3. Then if $f \leq \log m - 1$ and $p = \lceil P/2^f \rceil$, we have

$$T_p \leq T_P + (2^{f+1} - f - 2) \log n$$

Another technique that is useful in mapping any computation onto a limited number of processors $p < P$ is the *sweeping scheme* (Kuck et al., 1972). If the ith step of any parallel computation requires O_i operations using P processors, it can be executed on p processors in $\lceil O_i/p \rceil$ steps. This observation leads to the following:

Lemma 2 (Brent, 1974) If a computation C can be completed in T_P with O_P operations on P processors, then C can be computed in

$$T_p \leq T_P + (O_P - T_P)/p \quad \text{for} \quad p < P$$

To apply this technique directly on the algorithm of Theorem 3, the O_P value can be obtained by the summation of $2p(k)$ for $k = 2, 4, 8, \ldots, n$, where $p(k)$ is the number of processors required at each stage (Chen, 1975). The result of this technique can be found in Chen and Kuck (1975b).

Our third scheme for reducing the number of processors required for an $R\langle n,m\rangle$ system is called the *cutting scheme*. The idea is to cut the original system into a number of smaller systems and evaluate these in sequence, using the algorithm underlying Theorem 3 on each such system. We have used this scheme in Chen and Kuck (1975b) and Sameh *et al.* (1974a,b), and a detailed proof is given in Chen and Sameh (1975).

Corollary 3 Let $R\langle n,m\rangle$ and P be as in Theorem 3. Then any $R\langle n,m\rangle$ can be computed with $1 < p < P$ processors in

$$T_p \leq \begin{cases} 2\lceil m/p\rceil(n-1) & \text{for } 1 < p \leq m \\[6pt] \dfrac{\beta}{72} np^{-1/3}(\log^2 p + 27\log p + 144) + \dfrac{2mn}{p} & \text{for } m < p < m^2 \\[6pt] \dfrac{\beta}{72} np^{-1/3}(\log^2 p + 27\log p + 144) & \text{for } m^2 \leq p \leq m^3 \\[6pt] \beta\dfrac{m^2 n}{p}\left(\log m \log p + 2\log_2 p - \dfrac{5}{2}\log^2 m - \dfrac{7}{2}\log m + 1\right) & \text{for } m^3 < p < P \end{cases}$$

where $\beta(m,n,p)$ is a small constant.

For most practical $R\langle n,m\rangle$ systems in which m is very small compared to n, if the number of processors is also very limited then a new computational algorithm developed in Chen (1975) can be used more efficiently. This method gives the following time bounds.

Corollary 4 Let $R\langle n,m\rangle$ and P be as in Theorem 3. If $m < p < P$, then any $R\langle n,m\rangle$ can be computed in

$$T_p \leq (2m^2 + 3m)\frac{n}{p} + O(m^2 \log(p/m))$$

In summary, for $1 < p < P$, the time bound for evaluating a given $R\langle n,m\rangle$ system can be determined by choosing the minimum value obtained for Corollaries 2–4.

2.5 Constant-Coefficient Recurrences

In numerical computation, we are frequently faced with linear recurrences having constant coefficients, i.e., Toeplitz form matrices. For example, Eqs. (2)–(4) are such recurrences. Thus, Eq. (2) could be rewritten $x_i = 1x_{i-1} + a_i b_k$, and similarly for Eq. 3. Intuitively, we might expect to be able to compute such systems more efficiently than the more general recurrences we have been considering.

Indeed, this is the case, as we shall see below. We formalize the problem with the following definition which should be contrasted with Definition 2.

Definition 3 An *mth order linear recurrence system with constant coefficients* of n equations, $\tilde{R}\langle n,m \rangle$ is defined for $m \leq n - 1$ by

$$x_i = \begin{cases} 0 & \text{for} \quad i \leq 0 \\ c_i + \sum_{j=1}^{m} a_j x_{i-j} & \text{for} \quad 1 \leq i \leq n \end{cases}$$

If $m = n - 1$, we call the system a *general linear recurrence system with constant coefficients* and denote it $\tilde{R}\langle n \rangle$.

The fastest known method for solving an $\tilde{R}\langle n,m \rangle$ system can be summarized by the following theorem of Chen (1975). The proof follows the lines of Theorem 3, but avoids computations that are unnecessary due to the constant coefficients.

Theorem 4 Any $\tilde{R}\langle n,m \rangle$ can be computed in

$$T_P \leq (3 + \log m) \log n - (\log^2 m + \log m + 1)$$

with

$$P \leq \begin{cases} mn & \text{for} \quad m \ll n \\ n^2/4 & \text{for} \quad m \leq n \end{cases}$$

By exercising special care in avoiding redundant computations, the proof of Theorem 4 can be modified (Chen, 1975) to give us the following.

Corollary 5 Any $\tilde{R}\langle n,1 \rangle$ can be computed in

$$T_p \leq 2 \log n$$

with $P \leq n$.

By comparing Theorems 3 and 4, we see that while the time bounds are about the same, substantial processor savings can be made in the constant-coefficient case. In the case of small m, we have saved $O(m)$ processors, while in the general case we have saved a factor of $O(n)$ processors.

To test the quality of these bounds, we can compare them with some simple calculations. Consider the inner product of Eq. (2). This can obviously be handled using n processors (for the n multiplications) in $1 + \log n$ steps. Since we have been assuming the coefficient matrix and constant vector are set up before the recurrence solution begins, the multiplication is really outside our present scope, so just $n/2$ processors would be required for the summation.

The bound of Corollary 5 is thus high by a factor of two in each of processor count and time for this trivial recurrence. However, the recurrence method produces not only the inner product, but also all of the "partial inner products" $x_1, x_2, \ldots, x_{n-1}$, as well as x_n. Chen (1975) has also given other variations on the above to handle these special cases of evaluating only the remote terms of recurrences.

As a final example, note that the entire Fibonacci sequence of Eq. (4) can be evaluated (since $m = 2$) in

$$T_P \leq 4 \log n - 3$$

with $P \leq 2n$ for large n.

3. Program Analysis

In this section we discuss techniques for the analysis of whole programs. These techniques can be used to compile programs for parallel or pipeline computers. They can also be used to specify machine organizations for high-speed computation. Since we are really just studying the structure of ordinary serial programs, our results have interpretations for ordinary virtual memory machines and structured programming as well.

Our discussion is centered on methods developed and used by the author and his students. Several significant efforts in this general area were carried out elsewhere earlier. We will briefly sketch two of the most important of these.

The first major study of whole programs was carried out by Estrin and his students at UCLA in the 1960s. They studied graphs of programs in an attempt to isolate independent tasks for parallel execution. The lowest level object considered as a task was the assignment statement, while other tasks ranged in complexity up to whole subroutines. A number of papers (Estrin and Turn, 1963; Martin and Estrin, 1967; Russell, 1963) reported algorithms for the analysis of programs and the results of analyzing a limited number of real programs. This group also worked on various scheduling strategies for executing program graphs.

Another effort was initiated by Bingham, Fisher, and Semon at Burroughs in 1966. This group studied various aspects of the structure of programs and developed algorithms for the automatic detection of parallelism. They also investigated certain aspects of machine design related to this—particular attention was given to control unit features. Their work was described in a series of reports (Bingham *et al.*, 1966, 1968).

Our own effort has incorporated graphs of programs as well as the two key ideas of the previous section—tree-height reduction and fast recurrence evaluation. In this way we can carry parallel execution down to the level of individual operations in assignment statements. This is of course necessary if one wants to execute programs in the fastest possible way.

In order to formalize our discussion of program graphs and their manipulation, we now present a number of definitions.

Definition 4 An *assignment statement* is denoted $x = E$, where x is a scalar or array variable and E a well-formed arithmetic expression. A *block of assignment statements* (BAS) is a sequence of one or more assignment statements with no intervening statements of any other kind. Any BAS can be transformed by a process called *statement substitution* to obtain a set of expressions that can be evaluated simultaneously.

For example, the BAS

$$X = BCD + E, \quad Y = AX, \quad Z = X + FG$$

can be evaluated using one processor in six steps, ignoring memory activity. By statement substitution we obtain three statements, which can be transformed by tree-height reduction to obtain

$$X = BCD + E, \quad Y = ABCD + AE, \quad Z = BCD + E + FG$$

Since the resulting expressions can be evaluated simultaneously in three steps, we obtain a speedup of 2. By properly arranging the parse trees it may be seen that just five processors are required. Thus we have efficiency $E_5 = \frac{2}{5}$. In general, the number of processors required to evaluate a set of trees in a fixed number of steps may be minimized using an algorithm of Hu (1961). Note that the speedup here results from two effects: the simultaneous evaluation of independent trees and tree-height reduction by associativity, commutativity, and distributivity.

Definition 5 An IF statement is denoted $(C)(S_1, \ldots, S_n)$, where C is the *conditional expression* composed of arithmetic and logical operations and $S_1, \ldots, S_n$ are n different statements that may be assignment statements, IF statements, or loops such that control will be transferred to one of them depending on the value of C.

In many programs it is possible to find outside DO loops, rather large sets of statements consisting of many IF and GOTO statements with some interspersed assignment statements. Suppose we have a method of discovering sections of code in which the ratio of control (IF, GOTO) statements to arithmetic operations is greater than some small number. We call such a section of code an *IF block*. Given an IF block, it is straightforward to put it in a canonical form consisting of

Step 1: A set of assignment statements, all of which may be executed simultaneously.
Step 2: A set of Boolean functions, all of which may be evaluated simultaneously.
Step 3: A binary decision tree through which one path will be followed for each execution of the program. No Boolean function or arithmetic expression evaluation is included in the tree.
Step 4: A collection of blocks of assignment statements, each with a single variable or constant on the right-hand side. One such block is associated with each path through the tree.

The details of an algorithm for the discovery and transformation of an IF block to this canonical form are given by Davis (1972b). Note that the IF block may be a graph with or without cycles. Such graphs are converted to trees called IF trees in the cited references.

Definition 6 A *loop* is denoted

$$L = (I_1 \leftarrow N_1, I_2 \leftarrow N_2, \ldots, I_d \leftarrow N_d)(S_1, S_2, \ldots, S_s)$$

or

$$L = (I_1, I_2, \ldots, I_d)(S_1, S_2, \ldots, S_s)$$

where I_j is a *loop index*, N_j an ordered *index set*, and S_j a *body statement* that may be an assignment statement, an IF statement, or another loop. We use $\text{OUT}(S_j)$ and $\text{IN}(S_j)$ to denote for S_j the LHS (output) variable name and the set of RHS (input) variable names, respectively. We will write $S_j(i_1, i_2, \ldots, i_d)$ to refer to S_j during a particular iteration step, i.e., when the index variables of S_j are assigned the specific values $I_1 = i_1$, $I_2 = i_2, \ldots, I_d = i_d$. If S_i is executed before S_j, we will write $S_i <_0 S_j$. We say that the relation $<_0$ defines the *execution order* of the statements. If a loop execution leads to the execution of n statements, we sometimes denote their execution order by writing $Y_i: x_i = E_i, 1 \leq i \leq n$, implying that $Y_i <_0 Y_{i+1}, 1 \leq i \leq n - 1$.

Definition 7 Given a loop $L = (I_1 \leftarrow N_1, \ldots, I_d \leftarrow N_d)(S_1, \ldots, S_s)$, all possible data dependencies between statement pairs S_i and S_j are given by $\text{OUT}(S_i(k_1, \ldots, k_d)) \cap \text{IN}(S_j(l_1, \ldots, l_d)) \neq \emptyset$ for $S_i(k_1, \ldots, k_d) <_0 S_j(l_1, \ldots, l_d)$. Whenever this condition is satisfied, we say that S_j is *data* *dependent* on S_i and is denoted by $S_i \delta S_j$, where δ is a transitive relation. All of the data dependencies can be represented by a *data dependence graph* G_1 of s nodes for S_i, $1 \leq i \leq s$. For each $S_i \delta S_j$ there is an arc from S_i to S_j. Statement S_j is *indirectly data dependent* on S_i, denoted $S_i \Delta S_j$, if there exist statements $S_{k_1}, \ldots, S_{k_m}$ such that $S_i \delta S_{k_1} \delta \ldots \delta S_{k_m} \delta S_j$. Practical details on determining if $S_i \delta S_j$ can be found in Towle (1974).

Our definition of data dependence is much more delicate than the usual definitions (Bernstein, 1966; Fisher, 1967), which include the condition $OUT(S_i) \cap IN(S_j) \neq \emptyset$, i.e., they ignore subscripts and only check variable names. Thus statements like $S_i: A(I) = A(I+1) + B$ are said to be data dependent $(S_i \delta S_i)$. However, by Definition 7 we would not say $S_i \delta S_i$ because the values of $A(I+1)$ are not those from $A(I)$.

In terms of Definitions 6 and 7, we can further classify loops as follows.

Definition 8 We use D, for *data dependence* relations, to denote the set of loops with at least one $S_i \delta S_j$, $1 \leq i,j \leq s$. In other words, there is at least one E_k, $1 \leq k \leq n$, that is a function of x_{k-m_k}, for $m_k > 0$. If $L \in D$ and none of its S_i is a nonlinear function of x_j, $1 \leq j \leq s$, we call it a *linear dependence* and write $L \in LD$ $(LD \subset D)$. The complement of D is denoted $\bar{D}$, for nondependence relation.

Definition 7 can be applied to any $(d-u+1)$, $1 \leq u \leq d$, innermost nest of L as it is also a loop. This is described below.

Definition 9 Let L^u be the $(d-u+1)$ innermost nest of L, $1 \leq u \leq d$, i.e.,

$$L = (I_1, I_2, \ldots, I_d)(S_1, S_2, \ldots, S_s)$$
$$= (I_1, I_2, \ldots, I_{u-1})(I_u, I_{u+1}, \ldots, I_d)(S_1, S_2, \ldots, S_s)$$
$$= (I_1, I_2, \ldots, I_{u-1})(L^u)$$

Then for fixed values of $I_1, I_2, \ldots, I_{u-1}$, we can obtain all pairs of data dependence for L^u according to Definition 8 (note that now $k_1 = l_1, \ldots, k_{u-1} = l_{u-1}$), which defines graph G_u.

Example 1 Given a loop

L: DO S_2 I_1 = 1, 10
     DO S_2 I_2 = 1, 10
     DO S_2 I_3 = 1, 10
S_1: $A(I_1,I_2,I_3) = B(I_1-1,I_2,I_3)*C(I_1,I_2) + D*E$
S_2: $B(I_1,I_2,I_3) = A(I_1,I_2-1,I_3)*F(I_2,I_3)$,

the corresponding data dependence graphs G_1, G_2, and G_3 are

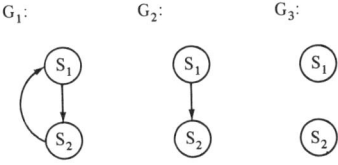

For the set of data-dependent loops, we can easily distinguish two cases: acyclic and cyclic graphs. Formally, we define these as follows:

Definition 10 An *acyclic dependence graph* is a dependence graph of s nodes, S_i for $1 \leq i \leq s$, with no pair (S_i, S_j) such that $S_i \Delta S_j$ and $S_j \Delta S_i$. A dependence graph that is not acyclic will be called *cyclic*.

Given a data dependence graph, we wish to partition it into blocks that contain only one statement or a cyclic dependence graph. Formally, we define these as follows:

Definition 11 On each dependence graph G_u, $1 \leq u \leq d$, for a given loop L we define a *node partition* π_u of $\{S_1, S_2, \ldots, S_s\}$ in such a way that S_k and S_l are in the same subset if and only if $S_k \Delta S_l$ and $S_l \Delta S_k$. On the partition $\pi_u = \{\pi_{u1}, \pi_{u2}, \ldots\}$ for $1 \leq u \leq d$, define a *partial ordering relation* α in such a way that $\pi_{ui} \alpha \pi_{ui}$ (reflexive), and for $i \neq j$, $\pi_{ui} \alpha \pi_{uj}$ iff there is an arc in G_u from some element of π_{ui} to some element of π_{uj}. The α relation is also antisymmetric and transitive. The π_{ui} are called π-blocks.

3.1 Wave Front Method

If there are cyclic dependencies in a DO loop, we may turn to our next method, the wave front method. This is a well-known method that effectively extracts array operations from the loop, and we can then apply the above bounds to these. If the maximum speedup given by the wave front method is insufficient, i.e., if the available processors are not all being used, we may turn to the recurrence method, which gives the fastest known speedup for such problems.

Example 2

```
L2:   DO  S₁  I = 1, N
          DO  S₁  J = 1, N
      S₁:  W(I,J) = A(I−1,J)*W(I−1,J) + B(I,J−1)*W(I,J−1)
```

For one or more assignment statements containing cyclic dependencies, the wave front method yields moderate speedups with high efficiency. The idea of this method can be illustrated by the loop L2 of Example 2 in which statement 10 has a cyclic dependence in that the LHS depends on RHS values computed earlier in the loop. Note that generally, one or more statements may form a cyclic dependence. This method proceeds as follows: if W(1,1) is computed from boundary values, then we can compute W(2,1) and W(1,2) in terms of W(1,1) and boundary values. Next we can compute W(3,1), W(2,2), W(1,3), and so on, as a wave front passes through the W array at a 45° angle. Thus we can compute this loop in $O(N)$ steps instead of the $O(N^2)$ serial steps required. The wave front method was first described in detail by Muraoka (1971) and was later used in Kuck et al. (1972) and also implemented in Lamport (1974). The formalization below removes some of the restrictions included in the original formulation.

In Chen et al. (1975b) a revised wave front algorithm is presented. This includes a method of determining the angle α at which the wave front passes through the array. It also includes a method for computing the speedup as a function of α. Note that these ideas can be extended to arrays of higher dimension, as well. However, the wave front method is of no value in one-dimensional arrays, since it degenerates to a serial computation in this case. A similar thing happens if α is slightly greater than 0° or slightly less than 90°. In such cases we may treat the cyclic dependence as a linear recurrence (assuming it is linear).

3.2 Loop Speedup Hierarchy

With the above fundamentals, it is possible to give some easy bounds on overall loop speedup in terms of the uniprocessor time T_1. We will present a simple hierarchy here based on the maximum known speedups for various classes of programs. Sharper bounds will be presented later in the chapter, based on more detailed loop parameters. The hierarchy of this section will provide good intuition for the following sections.

The simplest loop is $L \in \bar{D}$, which by Definition 8 has no dependence relation between any pair of statements. Thus, following the notation of Definition 6, all $x_i = E_i$, $1 \leq i \leq n$, can be computed in parallel. The following loop, which performs matrix addition and scalar product, has this property:

$$\text{DO} \quad S_2 \quad I_1 = 1, 10, 2$$
$$\text{DO} \quad S_2 \quad I_2 = 1, 10, 1$$
$$S_1: \quad G(I_1,I_2) = A(I_1,I_2) + B(I_1,I_2)$$
$$S_2: \quad Z(I_1,I_2) = C(I_1,I_2)*D(I_1,I_2)$$

The total time required by any $L \in \bar{D}$ is, by Theorems 1 and 2, $T_P \leq O(\log e)$, where e is the maximum number of atoms in E_i, $1 \leq i \leq n$. Hence, we have for $L \in \bar{D}$

$$S_p \geq T_1/O(\log e) = O(T_1)$$

Now, let us study a slightly more complicated loop $L \in LD$ such as one that performs the vector inner product:

$$\text{DO} \quad S_1 \quad I = 1, 10,$$

$$S_1: \quad T = T + A(I)*B(I)$$

For any $L \in LD$, if we precompute simultaneously all subexpressions in E_i, $1 \leq i \leq n$, that do not depend on any computed value in the loop, i.e., any x_i for $1 \leq i \leq n$, then the resultant statements $x_i = E_i'$, $1 \leq i \leq n$, can be treated as an $R\langle n,m \rangle$ system, where $m < n$ is the maximum of m_i (see Definition 8) for all i. The total computation time of any $L \in LD$ with $m \ll n$, or m independent of n, is therefore any preprocessing time needed to obtain the coefficients in $R\langle n,m \rangle$, which is $O(\log e)$ time steps by Theorems 1 and 2, plus the time to solve an $R\langle n,m \rangle$ system, which is stated in Theorem 3. Since $n \leq T_1 \leq ne$, we have a speedup for this subset of LD,

$$S_P \geq \frac{T_1}{O(\log m \log n) + O(\log e)} = O\left(\frac{T_1}{\log T_1}\right)$$

Next, consider the subset of loops that has $m \approx n$ or m a function of n. For example, given an upper triangular matrix A, to solve $Ax = b$ by the traditional back-substitution method, we may write a loop like

$$\text{DO} \quad S_1 \quad I = 10, 1, -1$$

$$X(I) = B(I)/A(I,I)$$

$$\text{DO} \quad S_1 \quad J = I + 1, 10, 1$$

$$S_1: \quad X(I) = X(I) - (A(I,J)/A(I,I))*X(J)$$

In this example, if we preprocess $B(I)/A(I,I)$ for all I, and $A(I,J)/A(I,I)$ for all I,J, we obtain an $R\langle n,n \rangle$ system. Since $m = n$, this is the worst-case loop of LD. Hence, we can say that the computation time of any $L \in LD$ is less than $O(\log e)$ plus the time stated in Theorem 3, i.e., for any $L \in LD$,

$$S_P \geq \frac{T_1}{O(\log^2 n) + O(\log e)} = O\left(\frac{T_1}{\log^2 T_1}\right)$$

Finally, we study a simple looking, but more complicated loop:

DO S_1 I = 1, 10,

S_1: X(I) = (X(I−1) + A/X(I−1))/2

This is a familiar iterative program for approximating $A^{1/2}$. For this loop, $L \in D$ but $L \notin LD$. Muraoka (1971) shows that by using statement substitution any loop with E_i being a dth degree polynomial of x_{i-1}, $d > 1$, can be speeded up at most by a constant factor. Later, Kung (1974) also studied this problem in a similar way. However, since we have been able to linearize a number of nonlinear recurrences, it remains an open question which techniques besides statement substitution may be used to speed up such loops.

Summarizing the above, we are able to classify all loops in terms of their best known speedups over serial computation time T_1, i.e.,

$$S_P = T_1/\alpha_i (\log T_1)^i \quad \text{for} \quad 0 \leq i \leq 2 \tag{6}$$

We call a loop *type i*, $0 \leq i \leq 2$, if its maximum speedup has the form of Eq. (6), or *type 3* if its maximum speedup is of a lower order of magnitude. This was also discussed in Kuck (1973).

By the wave front method we are at best able to achieve $T_P = O(T_1^{1/2})$, with $T_P = O(T_1)$ in the worse case. Thus we have $S_P \leq O(T_1^{1/2})$. Since the wave front method's speedup is always inferior to the recurrence method for such problems, this is consistent with our claim that Eq. (6) represents a maximum speedup hierarchy.

3.3 Loop Distribution

Now we turn to the problem of compiling parallel operations from serial loops that do not contain IFs and GOTOs (we will consider these later). There are two key ideas involved here: one is the reduction of data dependence, the other is the distribution of loop control over the loop statements. We give our loop distribution algorithm, which includes both of them and summarizes our handling of loops without IFs.

When constructing a data dependence graph, we wish to avoid any apparent dependencies that do not really hold for the given subscripts and index sets. This problem was first studied in a general way by Bernstein (1966) for unsubscripted variables. A powerful test for subscripted variables was given by Muraoka (1971). This has been refined by Towle (1974) and Chen *et al.* (1975b). By avoiding the inclusion of spurious data dependencies, we may be able to execute more statements in parallel on machines capable of executing multiple-array operations (e.g., the Texas Instruments' ASC). Also, we may be able to break cyclic dependencies, thereby reducing i in Eq. (6) and yielding higher speedup.

Another way to achieve statement independence is through statement substitution. This yields increased speedup, sometimes at the cost of redundant operations. It should be used with discretion and only in machines with a high degree of parallelism. For acyclic graphs, it is easy to demonstrate that we can perform statement substitution between any pair of nodes that have a dependence relation. As in a BAS (cf. Definition 4), we substitute for each LHS variable of S_i on the RHS of S_j, which is the cause of a dependence relation, the corresponding arithmetic expression on the RHS of S_i with all subscript expressions properly shifted. By applying statement substitution, the dependence relation is removed and a set of independent assignment statements results. Each of these represents a vector assignment statement, all of which can be executed simultaneously. Theorems 2 and 3 can be used to bound the time and processors.

In loops with acyclic graphs, we can thus reduce the graph for the entire loop to a set of independent nodes representing simultaneously executable array statements. However, in general, we must deal with cyclic graphs containing several interdependent nodes. Our loop distribution algorithm will be useful in handling these cases. By loop distribution we mean the distribution of the loop control statements over individual or collections of assignment statements contained in the loop. The idea of loop distribution was introduced by Muraoka (1971) and was later implemented in our FORTRAN program analyzer to measure potential parallelism in ordinary programs (Kuck *et al.*, 1972, 1974).

The purpose of distributing a given type i loop is to obtain a set of smaller size loops of type j, $0 \leq j \leq i$, which upon execution give results equivalent to the original loop. This is essentially to reduce α_i in Eq. (6) (and hence increase speedup) as much as possible. In fact, the loop distribution algorithm resembling the distribution algorithm for the reduction of tree height of an arithmetic expression may introduce more parallelism into a program loop than that obtained from an undistributed one. We now give the algorithm to accomplish this distribution as presented in Chen *et al.* (1975b). For simplicity, we assume all left-hand side variables are distinct in assignment statements.

3.4 Loop Distribution Algorithm

Step 1 Given a loop

$$L = (I_1, I_2, \ldots, I_d)(S_1, S_2, \ldots, S_s)$$

by analyzing subscript expressions and indexing patterns, construct a dependence graph G_u (cf. Definitions 7 and 9) for $1 \leq u \leq d$.

Step 2 On G_u, $1 \leq u \leq d$, establish a node partition π_u as in Definition 11.

Step 3 On the partition π_u, $1 \leq u \leq d$, establish a partial ordering relation as in Definition 11.

Step 4 Let the $(d-u+1)$ innermost nest of L be L^u, $1 \leq u \leq d$, i.e.,

$$L = (I_1, I_2, \ldots, I_d)(S_1, S_2, \ldots, S_s)$$
$$= (I_1, I_2, \ldots, I_{u-1})\{(I_u, I_{u+1}, \ldots, I_d)(S_1, S_2, \ldots, S_s)\}$$
$$= (I_1, I_2, \ldots, I_{u-1})(L^u)$$

Replace L^u according to π_u with a set of loops $\{(I)(\pi_{u1}), (I)(\pi_{u2}), \ldots\}$ where $(I) = (I_u, I_{u+1}, \ldots, I_d)$.

The condition of the partial ordering relation α ensures that data are updated before being used. Hence, any execution order of the set of loops that replaces L^u will be valid as long as this relation is not violated. Thus, for fixed values of $I_1, I_2, \ldots, I_{u-1}$, if $\pi_{ui} \alpha \pi_{uj}$ then loop $(I)(\pi_{ui})$ must be evaluated before $(I)(\pi_{uj})$; otherwise they may be computed in parallel. In general, we can also use statement substitution to remove this relation between some or all of the distributed loops. But, by not allowing statement substitution we have a somewhat simpler compiler technique, one that generally requires fewer processors and yields less speedup.

As an example of the use of our loop distribution, consider the following pseudo-FORTRAN program.

Example 3

```
           DO   S₅   I = 1, N
S₁:             A(I) = B(I)*C(I)
           DO   S₃   J = 1, N
S₂:             D(J) = A(I−3) + E(J−1)
S₃:             E(J) = D(J−1) + F
           DO   S₄   K = 1, N
S₄:             G(K) = H(I−5) + 1
S₅:             H(I) = SQRT(A(I−2))
```

Following step 1 of the Loop Distribution Algorithm, we obtain a dependence graph as shown in Fig. 5. We use brackets to denote loop nesting. For simplicity and speedup in this program, we only consider the case $u = 1$.

In step 2, we form the partition $\pi_1 = \{\pi_{11}, \pi_{12}, \pi_{13}, \pi_{14}\}$, where $\pi_{11} = \{S_1\}$, $\pi_{12} = \{S_2, S_3\}$, $\pi_{13} = \{S_4\}$, and $\pi_{14} = \{S_5\}$. These partitions are partially ordered on step 3 as follows: $\pi_{11} \alpha \pi_{21}$, $\pi_{11} \alpha \pi_{14}$ and $\pi_{14} \alpha \pi_{13}$. Since we are considering only the case $u = 1$ here, we ignore step 4.

PARALLEL PROCESSING OF ORDINARY PROGRAMS 151

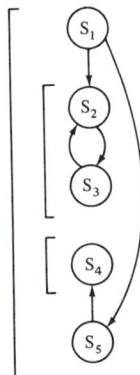

FIG. 5. Program graph (original G_1).

The result of this transformation is shown in Fig. 6. We could use this graph to compile array operations as follows. First, S_1 yields a vector multiply. Next, we can execute π_{12} or π_{14}. π_{12} leads to a linear recurrence of the form $R\langle N,3 \rangle$, which can be solved by the method of Theorem 3 by combining the D and E arrays as an unknown vector in which x_1 represents $D(1)$, x_2 represents $E(1)$, x_3 represents $D(2)$, x_4 represents $E(2)$, etc. π_{14} leads to the execution of S_5 as a vector of square roots. Finally, S_4 may be executed for all I and K simultaneously. Note that this requires the broadcasting of elements of the H array to all elements in the columns of G.

Here, the time required to execute π_{11}, π_{13}, and π_{14} is independent of N using $O(N)$ processors. The overall execution time is dominated by π_{12} and is $O(\log N)$, so this is a type 1 loop. The number of processors required to achieve this time is $O(N)$.

Notice that in this example we have avoided statement substitution.

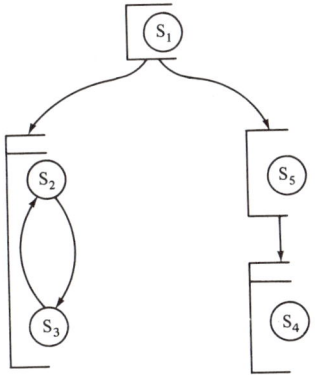

FIG. 6. Distributed graph.

Using statement substitution, we would have been able to obtain four π-blocks, all of which could be executed at once. This would require the execution of several different operations at one time, while the technique we used allows all operations at each step to be identical. Furthermore, very little additional speedup would be possible by this method since π_{12} dominates the time here.

3.5 IFs in Loops

To this point we have considered DO loops without conditional statements. The addition to DO loops of IF and GOTO as well as computed GOTO statements can cause major problems. In particular, data dependencies can be changed at execution time by the existence of such conditional statements. Thus, knowledge at compile time of what can be executed in parallel may be difficult to obtain. In the worst case, we may be forced by not knowing about control flow to compile loops for serial execution, which in fact can be executed in a highly parallel way.

In this section we will consider the addition to DO loops of IF and computed GOTO statements, denoted IFs. The first part of this section contains definitions and preliminary results concerning IFs. This leads to a distribution algorithm that allows for IFs. The importance of this algorithm is that using it we can often execute all of the DO loop simultaneously, or at worst, localize the part of the DO loop that will be done sequentially. Then we present a summary of the analysis of one year of CACM FORTRAN programs.

Before proceeding, we need a few definitions concerning IFs and control notions.

Definition 12 Statement S_j is an *immediate control successor* of S_i, denoted $S_i \gamma S_j$, if S_j is executed immediately after S_i. S_j is not unique when S_i is an IF. Statement S_j is a *control successor* of S_i, denoted $S_i \Gamma S_j$, if there exist statements $S_{k_1}, \ldots, S_{k_m}$ such that $S_i \gamma S_{k_1} \gamma S_{k_2} \gamma \ldots \gamma S_{k_m} \gamma S_j$.

Definition 13 Given a loop $L = (I_1 \leftarrow N_1, \ldots, I_d \leftarrow N_d)(S_1, \ldots, S_s)$ with $S_i = (C)(S_{i_1}, \ldots, S_{i_n})$; the *jth follower*, $1 \leq j \leq n$, of IF statement S_i, denoted $F_j(S_i)$, is the set $\{S_k \mid S_k = S_{i_j} \text{ or } S_{i_j} \Gamma S_k\}$. We will refer to an arbitrary jth follower as a *follower*. The set of *common followers* of IF statement S_i, denoted $CF(S_i)$, is the set $\{S_k \mid S_k \in \bigcap_{j=1}^{n} F_j(S_i)$ such that if S_i is executed then S_k is executed$\}$. The set of *parent IFs* of statement S_k, denoted $PIF(S_k)$, is the set $\{S_l \mid S_l$ is an IF, $S_l \Gamma S_k$, and there is no IF statement S_m such that $S_l \Gamma S_m \Gamma S_k$ where $S_k \in CF(S_m)\}$. When there is more than one IF in the loop, it is possible that some of the followers will resemble trees.

Example 4

$$\text{DO } S_5 \quad I_1 = 5, 14, 1$$
$$\text{DO } S_5 \quad I_2 = 5, 14, 1$$

S_1: IF $I_1 > I_2$ THEN $(S_2:) A(I_1,I_2) = A(I_1-2,I_2-2) + A(I_1-4,I_2-4)$
$$+ A(I_1+2,I_2+2)$$
$$+ A(I_1+4,I_2+4)$$

S_3: IF $I_1 < I_2$ THEN $(S_4:) B(I_1,I_2) = B(I_1-1,I_2)*C(I_1,I_2)$
$$+ B(I_1-1,I_2)*D(I_1,I_2)$$

S_5: IF $I_1 = I_2$ THEN $(S_6:)$ IF $\text{MOD}(I_1,2) = 0$
$$\text{THEN } (S_7:) \ E(I_1,I_2) = E(I_1-1,I_2-1) + F(I_1,I_2)$$

In Example 4, we have

$$F_{11} = \{S_2,S_3,S_4,S_5,S_6,S_7\}, \qquad F_{12} = \{S_3,S_4,S_5,S_6,S_7\}$$

$$F_{31} = \{S_4,S_5,S_6,S_7\}, \qquad F_{32} = \{S_5,S_6,S_7\}$$

$$F_{51} = \{S_6,S_7\}, \qquad F_{52} = \emptyset$$

$$F_{61} = \{S_7\}, \qquad F_{62} = \emptyset,$$

$$CF(S_1) = \{S_3,S_4,S_5,S_6,S_7\}, \qquad CF(S_3) = \{S_5,S_6,S_7\}$$

$$CF(S_5) = \emptyset \qquad CF(S_7) = \emptyset$$

$$PIF(S_2) = PIF(S_3) = S_1, \qquad PIF(S_4) = PIF(S_5) = S_3$$

$$PIF(S_6) = S_5, \qquad PIF(S_7) = S_6$$

Definition 14 Given a π-block π_{ui} and IF statement S_j in π_{ui}, the kth *control path* with respect to S_j through π_{ui} is the set

$$\{S_l \in \pi_{ui} \mid S_l \ \Gamma \ S_j \quad \text{or} \quad (S_l \in F_k(S_j) \quad \text{and} \quad S_l \neq S_j)\}$$

We will refer to an arbitrary jth control path as a *control path*. Note that the number of control paths through π_{ui} is the same as the number of followers of S_j.

Example 5

```
        DO  S₇  I = 1, N
S₁:     A(I) = B(I−2) + C(I)
S₂:     IF (A(I−1).EQ.0)    THEN DO
S₃:                         B(I) = 3
S₄:                         D = .FALSE.
                            END
                            ELSE DO
S₅:                         E(I) = E(I−3) + 1
S₆:                         D = .TRUE.
                            END
S₇:     F(I) = 0
```

Using Example 5 we will point out the differences between followers and control paths: $F_1(S_2) = \{S_3, S_4, S_7\}$, $F_2(S_2) = \{S_5, S_6, S_7\}$, and $CF(S_2) = \{S_7\}$. In the π-partition $\pi_1 = \{\{S_1, S_2, S_3\}, \{S_4\}, \{S_5\}, \{S_6\}, \{S_7\}\}$ notice that $F_1(S_2)$ is contained in three π-blocks and $F_2(S_2)$ is not in the same π-blocks as $F_1(S_2)$. There are two control paths in $\{S_1, S_2, S_3\}$. One control path $\{S_1, S_3\}$ contains a statement not in any follower of S_2 and not all the statements in $F_1(S_2)$. The other control path $\{S_1\}$ does not contain any statements of $F_2(S_2)$. In general, a control path can contain statements not in any follower of the IF and does not have to contain any statements of a follower.

In an IF-free DO loop L, $L \in D$, we know that the data dependences for each iteration do not change as a function of the input data. The addition of IFs can give rise to several distinct data dependences for different input data sets. The data dependences on different iterations can be distinct for all iterations, some iterations, or only one iteration. Thus we may have statements that can have several different combinations of data dependence.

Example 6

```
        DO  S₅  I = 1, N
S₁:     IF C(I−1) = D(I)   THEN (S₂:) A(I) = 3 P(I)
                           ELSE DO
S₃:                        A(I) = 4*Q(I)
S₄:                        B(I) = R(I) + 1
                           END
S₅:     C(I) = A(I) + B(I−1) + 2
```

Definition 15 The set of different combinations of data dependence into statement S_i is called the *data dependence combinations* of statement S_i and is denoted DDC_i. The number of followers of S_j that contain S_i is denoted f_{ji}.

Statement S_5 in Example 6 can be computed in four different ways. First, the value of A(I) can be from S_2 and B(I−1) from outside the DO loop. Second, the value of A(I) can be from S_2 and B(I−1) from S_4. Third, the value of A(I) can be from S_3 and B(J−1) from S_4. Fourth, the value of A(I) can be from S_3 and B(I−1) from outside the DO loop.

Using Definitions 8, 12, 13, and 15, we can classify IFs into three types:

Definition 16   Given a loop $L = (I_1 \leftarrow N_1, \ldots, I_d \leftarrow N_d)(S_1, \ldots, S_s)$ and IF $S_i = (C)(S_{i_1}, \ldots, S_{i_n})$, $1 \leq i \leq s$, we say S_i is

(a) *Type A* iff there does not exist S_j, $1 \leq j \leq s$, such that $S_j \, \delta \, S_i$ and $\{I_1, \ldots, I_d\} \cap \text{IN}(S_i) = \emptyset$.

(b) *Type B* iff one of the following holds:
   (1) All but one of $F_j(S_i)$ branch out of the loop.
   (2) For each $S_k \in \bigcup_{j=1}^n F_j(S_i)$ such that $S_k \, \Delta \, S_i$, $|DDC(S_k)|/f_{ik} \leq 1$ and each of the data dependence combinations of S_k only include data dependence on the statements in a single follower of S_i and/or statements not in any follower of S_i.

(c) *Type C* iff S_i is not type A or type B.

Type B IFs can be further subdivided. A *prefix type B IF* is a type B IF that is not data dependent on any statement in its followers. *Postfix type B IFs* are all other type B IFs.

Next we will discuss compiler algorithms for array machines. These machines have two characteristics of which we want to take advantage. First, these machines operate on whole arrays. Thus we need to transform programs to operate on the whole array at once rather than element by element. Second, these machines can selectively omit certain elements of an array during array operations. We define *mode bits* as the indicators of which array elements are to be operated on. Thus we want to transform IFs to generate mode bits. Both of these characteristics let us obtain speedups over uniprocessor machines.

As we saw earlier for IF-free loops, by distributing DO loop indices over π-blocks we are able to transform a given loop into one or more loops each containing a vector or recurrence operation. In Chen et al. (1975a) we gave a modification of that algorithm to allow IFs. The first goal of the algorithm is to localize data dependence and the effects of IFs. Second, the algorithm handles the IFs in four different ways.

(1) Type A IFs are the easiest to handle. One loop is compiled for each follower and an IF is used at execution time to select which loop to execute.

(2) Prefix type B IFs use mode bits to "prefix" the body statements. The IF is used only to set up the mode bits. The mode bits are set up once and then used by the body statements as necessary.

(3) Postfix type B IFs require execution of each control path for the full DO loop index set. Then we postfix by merging the outputs from each control path.

(4) Type C IFs are executed serially.

Since the type A IF depends on variables not set inside the loop, such IFs can be removed from loops trivially. However, good programmers seldom write such statements, so this is a moot point.

In the prefix type B IF, we set up the π-block containing the IF and the other π-blocks that are α-dependent on it to be executed for the full index set. However, before these π-blocks are executed we precompute (at compile or run time) which follower will be taken on each particular iteration of the DO loop. This is expressed as a vector of mode bits for each follower. A vector of mode bits is a mask that is applied to the index set for a given operation. In this way we can selectively omit certain elements at run time. The end result is that each statement is executed only for the proper elements. By precomputing these mode bits, we are able to fix the results a priori, and hence the name prefix type B.

As an example of a prefix type B IF, consider the following program:

```
        DO  S  I = 1, N
        IF (I≤5)  THEN A(I) = B(I) + C(I)
        ELSE A(I) = B(I)/C(I)
    S:  CONTINUE
```

Let $M_i[a,b]$ be a vector of mode bits denoting vector elements from a to b, inclusive. Then we can compile the above as

```
        M1 = [1,5]
        M2 = [6,N]
    DO  SIM{A(M1) = B(M1) + C(M1), A(M2) = B(M2)/C(M2)}
```

where DO SIM indicates that the bracketed statements can be executed as array statements and simultaneously.

The postfix type B IFs are more complicated. Using only the statements in the π-block that contains the IF, we compute all control paths in parallel for the full index set. Using these results we evaluate the IF. Finally, the results are merged to produce the correct results and a set of mode bits are passed on to other π-blocks. The details of the test and merge are now given. What we want to do is find which follower is taken for each iteration. Thus given the outputs for each control path for each iteration, we want to thread our way through the outputs, picking up the proper results. It is possible to do this recursively by using the previously selected results and the results from the current iteration to determine which follower is to be taken. Using subscripts to denote control path, in Example 7 we compute $A_1(I) = D(I)$ and $A_2(I) = B(I)*C(I)$ for all values of the index set. Let M_1 and M_2 be the vector of mode bits for followers 1 and 2, respectively. Whenever $M_i(j)$ is a 1, then the statements in the ith follower are executed on the jth iteration in the serial program.

Example 7

```
        DO S I = 6, N
        IF  A(I-3) = 5  THEN A(I) = D(I)
                        ELSE A(I) = B(I)*C(I)
S:  CONTINUE
```

It should be noted, in general, that ANDing of any two distinct vectors of mode bits associated with an IF statement results in a vector of 0 bits. The ORing of all the vectors results in a vector of 1 bits, corresponding to the iterations on which the IF statement is executed in the serial program.

In Example 7, control path 1 is taken whenever we were on control path 1 three iterations ago and the output was 5, or we were on control path 2 three iterations ago and the output was 5. Control path 2 is taken in either case if the output was not 5. This can be expressed as the following coupled recurrence relation:

$$M_1(I) \leftarrow (A_1(I-3) = 5 \ \& \ M_1(I-3)) \lor (A_2(I-3) = 5 \ \& \ M_2(I-3))$$

$$M_2(I) \leftarrow (A_1(I-3) \neq 5 \ \& \ M_1(I-3)) \lor (A_2(I-3) \neq 5 \ \& \ M_2(I-3))$$

The techniques to solve this recurrence are described in Chen and Kuck (1975a) with specific reference to this application. This is a bit level recurrence and can be done in $O(\log n)$ gate delays, where n is the number of iterations. In reality, we could approximate the $\log n$ gate delays by one clock, i.e., one time step.

Finally, we mask A_1 with M_1, A_2 with M_2, and merge the results to get the proper elements of A. Also M_1 and M_2 are passed on to other π-blocks as needed.

We should point out that postfix type B loops yield the same speedups as prefix type B loops, in general. The difference is that since more processors are required for redundant operations here, postfix type B loops generally have lower efficiencies.

As a test of the usefulness of our methods, we have analyzed the 16 FORTRAN programs that appeared in 1973 in the CACM Algorithms Section. Nested DOs were counted as one loop at the outermost level.

TABLE I

1973 CACM DO Loop Summary

	Recurrence type			
IF type	0	1	2	3
No IF	51	24	2	3
A	0	0	0	0
Prefix B	24	6	1	1
Postfix B	3	8	1	0
C	0	1	1	0

There were a total of 124 such DO loops. Each loop was characterized in terms of the worst recurrence type [cf. Eq. (6)] and worst IF type it contained. Table I is a summary of our results.

We observe that type A and prefix type B IFs together with recurrence types 0 and 1 can be handled with good speedup and efficiency. This accounts for 85% of the loops. Four programs (type 3 and type C) are disasters for our methods and in part must be handled serially. The remaining programs can be handled by the postfix and wave front (type 2) methods. Overall, this seems to imply that the methods given would be very effective for the general mix of CACM FORTRAN algorithms.

4. Machine Considerations

Since the early 1960s, we have seen a sequence of high-speed machines that have some kind of multioperation capability. The CDC 6600 of the 60s was succeeded by the 7600 in the early 70s. IBM introduced the 360/91 and its successors. The 7600 and 360/91 are both pipelined machines and achieve high performance by operating on arrays of data. Their instruction sets are rather traditional, however. In contrast, the pipelined Control Data STAR (Hintz and Tate, 1972) and Texas Instruments ASC (Watson and Carr, 1974) both have vector instruction sets, which should make compilation for them substantially easier.

On the other hand, the Burroughs ILLIAC IV (Barnes et al., 1968) is a parallel array machine, but its instruction set is also traditional in nature. Vectors must be broken up into partitions of size 64 and loops performed over a sequence of such partitions. The Goodyear Aerospace STARAN IV (Batcher, 1973) is a parallel array of processors, each of which operates in a bit-serial fashion. This is an example of an associative processor.

It is interesting to note that the highest speed pipeline processors, the STAR and ASC, both resort to parallelism by providing several parallel pipelines to achieve their desired operating speeds.

The processing speedups achieved by all of these machines are due to parallelism between operations as well as parallelism between memory and processor activities. We shall discuss memories, alignment networks, and control units later. Our point here is that in order to compile ordinary serial languages for these processors, two things are desirable: (1) powerful translation techniques to detect parallelism, and (2) array-type machine languages.

The main contributions to program speedup discussed in Section 3 arise from our loop distribution procedure. This leads to array operations and recurrences. Both of these are well suited for computation on machines that must perform the same operation on many data elements to achieve high performance. Thus, the methods of Section 3 could serve as compiler algorithms for such machines.

Some time ago, we implemented a comprehensive analyzer of FORTRAN programs. It used algorithms like those of Sections 2 and 3, although some of the techniques were much more primitive than those discussed here. Details of our algorithms and results may be found in Kuck (1973), Kuck et al. (1972, 1974), and Muraoka (1971). We will summarize a few points very briefly.

Altogether some 140 ordinary FORTRAN programs, gathered from many sources, were analyzed. The programs ranged from numerical computations on two-dimensional arrays (e.g., EISPACK) to essentially nonnumerical programs (e.g., FORTRAN equivalents of GPSS blocks). We set all loops to 10 or fewer iterations and analyzed all paths through the programs, computing T_1, T_p, S_p, E_p, etc. These were averaged over all traces and also over collections of programs. A plot of our results for S_p versus p is shown in Fig. 7. Some of the points are labeled with the name of a collection of programs.

Our experiments lead us to conclude that multioperation machines could be quite effective in most ordinary FORTRAN computations. Figure 7 shows that even the simplest sets of programs (GPSS, for example, has almost no DO loops) could be effectively executed using 16 processors. The overall average (ALL in Fig. 7) is 35 processors when all DO loop limits are set to 10 or less. As the programs become more complex, 128 or more processors would be effective in executing our programs. Note that for all of our studies, $T_1 \leq 10{,}000$, so most of the programs would be classed as short jobs in a typical computer center. In all cases, the average efficiency for each group of programs was no less than 30%. While we have not analyzed any decks with more than 100 cards, we would expect extrapola-

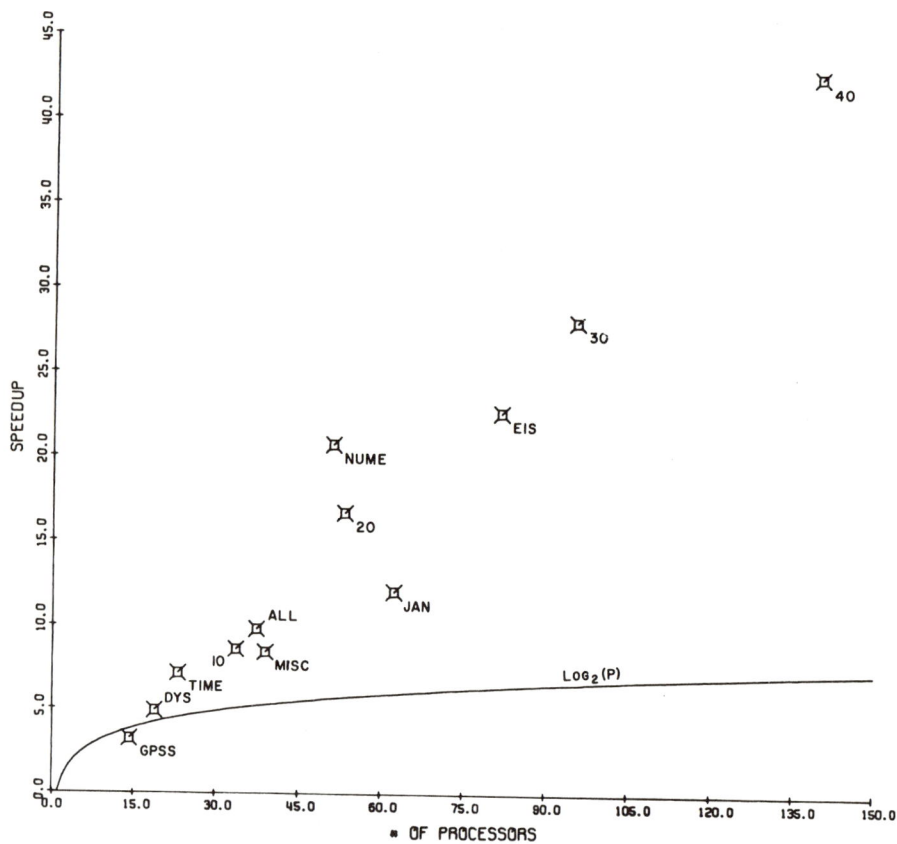

FIG. 7. Speedup vs. processors.

tions of our results to hold. In fact, we obtained some decks by breaking larger ones at convenient points.

These numbers should be contrasted with current computer organizations. Presently, two to four simultaneous-operation general purpose machines are quite common. The pipeline, parallel, and associative machines mentioned above perform 8 to 64 simultaneous operations, but these are largely intended for special purpose use. Thus, we feel that our numbers indicate the possibility of perhaps an order of magnitude speedup increase over the current situation.

Furthermore, we took a subset of the programs, again a random cross section, and varied the DO loop limits from 10 to 40. The points 10, 20, 30, 40 correspond to the results. We conclude that for our sample or ordinary FORTRAN programs, speedup is a linear function of T_1 and hence p.

This is quite different from some of the folklore that has arisen about parallel computation, (Amdahl, 1967; Flynn, 1972; Minsky, 1970) [e.g., $S_p = O(\log p)$]. We will next give an outline of two commonly held beliefs about machine organization.

Let us assume that for $0 \leq \beta_k \leq 1$, $(1-\beta_k)$ of the serial execution time of a given program uses p processors, while β_k of it must be performed on $k \leq p$ processors. Then we may write

$$T_p = \frac{\beta_k T_1}{k} + (1-\beta_k)\frac{T_1}{p}$$

$$E_p = \frac{T_1}{(p/k)\beta_k T_1 + (1-\beta_k)T_1} = \frac{1}{1 + \beta_k((p/k) - 1)}$$

For example, if $k = 1$, $p = 33$, and $\beta_1 = \frac{1}{16}$, then we have $E_{33} = \frac{1}{3}$. This means that to achieve $E_{33} = \frac{1}{3}$, $\frac{15}{16}$ of T_1 must be executed using all 33 processors, while only $\frac{1}{16}$ of T_1 may use a single processor. While $E_{33} = \frac{1}{3}$ is typical of our results (see Fig. 7), it would be extremely surprising to learn that $\frac{15}{16}$ of T_1 could be executed using fully 33 processors. This kind of observation led Amdahl (1967) and others (Chen, 1971; Senzig, 1967) to conclude that computers capable of executing a large number of simultaneous operations would not be reasonably efficient—or, to paraphrase them, "Ordinary programs have too much serial code to be executed efficiently on a multioperation processor."

Such arguments have an invalidating flaw, however, in that they assume $k = 1$ in the above efficiency expression. Evidently no one who repeated this argument ever considered the obvious fact that k will generally assume many integer values in the course of executing most programs. Thus, the expression for E_p given above must be generalized to allow all values of k up to some maximum.

The technique used in our experiments for computing E_p is such a generalization. For some execution trace through a program, at each time step i, some number of processors $k(i)$ will be required. If the maximum number of processors required on any step is p, we compute the efficiency for any trace as

$$E_p = \sum_{i=1}^{T_p} k(i)/pR_pT_p$$

assuming p processors are available. Apparently no previous attempt to quantify the parameters discussed above has been successful for a wide class of programs. Besides Kuck et al. (1974) the only other published results are by Baer and Estrin (1969), who report on five programs.

Another commonly held opinion, which has been mentioned by Minsky (1970), is that speedup S_p is proportional to log p. Flynn (1972) further discusses this, assuming that all the operations simultaneously executed are identical. This may be interpreted to hold (1) over many programs of different characteristics, (2) for one fixed program with a varying number of processors, or (3) for one program with varying DO loop limits. That the above is false under interpretation 1 for our analysis is obvious from Fig. 7. Similarly, it is false under interpretation 2 as the number of processors is varied between 1 and some number as plotted in Fig. 7. As p is increased still further, the speedup and efficiency may be regarded as constant or the speedup may be increased at a decreasing rate together with a decreasing efficiency. Eventually, as p becomes arbitrarily large, the speedup becomes constant and in some region the curve may appear logarithmic. Under interpretation 3, there are many possibilities—programs with multiply nested DO loops may have speedups that grow much faster than linear, and programs without DO loops, of course, do not change at all.

One of Flynn's arguments in support of such behavior concerned branching inside loops. For example, if on each pass through a loop we branched down some new path, not taken on any other iteration, then indeed we might have disastrous results. However, we have not observed such intense splitting; in fact, most computations that do branch inside a loop come together in common followers rather quickly. Furthermore, there are usually relatively few distinct paths through a loop in most cases. The results of Table I lend further support to our conclusion that IFs in loops do not pose a serious practical problem.

Abstractly, it seems of more interest to relate speedup to T_1 than to p. Based on our data, we offer the following observation: for many ordinary FORTRAN programs (with $T_1 \leq 10{,}000$) we can find p such that

(1) $\quad T_p = \alpha \log_2 T_1 \quad$ for $\quad 2 \leq \alpha \leq 10$

and

(2) $\quad p \leq T_1/0.6 \log_2 T_1$

such that

(3) $\quad S_p \geq T_1/10 \log_2 T_1 \quad$ and $\quad E_p \geq 0.3$

The average α value in our experiments was about 9. However, the median value was less than 4, since there were several very large values.

In terms of our present theoretical results, it is not hard to justify such estimates. Consider, for example, Corollary 4, which is intended for solving $R\langle n,m \rangle$ systems with small n using a limited number of processors. Let us approximate the times by

$$T_1 \approx mn \quad \text{and} \quad T_p \approx 2m^2n/p \approx 2mT_1/p$$

since most programs have $m = 1$ or $m = 2$. Following the observation, we choose $p \approx T_1/\log T_1$, so

$$T_p \approx 2m \log T_1, \qquad S_p \approx T_1/2m \log T_1, \qquad E_p \approx 1/2m$$

all of which agree reasonably with the observation.

We should point out that our previous analyzer allowed each processor to be executing a different operation on any time step. This could degrade our results, possibly by a factor of two. However, the newly discovered algorithms perform better than the ones we used in our old analyzer. We are currently implementing a new analyzer with which we expect to obtain better results than those summarized above.

For a more complete discussion of theoretical bounds on the time and processors required for executing whole FORTRAN loops, see Chen (1975) and Chen et al. (1975b). These references show how certain details about overall program graphs can be combined with the results of Section 3 to obtain loop bounds. From these, whole program bounds can be obtained.

4.1 Control Units

A well-designed control unit is one that never gets in the way of the processor(s) and memories. In other words, it operates fast enough to be able to supply instructions whenever they are needed in the processing and moving of data. Control units tend to become complex, mainly in a timing sense, because they may have a number of tasks to control.

One way to ease some control unit difficulties is to use parallelism at the control unit level. A multiprocessor is an example; several complete control units are used. This may be rather expensive, so the multifunction, pipeline, and parallel processor machines use one shared control unit. Such control units often contain a number of independently operating parts. For example, the first use of pipelining was in control units (Buchholz, 1962). A detailed study of the control unit of any high-speed computer will reveal a number of simultaneously operating, independent functions. While this may allow the functions to operate more slowly, it also causes some synchronization problems.

As we mentioned in our processor discussion, the level of machine language is very important in modern, high-speed computers. Vector instruction sets make compiler writing easier. They also focus control unit design on the correct questions, namely, to execute vector functions at high speed.

Control units for high-speed computers must handle the traditional functions, including instruction decoding and sequencing, I/O and interrupt handling, and address mapping and memory indexing. In addition, we can list several new functions. For one, memory indexing becomes some-

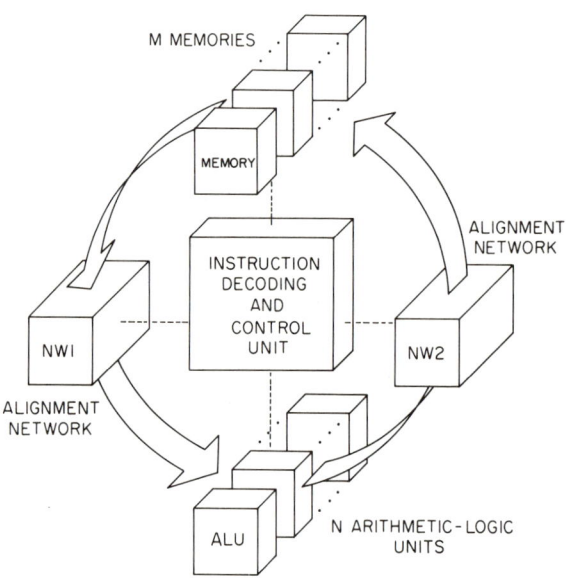

Fig. 8. Overall machine organization.

what more complex when whole arrays are being accessed in large parallel memories. Also, array computers (parallel or pipeline) often rely on the control unit for scalar computations. Broadcasting of scalars to an array must also be handled. Special control features such as IF tree processing (Davis, 1972a) can be effectively handled in the control unit. Special stacks and queues may be required to handle a number of processors and programs in rapid succession. Indeed, instruction level multiprogramming may even be attempted.

Rather than discuss any of these in detail, we simply refer the reader to a detailed study of the several high-speed machine papers mentioned earlier.

We conclude this section with the computer organization of Fig. 8. The control unit can really be regarded as four control units, one for each of the four other major subsystems shown. The operation of this machine can be regarded as a pipeline from memory to memory. For move instructions (memory to memory) the processors can be bypassed.

Figure 8 represents parallelism at a number of levels: within the control unit, processors, memories, and data alignment networks. Also, it contains parallelism in the simultaneity of operation of each of these, which forms a pipeline. Note that pipelining can also be used within each of the five major subsystems to match bandwidths between them.

The details of accessing parallel memories and of aligning the accessed data will be discussed in the next section.

4.2 Parallel Memory Access

As effective speeds of processing units have increased, memory speeds have been forced to keep up. This has partly been achieved by new technologies (magnetic cores to semiconductors). But technology has not been enough, as evidenced by the fact that in 1953, the first core memory operating (in Whirlwind I) had an 8-μsec memory cycle time. Today, most computer designers cannot afford to use memories much faster than 100 nsec. Thus, we have achieved an increase of only two orders of magnitude in memory speed over the past twenty-odd years.

In the same period, the fastest processor operation times have advanced from a few tens of microseconds to a few tens of nanoseconds, or three orders of magnitude. Memory system speeds have kept up with processors only through the use of parallelism at the word level. In the late 1950s, ILLIAC II and the IBM STRETCH introduced the first two-way interleaved memories. At the present time, high-speed computers have on the order of 100 parallel memory units. If a word can be fetched from each of m memory units at once, then the effective memory bandwidth is increased by a factor of m.

4.3 Array Access

Parallel memories are particularly important in array computers (parallel or pipeline). Thus, if a machine has m memory units we can store one-dimensional arrays across the units as shown in Fig. 9, for $m = 4$. While

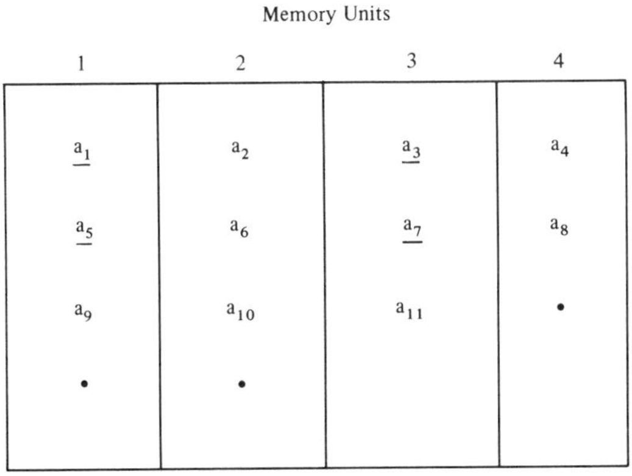

Memory Units

1	2	3	4
$\underline{a_1}$	a_2	$\underline{a_3}$	a_4
$\underline{a_5}$	a_6	$\underline{a_7}$	a_8
a_9	a_{10}	a_{11}	•
•	•		

Fig. 9. One-dimensional array storage.

the first m operands are being processed, we can fetch m more, and so on. But, if the array is indexed such that, say, only the odd elements are to be fetched, then the effective bandwidth is cut in half due to access conflicts as shown in the underlined elements of Fig. 9. These conflicts can be avoided by choosing m to be a prime number. Then, any index distance relatively prime to m can be accessed without conflicts.

Many programs contain multidimensional arrays. These can lead to more difficult memory access problems, since we may want to access rows, columns, diagonals, back diagonals (as in the wave front method of Section 3), square blocks, and so on. For simplicity, consider two-dimensional arrays and assume we want to access n element partitions of arrays from parallel memories with m units.

Consider the storage scheme shown in Fig. 10, where $m = n = 4$. Clearly, using this storage scheme we can access any row or diagonal (e.g., the circled main diagonal) without conflict. But all the elements of a column (e.g., the underlined first column) are stored in the same memory unit, so accessing a column would result in memory conflicts, i.e., we would have to cycle the memories n times to get the n elements of a column.

In order to allow access to row and column n-vectors, we can *skew* the data as shown in Fig. 11 (Kuck, 1968). Now, however, we can no longer access diagonals without conflict. It can be shown, in fact, that there is no way to store an $m \times m$ matrix in m memories when m is even, so that arbitrary rows, columns, and diagonals can be fetched without conflicts. However, as we shall see, by using more than m memories we can have

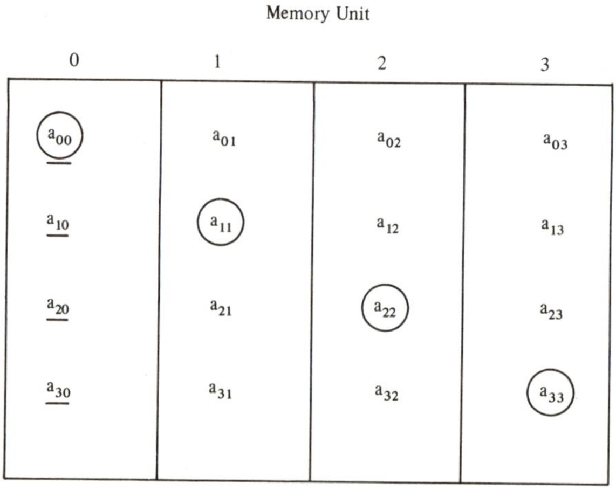

Memory Unit

0	1	2	3
a_{00}	a_{01}	a_{02}	a_{03}
a_{10}	a_{11}	a_{12}	a_{13}
a_{20}	a_{21}	a_{22}	a_{23}
a_{30}	a_{31}	a_{32}	a_{33}

FIG. 10. Straight storage ($m = 4$).

Memory Unit

	0	1	2	3
	(a₀₀)	a₀₁	a₀₂	a₀₃
	a₁₃	a₁₀	(a₁₁)	a₁₂
	(a₂₂)	a₂₃	a₂₀	a₂₁
	a₃₁	a₃₂	(a₃₃)	a₃₀

FIG. 11. Skewed storage ($m = 4$).

conflict-free access to any row, column, or diagonal, as well as other useful m-vectors.

It is easy to show that if $m = 2^{2k} + 1$, for any integer k, we have conflict-free access to rows, columns, diagonals, back diagonals, and square blocks. For an example with $k = 1$, see Fig. 12. This and other similar results are discussed in Budnik and Kuck (1971). If m is not a power of two, certain difficulties arise in indexing the memory. Also, note that the elements of various partitions are accessed in scrambled order. A crossbar switch could be used to unscramble the data, but much cheaper schemes can be

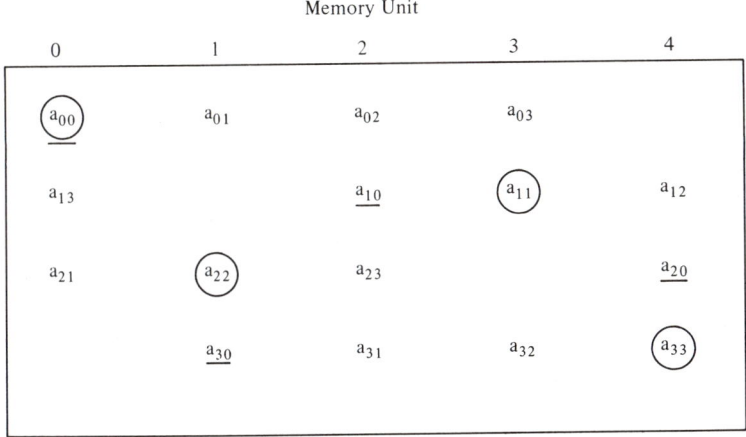

FIG. 12. Skewed storage ($m = 5$).

devised. The question of unscrambling the accessed elements using a rather simple network is discussed by Swanson (1974).

In order to simplify indexing and unscrambling, systems of the form $m = 2n$ were considered by Lawrie (1973, 1975). He shows that conflict-free access to a number of partitions is possible using such a memory. We illustrate this in Fig. 13 with $m = 2n = 8$. We will discuss data alignment networks for unscrambling the data accessed in such a memory later in this section.

In order to implement a skewing scheme, we must have a properly designed parallel memory system. In particular, each of the m memory units must have an independent indexing mechanism. This allows us to access a different relative location in each memory unit. It is interesting to observe that several presently existing high-speed computers have handled their parallel memories in different ways.

The Control Data STAR, for example, does not allow independent indexing of each memory unit. Instead, it has an instruction by which arrays can be physically transposed in memory to provide access to, say, rows and columns. The transpose time is essentially wasted time and some algorithms for these machines are slowed down by as much as a factor of two in this way.

ILLIAC IV has independent index registers and index adders on each of $m = 64$ memories. Since it has 64 processors, access to partitions of $n = 64$ elements is usually required. Thus the skew scheme of Fig. 11 is easily implemented. Of course, since m is even, conflict-free access to rows, columns, and diagonals is impossible. But as Fig. 11 shows, diagonals may be accessed in just two memory cycles.

4.4 Parallel Random Access

The execution of FORTRAN-like programs frequently leads to memory access requirements that include one-dimensional arrays and various partitions of multidimensional arrays, as we have been discussing. However, we sometimes face access problems that have much less regularity.

For example, consider the subscripted subscript case:

$$\text{DO } I = 1, N$$
$$X(I) = A(B(I))$$

Here, we have no idea at compile time about which elements of A are to be fetched, assuming that B was computed earlier in the program. This easily generalizes to multidimensional arrays. Frequently, table lookup problems are programmed in this way.

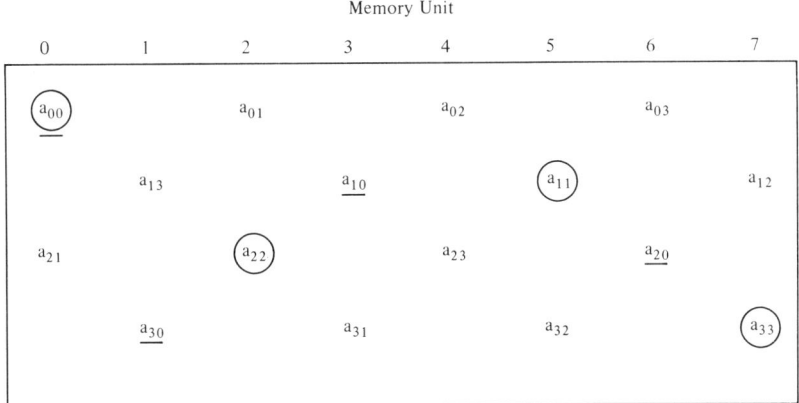

Fig. 13. Skewed storage ($m = 2n = 8$).

To deal with this kind of memory access problems is in general to deal with random access to a parallel memory. Note that this is a problem that has been given a good deal of attention for multiprocessor systems using rather abstract models of various kinds. There are two key questions on which the validity and usefulness of these models turn:

(1) What kind of data dependence is assumed in the memory access sequence?

(2) What kind of queueing mechanism is assumed for retaining unserviced accesses?

In these terms, we briefly summarize some of the results. Hellerman's model (1967) can most reasonably be interpreted to assume no data dependence between successive memory accesses and to have no provision to queue conflicting addresses. It is also a steady state model, ignoring control dependence. Thus, it scans an infinite string of addresses, blocking when it finds the first duplicate memory unit access request.

In various models, Coffman and his co-workers (1971; Burnett and Coffman, 1970, 1973) extended the above to include a type of queueing and to separate data access from instruction accesses. These papers further introduced address sequences that were not necessarily uniformly distributed. These models also assumed that no data dependences existed in the address sequence.

Ravi (1972) introduced a model that was more realistic for multiprocessor machines. He allows each processor to generate an address and computes the number of them that can be accessed without conflict, in a steady state sense. Effectively he assumes a sequential data dependence in the addresses generated by each processor.

In Chang et al. (1975) the above results are extended in several ways. First, it is shown analytically that the model of Ravi (1972) yields an effective memory bandwidth that is linear in the number of memory units. Several models are given with queues in the processors and in the memories, to show the differing effects on bandwidth of such queues and methods used for managing the queues. Several types of data dependences are assumed to exist, some as in the Ravi model and others that include dependences between the processors. In all of these models, we show that the effective bandwidth of m memories can be made to be $O(m)$. The models are useful for either multiprocessor or parallel machines.

Thus, we conclude that for parallel or multiprocessor machines, the proper use of m parallel memories can lead to effective bandwidths that are $O(m)$. This is much more encouraging than the $O(m^{1/2})$ that was derived from earlier, more naive models.

4.5 Alignment Networks

Finally, we consider the problem of interconnecting the processors and memories we have been examining. Data alignment requirements depend on the programs to be run and the machine organization. A simple way to connect several memories to a processor is to use a shared bus. For higher speed operation, multiprocessors often use a crossbar switch that allows each processor to be connected to a different memory simultaneously. In the ILLIAC IV array, the ith processor can pass data to processors $i \pm 1$ and $i \pm 8$, modulo 64. Here all processors must route data the same distance in a uniform way.

None of the above techniques is well suited to a high-performance parallel computer. Indeed, the alignment network should be driven by an independent control unit, to operate concurrently with the processor and memory operation. The requirements include more than uniform shifts and at times even more than permutations. Often broadcasts are needed, including partial and multiple simultaneous broadcasts, e.g., $n^{1/2}$ numbers, each broadcast to $n^{1/2}$ processors for matrix multiplication in an n-processor machine (Lawrie, 1975).

The alignment network should be able to transmit data from memory to memory and processor to processor as well as back and forth between memories and processors. The connections it must provide are derived from two sources. For one, it must be able to handle the indexing patterns found in existing programs, for example, the uniform shift of 5 necessary in A(I) + A(I+5). For another, it must be able to scramble and unscramble the data for memory accesses. For example, to add a row to a column, one of the partitions must be "unskewed." More details can be found in Kuck (1973) and Lawrie (1973, 1975).

With a crossbar switch we can perform any one-to-one connection of inputs to outputs, and with some modification we can also make one-to-many connections for broadcasting. The switch can be set and data can be transmitted in $O(\log n)$ gate delays. However, the cost of such a switch is quite high, namely, $O(n^2)$ gates. Thus for large systems, a crossbar alignment network is out of the question.

Another possibility is the rearrangeable network. It is shown by Beneš (1965) that such a switch, with the same connection capabilities as a crossbar, can be implemented using only $O(n \log n)$ gates. The time required to transmit data through the network is just $O(\log n)$. Unfortunately, the best known time to set up the network for transmission is $O(n \log n)$ (Opferman and Tsao-Wu, 1971). This control time renders the network impractical as an alignment network, unless all connection patterns could be set up at compile time.

The Batcher (1968) sorting network is another possibility. Not only can it perform the connections of a crossbar switch, it can also sort its inputs, if desired. This network has $O(n \log^2 n)$ gates, so it is an improvement over the crossbar. However, it requires time of $O(\log^2 n)$ gate delays for control and data transmission, making it faster than the Beneš approach.

As a final possibility, the Ω-network (Lawrie, 1975) proposed specifically for this purpose can be controlled and transmit data in $O(\log n)$ gate delays, but contains only $O(n \log n)$ gates. Thus it has the speed of a crossbar with the cost of a Beneš network. Its shortcoming is that it cannot perform arbitrary interconnections. However, as discussed above, we seek an alignment network that can handle the requirements posed by program subscripts and memory skewing schemes. Lawrie has examined a number of such questions and the Ω-network satisfies many of them.

It is interesting to note that the Ω-network consists of a sequence of identical interconnection paths called *shuffles* (see, e.g., Lawrie, 1975; Pease, 1968). We call transmission from left to right a shuffle and from right to left an *unshuffle*. It can be shown that the Beneš and Batcher networks, as well as the Ω-network, can all be constructed from a series of shuffle and unshuffle interconnections of 2×2 switching elements. The switching elements are basically 2×2 crossbars. In the Batcher network, they have the further capability of comparing their inputs and switching on this basis. In the Ω-network, they can also broadcast either of their inputs to both outputs.

4.6 A Cost Effectiveness Measure

One important motivation for studying the structure of parallel algorithms is to determine computer architectures for effectively executing these algorithms. We are interested in computer requirements as measured in terms such as number of processors, type of processors, number of memories, and type of interconnections. We measure the effectiveness of an architecture for some algorithm in terms of its speedup over a single processor and the efficiency of the evaluation of that algorithm.

In Section 3, we defined speedup categories as a way of characterizing parallel algorithms. These were given in terms of T_1 rather than, say, n, the size of some array, in order to compare dissimilar algorithms. Such a hierarchy is useful for comparing algorithms, but it may not be useful as a quality or effectiveness measure for machine computation. In practice, which algorithm one chooses depends on many factors, an important one being the number of processors available.

The speedup types mentioned above are useful in algorithm selection if one has a machine that is relatively very large compared to the sizes of his problems. But categorizing algorithms on the basis of speedup alone is unsatisfactory in general, since efficiency is important if unlimited processors are not available. On the other hand, using efficiency as the sole measure of effectiveness is too conservative, since a serial computation always has maximum efficiency, i.e., $E_1 = 1$. Thus, we turn to a measure that includes both effectiveness and cost.

The cost of a computation is clearly related to the number of processors required and the time they must be used. We will assume the processor $\times$ time product reasonably represents cost, so we define cost as $C_p = pT_p$.

Assume that we have two algorithms A_1 and A_2, which compute the same function using p_1 and p_2 processors, respectively. Thus, we should decide which algorithm to use on the basis of $\max(S_{p_1}/C_{p_1}, S_{p_2}/C_{p_2})$, the ratios of effectiveness to cost.

We can rewrite this measure as

$$S_p/C_p = S_p/pT_p = E_p/T_p$$

Note that since $E_p \leq 1$ and $T_p \geq 1$, $E_p/T_p \leq 1$; hence, $S_p/C_p \leq 1$.

Another way of viewing this measure is to write

$$E_p/T_p = E_p S_p/T_1$$

Note that for a given function, T_1 is fixed so for various parallel algorithms we are attempting to maximize the product of efficiency and speedup. Since $E_p \leq 1$ and $S_p \leq T_1$, division by T_1 is simply a normalization of the maximum product to unity.

In Fig. 14 we present a summary of S/C values for a number of parallel

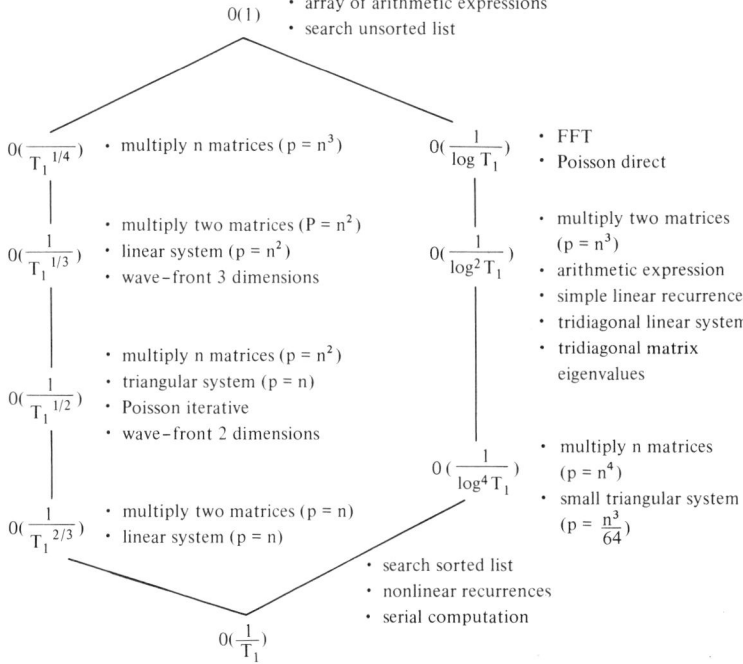

FIG. 14. S_p/C_p classes. (Note: all arrays $n \times n$.)

computations. This is discussed in detail in Kuck (1974). We shall make a few summary remarks here.

Generally speaking, the best parallel algorithms in the S/C sense are at the top and the worst are at the bottom. The column at the left represents algorithms running on machines in a less than maximum possible speedup way. The right column contains the best known speedups, in general.

By studying various algorithm and machine organizations for a given problem, we could hope to maximize the S/C measure for some set of computations. For example, the problem of multiplying n matrices is shown in three places, for $p = n^2$, $p = n^3$, and $p = n^4$. Note that S/C is maximum for $p = n^3$, less than the maximum possible speedup for this problem. In Kuck (1974) several algorithms are compared in this way.

Finally, we point out that for an analysis such as the one we have presented here to be practically meaningful, some machine details must also be included. Analyses similar to the above may be performed on various parts of a computer system. For example, bit-serial and bit-parallel arithmetic units may be compared in a similar way. Various interconnection networks can also be studied in this way. Thus we would be able to make tradeoffs in parallelism from the level of arithmetic algorithms (i.e., hardware) up through the level of computational algorithms (i.e., programs). Consider the extra gates required for carry lookahead arithmetic over bit-serial arithmetic. These could be more cost-effectively used in multiple microprocessors in a machine properly designed for some set of algorithms.

5. Conclusions

Parallelism in machine organization has been observed and exploited since the time of Babbage (Kuck *et al.*, 1972). Since the early 1960s, multi-operation machines have existed in implementations like the CDC 6600, CDC STAR, TI ASC, Burroughs ILLIAC IV, and so on. Compilers for these machines have been uniformly difficult to write—mainly for two reasons. First, it has been difficult in ordinary programs to discover operations that can be executed simultaneously on such machines. Second, the organizations of these machines have often made it difficult to implement array operations in efficient ways.

In this chapter we have discussed both of these problems. The first can be solved by using several compilation techniques aimed at parallelism detection and exploitation. This involves building a dependence graph in a careful way and then being able to compile trees, recurrences, and IF statements for execution in fast ways. For most ordinary FORTRAN programs, this will probably lead to theoretical speedups that grow (nearly) linearly in the number of processors used in a computation.

The second problem is closely related to the first. If one can transform most programs into array form, then proper hardware is necessary to support their fast execution. This means we must have a control unit capable of executing array instructions in a more or less direct way. For example, sufficiently many registers are required to contain all of the relevant parameters of loops, their indexing, and array subscripting. Furthermore, we must have a high-bandwidth memory that provides conflict-free access to arrays and various commonly needed partitions. We must also be able to align such partitions with others for processing. Finally, sufficiently high processing bandwidth must be provided—most likely by a combination of parallel and pipeline techniques. To complete the circle, the control unit must be sufficiently pipelined to provide a continuous flow of data in a memory to memory (or register to register) way.

While many aspects of the problem are well understood now, no machine exists that combines all of the necessary features in an adequate way. These ideas are generally regarded as techniques for very high-speed computation. However, the supercomputers of one day are often the ordinary computers of a later day and perhaps the minicomputers of the future. Clearly, good architectural ideas for machine speedup and ease of compiler writing will be widely useful. Indeed, with the arrival of 16-bit microprocessors, we seem to be quite close to the time when large numbers of simple processors can be used as components in one superprocessor.

We emphasize the need for program analysis to determine which machine organizations are useful for various classes of programs. In this chapter we have concentrated on FORTRAN-like programs. The techniques described here have been adapted to other languages. For example, in Davis (1972b), all of the important blocks of GPSS were analyzed. Using these results, a machine organization was proposed for the fast execution of GPSS programs. Since little arithmetic is involved, designs for the memory, control unit, and alignment network were emphasized.

Similarly, in Strebendt (1974), a number of COBOL programs were analyzed using these techniques. There the memory hierarchy requirements became obvious. Also, the ability to execute one program on a number of successive, independent data sets was necessary. Again, little arithmetic was required. The control unit became a key to obtaining high performance—too much complexity in the control unit was a danger.

We have also attempted to exploit parallel and pipeline techniques in information retrieval and file-processing problems (Hollaar, 1975; Stellhorn, 1974). Here, since there are no standard programming languages, standard algorithms (e.g., list-merging) were studied.

It seems clear that by combining the control notions discussed in this chapter with various data structure transformations, other programming languages could be analyzed and good machine parameters discovered. For example, instead of arithmetic tree height reduction and fast recurrence handling methods, various string manipulations or tree and graph algorithms could be used—these could be interpreted in appropriate languages, e.g., SNOBOL, LISP, etc.

Another approach to machine design is to avoid programs and go directly to the algorithms themselves. We have carried out the direct analysis of several algorithms including (Sameh *et al.*, 1974a,b; Sameh and Kuck, 1975a,b). In general, better speedup results can be obtained in this way since one avoids the difficulties of programming language artifacts. In fact, while few nonlinear recurrences are found in real programs, we often are limited in obtaining faster numerical algorithms by nonlinear recurrences. By hand, the algorithm is reorganized into a potentially fast form, which contains a nonlinear recurrence and, hence, cannot be handled by known methods.

While some nonlinear recurrences can be treated analytically and others can be shown to be intractable, this area is generally not well understood.

The hand analysis of whole algorithms provides good nonlinear recurrence research problems. Of course, even if we cannot analytically speed up nonlinear recurrences, this does not mean that there is no hope. In fact, hardware tricks can be used to get around some nonlinearities. At the bit level, several examples of this are discussed in detail in Chen and Kuck(1975a), for example, binary multiplication.

To summarize, we have been discussing the structure of programs, the structure of machines, and the relation between the two. To discover ultimate-speed machines, or just to find low-cost, high-performance machine designs, such studies are important. By obtaining a better understanding of the structure of real programs we can determine good compiler algorithms for exotic machine organizations. Furthermore, there are benefits for standard machines; for example, we can hope to improve paging performance for virtual-memory machines by understanding the control and data flow. Also, by transforming a program into simpler forms—for example, removing IFs from loops and bringing out the array nature of programs—we can hope to aid programmers in understanding and debugging their programs. Finally, by viewing compilation in a broad way we can see that certain traditional speedup techniques of logic design are identical to methods useful in compilers for multioperation machines. These include tree height reduction and fast linear recurrence solving.

Acknowledgments

I am particularly indebted to S. C. Chen, Duncan H. Lawrie, Ahmed H. Sameh, and Ross A. Towle for discussions about these ideas.

References

Amdahl, G. M. (1967). Validity of the single processor approach to achieving large scale computing capabilities. *Proc. AFIPS Conf., 1967* pp. 483–485.

Baer, J. L., and Bovet, D. P. (1968). Compilation of arithmetic expressions for parallel computations. *Proc. IFIP Congr., 1968* pp. 340–346.

Baer, J. L., and Estrin, G. (1969). Bounds for maximum parallelism in a bilogic graph model of computations. *IEEE Trans. Comput.* **c-18,** 1012–1014.

Barnes, G., Brown, R., Kato, M., Kuck, D. J., Slotnick, D., and Stokes, R. (1968). The ILLIAC IV computer. *IEEE Trans. Comput.* **c-17,** 746–757.

Batcher, K. E. (1968). Sorting networks and their applications. *Proc. AFIPS Spring Jt. Comput. Conf., 1968* pp. 307–314.

Batcher, K. E. (1973). STARAN/RADCAP hardware architecture. *Proc. Sagamore Conf. Parallel Process., 1973* pp. 147–152.

Beatty, J. C. (1972). An axiomatic approach to code optimization for expressions. *J. Assoc. Comput. Mach.* **19,** 613–640.

Beneš, V. E. (1965). "Mathematical Theory of Connecting Networks and Telephone Traffic." Academic Press, New York.

Bernstein, A. (1966). Analysis of programs for parallel processing. *IEEE Trans. Electron. Comput.* **ec-15,** 757–763.

Bingham, H. W., Fisher, D. A., and Semon, W. L. (1966). "Detection of Implicit Computational Parallelism from Input-Output Sets," ECOM-02463-1, AD645438.

Bingham, H. W., Reigel, E. W., and Fisher, D. A. (1968). "Control Mechanisms for Parallelism in Programs," ECOM-02463-7.

Brent, R. (1974). The parallel evaluation of general arithmetic expressions. *J. Assoc. Comput. Mach.* **21**, 201–206.

Brent, R., and Towle, R. (1975). On the time required to parse an arithmetic expression for parallel processing. (Submitted for publication.)

Buchholz, W. (1962). "Planning a Computer System." McGraw-Hill, New York.

Budnik, P., and Kuck, D. J. (1971). The organization and use of parallel memories. *IEEE Trans. Comput.* **c-20**, 1566–1569.

Burnett, G. J., and Coffman, E. G., Jr. (1970). A study of interleaved memory systems. *Proc. AFIPS Spring Jt. Comput. Conf., 1970* pp. 467–474.

Burnett, G. J., and Coffman, E. G., Jr. (1973). A combinatorial problem related to interleaved memory systems. *J. Assoc. Comput. Mach.* **20**, 39–45.

Chang, D., Kuck, D. J., and Lawrie, D. (1976). On the effective bandwidth of parallel memories. (Submitted for publication in *IEEE Trans. Comput.*).

Chen, S. C. (1975). Speedup of iterative programs in multiprocessor systems. Rep. No. 75-694. Ph.D. Thesis, Department of Computing Science, University of Illinois, Urbana.

Chen, S. C., and Kuck, D. J. (1975a). Combinational circuit synthesis with time and component bounds. (Submitted for publication.)

Chen, S. C., and Kuck, D. J. (1975b). Time and parallel processor bounds for linear recurrence systems. *IEEE Trans. Comput.* **c-24**, 701–717.

Chen, S. C., and Sameh, A. H. (1975). On parallel triangular system solvers. *Sagamore Comput. Conf. Parallel Process., 1975* pp. 237–238.

Chen, S. C., Kuck, D. J., and Towle, R. (1975a). Control and data dependence in ordinary programs. (Submitted for publication.)

Chen, S. C., Kuck, D. J., and Towle, R. (1975b). Time and parallel processor bounds for Fortran-like loops. (Submitted for publication.)

Chen, T. C. (1971). Unconventional superspeed computer systems. *Proc. AFIPS Spring Jt. Comput. Conf., 1971* pp. 365–371.

Coffman, E. G., Jr., Burnett, G. J., and Snowdon, R. A. (1971). On the performance of interleaved memories with multiple-word bandwidths. *IEEE Trans. Comput.* **c-20**, 1570–1572.

Davis, E. W., Jr. (1972a). Concurrent processing of conditional jump trees. *Compcon 72, IEEE Comput. Soc. Conf. Proc., 1972* pp. 279–281.

Davis, E. W., Jr. (1972b). A multiprocessor for simulation applications. Rep. No. 72-527. Ph.D. Thesis, Department of Computing Science, University of Illinois, Urbana.

Estrin, G., and Turn, R. (1963). Automatic assignment of computations in a variable structure computer system. *IEEE Trans. Electron. Comput.* **ec-12**, 755–773.

Fisher, D. (1967). "Program Analysis for Multiprocessing," TR-67-2. Burroughs Corp.

Flynn, M. (1972). Some computer organizations and their effectiveness. *IEEE Trans. Comput.* **c-21**, 948–960.

Hellerman, H. (1967). "Computer System Principles." McGraw-Hill, New York.

Hintz, R. G., and Tate, D. P. (1972). Control Data STAR-100 processor design. *Proc. IEEE Comput. Soc. Conf., 1972* pp. 1–4.

Hollaar, L. A. (1975). A list merging processor for inverted file information retrieval systems. Rep. No. 75-762. Ph.D. Thesis, Department of Computing Science, University of Illinois, Urbana.

Hu, T. C. (1961). Parallel sequencing and assembly line problems. *Oper. Res.* **9**, 841–848.
Knuth, D. E. (1970). "An Empirical Study of FORTRAN Programs," Rep. No. CS-186. Department of Computing Science, Stanford University, Stanford, California.
Kraska, P. W. (1972). Parallelism exploitation and scheduling. Rep. No. 72-518. Ph.D. Thesis, Department of Computing Science, University of Illinois, Urbana.
Kuck, D. J. (1968). ILLIAC IV software and application programming. *IEEE Trans. Comput.* **c-17**, 758–770.
Kuck, D. J. (1973). Multioperation machine computational complexity. *In* "Complexity of Sequential and Parallel Numerical Algorithms" (J. Traub, ed.), pp. 17–47. Academic Press, New York.
Kuck, D. J. (1974). On the speedup and cost of parallel computation. *In* "Complexity of Computational Problem Solving" (R. Anderson and R. Brent, eds.). Australian National University, Canberra (to be published).
Kuck, D. J., and Maruyama, K. (1975). Time bounds on the parallel evaluation of arithmetic expressions. *SIAM J. Comput.* **4**, 147–162.
Kuck, D. J., and Muraoka, Y. (1974). Bounds on the parallel evaluation of arithmetic expressions using associativity and commutativity. *Acta Inf.* **3**, 203–216.
Kuck, D. J., Muraoka, Y., and Chen, S. C. (1972). On the number of operations simultaneously executable in FORTRAN-like programs and their resulting speed-up. *IEEE Trans. Comput.* **c-21**, 1293–1310.
Kuck, D. J., Budnik, P., Chen, S. C., Davis, E., Jr., Han, J., Kraska, P., Lawrie, D., Muraoka, Y., Strebendt, R., and Towle, R. (1974). Measurements of parallelism in ordinary FORTRAN programs. *IEEE Comput.* **7**, 37–46.
Kung, H. T. (1974). New algorithms and lower bounds for the parallel evaluation of certain rational expressions. *Proc. 6th Annu. ACM Symp. Theory Comput., 1974.*
Lamport, L. (1974). The parallel execution of DO loops. *Commun. ACM* **17**, 83–93.
Lawrie, D. (1973). Memory-processor connection networks. Rep. No. 73-557. Ph.D. Thesis, Department of Computing Science, University of Illinois, Urbana.
Lawrie, D. (1975). Access and alignment of data in an array processor. *IEEE Trans. Comput.* **c-24**, 1145–1155.
Martin, D., and Estrin, G. (1967). Models of computations and systems—evaluation of vertex probabilities in graph models of computations. *J. Assoc. Comput. Mach.* **14**, 281–299.
Maruyama, K. (1973). On the parallel evaluation of polynomials. *IEEE Trans. Comput.* **c-22**, 2–5.
Minsky, M. (1970). Form and content in computer science. *J. Assoc. Comput. Mach.* **17**, 197–215.
Muller, D. E., and Preparata, F. P. (1975). "Restructuring of Arithmetic Expressions for Parallel Evaluation," Rep. No. R-676. Coordinated Science Lab., University of Illinois, Urbana.
Muraoka, Y. (1971). Parallelism exposure and exploitation in programs. Rep. No. 71-424. Ph.D. Thesis, Department of Computing Science, University of Illinois, Urbana.
Muraoka, Y., and Kuck, D. J. (1973). On the time required for a sequence of matrix products. *Commun. ACM* **16**, 22–26.
Opferman, D. C., and Tsao-Wu, N. T. (1971). On a class of rearrangeable switching networks. *Bell Syst. Tech. J.* **50**, 1579–1618.
Pease, M. C. (1968). An adaptation of the fast Fourier transform for parallel processing. *J. Assoc. Comput. Mach.* **15**, 252–264.

Ravi, C. V. (1972). On the bandwidth and interference in interleaved memory systems. *IEEE Trans. Comput.* **c-21,** 899–901.

Russell, E. C. (1963). Automatic assignment of computational tasks in a variable structure computer. M.S. Thesis, University of California, Los Angeles.

Sameh, A. H., and Brent, R. P. (1975). Solving triangular systems on a parallel computer. (Submitted for publication in *SIAM J. Num. Anal.*).

Sameh, A. H., and Kuck, D. J. (1975a). Linear system solvers for parallel computers. (Submitted for publication.)

Sameh, A. H., and Kuck, D. J. (1975b). Rep. No. 75-701. Department of Computing Science, University of Illinois, Urbana.

Sameh, A. H., Chen, S. C., and Kuck, D. J. (1974a). Parallel direct Poisson and biharmonic solvers. (Submitted for publication in *Computing*).

Sameh, A. H., Chen, S. C., and Kuck, D. J. (1974b). Rep. No. 74-684. Department of Computing Science, University of Illinois, Urbana.

Senzig, D. (1967). Observations on high-performance machines. *Proc. AFIPS Fall Jt. Comput. Conf., 1967* pp. 791–799.

Stellhorn, W. H. (1974). A specialized computer for information retrieval. Rep. No. 74-637. Ph.D. Thesis, Department of Computing Science, University of Illinois, Urbana.

Strebendt, R. E. (1974). Program speedup through concurrent record processing. Rep. No. 74-638. Ph.D. Thesis, Department of Computing Science, University of Illinois, Urbana.

Swanson, R. C. (1974). Interconnections for parallel memories to unscramble p-ordered vectors. *IEEE Trans. Comput.* **c-23,** 1105–1115.

Towle, R. (1974). Control structures inside DO loops. Ph.D. Thesis proposal. Department of Computing Science, University of Illinois, Urbana.

Watson, W. J., and Carr, H. M. (1974). Operational experiences with the TI advanced scientific computer. *Natl. Comput. Conf., 1974* pp. 389–397.

Winograd, S. (1975). On the parallel evaluation of certain arithmetic expressions. *J. Assoc. Comput. Mach.* **22,** 477–492.

The Computational Study of Language Acquisition

LARRY H. REEKER

Department of Computer Science
University of Arizona
Tucson, Arizona

1. The Problem 181
   1.1 Grammatical Theories 182
   1.2 Structural Learning and Generalization 184
   1.3 Transformational Grammars 185
   1.4 Innateness 186
   1.5 Grammatical Inference 187
   1.6 Language-Learning Phenomena 190
2. Modeling Language Acquisition 191
   2.1 Noncomputational Models 191
   2.2 Computational Models 191
3. The Problem-Solving Theory 196
   3.1 Basic Features of the Theory 196
   3.2 An Exemplary Grammar and System 197
   3.3 An Example of Acquisition 207
   3.4 The Generalization Process 216
   3.5 Generalization and Transformations 222
4. Conclusion 223
5. Appendix: Grammar Representation 224
   5.1 Surface Representation 224
   5.2 The Semantic Mapping 226
   5.3 Semantic Dependency Notation 228
   References 235

1. The Problem

In its most straightforward form, the problem to which this chapter addresses itself is the following: How is it possible to supply to a computer program a set of utterances in some language and have the program produce as output a grammar that can generate not only the utterances supplied, but the rest of the language, as well? More specifically, however, we shall be interested in natural languages, such as English, where the grammar has both syntactic and semantic dimensions; and ultimately, we want the program to model the way that children acquire such languages. These last codicils provide more structure to the problem and, at the same time, complicate it. Since total success in the enterprise that we have outlined is some distance away, we shall explore some of the different approaches to the language acquisition problem and examine the utility of partial successes in the area. Among other things, it will be seen that the major problems of computational linguistics must be faced in the task of language acquisition simulation, and that more general problems of learning also become important.

In dealing with the syntactic and semantic dimensions of languages (the term "language" meaning natural language in this chapter, unless otherwise qualified), we are specifically excluding the phonological system (except for some brief remarks, to be included later). To divide the systems of language in this way entails the assumption that the details of phonological learning do not affect grammatical learning in any essential way. Such an assumption is widely held and seems to be warranted by observation. We shall also exclude from consideration the learning of the meanings of individual words (which we might call "semantic acquisition"). While semantic acquisition is part of language acquisition, the problem to which this chapter addresses itself is that of learning a grammar that maps sentences in a natural language into meaning representations. We might call this "grammatical acquisition" or "syntactic acquisition," or—having excluded phonological and semantic learning—merely "language acquisition."

1.1 Grammatical Theories

A basic problem of computational linguistics is to find three interacting components for languages and to describe each of them in a manner that is computationally tractable. These three components are: (1) a representation for the surface syntactic structure of the language; (2) a representation for the meanings expressible in the language; (3) a semantic mapping between the surface structure and the meanings (Fig. 1). Similarly, a human

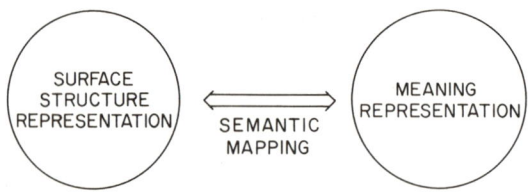

FIG. 1. The components of a natural language grammar.

speaker is able to produce a sentence corresponding to an idea or meaning, and to obtain meanings from sentences. Thus what he learns is, in fact, a complex set of correspondences between sentences and meanings.

Contemporary linguistic theories can shed some light on the space of possible grammatical theories, since some models have been shown to be inadequate for the complexities of natural languages. It is not necessarily true, however, that linguistic theories have any direct correspondence to the systems that are acquired by the human being. We can refer to the grammar that is acquired by a human as the "mental grammar," and since it is the mental grammar that will be of primary importance in this chapter, the term "grammar" used by itself will denote that construct, when there appears to be no danger of confusion.

For the surface structure description, a number of standard devices are available, including context-free and context-sensitive phrase structure grammars. These grammars generate sets of strings, along with structural descriptions for the strings in the set (the latter usually called "phrase markers"). For persons unfamiliar with these concepts, a short discussion is included in the Appendix. Transformational grammars, discussed below, are an economical alternative to phrase structure grammars.

The issue of meaning representation ("semantic representation" is also used in the literature) in a grammatical theory is one of immense importance; yet for the mental grammar, the meaning representation is a total unknown. As a conjecture, we might imagine that when a speaker of English hears "The chair is on the table," he may form some sort of image in his mind, although the image must be incomplete, since the sentence does not indicate whether the chair is standing or lying on its side, etc. For a number of obvious reasons, direct representation as an image is difficult within a computational system (or otherwise, for that matter, since it introduces all sorts of additional nonlinguistic problems). It should be possible to face the important issues of language acquisition with a simplified representation.

Meaning representations may involve the use of a notation that expresses meaning in terms of a small number of primitive elements, whose meanings are assumed to be known, together with the meanings of primitive relationships. It is possible, however to have a meaning representation in which the elements and relations are not totally primitive. In particular, it is possible to express the meaning of one language in terms of another, which may be a natural language or an artificial one. For most purposes, it is desirable that the meaning representation be carefully defined itself, perhaps in terms of the truth value of each proposition within it, or some other very simple representation. There are, therefore, various levels of meaning representation, some more primitive than others, which might be chosen as a component of a system. It is probably not essential in modeling early language acquisition that the representation be extremely primitive, but it is essential that it be rich enough.

From a computational point of view (and perhaps from any point of view), the most sophisticated meaning representation is that of Schank (1969, 1973). The representation used later in this chapter and discussed in detail in the appendix is similar to that of Schank, but is preferred for illustrative purposes because it is simpler. It also has been used within a computational system discussed later.

1.2 Structural Learning and Generalization

Postponing for the time a further consideration of grammatical specification, let us consider the case of an individual, say Alice Smith, acquiring a grammar of English. Whatever Alice's mental grammar will eventually consist of, it must not have been totally present at birth, since Alice could equally well have been brought up in a Hopi or Vietnamese community, in which case she would have learned Hopi or Vietnamese, rather than English. Therefore, the grammar of English must have been induced from utterances heard by Alice. Yet even if Alice were to remember every sentence she had heard, along with its meaning, that would not account for Alice's eventual ability to understand and produce sentences that she had never previously heard. (Parenthetically, if she were to store all sentences she heard, the retrieval problems would soon become intractable.) Alice's grammar must consist of some more general knowledge that she has obtained from her experiences with English sentences.

The sentences "He walked" and "He talked" are both of the form "He X," where X represents either "walked" or "talked," and this fact can be reflected in the surface grammar

$$S \rightarrow he\ X, \quad X \rightarrow walked\ |\ talked$$

Notice, however, that such a grammar cannot be written until there has been a structural analysis of the sentence. To see this fact, consider the sentence "He walked and talked." This might be expressed as "He X" also, but in the absence of any evidence to the contrary, the language learner might just as well analyze it as "He walked and X," or even "He walked X," which would lead to a bad generalization, or to no generalization at all.

As this process of structural analysis goes on, it will interact with generalization to form a surface grammar; but the formation of the surface grammar must also be chastened by the semantic rules that form a part of the mental grammar. The sentences "They eat fish," "They may fish," and "They and I fish" can be generated by the following very economical surface grammar:

$$S \rightarrow \text{They X fish}, \qquad X \rightarrow \text{eat} \mid \text{may} \mid \text{and I}$$

Clearly, any economy gained in such a surface specification is no compensation for the difficulty that will be encountered in trying to specify the semantics of these sentences, if that semantic specification must be based on the surface grammar. (It has often been said that the surface grammar should specify a "reasonable" or "intuitive" phrase marker for each sentence generated. The necessity of a semantic mapping has a lot to do with what might be considered "reasonable" or "intuitive.")

The process of determining the structure of the sentences that are observed is an important part of the language learning process, and it is not easy to see how it is done. It is this process that the author has referred to as "structural learning" and that term will be used in this chapter. The process of generalization also has its mysteries. How might a decision be made to form a generalization from "He walked" and "She talked"? Or should such a generalization be made? One of the first lessons that is learned in attempting computer simulations of language acquisition is that generalization is very easily overdone. Using the "obvious" sorts of heuristics and any reasonably large input, some very strange sentences will quickly be generated by the resulting grammars!

1.3 Transformational Grammars

Linguistic transformations take phrase markers and map them into other phrase markers, as in the active–passive transformation (Fig. 2). Arguments can be made for transformations in the surface (syntactic) representation, and as devices for specifying the semantic mapping.

At the syntactic level, it can be argued that transformations describe the sentences of a language more elegantly and economically than other devices, such as context-free grammars. This argument, as presented by Chomsky in "Syntactic Structures" (1957), led to the original popularity

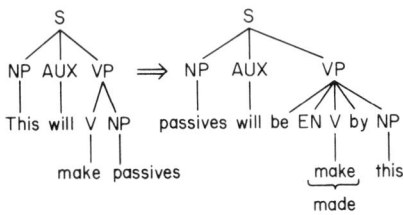

FIG. 2. Example of the active–passive transformation.

of transformational grammars among theoretical linguists. Certainly anyone who has tried to write a context-free grammar (or even a context-sensitive grammar) for use in a computational situation will appreciate the economy afforded by transformations. In the active–passive case, for instance, it is necessary, in a context-free grammar, to write separate sets of rules for active and passive sentences that largely duplicate one another. The alternative, to write one set for, say, active sentences, then to specify that passives are like actives except that subject and object noun phrases are switched around, etc., is essentially transformational.

An argument can also be made for a set of transformations as the device that performs the mapping of surface structure to semantic representation. This argument is partially implicit in Katz and Postal (1964) and Chomsky (1965), where transformations are combined with "interpretation rules" as the mapping device, and is carried to completion by the "generative semanticists" (e.g., Lakoff, 1970; McCawley, 1968a; Postal, 1970), who argue that it is not possible to separate aspects of economical syntactic specification from semantic mapping.

Although the transformational literature contains references to a "language acquisition device" (Chomsky, 1965) and apparent references to mental grammars, the persuasive arguments for transformational grammars are arguments for a particular "theory of language," rather than for a mental grammar. While it does not appear that constraints on human intellectual organization or human learning abilities preclude the internalization of a transformational grammar, it may be that they facilitate the learning of some other sort of grammar, so it must not be assumed that a mental grammar must be transformational. Nevertheless, the arguments from economy of syntactic description seem to say something about the space of possible mental grammars: A context-free grammar appears quite adequate to deal with early syntactic acquisition, yet the number of rules that would be necessary to characterize even the surface syntax of a four-year-old's language is so large as to suggest that richer mechanisms must be available within the mental grammar. Nobody has presented strong evidence as to just what these mechanisms are.

1.4 Innateness

In acquiring a grammar, the child must bring to bear some learning mechanisms, and the purpose of language acquisition modeling is to delineate hypotheses as to the nature of these mechanisms. A basic philosophical controversy through the ages has centered on the question of whether learning mechanisms actually begin with a clean slate and discover knowledge in the outside world (extreme empiricism) or whether the forms of knowledge are so highly constrained that learning is largely a process of using the environment to stimulate already present knowledge (extreme rationalism).

A less extreme rationalist position on language learning would be that humans are predisposed to acquire languages of a highly specific sort; that Navaho, Hungarian, Swahili, and Maori share features that make them learnable, as against various otherwise reasonable but unlearnable alternative (nonexistent) languages (Chomsky, 1965). A "typical" empiricist would maintain that any predisposition to learn languages with features of existent languages, as against other conceivable languages, is dictated by the means of discovering knowledge—the learning mechanisms themselves. He might also grant that there are limitations upon the way that the human brain organizes knowledge, and that information about these limitations can be obtained by experimentation and observation.

As the less extreme positions are taken, it becomes more difficult to differentiate the empiricist from the rationalist on the issue of innateness. Within the context of linguistics, the rationalist position has sometimes been identified with the claim that innate knowledge of a specifically linguistic sort is needed to acquire language, in addition to any general learning propensities or predispositions to structure knowledge (other than linguistic knowledge) in particular ways. In this form, the author has argued elsewhere, the claim is not supported by the evidence (Reeker, 1975). Many of the supposed arguments for this "neorationalist" position have been supported by appeal to impoverished models of acquisition—models that do not take account of all of the information available to the language learner.

Although there is still controversy concerning the amount of innate linguistic knowledge that must be brought to bear in the language acquisition task, it is probably safe to say that nobody really knows the answer. The position taken in this chapter is to try to model the acquisition process without presupposing any purely linguistic knowledge. Some of the mechanisms of the models most certainly place conditions on the types of languages that can be learned; but these mechanisms also look general enough to deal with other types of learning.

1.5 Grammatical Inference

The problem of acquiring a surface description of a language based upon a set of utterances is known as the grammatical inference problem. Again, it is not the grammar of Fig. 1 that is being acquired in grammatical inference, but the surface structure description alone. The literature of grammatical inference, because it is dealing with a somewhat different task from what we mean by language acquisition, tells us little about how language acquisition takes place.

Some of the first work on the grammatical inference problem was due to Gold (1967), who defined the concept of "identifiability in the limit." A grammatical inference procedure is said to identify a language L in the limit if it eventually produces a single grammar that generates L. Gold showed that for a wide variety of languages (in fact, the recursive languages), such a procedure exists. He not only gives such a procedure, but shows that there is no procedure available that is faster in every case than the one he gives. The procedure requires negative instances also (strings not in L), and Gold shows that without these negative instances, even very simple (finite state) languages cannot be consistently identified in the limit by *any procedure*. [A very fine survey of the literature of grammatical inference is that of Biermann and Feldman (1972).]

How much of this is relevant to the language acquisition problem? At first glance, it appears that a good deal of it is relevant; a closer examination reveals that most of it is not. Certainly, a syntactic component must be inferred by the language learner; that is, he does internalize a knowledge of which sentences are grammatical and which are not. But the situation in which he finds himself is a different one, because of the fact that he has semantic information available. Thus, decisions regarding both structural analysis and generalization can be made on the basis of this additional information. In addition, of course, not only the surface syntax is being learned, but the semantic mapping. It thus appears that Gold's results concerning the learning procedure are not directly relevant to our problem. A number of more practical procedures are available for inferring grammars of various subsets of the context-free languages, but all deal with surface structure only.

Gold's negative result, however, may have more to say about language acquisition. What it says is that information concerning negative instances is needed. One source for such negative information is explicit corrections, of course. The child is told that a sentence that he produces is wrong. Observation seems to indicate that such explicit corrections are not frequent enough to play a major role in acquisition (Brown, 1973). Another source of negative information is available if the child's sentences are not understood, or produce the wrong response. Yet for acquisition to take place, it does not appear to be wholly necessary for the child to be able to speak. How, then, does the child acquire the negative information needed to correct mistakes of overgeneralization?

It seems to be the case that the child actually makes fewer mistakes of generalization than could be expected, and that when he does, the mistaken forms are gradually replaced by equivalent forms in more common use. Thus the form "he goed" is replaced gradually by "he went" without any explicit corrections, merely because the common form that the child hears is the latter. This is not to say that corrections never have any effect, merely that the child does not keep using each form that he induces, but replaces early forms with new ones.

A fundamental difference between the type of situation postulated by Gold and the situation of the child acquiring grammar is that the child does not directly acquire full sentences that will remain in the syntactic portion of his mental grammar. To put this another way, in acquiring the surface syntax of L, the child acquires a succession of grammars $G_1, G_2, \ldots,$ where it need not be the case that $L(G_i) \subseteq L$, or even that $L(G_i) \cap L$ is nonnull. More concretely, such sentences as "daddy milk," "daddy bring milk," etc., may be generated by the earlier grammars, although they are most definitely not a part of L; and these child sentences along with their meaning representations form not wrong sentences to be rejected, but sentences to be built on in acquiring a grammar for L. A different type of approximation is taking place from that envisioned in the surface grammars of grammatical inference systems. We shall see that the difference between acquiring "adult" sentences and acquiring "child languages" that eventually get more like adult languages carries over to computer simulations. Systems that seek to acquire full sentences of the language will be termed "sentence-acquiring" systems.

Within the area of grammatical inference we should also take note of the work of Hamburger, Wexler, and Culicover, who have considered the inference of transformational grammars. Wexler and Hamburger (1973) reach the conclusion that, using Gold's learnability criteria, a transformational grammar (even based upon a fixed context-free base and subject to several limitations on form) is not identifiable from surface data alone.

Hamburger and Wexler (1973) consider the same task, with the learner given pairs, consisting of surface string (but not surface phrase marker) and base phrase marker. In some theories, the base phrase marker contains all the information necessary for semantic interpretation (or may even be a form of meaning representation), so this could be equivalent to providing surface string-meaning pairs. They show that this information leads to identifiability, and they provide a procedure guaranteed to achieve that end. The procedure is basically this: The deep phrase marker is acted upon by the available transformations (initially, none) to produce a surface form, and this is compared to the given surface form. If it is identical, then no change is made in the grammar. If an identical surface form is not produced, then either a new transformation will be added or one that was applied will be removed from the grammar. Notice that this procedure learns grammars for full sentences, rather than for child language.

An interesting aspect of the work of this group is the series of publications beginning with Culicover and Wexler (1973), which seeks to derive constraints on possible transformations from their theory of learnability. Ultimately, language acquisition models will provide constraints on the form of possible grammars for natural language. This is important because, as Peters (1972) has pointed out, the lack of such constraints means that "the principal available type of empirical data cannot play the decisive role one might expect it to in selecting either the particular grammars or the theory of grammars."

1.6 Language-Learning Phenomena

The literature on child language is now very extensive, containing statistical studies, experiments, longitudinal studies of individual children, and a good deal of anecdotal material. The interested reader can gain access to this literature through Brown (1973), Dale (1972), or Bowerman (1973), among other sources. Many clues to the phenomena of interest have been included in the discussion above [for a more thorough discussion, see Reeker (1974)].

The earliest child language consists of single words. The child learns both a phonetic representation and a meaning for these words. (We will refer to the learning of individual word meanings as semantic acquisition, to distinguish it from learning a grammar—syntactic acquisition—although the latter task, as specified earlier, also deals with meanings.)

Phonological and semantic acquisition continue as the child learns to put words together. It may be that the first combinations of two words are merely formed by juxtaposition of words representing two meanings that the child wants to express simultaneously, without any reference to a mental grammar. Some of the early two- and three-word utterances are also holophrases, learned in a manner analogous to a single word. But at some point, a systematic knowledge of a language begins to form; and although this language is not the same as the adult language, it serves the child's needs as he develops successively more "adultlike" languages. Eventually, of course, the mental grammar is capable of producing and understanding full adult sentences (for purposes of this statement we include various sentence fragments among the sentences also). Jesperson (1922) quotes an old Slavonic proverb, "If you wish to talk well, you must murder the language first." This proverb applies aptly to the child's early attempts to talk.

2. Modeling Language Acquisition

2.1 Noncomputational Models

A number of models of syntax learning based on conditioning have been proposed by behavioral psychologists (Skinner, 1957; Jenkins and Palermo, 1964; Osgood, 1963; Piezer and Olmstead, 1969; Braine, 1963). These are really psychological theories of surface grammar inference with assumptions enough different from what we have assumed as the task of syntactic acquisition that it is difficult to fit these into the same framework [for an attempt, see Reeker (1974)]. They appear, if anything, to account for possible ways in which a grammar becomes internalized, rather than how it is discovered, although some of them address the learning of positions in a sentence (e.g., Braine, 1963). All of these models assume reinforcement of correct production by the child.

Linguists' models have tended to stress the paradigm of linguistic field work: observe and compare utterances, form hypotheses concerning grammars, test those hypotheses. They have also, as mentioned earlier, tended to contain a significant portion of innate linguistic knowledge. Again, they have been primarily of a grammatical inference sort, although with more concern for generating an "appropriate" syntactic structure (which, as pointed out earlier, is a nod toward the semantic mapping). Within the hypothesis testing paradigm, there has generally been little concern for how the hypothesis testing component might function. Certainly it is not a conscious process. There has also been too little concern with the role of the child's emerging grammar in helping him to acquire a later grammar. [For a critique of Chomsky's writings in this respect, see McCawley (1968b) and Reeker (1974).]

2.2 Computational Models

We will now briefly review a series of computational models of the language acquisition process. These models share the usual virtues of computational models, in addition to the fact that they can be run to simulate the acquisition process. They also share some of the deficiencies and dangers of the computer simulation approach (Chandrasekaran and Reeker, 1974). In the field of language acquisition research, however, the available computational models represent the most explicit available models. Given the apparent complexity of the language acquisition task, it may be that computational models are not only helpful, but necessary to an understanding of the process.

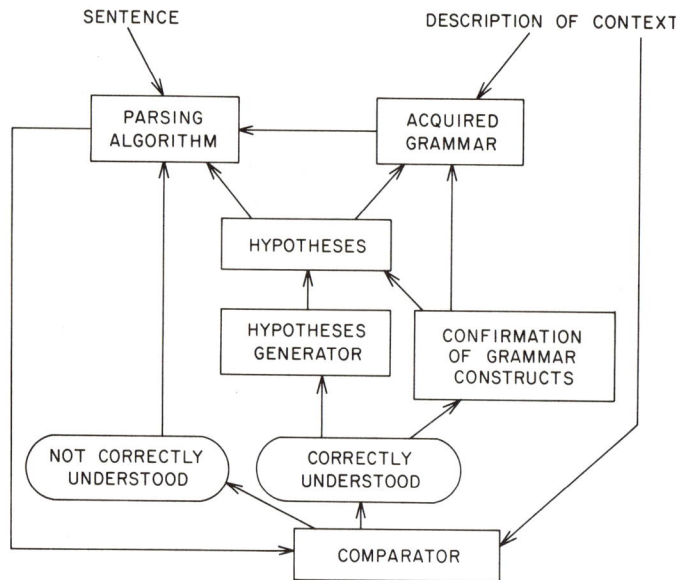

Fig. 3. Kelley's language acquisition system.

2.2.1 Kelley's System

A pioneering effort in the field is that of Kelley (1967). Kelley's model (Fig. 3) is firmly rooted in the hypothesis testing tradition, with no outside reinforcement required. Three stages, each characterized by a different initial hypothesis, are considered:

1. Each sentence consists of a surface structure "thing" with the (deep structure) function "concrete reference of the sentence."
2. A second type of lexical item, "action," and another semantic function, "modifier of the sentence," are available.
3. A new functional relation, "subject of the sentence," is introduced.

Kelley's system is interesting in a number of ways. It is not a sentence-acquiring system, but learns successively more accurate approximations to adult sentences. Semantics are embodied in the notions of functional relationship and type of lexical item, although it is not clear that the particular relationships chosen are the appropriate ones. One drawback to the system is the fact that adult sentences must be fully understood by the child in order either to generate hypotheses or augment the grammar. It appears that most adult sentences are imperfectly understood by children in the early acquisitional stages.

There is no procedure for using negative information to disconfirm anything that has been learned, but only for failing to confirm. Rules that are not used (i.e., reconfirmed) are assumed to drop out eventually, which, as pointed out earlier, is an effect not considered in Gold's studies that may obviate the use of negative examples.

The program has access to a parse of the adult input sentence, which probably gives it more information than is realistic. This is assumed to model the available semantic information, which raises questions about the close relationship between the grammar and the functional relationships. Nevertheless, Kelley's system deserves more attention than it has obtained.

2.2.2 Siklóssy's System

Siklóssy (1972) presents a program for learning a natural language by presentation of graded pairs of sentences and corresponding meanings, analogous to the presentation in a language-through-pictures text, or for that matter, to an immersion language-learning situation. The meanings in Siklóssy's program are expressed in terms of a formal language similar to that of Reichenbach (1947), and similar in appearance to a representation in prefix form of the semantic dependency trees used later in this chapter (see appendix). The central structure of the program is a semantic mapping *pattern*, which matches a formal language (meaning) structure and specifies a translation into the natural language (a surface structure).

When all is said and done, Siklóssy's program is unable to acquire a very extensive language. Part of the problem may be that it is a sentence-acquiring program, intended as a model of an adult learning a second language. One of the advantages of the child language learner, of course, is that he can use his incomplete versions of the sentences in the language, omitting the informationless portions, whereas the second-language learner may encounter much less sympathy when he "murders the language." The careful sequence of presentation used in Siklóssy's examples should help to overcome some of the difficulties thus engendered, but it is clearly (as pointed out by Siklóssy) not enough. Additionally, the theory of language embodied in the pattern-matching-and-interpretation feature is a very simple one, which might work for early acquisition but clearly has trouble with anything very complex. Inclusion of a more extensive theory would undoubtedly improve the learning, although it might result in severe time problems. It is an interesting feature of the program that rules of surface syntactic structure are intermixed with the semantic mapping rules.

The most interesting and important thing about Siklóssy's model is not its performance in actual simulation, but the underlying hypotheses involving the presentation and analysis of corresponding syntactic and semantic structures in acquisition. These were obtained, in part, at least, by Siklóssy's examination of his own intuitions concerning extensive second-language learning experiences. Clearly, there are similarities between these experiences and the phenomena of child language acquisition, though there are some differences as well.

2.2.3 Anderson's System

An interesting computer simulation of language acquisition is described in Anderson (1974, 1975). The program is called LAS and uses as a meaning representation a version of the HAM memory system described in Anderson and Bower's "Human Associative Memory" (1973). Grammars learned by LAS are basically context free, but to facilitate processing, they are encoded in a restricted form of network grammar (Woods, 1970; Simmons, 1973). The network also acts to perform the semantic mapping; that is, it translates from the HAM network into the sentence, and vice versa. The overall scheme of LAS is shown in Fig. 4.

The induction portion of LAS is the portion labeled LEARNMORE in Fig. 4. The tasks to which LEARNMORE addresses itself are structural learning and generalization. LEARNMORE receives as input a sentence and a HAM structure expressing the meaning of the sentence (actually, some structural information about the sentence also has to be given), and it produces a network grammar that encodes both surface structure and semantic mapping. This portion of the program preserves generalizations in the grammar as new sentences are added and merges rules or components

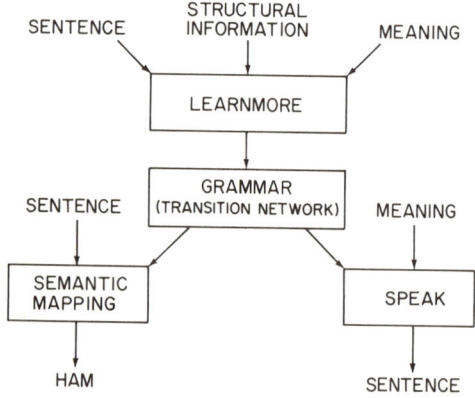

FIG. 4. Anderson's language acquisition system.

of rules if they serve identical semantic functions. A generalization program tries further to merge rules (networks).

Anderson's program is a sentence-learning program, but in many other respects, it is similar to the PST program discussed below in more detail. LAS is part of an ongoing experimental project, and it is reasonable to expect further important developments from that project. An informative presentation of the problems of generalization is contained in Anderson (1974), along with some ideas for their solution. Again, similar ideas are discussed below in connection with PST.

2.2.4 Other Systems

A program that uses problem solving in language acquisition is that of Harris (1972). This program is written within the context of a "robot," equipped with preprogrammed capabilities. These capabilities form the semantic concepts to which utterances must be related by the grammar. Learning takes place in three separate phases. The first phase of Harris' program pairs words and concepts. It does not appear to be a realistic model of the child's learning situation, but it does provide the sorts of pairings that the child needs for later acquisition; so it might be considered as more of an initialization process for a model of later acquisition. Such phrases as "right of" are considered to be idioms, and treated holophrastically, which begs some interesting questions.

Phase 2, the grammatical acquisition portion, is given as input pairs consisting of a sentence and a representation of the "parts of speech" of the words in the sentence. The "parts of speech" are more or less meaning oriented [a kind of "semantic counterpart of syntax," in the sense of Thompson (1963)]. This fact should simplify the overall grammar but is simply not realistic either with respect to a plausible description for a natural language or to input actually received by children. Harris' program is a sentence-acquiring program.

A system with the acronym METQA (for "Mechanical Translator and Question Answerer") is discussed by Jordan (1972). The program is based on an associative network. The translation-learning phase is of some interest, in that the input is a string from the source language and another from the target language (i.e., the one into which the source language text is to be translated). The target language sentence could be considered to be a meaning representation (although another natural language provides a rather complex meaning representation). The system is an unusual one, but its results are not particularly impressive (perhaps because the translation task is a rather complex one). It would be interesting to see the approach applied to first-language acquisition.

McMaster (1975) has described a projected Comprehensive Language Acquisition Program (CLAP). A subset called VAS (Vocabulary Acquisition System) is described in more detail. VAS works within a "blocks world" environment similar to that of Winograd (1973). VAS focuses on the problem of acquiring initial word–concept pairs and is interesting from that point of view. It has no syntactic acquisition capabilities. The remainder of CLAP (the portion that would acquire syntax) is based on a description of possible mechanisms of acquisition by Schwarcz (1967). In this author's view, McMaster's proposed system is trying to deal with several types of learning at once, and the result is an overly complex system in which it is difficult to discern a clear model for any of the aspects of learning. There are nevertheless some interesting ideas in McMaster's report, as in the Schwarcz article.

3. The Problem-Solving Theory

The problem-solving theory (PST) (Reeker, 1971) holds that natural language syntax acquisition is a product of the child's attempts to use and understand the language. The current computer implementation is the second in what is envisioned as a series of successively more detailed simulations, or "instances," of PST. Some components of the present system (e.g., the reduction component) are only empirically based approximations at present, and will eventually be replaced with simulations of postulated underlying processes. The simulation project for the problem-solving theory is thus taking what is sometimes described as a "top-down" approach to systems building. A discussion of extensions to the present system may be found in Reeker (1974).

3.1 Basic Features of the Theory

According to PST, the child acquires a succession of mental grammars through his attempts to connect the surface structure of the sentences that he hears to a meaning representation. At any time t, he tries to make this connection through his own grammar at time t, and if learning takes place, he has a new grammar at time $t + 1$. The changes made in the grammar are a reflection of changes made in the child's individual sentences, in order to bring them in closer accord with what the child is able to perceive of the adult sentence. A meaning description, which both constrains the child's production and provides an appropriate semantic mapping for any new structures produced, is given along with an "adult" sentence input.

The semantic mapping is specified from surface structure to meaning representation, and the present system uses a rather laborious process to go in the other direction (meaning to surface). The notation used for the mapping and for the meaning representation is discussed in the appendix.

The expository device used below is to provide a grammar at time t and to see how it is modified by the input, providing a new grammar sometime later. Since primary attention is being paid to structural learning, generalizations are preserved, but no new ones are added. In a real situation, of course, generalization would take place within the same time span as the structural learning. Some alternative approaches to various of the subsystems are discussed, but those chosen reflect those used in the present simulation instance.

3.2 An Exemplary Grammar and System

The particular mental grammar that we shall assume at the beginning of this illustration generates only a finite language. One might consider this grammar to be only an illustrative fragment of a larger grammar, although children certainly do exhibit finite grammars at some point in time. It may also be relevant that grammarians have found motivation for including recursion only with respect to embedding sentences in the deep structure—and embedding is a relatively late acquisitional phenomenon.

Although these considerations may lend plausibility to the example, our primary interest is in providing some mental grammar that constrains the child's sentential output, so that we may consider how the grammar might be augmented on the basis of input tokens. The grammar below will be called IG (for "initial grammar"). It reflects a mixture of under- and overgeneralization.

We first provide a surface syntax for IG, in standard context-free notation, as follows:

$$S \rightarrow N_0 V_0 \mid N_1 N_2 \mid MN \mid N$$
$$N_0 \rightarrow \text{he} \mid \text{doggy} \mid N_1$$
$$N_1 \rightarrow N_3 \mid M_3$$
$$N_3 \rightarrow \text{Daddy} \mid \text{Mommy}$$
$$N_2 \rightarrow \text{sock}$$
$$M \rightarrow M_1 \mid M_2$$
$$M_1 \rightarrow \text{big} \mid \text{blue} \mid \text{more}$$
$$M_2 \rightarrow \text{that}$$
$$M_3 \rightarrow \text{my}$$
$$V_0 \rightarrow \text{bye-bye}$$
$$N \rightarrow \text{boat} \mid \text{man} \mid \text{flower}$$

In order to specify semantic correspondences, we need some additional notation. Let us assume that primitive concepts (primitive for the purpose of this example, that is) are denoted by uppercase English words. These are joined together, using a semantic dependency notation, to form the complex concepts expressed by surface strings. The semantic dependency notation, explored in more detail in Reeker (1975), is stripped to its bare essentials, with selectors, higher performatives, and time arguments omitted, for the purpose of the example. The semantics of a particular class, represented by a sequence of nonterminals W in the surface grammar is denoted $\text{Sem}(W)$. In cases where W is a single nonterminal symbol that appears as the left-hand side of a rule

$$W \to W_1 \mid W_2 \mid \ldots$$

we will write $\text{Sem}(W \to W_1)$, $\text{Sem}(W \to W_2)$, etc. The notation $\text{Sem}(W)$ means that one of the $\text{Sem}(W \to W_i)$ will be chosen. These situations should be amply illustrated by IG, whose semantics are expressed as

$$\text{Sem}(S \to N_0 V_0) = \begin{array}{c} \text{Sem}(V_0) \\ | \\ \text{Sem}(N_0) \end{array}$$

$$\text{Sem}(S \to N_1 N_2) = \begin{array}{c} \text{BELONG (to)} \\ \diagup \quad \diagdown \\ \text{Sem}(N_2) \quad \text{Sem}(N_1) \end{array}$$

$$\text{Sem}(S \to MN) = \begin{array}{c} \text{Sem}(M) \\ | \\ \text{Sem}(N) \end{array}$$

$$\text{Sem}(S \to N) = \text{Sem}(N)$$

$$\text{Sem}(\text{bye-bye}) = \text{GO.OUT}$$

The remainder of the semantics is straightforward: If q is a terminal string and Q is the same string in uppercase letters, then $\text{Sem}(W \to q) = Q$. If q is nonterminal, then $\text{Sem}(W \to q) = \text{Sem}(q)$.

The instance of PST which we shall use to modify IG has a form shown in Fig. 5. As the diagram indicates, the meaning derived from the situation, and sometimes from portions of the adult sentence, is used in consulting the grammar to produce the child's version of the adult sentence (ChS and AdS, respectively). The reduced sentence (RS) also plays a role in the process, helping to select appropriate lexical items.

The reduced sentence and child sentence are compared, and if a difference is obtained, the table of connections and changes is consulted. This table provides a change in ChS that will bring it more closely in line with RS, and it also indicates a grammatical change. The situational semantics determine the correlated semantics for any new surface grammatical structures. Below we consider in more detail some of these features.

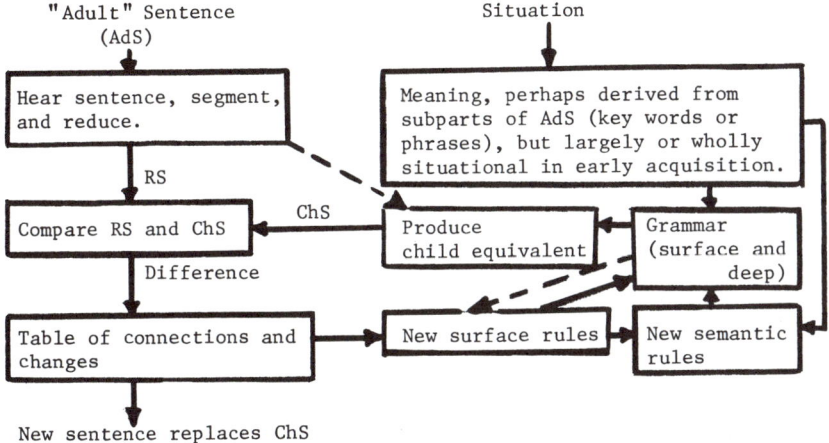

Fig. 5. Components of PST and their interactions.

3.2.1 The Reduction Process

Upon hearing an utterance by an adult (or another child, for that matter, although we will use the term "adult sentence" throughout this discussion), a child will often vocalize an imitation of the adult sentence. These imitations tend to be in a shortened form, presumably because of limitations on the child's short-term memory. In PST, these reductions (not necessarily enunciated) are important in providing sentences short enough for comparison with the child's own productions. The question to which we must now turn our attention is, "How are the reductions made?"

One possibility is that reductions are performed after analyzing the adult sentences through some sort of grammatical process. Such a "reduction grammar" need not be a grammar of the sort that PST is designed to acquire, that is, a means of connecting surface structure to semantics. It might be induced by the surface features alone, coupled with a distinction between meaningless and meaningful constructions. We will not detail such a procedure, however, because we feel that the process of reduction is more fruitfully described as a heuristic process. [For some recent thoughts on reduction models, see Clark (1975).]

In this instance, we have avoided the complexities of the reduction process, using a set of empirically derived rules for children's reductions:

(1) Eliminate pure function words and inflections,
(2) Eliminate any meaningless (to the child) words,
(3) Eliminate the initial portion of the sentence.

These heuristics are applied as long as the observed sentence is too long for the short-term memory, providing an effect that we might characterize as "filtering," as opposed to deliberate reduction.

If the PST presents anything like the correct picture of acquisition, as we contend it does, then this filtering process is very important and deserves a careful empirical investigation. Is it really the process that is reflected in surface reductions, as we have assumed? Can more definite heuristics be given? The fact that adults can do a good job of producing childlike reductions (after a bit of practice) indicates that there are some fairly definite heuristics available. It has, however, been observed by the author that two different reductions of the same sentence will be uttered within a few minutes of one another (e.g., "You want Daddy's pen?" repeated as both "want pen" and "Daddy pen"—both accompanied by reaching). This fact may indicate that the child has learned something, but it may also indicate that the heuristics are applied in an unordered manner, that situational context may change the meaningfulness of words, or that slight differences in stress or intonation in the adult sentence can influence the reductions. Different reductions may turn out to give alternate paths of grammar acquisition, but some of them may also lead nowhere; that is, the problem solving fails.

3.2.2 Matching the Reduced Sentence

The process by which the child sentence is generated and matched to the reduction is itself an important aspect of PST. We have said that the child has obtained some feeling for the meaning of the reduced adult sentence, through context, individual words, and perhaps other aspects of the sentence. Therefore, he can presumably use these semantics to produce a surface approximation (including the structural description of this approximation, which he will keep around for use in producing the new grammatical rules). Since he also has a string of words in his memory (the reduced sentence itself), he may try to parse that string or, failing that, to parse variations on it (systematically deleting portions or permuting portions, etc.). These, then, are the polar alternatives, which we shall label as semantics-driven and syntax-driven, respectively.

It should be clear that the semantics-driven approach will have to consult the surface string in order to produce an approximation, rather than a mere paraphrase. In the syntax-driven process, the semantics must also be consulted, since we require in general (the exception being analogy—see discussion below) that the approximation have a semantic tree (meaning representation) identical to a subtree (preferably a whole tree, otherwise a proper subtree) of the semantic tree for the (reduced) adult sentence.

Figure 6 gives a slight oversimplification of the present system's syntax-driven approach. The "analogy" portion is not implemented at present; instead, the match fails at that point. The basic idea is to match as much of the reduced sentence as possible. If the reduction is AwB and the approximation is AB, then PST tries to insert the string w. But it may be that $\mathrm{Cl}(AB)$, $\mathrm{Cl}(A)$, $\mathrm{Cl}(w)$, and $\mathrm{Cl}(B)$ are not all classes that occur, in which case PST will fail. If w is a single new lexical item, it may be added to the child's vocabulary as a class; more precisely, if length$(w) = 1$, then add a new class $\mathrm{CL}(w) = X_w \rightarrow w$.*

3.2.3 Comparison and Difference Reduction

As indicated in Fig. 5, the child sentence and the reduced sentence are compared, yielding a difference that is remedied in a manner indicated by the table of connections and changes (Table I). This table also provides a grammatical change and can thus be considered as the heart of the structural learning system. In Table I, which is used in this instance of PST, the first column indicates the difference as a schematic form of the reduced sentence, followed by a diagonal, followed by a schema of ChS. The sentence change is indicated in English in the second column. In the third column is given the associated surface grammar change. The notation, using $\mathrm{Cl}(x)$ as a class containing x, is explained below. In general, W, X, Y, and Z could be strings of lexical items. However, only single lexical items (including inflectional morphs and holophrases) are added, replaced, deleted, or permuted.

The following additional provisions pertain to the table of connections and changes:

(1) $\mathrm{Cl}(W)$, where W is a string, represents the largest class containing W; thus it stands for the highest nonterminal dominating only the string W in some tree of the grammar—when it appears on the *left-hand side* of a rule.

(2) $\mathrm{Cl}(W)$ represents the smallest class containing W if it appears on the *right-hand side* of a rule.

(3) If an appropriate class is not found within the mental grammar [to match $\mathrm{Cl}(W)$], it is added, provided W is a *single lexical item* (this includes

---

* Most sentences that the child hears will result in failure for one reason or another: lack of even partial understanding, distraction (which spoils the reduction process), or a surface grammar not advanced enough to allow solution. This feature of PST is quite plausible, in view of the slowness of early syntactic acquisition. In fact, if it were not for these failures, the mechanisms of PST might be powerful enough to produce learning of unrealistic rapidity.

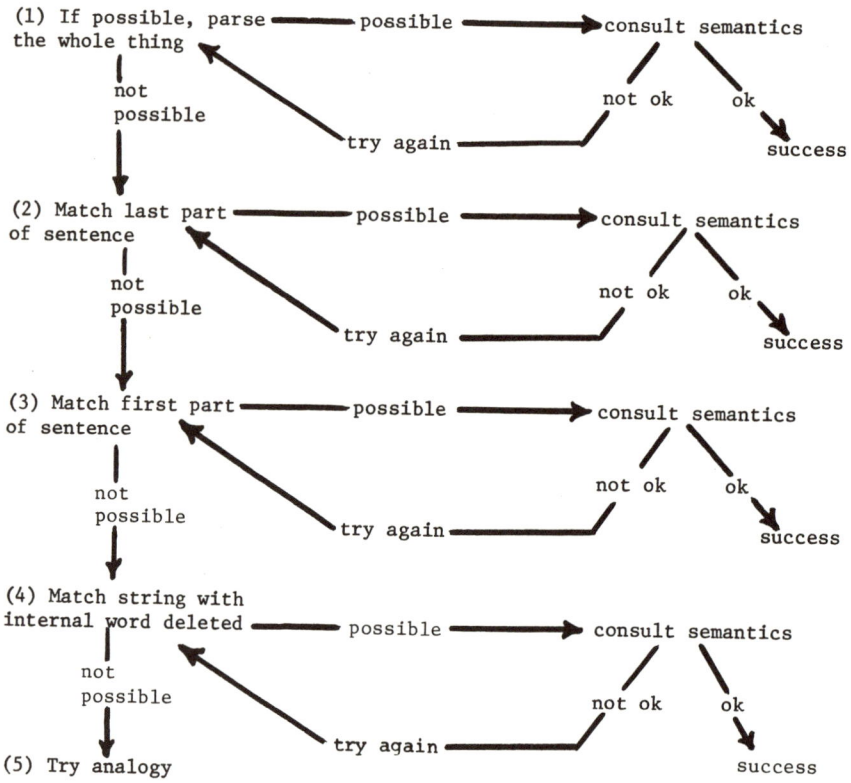

Fig. 6. A matching routine for PST.

holophrases that function as single lexical items). If this condition is not met, the grammar change fails.

(4) Deletion and permutation are semantics-preserving processes. Prefix, suffix, and infix need not be semantics preserving.

(5) Replacement is only used if the semantics of the resulting semantic tree agrees with the situational semantics, and only if none of the others applies. Otherwise, the first applicable difference is applied.

The requirements on C1 express the conservativeness of generalization that we are assuming. We will have more to say on generalization after the example. The requirements on deletion and permutation are consonant with the usual assumptions in transformational grammar that transformations preserve meaning. This allows the recoverability of the original structure from the meaning representation. For deletion, holding the semantics the same usually requires an identical undeleted term somewhere

TABLE I
TABLE OF CONNECTIONS AND CHANGES

Reduction (RS) /child form (ChS)	Sentence change	Grammar change
ZX/X	Prefix Z	$Cl(X) \to Cl(Z)\ Cl(X)$
XZ/X	Suffix Z	$Cl(X) \to Cl(X)\ Cl(Z)$
XYZ/XZ	Infix Y in X–Z	$Cl(XZ) \to Cl(X)\ Cl(Y)\ Cl(Z)$
XQZ/XYZ	Replace Y by Q in X–Z	$Cl(XYZ \to Cl(X)\ Cl(Q)\ Cl(Z)$
XZ/XYZ (Condition: meaning of both RS and ChS must be same)	Delete Y in X–Z	$Cl(XYZ) \to Cl(X)\ Cl(Z)$
$WXYZ/WYXZ$ (Condition: meaning of both RS and ChS must be same)	Permute X, Y in W–Z	$Cl(WXYZ) \to Cl(W)\ Cl(Y)\ Cl(X)\ Cl(Z)$

in the surface structure that the semantic structure can match; but there are also conventional situations where one of a finite list of terms—fixed for the grammar—may be deleted. This is the standard "condition on recoverability of deletions," which seems reasonable for any mental grammar.

The process by which a difference is obtained is simplified by our assumption that single lexical items are added, replaced, deleted, or permuted. The reduced sentence RS is compared word-to-corresponding-word, on the basis of the lexical correspondence used to produce the matching ChS. If pieces of RS larger than a single lexical item differ from ChS, then no problem solving takes place.

3.2.4 Semantics for the New Sentence

Rephrasing the description we used earlier, we might say that a sentence is understood by the child when he is able to relate it to a meaningful situation and to what he already knows of the language; that is, to place it systematically within his mental grammar (the purpose of the mental grammar being to systematize the relationship between the set of sentences of the language and the space of possible situations, which also systematizes the relationship between the various sentences). Until the child becomes aware of the need to understand, in the sense mentioned, he does not acquire *language*, although he may imitate the sounds about him and even seem to be using them appropriately in individual situations. The essence of language is its system, and in understanding the child is building the system. After augmenting his surface structure grammar, it is therefore essential that the new structures be related systematically to meaning.

The dual aspects of the relationship between the semantics and the surface structure are the determination of meaning from syntactic structure and the determination of a syntactic surface structure from a meaning representation. Possible mechanisms for the determination of meaning include (1) analysis-by-synthesis (as in the motor theory of speech perception); (2) modifications of analysis-by-synthesis using surface and contextual clues to answer the obvious objections based on time; (3) parsing in terms of the context-free grammar, using syntax-directed interpretation; (4) reverse transformations, with meanings attached to the transformations, perhaps coupled with context-free parsing; (5) mixtures of the various approaches; (6) surely others.

For getting from semantic structure to surface structure, a similar array of alternatives is available. But perhaps the only thing that is really clear at this time is that children do produce sentences that say what they want to say—that is, there is a mechanism that moves from semantic structure to surface structure.

For the purposes of our example, we have attached interpretive rules to surface productions and specified the syntax of these rules. Thus if we had

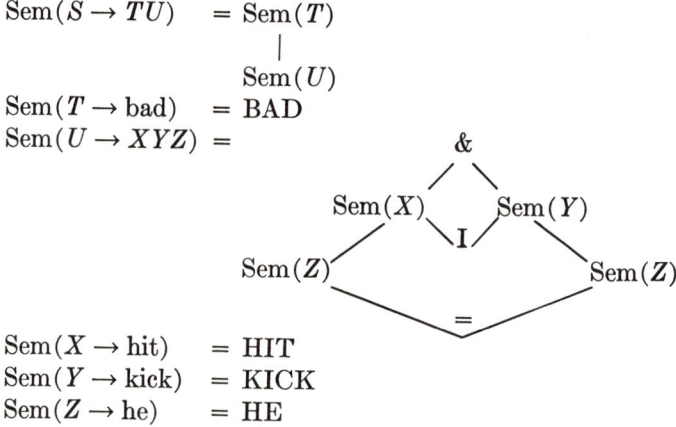

$$\text{Sem}(S \rightarrow TU) = \text{Sem}(T) \mid \text{Sem}(U)$$

$$\text{Sem}(T \rightarrow \text{bad}) = \text{BAD}$$

$$\text{Sem}(U \rightarrow XYZ) =$$

$$\text{Sem}(X \rightarrow \text{hit}) = \text{HIT}$$
$$\text{Sem}(Y \rightarrow \text{kick}) = \text{KICK}$$
$$\text{Sem}(Z \rightarrow \text{he}) = \text{HE}$$

Then a structure that on the surface looked like

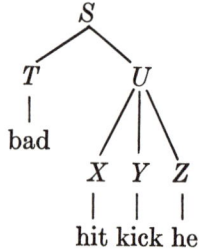

would have the semantics

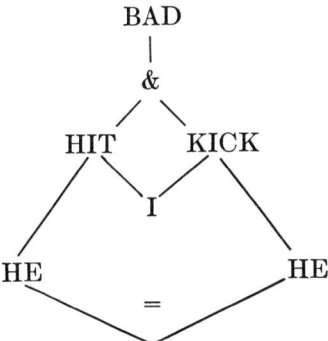

Of course, the surface string "bad hit kick me" sounds more like pidgin English than it does any English equivalent, e.g., "His hitting me and my kicking him is bad." This is why the syntax and the semantics must simultaneously be involved in the structural learning process. It is the task of structural learning to produce English, rather than pidgin English, when the child is exposed to English.

When a new surface structure is formed, PST associates with it a semantic structure, the semantics basically being that of the situation, perhaps including clues from the adult sentence, as discussed above. If we start, for instance, with the semantics

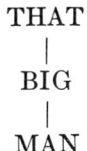

(one of our examples below), we can first project this meaning onto lexical items from the sentence, looking for a word x such that sem(x) = MAN (presumably in the same manner as when the child wants to utter a sentence with the concept MAN). Now we look at the form obtained for the surface grammar: $S \rightarrow M_2 M_1 N$. These are the classes that must be used in specifying the semantics. From our lexical item search, we have a tree with the form

$$\begin{array}{cc} \text{Sem(Cl(that))} & \text{Sem}(M_2) \\ | & | \\ \text{Sem(Cl(big))} \quad \text{or} \quad \text{Sem}(M_1) \\ | & | \\ \text{Sem(Cl(man))} & \text{Sem}(N) \end{array}$$

The only other requirement on the semantic structure assigned is that it be consistent with the rest of the grammar. Thus if $S \to M_2M_1N$ is not new, then the earlier specification of $\text{Sem}(S \to M_2M_1N)$ will be precisely the same. Furthermore, as we shall see, generalization can only take place if the semantics can remain consistent. If M_1N is found in many different constructions, we would like to have the surface grammar reflect that distributional fact and thus allow generalizations involving M_1N. In terms of the surface grammar, this would be done by replacing M_1N by a symbol R throughout the grammar and adding the rule $R \to M_1N$. But this can only take place if the semantics of M_1N are the same at each point of replacement. Then we can also replace the subtree

$$\begin{array}{c} \text{Sem}(M_1) \\ | \\ \text{Sem}(N) \end{array}$$

by $\text{Sem}(R)$, and add the semantic rule

$$\text{Sem}(R \to M_1N) = \begin{array}{c} \text{Sem}(M_1) \\ | \\ \text{Sem}(N) \end{array}$$

In the general case, then, some subtree of the situational semantics has brought about the child sentence. Call this subtree Γ and the full tree Δ. Now if the sentence produced from Γ is X and the reduction of the adult sentence has produced YX, then "prefix" may be used. The semantics associated with YX will be Δ, i.e., $\text{Sem}(YX) = \Delta$. The semantics of the more general entity YX will be $\text{Sem}(\text{Cl}(YX) \to \text{Cl}(Y)\,\text{Cl}(X)) = \text{Subst}\,(\Delta/\Gamma \leftarrow \text{Sem}\,\text{Cl}(X))$, that is, it merely substitutes the semantics of $\text{Cl}(X)$ for Γ in Δ.

In the case of the suffix operation, the result is entirely analogous. With the infix operations the new surface rule is $\text{Cl}(XZ) \to \text{Cl}(X)\,\text{Cl}(Y)\,\text{Cl}(Z)$, but the semantics $\text{Sem}(XZ)$ is a single subtree in the deep structure. This is the situation usually thought of as a *discontinuous constituent* on the surface of the sentence.

For the semantics-preserving changes, there is no problem of adding new meanings for the surface grammar rules produced.

3.2.5 Internalization

While disclaiming any intention of exploring the internalization or mechanization problem *per se*, we are nevertheless making some assumptions about the nature of learning. We assume, for instance, that nothing is retained from a failed attempt at problem solving, so an instance of structure must be discovered in a single successful problem-solving event. In other words, the structure is not known before the problem-solving attempt, but if the attempt is successful, the structure is learned. This "all-or-none" assumption has many adherents in psychology [see Gregg and Simon (1967) for a survey of the area]. We are also assuming that constant use may make the access to a particular structure more automatic, while structures not used may become less and less "natural." This is analogous to a language not spoken in years, which is nevertheless available for use if one is again put in a position where it is useful. Whether or not portions can be totally forgotten will not be one of our concerns here.

3.3 An Example of Acquisition

The "adult" input sentences for our example will be as follows:

(1)   That's a big man
(2)   Here's a big blue boat
(3)   Daddy's going bye-bye
(4)   I want the boat
(5)   I want it
(6)   Daddy is going
(7)   I am going
(8)   I want to go
(9)   You go
(10) I want you to go
(11) That's not a big man
(12) I do not want it

These sentences illustrate a number of common phenomena: single and multiple modification, negation, and rudimentary embedding.

The scheme we will use for illustrating the process for each sentence is as follows:

Input sentence
Situational semantics (with relevant portion indicated by brace)
Reduction
Child equivalent
Difference between RS and ChS in a simplified notation
Sentence change
Surface syntax to be added (in Cl notation and in terms of grammar)
Semantics of the new syntax

Comments will be appended to examples and interspersed between them.

Sentence 1: That's a big man.
Meaning: THAT
     |
     BIG
     |
     MAN
Reduction: That big man
Child equivalent: big man
Difference: That-
Change: PREFIX That
Surface syntax: Cl(big man) → Cl(that) Cl(big man)
                    $S \to M_2 M_1 N$
Semantics: $\text{Sem}(S \to M_2 M_1 N) = \text{Sem}(\text{Cl}(\text{That})) = \text{Sem}(M_2)$
                                | |
                         Sem(Cl(big))   Sem(M_1)
                                | |
                         Sem(Cl(man))   Sem(N)

Sentence 2: Here's a big blue boat.
Meaning: BIG ⎧ BLUE
            ⎨ /
            ⎩ BOAT
Reduction: big blue boat
Child equivalent: blue boat
Difference: big-
Change: PREFIX Big
Surface syntax: Cl(blue boat) → Cl(big) Cl(blue boat)
                    $S \to M_1 M_1 N$
Semantics: $\text{Sem}(S \to M_1 M_1 N) = \text{Sem}(\text{Cl}((\text{big}))\quad \text{Sem}(\text{Cl}(\text{blue}))$
                                              \/
                                      Sem(Cl(boat))

                    Sem(M_1)   Sem(M_1)
                           \/
                       Sem(N)

Now the child can certainly generate also *blue big boat*. This is an effect of earlier overgeneralization indicated in IG. It may simply have been inaccurate to indicate such overgeneralization in the specific case in point; but let us consider what might happen if the child generates "blue big boat."

First, there may be negative feedback, such as misunderstanding of the sentence. More helpful, however, are overt or implied corrections ("you mean. . ." or "oh, a big blue boat?"). The results of the child's comparing a correct form with his form will be a permutation, and a class cleavage must take place.

Example: You mean a big blue boat?
Reduction: big blue boat
Just-produced equivalent: blue big boat (*note:* meaning preserving)
Difference: big blue versus blue big
Change: PERMUTE
Surface syntax:
Cl(blue big boat) → Cl(big) Cl(blue) Cl(boat)
$S \to M_{11}M_{12}N$
$M_{11} \to$ big   (Situation renders change obligatory.)
$M_{12} \to$ blue
$M_1 \to M_{11} \mid M_{12} \mid \ldots$
Semantics: $\text{Sem}(S \to M_{11}M_{12}N) = \text{Sem}(M_{11}) \quad \text{Sem}(M_{12})$
$$\searrow \swarrow$$
$$\text{Sem}(N)$$

This use of PST is not, in fact, included in the present system, but it does provide a means of eliminating certain errors, and thus deserves empirical exploration.

Returning to the example sentences:

Sentence 3: Daddy's going bye-bye.
Meaning: $\begin{cases} \text{GO.OUT} \\ \mid \\ \text{DADDY} \end{cases}$
Reduction: Daddy go bye-bye
Child equivalent: Daddy bye-bye
Difference: -go-
Change: INFIX go
Surface syntax: Cl(Daddy bye-bye) → Cl(Daddy) Cl(go) Cl(bye-bye)
$S \to N_3 V_1 V_0 \quad (V_1 \to \text{go})$
Semantics: $\text{Sem}(S \to N_3 V_1 V_0) = \text{Sem}(\text{Cl}(\text{GO.OUT})) = \text{Sem}(V_0)$
$$\mid \qquad\qquad \mid$$
$$\text{Sem}(\text{Cl}(\text{Daddy})) \quad \text{Sem}(N_3)$$

Note that V_1 has no special meaning attached to it at this point.

Meaning: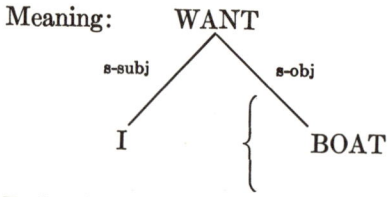

Reduction: Want boat
Child equivalent: boat
Difference: Want-
Change: PREFIX Want
Surface syntax: Cl(boat) → Cl(want) Cl(boat)
$\qquad\qquad\qquad\qquad S \to V_3 N \qquad\qquad (V_3 \to \text{want})$
Semantics: $\text{Sem}(S \to V_3 N) = \text{Sem}(\text{Cl(want)}) = \text{Sem}(V_3)$
$\qquad\qquad\qquad\qquad\qquad\qquad\qquad\qquad\quad\quad\;\diagup\;\diagdown\qquad\qquad\;\;\mid\diagdown$
$\qquad\qquad\qquad\qquad\qquad\qquad\qquad\qquad\quad I\;\;\text{Sem}(\text{Cl(Boat)})\quad I\;\;\text{Sem}(N)$

"Want" in child language is always used with subject "I" implied. Notice that a new class was added for the verb "want."

Sentence 5: I want it.
Meaning: { WANT
$\qquad\qquad\qquad\;\;|$
$\qquad\;\; I\;\;\; X$
Reduction: want it
Child equivalent: want boat
Difference: it versus boat
Change: REPLACE boat BY it
Surface syntax: Cl(want boat) → Cl(want) Cl(it)
$\qquad\qquad\qquad\qquad S \to V_3 N$
$\qquad\qquad\qquad\qquad N \to \text{it}$
Semantics: See sentence 4.

Notice that replacement is semantics preserving and adds a lexical item to the same class as the item it replaces. The X above stands for the actual antecedent (presumably "BOAT," in this instance).

Sentence 6: Daddy is going.
Meaning: { GO.OUT
$\qquad\qquad\quad\;\;\;|$
$\qquad\qquad\;\;$ DADDY
Reduction: Daddy go
Child equivalent: Daddy go bye-bye
Difference: child form has bye-bye
Change: DELETE bye-bye

Surface syntax: Cl(Daddy go bye-bye) → Cl(Daddy) Cl(go)
$$S \to N_3 V_1$$
Semantics: $\text{Sem}(S \to N_3 V_1) = \text{Sem}(\text{GO.OUT}) = \text{Sem}(V_1)$
| |
$\text{Sem}(\text{Cl}(\text{Daddy}))$ $\text{Sem}(N_3)$

Note that the old "Daddy go bye-bye" form will gradually be used less, although it will still be available for interpretation purposes. "GO.OUT" will now be one of the meanings of the lexical item "go."

The process known as "analogy" may be mirrored within PST also, by the use of the REPLACE operation. Although we have included it in the example (sentences 5 and 7, specifically), it is not clear that it ought to be included. Replacement is not necessary in view of the scheme for generalization that has been indicated. Furthermore, the whole process of analogy seems alien to the system presented, since it requires that the child generate a ChS different in meaning from the sentence he is presented. In this particular, sentence 5 differs from sentence 7, since the antecedent of "it" may actually be "boat." Therefore, it is possible that analogy should be included with the proviso that the generated child equivalent have the same meaning as the adult sentence. The constraint used in this instance [(5) in Section 3.2.3] is weaker.

Sentence 7: I am going.
Meaning: $\begin{cases} \text{GO} \\ | \\ \text{I} \end{cases}$

Reduction: I go
Child equivalent: Daddy go
Difference: Daddy versus I
Change: REPLACE Daddy BY I
Surface syntax: Cl(Daddy go) → Cl(I) Cl(go)
$$S \to N_3 V_1$$
$$N_3 \to I$$

Semantics: See sentence 6

Sentence 8: I want to go.
Meaning:

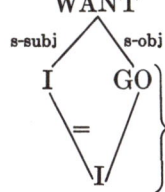

Reduction: I want go

Child equivalent: I go
Difference: -want-
Change: INFIX want
Surface syntax: Cl(I go) → Cl(I) Cl(want) Cl(go)
$$S \to N_3 V_3 V_1$$
Semantics:

$\text{Sem}(S \to N_3 V_3 V_1) = \text{Sem}(\text{Cl}(\text{want}))$ = $\text{Sem}(V_3)$

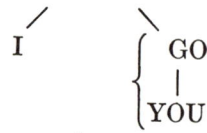

     Sem(Cl(I))   Sem(Cl(go))   Sem(N_3)   Sem(V_1)
        \= | \= |
          Sem(Cl(I))   Sem(N_3)

Sentence 9: You go. Exactly analogous to sentence 7, but no reduction required.

Sentence 10: I want you to go.
Meaning: WANT
                 /   \
           I   { GO
                       |
                      { YOU

Reduction: want you go
Child equivalent: you go
Difference: want-
Change: PREFIX want
Surface syntax: Cl(you go) → Cl(want) Cl(you go)
$$S \to V_3 N_4 V_1$$
Semantics:

$\text{Sem}(S \to V_3 N_4 V_1) = \text{Sem}(\text{Cl}(\text{want}))$ = $\text{Sem}(V_3)$

            /   \   /   \
        I   Sem(Cl(Go))   I   Sem(V_1)
                    | |
            SemCl(you)   Sem(N_4)

Sentence 10 could cause further grammar modification if presented later when the child's short-term memory was sufficient to remember "I want you go." The surface structure then obtained would (by precisely the same processes) be $S \to N_3 V_3 N_4 V_1$, where

$\text{Sem}(S \to N_3 V_3 N_4 V_1) = \text{Sem}(V_3)$
                                    /   \
                         Sem(N_3)   Sem(V_1)
                                           |
                                      Sem(N_4)

COMPUTATIONAL STUDY OF LANGUAGE ACQUISITION   213

If at the time of first presentation, the child's short-term memory had been adequate, an augmented instance of PST might have produced the more advanced grammar immediately, in two steps. The possibility of multistep derivations needs to be explored in more detail.

Sentence 11: That's not a big man.
Meaning: NEG
                |
          $\begin{cases} \text{THAT} \\ | \\ \text{BIG} \\ | \\ \text{MAN} \end{cases}$

Reduction: that not big man
Child equivalent: That big man
Difference: -not-
Change: INFIX not
Surface syntax: Cl(that big man) → Cl(that) Cl(not) Cl(big man)
$$S \rightarrow M_2 Ng M_{11} N$$
$$Ng \rightarrow \text{not}$$
Semantics:
Sem$(S \rightarrow Ng M_{11} N)$ = Sem(Cl(not))   Sem(Ng) = NEG   Sem(Ng)
                                           | |
                                   Sem(Cl(that))   Sem(M_2)
                                           | |
                                   Sem(Cl(big))   Sem(M_{11})
                                           | |
                                   Sem(Cl(man))   Sem(N)

Notice that a new class Ng is added here. As specified earlier, this happens anytime Cl(X) is used, where X is a single lexical item.

Sentence 12: I do not want it.
Meaning: NEG
              |
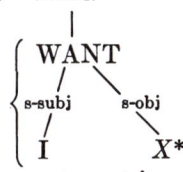

Reduction: not want it
Child equivalent: want it
Difference: not-

---

* That is, whatever it refers to in the situation.

Surface syntax: Cl(want it) → Cl(not) Cl(want it)
$S \to NgV_3N$

Semantics:
Sem$(S \to NgV_3N)$ = Sem(Cl(not)) = Sem(Ng)
                    | |
                Sem(Cl(want it))   Sem(V_3)
                                    s-subj / \ s-obj
                                    I   Sem(N)

The new grammar (NG) which has been obtained in our example is indicated below. Comparison of NG with IG provides an indication of the structural information obtained from the 12 sentences, although it does not indicate the extent of the generalization that may have taken place (a topic to be discussed in the next section).

Surface Syntax of NG
$S \to M_2M_1N \mid M_{11}M_{12}N \mid V_3N_4V_1 \mid M_2NgM_{11}N \mid NgV_3N \mid V_3N$
$\mid N_3V_1 \mid N_3V_3V_1 \mid N_3V_1V_0 \mid N_0V_0 \mid N_1N_2 \mid MN \mid N$
$M_{11} \to$ big
$M_{12} \to$ blue
$M_1 \to M_{11} \mid M_{12} \mid$ more
$Ng \to$ not
$N \to$ it
$N_3 \to$ I $\mid$ Daddy $\mid$ Mommy $\mid N_4$
$N_0 \to$ he $\mid$ doggy $\mid N_1$
$N_1 \to N_3 \mid M_3$
$N_2 \to$ sock
$M_2 \to$ that
$M_3 \to$ my
$V_0 \to$ bye-bye
$N \to$ boat $\mid$ man $\mid$ flower
$V_1 \to$ go
$V_3 \to$ want
$N_4 \to$ you
$M \to M_1 \mid M_2$

Correlated Semantics of NG
Sem$(S \to M_2M_1N)$ = Sem(M_2)
                       |
                       Sem(M_1)
                       |
                       Sem(N)

$\mathrm{Sem}(S \to M_{11}M_{12}N) = \mathrm{Sem}(M_{11}) \quad \mathrm{Sem}(M_{12})$
$$\diagdown\diagup$$
$$\mathrm{Sem}(N)$$

$\mathrm{Sem}(S \to N_3V_1V_0) = \mathrm{Sem}(V_0)$
$$|$$
$$\mathrm{Sem}(N_3)$$

$\mathrm{Sem}(S \to V_3N_4V_1) = \mathrm{Sem}(V_3)$
$$\diagup\quad\diagdown$$
$$\mathrm{I} \qquad \mathrm{Sem}(V_1)$$
$$|$$
$$\mathrm{Sem}(N_4)$$

$\mathrm{Sem}(S \to M_2NgM_{11}N) = \mathrm{Sem}(Ng)$
$$|$$
$$\mathrm{Sem}(M_2)$$
$$|$$
$$\mathrm{Sem}(M_{11})$$
$$|$$
$$\mathrm{Sem}(N)$$

$\mathrm{Sem}(Ng) = \mathrm{NEG}$

$\mathrm{Sem}(S \to N_3V_3V_1) = \mathrm{Sem}(V_3)$
$$\diagup\quad\diagdown$$
$$\mathrm{Sem}(N_3) \quad \mathrm{Sem}(V_1)$$
$$\diagdown = \diagup$$
$$\mathrm{Sem}(N_3)$$

$\mathrm{Sem}(S \to NgV_3N) = \mathrm{Sem}(Ng)$
$$|$$
$$\mathrm{Sem}(V_3)$$
$$\diagup\quad\diagdown$$
$$\mathrm{I} \qquad \mathrm{Sem}(N)$$

$\mathrm{Sem}(S \to N_0V_0) = \mathrm{Sem}(V_0)$
$$|$$
$$\mathrm{Sem}(N_0)$$

$\mathrm{Sem}(S \to N_3V_1) = \mathrm{Sem}(V_1)$
$$|$$
$$\mathrm{Sem}(N_3)$$

$\mathrm{Sem}(S \to V_3N) = \mathrm{Sem}(V_3)$
$$\diagup\quad\diagdown$$
$$\mathrm{I} \quad \mathrm{Sem}(N)$$

$$\text{Sem}(S \rightarrow N_1 N_2) = \begin{array}{c} \text{BELONG} \\ \diagup \diagdown \text{(to)} \\ \text{Sem}(N_2) \text{Sem}(N_1) \end{array}$$

$$\text{Sem}(S \rightarrow MN) = \begin{array}{c} \text{Sem}(M) \\ | \\ \text{Sem}(N) \end{array}$$

$$\text{Sem}(S \rightarrow N) = \text{Sem}(N)$$

$$\text{Sem}(V_0) = \text{Sem(bye-bye)} = \text{GO.OUT}$$

$$\text{Sem}(V_1) = \text{Sem(go)} = \text{GO.OUT}$$

Other lexical items may be assumed to represent semantic primitives, as in our presentation of IG. The selectors are not indicated but should be clear enough in this example.

3.4 The Generalization Process

In our illustration of PST, we have been examining only the mechanisms that derive structural information from the raw empirical data. One important job of these mechanisms is to provide structures that can be generalized. It is therefore appropriate for us to examine the generalization process within the context of the information furnished by PST.

Within PST itself, we chose to keep generalization to a minimum. Nevertheless, PST deals with classes of lexical items, rather than merely with individual items, so whatever concurrent generalization takes place is preserved by the problem-solving process. This feature preserves the combinatorial growth possibilities so essential to any realistic grammatical system.

A particular generalization mechanism discussed earlier is that of analogy (replacement) within PST. The mechanisms we will now discuss should be thought of as separate from the structural learning process, and are not presently included in the system.

Before considering in generality the generalization process, let us look at a specific example of something that really *ought* to be generalized. Suppose the structure "big man" in our example above is paralleled by the learning of a structure for "little boy," and that after this structure has been learned, one has in the grammar

$$S \rightarrow M_{13} N', \quad \text{Sem}(S \rightarrow M_{13} N') = \begin{array}{c} \text{Sem}(M_{13}) \\ | \\ \text{Sem}(N') \end{array}$$

where $\text{Cl(little)} = M_{13}$ and $\text{Cl(boy)} = N'$. Now we would like to combine

M_{13} with M_{12} and N with N', and we might ask ourselves why we would like to do so. There seem to be three criteria, the first being that the classes must participate in identical surface structures. This criterion is the one usually applied when writing "child grammars," such as the "pivot grammars" [which, as maintained in Reeker (1974), are of dubious utility because only this one criterion has been applied].

The other criteria we shall term semantic coherence and consistency. These criteria tend to be assumed by all linguistic fieldworkers, but they also tend to remain unstated. Semantic coherence means that any structure to be grouped under a single syntactic category should be "a single piece" of a sentence semantically. That is, its semantic tree should be a connected subtree of the semantic tree of the sentence. Semantic consistency requires that the semantic tree of the class be identical in every tree in which it appears as a subtree.

There may be another criterion operative, which we could call semantic commonality. In the example we have been using, one of the compelling reasons for generalization is that "man" and "boy" have a good deal in common semantically. But how much they must have in common is problematical. If too much is required, they will never be generalized; if too little, massive overgeneralization could result. The problem of when to take the inductive leap is a problem shared by all sorts of learning phenomena, and not one that we want to attack in the present instance. Some of the complications involve the fact that "man" and "boy" are not semantic primitives, although both share the properties (to use feature notation) [+ human], with whatever that implies ([+animate], [−abstract], etc.). But we do not know how much of the semantic representation is relevant to the child at any point in time. [±male] is a relevant linguistic feature also, but children of three and four sometimes do not distinguish the gender of their pronouns.

Basically, though, we can say that all of the semantics relevant to grammatical structures with which the child is familiar must be coherent and consistent; more formally, if a surface generalization can be made on the basis of combining classes X and Y, then it must be the case that the correspondence $\varphi: X \to Y$ commutes with the mapping from surface to semantic structures (i.e., the mapping $(\lambda x) [\text{Sem}(x)]$). In the example, since $S \to M_{12}N$ and $S \to M_{13}N'$, we can make the surface generalization

$$S \to M_{123}N_0, \qquad M_{123} \to M_{12} \mid M_{13}, \qquad N_0 \to N \mid N'$$

Then if the correspondence (i.e., the relation of being grouped into the same superclass) is φ, $\varphi(M_{12}) = M_{13}$ and $\varphi(N) = N'$, we check to see if, for example, $\text{Sem}(\varphi(M_{12}N)) = \varphi(\text{Sem}(M_{12}N))$. The following diagram commutes:

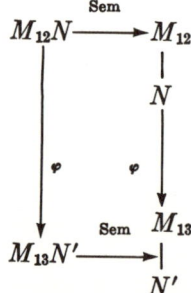

This commutation criterion forms a general test for semantic consistency within the grammar extant at any particular time and can be used on candidates for generalization.

There is actually no reason that constituents need to be in identical positions in order for generalization to take place. Thus if

$$X \to X_1X_3X_4 \mid X_1X_6, \quad \text{and} \quad Y \to X_3X_4X_5 \mid X_6X_5$$

then it may be possible to generalize:

$$X \to X_1Z, \quad Y \to ZX_5, \quad \text{and} \quad Z \to X_3X_4 \mid X_6$$

provided the semantics of the two situations are coherent and consistent. Thus if

$$\text{Sem}(X) = \text{Sem}(X_1)$$
$$\diagup \qquad \diagdown$$
$$\text{Sem}(X_3) \qquad \text{Sem}(X_4)$$

the semantics of X_3X_4 are not coherent, so the generalization would not take place. Similarly, if

$$\text{Sem}(X \to X_1X_3X_4) = \text{Sem}(X_1)$$
$$\mid$$
$$\text{Sem}(X_3)$$
$$\mid$$
$$\text{Sem}(X_4)$$

but

$$\text{Sem}(Y \to X_3X_4X_5) = \text{Sem}(X_5)$$
$$\mid$$
$$\text{Sem}(X_4)$$
$$\mid$$
$$\text{Sem}(X_3)$$

then no generalization can take place because the semantics of $Z \to X_3X_4$ could not be consistent.

In the example used to illustrate the instance of PST, we obtained

$$S \to MN \mid N \mid M_2M_1N \mid M_{11}M_{12}N$$

Since N is involved in each of these, it might be possible to generalize to $S \to XN$, and upon consulting the semantics, this turns out to be quite possible for the first three structures above. It may be verified that the semantics are consistent, as

$$\text{Sem}(S \to XN) = \begin{array}{c} \text{Sem}(X) \\ \mid \\ \text{Sem}(N) \end{array}$$

In the case of $S \to M_{11}M_{12}N$, however, the semantics are

$$\begin{array}{cc} \text{Sem}(M_{11}) & \text{Sem}(M_{12}) \\ \diagdown & \diagup \\ & \text{Sem}(N) \end{array}$$

So $M_{11}M_{12}$ would have an incoherent semantics, and no generalization can take place.

The surface grammars produced by the present instance of PST do not involve self-embedding and are thus weakly equivalent to some right linear grammar. Thus we must concern ourselves with the weak generative arguments to which finite state surface grammars fall prey. The strong generative arguments are concerned with whether the information provided by the grammar accords with grammatical intuitions, and we contend that if we can meet the weak generativity conditions, then we also can meet strong generativity conditions, on the basis of the semantic correspondences that PST provides.

The argument against weak adequacy of finite state grammars are concerned with the fact that they cannot generate indefinite-depth nested dependencies, of which languages of well-formed bracketings are cases in point. These are represented by grammars containing rules like $S \to [S]S$. It should be clear that if $S \in (\Sigma \cup \{[,]\})^*$, for $\Sigma \cap \{[,]\} = \emptyset$, then the set generated by this grammar can be intersected with $\{[^*\Omega]^*\Omega' \mid \Omega,\Omega' \in \Sigma^*\}$ to produce $\{[^i\Omega]^i\Omega' \mid \Omega,\Omega' \in \Sigma^*\}$, and the pumping theorem for finite state languages readily yields the result that this is not finite state. Since regularity is preserved under intersection, the bracketing language is not finite state.

One answer to this problem is to point out that in ordinary speech the depth of embedding is bounded, and if an individual is provided with pencil and paper to figure out the structure of deeper sentences, he does so by analogy; that is, he learns as he works that he can always go one embedding deeper. Since this has a somewhat unsatisfactory ring (but remember that we are talking about an individual's mental grammar, not a generalization for the whole language, so it may not be as unsatisfactory as it sounds), we will consider the case of generalization on a typical bracketing grammar involving "if ... then" below.

Suppose we have, for instance

$$S \rightarrow \text{if } T \text{ then } U$$

$$\text{Sem}(S \rightarrow \text{if } T \text{ then } U) = \begin{array}{c} \supset \\ / \quad \backslash \\ \text{Sem}(T) \quad \text{Sem}(U) \end{array}$$

Then we have

$$S \rightarrow \text{if } T \text{ then if } U \text{ then } V$$

$$\text{Sem}(S \rightarrow \text{if } T \text{ then if } U \text{ then } V) = \begin{array}{c} \supset \\ / \quad \backslash \\ \text{Sem}(T) \quad \supset \\ \quad\quad / \quad \backslash \\ \quad\quad \text{Sem}(U) \quad \text{Sem}(V) \end{array}$$

This can be generalized by allowing

$$S \rightarrow \text{if } T \text{ then } W \qquad \text{Sem}(S) = \begin{array}{c} \supset \\ / \quad \backslash \\ \text{Sem}(T) \quad \text{Sem}(W) \end{array}$$

$$W \rightarrow \text{if } U \text{ then } V \qquad \text{Sem}(W) = \begin{array}{c} \supset \\ / \quad \backslash \\ \text{Sem}(U) \quad \text{Sem}(V) \end{array}$$

and then

$$X \rightarrow \text{if } Q \text{ then } R, \quad Q \rightarrow T \mid U, \quad R \rightarrow W \mid V$$

But consider the case

$$S \rightarrow \text{if if } W' \text{ then } V' \text{ then } Q'$$

This particular case does not occur in English, but the sort of bracketing it illustrates is not uncommon (e.g., "If your mother's coming to visit means that if I so much as open my mouth I'll be criticized, then I'll move out right now").

This must have the semantics

$$\text{Sem}(S \rightarrow \text{if if } W' \text{ then } V' \text{ then } Q') = \begin{array}{c} \supset \\ / \quad \backslash \\ \supset \quad \text{Sem}(Q') \\ / \quad \backslash \\ \text{Sem}(W') \quad \text{Sem}(V') \end{array}$$

Again we must allow

$S \to \text{if } R' \text{ then } Q'$ $\text{Sem}(S) = \supset$ with branches $\text{Sem}(R')$, $\text{Sem}(Q')$

$R' \to \text{if } W' \text{ then } V'$ $\text{Sem}(R') = \supset$ with branches $\text{Sem}(W')$, $\text{Sem}(V')$

Then

$$Y \to \text{if } P \text{ then } P', \quad P \to R' \mid W', \quad P' \to Q' \mid V'$$

but on the basis of our earlier generalization, we can have

$$Z \to \text{if } L \text{ then } L', \quad L \to P \mid Q, \quad L' \to P' \mid R$$

or essentially,

$$L \to R' \mid W' \mid T \mid U \mid T', \quad L' \to Q' \mid V' \mid W \mid V \mid U'$$

These generalizations represent a lot of different possibilities quite economically; and if it could be shown that each of the right-hand sides is equivalent to S, it would not be difficult to add mechanisms to form the ultimate generalization:

$$S \to \text{if } S \text{ then } S$$

This would be semantically consistent and coherent, according to the criteria we have given.

One problem with such a generalization involves the fact that our notation for this example is oversimplified. There really are conditions that relate the antecedent and the consequent in sentences of the form we have been discussing. Thus, "if it rains, I went yesterday," with the straightforward meaning (not "if it rains, tell them I went yesterday") violates a constraint on the relative times of the embedded sentences. Thus if the syntactic generalization that has been sketched above is really to remain semantically coherent, some additional mechanism for noting such side conditions is necessary. In transformational grammar, there may, in general, be conditions on the constituents of the structural descriptions that must be met if a structural change is to take place. But note that this is a problem of generalization, and as such, one would expect to find it in various areas of learning.

As another example of how one can generalize more if one "strips away" semantic conditions (presumably "remembering" them in some other form), consider the case in our example:

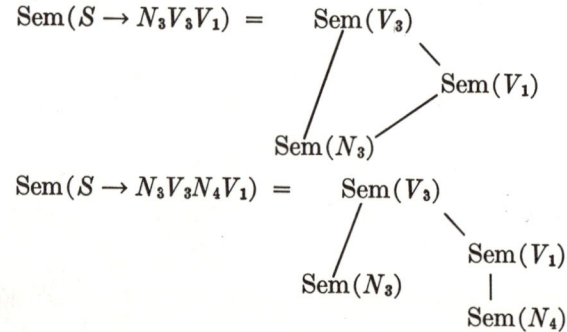

Will these be generalized so that N_3 and N_4 can be combined? Surface generalization $S \to N_3 V_3 X$ does not allow the expression of the identity of argument of V_3 and V_1 (as the reader may readily verify). If we want to be able to generalize these, it is necessary to remove the condition on identity of arguments from the representation. One alternative solution is that the derivation of "I want go" actually come about from something like "I want I go." This requires deletion, which must be semantics preserving, so we would have the upper tree above derived after the lower one. It must then be the case that the generalization of N_3 and N_4 has taken place previous to that time to allow for the identity of the two concepts. The more straightforward solution is merely to suspend the identity condition and use the mechanisms sketched above.

In the general case, it may turn out that some evidence of self-embedding within the mental grammar comes to light. If so, it is evidence of a generalization mechanism that proceeds from

$$\varphi \stackrel{*}{\Rightarrow} AXB, \qquad S \to \varphi \mid X, \qquad \text{and} \qquad \text{Sem}(\varphi \stackrel{*}{\Rightarrow} A\varphi B) \cong \text{Sem}(\varphi \stackrel{*}{\Rightarrow} AXB)$$

where $\text{Sem}(\varphi)$ is compatible with $\text{Sem}(X)$, to the generalized form. The work of Klein and his associates (Klein and Kuppin, 1970) on an automated fieldworker provides some possible solutions to the generalization of the more powerful devices that may turn out to be necessary in the surface component of the mental grammar, although they do not use semantic criteria.

3.5 Generalization and Transformations

A transformational grammarian may—for the sake of the economy of his theory—make generalizations that the child just does not make. But his decisions, which he codifies in terms of transformations from the deep to the surface structure, are made on the basis of criteria very similar to those we have enunciated above. Any time the deep-surface correspondence is formalized, these generalizations can be made, irrespective of whether or not a person's mental grammar would contain them. People's mental grammars probably even differ, one from another, on the basis of the generalizations that have been made. This would not, after all, affect the structural information relevant to either surface or semantic structure, although it could conceivably have an effect on the efficiency of linguistic performance.

We close this section by pointing out that in the usual transformational grammar, we are given a means of generating deep structure and a set of transformations. These together induce a surface structure that may be codified in terms of another grammar. We have instead employed the alternative of providing a surface grammar, a set of meaning representations, and some correspondences between them. This method of specifying semantics can be extended to cases where the surface structure is specified by a transformational grammar, and an instance of PST now being developed will incorporate such mechanisms.

4. Conclusion

This chapter has included a discussion of the problems involved in language acquisition modeling, a summary of the computational efforts in that direction, and a closer examination of one particular ongoing modeling effort. It is the author's belief that computational models will play a crucial role in developing satisfactory theories of the language acquisition process. This conviction is based on the complexity of both the grammatical system and the various learning processes that must interact in the acquisition task.

The purpose of the type of modeling with which this chapter has been concerned is both theoretical and experimental. The experimental function is realized when the model is run as a simulation of behavior, and the output for particular inputs is examined to see if it is consistent with available empirical data. At the present time, this function of computational model-building is less important within the language acquisition domain than the theoretical function, yet it is always available as a chastening influence on overextravagant claims for a model. Seemingly reasonable heuristics in such areas as generalization can be seen, upon simulation, to lead to unreasonable output data.

Within the theoretical domain, computational models have a number of well-known advantages, including that of forcing explicitness. In facing the details concerning the components of a theory and their interactions, the possibility or impossibility of a particular hypothesized entity often becomes clear without running a simulation at all. The really important feature of computational models in exploring language acquisition lies in their ability to express in a flexible manner the complex interactions among the evolving grammar, the learning processes, and the input data.

It should be clear that the models examined in this chapter have a long way to go; yet they have also progressed in their sophistication in the past few years, and currently represent the best-delineated available attempts at explaining the syntactic acquisition task. Although this chapter has not treated phonological or semantic acquisition, computational models provide an equally promising tool in those areas. [For some remarks on PST and phonology, see Reeker (1974).]

Learning a natural language is perhaps the supreme mental accomplishment of the average human being. Attempts to delineate how this accomplishment takes place provide a fascinating field for research, with important practical implications. The computer can be an important part of research endeavors in language acquisition and may be essential in the eventual unraveling of this portion of the mind's secrets.

5. Appendix: Grammar Representation

The purpose of this appendix is to explain the notation used within the chapter for surface structure representation, for meaning representation, and for the semantic mapping. The latter two will be explored in more detail, since they are less likely to be familiar to the reader than surface syntactic representation.

5.1 Surface Representation

The type of grammar used in the earlier exposition, and in PST, for surface structure representation is a *context-free phrase structure grammar*. This type of grammar specifies a set of sentences in a language and provides a description for each of them by generating the sentences and their descriptions. The description is called a *phrase marker*. The term "context free" will be used below without "phrase structure" for economy of expression.

A context-free grammar includes

1. A symbol S, standing for "sentence."
2. A set of *nonterminal symbols*, including S, representing grammatical categories in the language (e.g., NP for "noun phrase," VP for "verb phrase," AUX for "auxiliary," V for "verb," N for "noun").

3. A set of *terminal symbols*, consisting of words in the language, as well as certain prefixes, suffixes, etc.

4. A set of *productions*, or *generation rules*, which generate the phrase markers (and the sentences that the phrase markers represent). These rules are of the form

$$X \to Y_1 \cdots Y_n \quad (n \geq 1)$$

where X is a nonterminal symbol and $Y_1, \ldots, Y_n$ are either nonterminal or terminal symbols.

The generation of a sentence and its phrase marker according to the rules of the grammar may be described as follows:

(1) Start with (S).
(2) For each rule $X \to Y_1 \cdots Y_n$, (X) may be replaced by

$$\begin{array}{c} (X) \\ \diagup \quad \diagdown \\ (Y_1) \cdots (Y_n) \end{array}$$

Each pair of parentheses represents a *node*, and the terminal or nonterminal symbol within the parentheses is said to *label* the node.

A *proper* phrase marker according to the grammar is one that (1) is built as above; (2) has one or more lines emanating downward from every node that is labeled with a nonterminal symbol; and (3) has no lines emanating downward from nodes labeled with terminals.

As an example, the tree shown on the left in Fig. 2 (with parentheses deleted) is a proper phrase marker according to a grammar containing the rules

$$S \to NP\ AUX\ VP$$
$$VP \to V\ NP$$
$$NP \to THIS$$
$$NP \to PASSIVES$$
$$AUX \to WILL$$
$$V \to MAKE$$

S, NP, AUX, VP, and V are nonterminals, and THIS, WILL, MAKE, and PASSIVES are terminals. As illustrated in this example, a sentence generated by a grammar is obtained from a proper phrase marker by reading the nodes labeled by terminals from left to right. Multiple rules with the same nonterminal to the left of the arrow are often combined. In the chapter, the vertical bar notation is used, so the two NP's above would be combined as

$$NP \to THIS\ |\ PASSIVES$$

An extension of the context-free grammar is the *context*-sensitive grammar, which allows productions of the form

$$X \to Y_1 \cdots Y_n \quad \textit{in context } Z\text{-}W$$

or equivalently,

$$ZXW \to ZY_1 \cdots Y_n W$$

The process of generating a phrase marker using a context-sensitive grammar is more involved and will not be described here. Context-sensitive grammars provide a natural and economical means of expressing certain linguistic phenomena, such as subject–verb agreement. They can also generate languages that context-free grammars cannot, although this fact is less important from the standpoint of natural languages.

Transformational grammars may also be used to specify surface representation. Such a grammar consists of (1) a context-free grammar, which generates a set of *base phrase markers*, and (2) a set of transformations (see Fig. 2), which map phrase markers to phrase markers. A transformational derivation consists of a series of phrase markers $P_1, \ldots, P_n$, where P_1 is a base phrase marker, each P_{i+1} is derived by a transformation from P_i, and no further obligatory transformation can be used on P_n. P_n is then called the *final derived phrase marker*. If a transformational grammar were used for surface representation, the structural description used as input to the semantic mapping might consist of $P_1, \ldots, P_n$, of P_n alone, or of P_1 alone, depending upon how the transformational grammar and semantic mapping have been defined. It is not known if there are empirical considerations that favor one formulation over another.

A number of standard references are available on context-free, context-sensitive, and transformational grammars (for example, Bach, 1974).

5.2 The Semantic Mapping

The semantic mapping, connecting surface descriptions to meaning representations, is the heart of the grammar, yet its form depends very much on the surface description and meaning representation chosen. One possibility is to use diagrams that look like phrase markers for the meaning representation, and to use transformations of the sort described above to effect the mapping. This is the alternative advocated by the generative semanticists (see Section 1.3). This section will be devoted to describing the inductive mapping of phrase markers into semantic dependency notation, as used in PST.

It is a standard practice in mathematical logic to specify truth value of well-formed formulas inductively, in parallel with the syntactic definition. This method is often associated with Tarski (1956). Since truth values provide the meanings of logical formulas, the inductive definition represents the semantic mapping. As an example, consider an English-like logic with propositions defined by

(1) $S \to$ It is not the case that S.
(2) $S \to$ Both S and S.
(3) $S \to$ Either S or S.
(4) $S \to$ Black is white.
(5) $S \to$ White is white.

This language is not a very rich one, but it allows the generation of an infinite number of sentences. The truth value for all of these sentences can be specified succinctly as follows:

(1) When production 1 is applied, the value of the left-hand S is "true" just in case the value of the right-hand S is "false."
(2) When production 2 is applied, the value of the left-hand S is "true" just in case both of the right-hand S's are "true."
(3) When production 3 is applied, the value of the left-hand S is "true" in case either or both of the right-hand S's is "true."
(4) When $S \to$ Black is white, the value of the left-hand S is "false."
(5) When $S \to$ White is white, the value of the left-hand S is "true."

The effect of applying these definitions is to begin at the bottom nodes of the phrase marker and work up, until the meaning of the top S is determined.

This method of specifying semantics can be elaborated by defining attributes other than "truth value" at each node, and using combinations of those attributes to define values of the attributes at nodes above. A further elaboration allows for defining attributes based on nodes above, rather than below. These latter are called inherited attributes, and those that move up from below are called synthesized attributes by Knuth (1968).

In view of the available elaborations of attribute semantic mappings, those used in PST are relatively simple. Only a single attribute "Sem" is used, and it is synthesized. The values of Sem are semantic dependency trees rather than truth values, so that a good deal of information is expressed in the single attribute. There are expressive limitations to this limited form of attribute specification, and a more elaborate form will probably be needed in the future, but the method does not impose any unreasonable restriction on the early grammars that have been studied. Furthermore, it is not inordinately cumbersome to reverse the mapping, a consideration that is not inconsequential when considering a mental grammar model.

The particular notation used may be illustrated by the rule

$$X \rightarrow YZ \mid XR$$

with the semantic mapping

$$\text{Sem}(X \rightarrow YZ) = \begin{array}{c} \text{Sem}(Y) \\ | \\ \text{Sem}(Z) \end{array}$$

$$\text{Sem}(X \rightarrow XR) = \begin{array}{c} \text{Sem}(R) \\ | \\ \text{Sem}(X) \end{array}$$

The notation $\text{Sem}(X \rightarrow YZ)$ can be read as "the dependency representation of X when the production $X \rightarrow YZ$ is applied." For the phrase marker portion

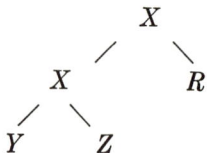

the meaning would be given by

$$\begin{array}{c} \text{Sem}(R) \\ | \\ \text{Sem}(Y) \\ | \\ \text{Sem}(Z) \end{array}$$

Notice that a convention has been included that a meaning representation be joined at the top, so that $\text{Sem}(Y)$, rather than $\text{Sem}(Z)$, is joined to $\text{Sem}(R)$.

5.3 Semantic Dependency Notation

The notation used to express meaning in this chapter is a simplified version of a specification advocated by the author (Reeker, 1969), which was originally developed for a computerized system for semantics research. It incorporates a number of insights into the semantics of natural language gained through research in logic and in language—particularly within the generative semantics school—and some experience in language description derived from research in computer languages.

The design criteria for the notation, within the context of the system mentioned above were (1) that it be adequate for the expression of any known linguistically expressible semantic structure, and (2) that it be restrictive enough in framework to force meaningful system-building and comparison of alternatives by users of the system.

With these criteria in mind, and after surveying a large amount of linguistic semantics literature, we have chosen basically the dependency notation (Hays, 1964; Robinson, 1970; Schank, 1969), because it seems particularly natural for expressing semantics, simplifying structural descriptions because:

(1) The grammatical categories are redundant at the lowest level of semantics. The only categories at that level are "predicate" and "argument." This is a consistent fact in generative semantics deep structures, where the categories employed are S, NP, and VP, but where the occurrence of the symbols for these categories is entirely predictable.

(2) The concept of a natural ordering is meaningless at the semantic level. It is just not meaningful to ask which of the arguments of a verb "comes first," since there is no temporal or spatial relationship involved. Thus any order *imposed* is merely for the purpose of *selecting* an argument. We shall use selectors, which may be thought of as deep structure cases (in the sense of Fillmore).

Both grammatical categories and order are language-dependent phenomena, which should not, therefore be in the semantics.

The type of dependency notation being used here is analogous to operator trees often used for storing arithmetic expressions in a computer. Further, the Polish and reverse Polish expressions can be read directly from the trees. Thus

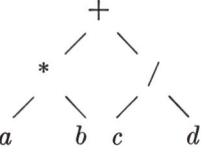

has Polish expression $+*ab/cd$ and reverse Polish $ab*cd/+$. The function of the selectors (mentioned above) is seen in considering the subtree

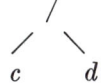

The order of the operands is important here only in the sense that a *convention* specifies that the dividend be listed first, the divisor second. The necessity of this order disappears if we add selectors to the edges:

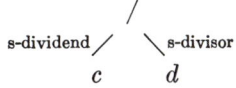

The mnemonic s for selector is as employed in the Vienna Definition Language (Lucas et al., 1968) for programming languages (although the Vienna Definition Language does not use dependency trees).

Each predicate in a semantic system has a characteristic number of arguments, and nouns may be considered as a special case of predicates without arguments.* Boolean connectives can be employed and have either one or two arguments (though the usual case can be made for allowing "and" to have an indefinite number of arguments—and maybe "or" also). Modals have one argument, which is another predicate. It appears that verbals all have a time argument, in addition to any others they may possess.

The notion of a time argument leads us to the notion of tense. Tense may be expressed by the relationship between the time argument of the sentence's main verb and the time of the speech act. To express these relationships, the notion of *lower node condition* may be used. A lower node condition is a relationship between two items in the dependency tree that is not shown directly within the tree. One of the most common lower node conditions is identity of reference, symbolized by "=," or by running two branches into a single node. Thus "John cut himself" might be denoted (without tense) as

```
        CUT                        CUT
   s-subj/  =  \s-obj    or   s-subj(      )s-obj
   JOHN────────JOHN                  JOHN
```

For the purpose of comparing times, the operators < (earlier) and > (later) are also needed (we will use = with time, also). Finally, in order to give a time to the speech act, the act itself is symbolized as a (performative) predicate, following the suggestion of Ross (1970). Thus with tense, "John cut himself" would be

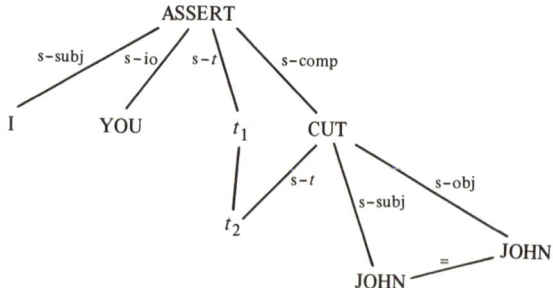

To a certain extent, Fillmore's generative lexicography approach was

---

* Although Bach (1968) has made a well-known suggestion to the contrary.

aimed at this type of thing and is easily (and to some advantage) placed within the semantic dependency notational system. To use one of his examples (1971),

CRITICIZE [Judge, Defendant, Situation (for)]
Meaning: SAY [Judge, X, Addressee]
X = BAD [situation]
Presupposition: RESPONSIBLE [Defendant, Situation]
Presupposition: ACTUAL [Situation]

We shall illustrate a possible treatment of presupposition also in presenting the tree representing this lexical item (time omitted)

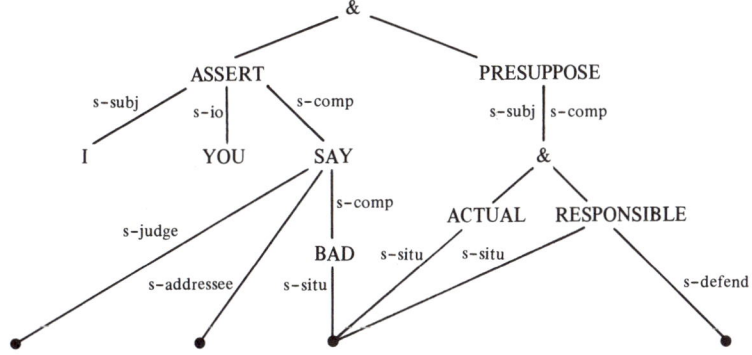

Thus "John criticized me for my laziness" might be given the meaning specification:

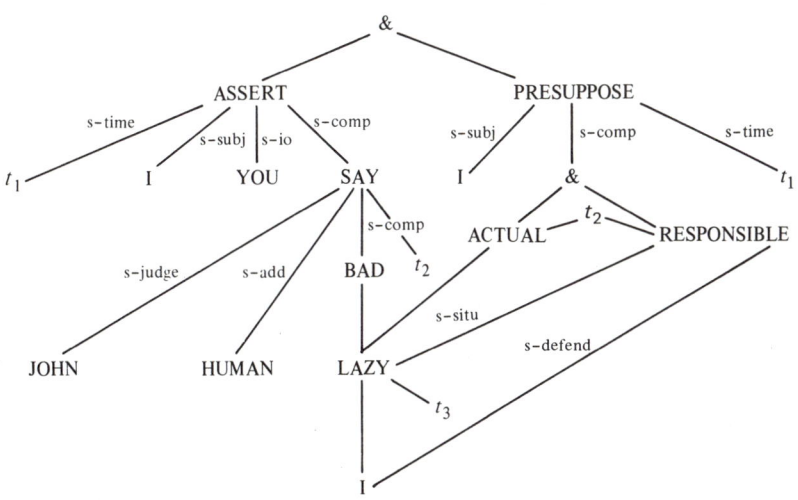

Adjectives, are, as illustrated, merely predicates, equivalent to verbs. The adjectival nature of certain predicates is a language-dependent phenomenon in some cases; but in general, adjectival predicates have a single argument besides "time." Adverbials are adjectivals whose arguments are predicates.

Adverbial phrases often require more precise specification of time than has been indicated above. After consulting a number of references,* and dealing with many examples, it is clear that time must be treated as a duration, with a beginning and an end. In the common "point of time" cases, the beginning and end of the time period are identical, but in cases such as "he sprained his ankle while running," the time argument of "sprain" must be within the period described by "run," as indicated in

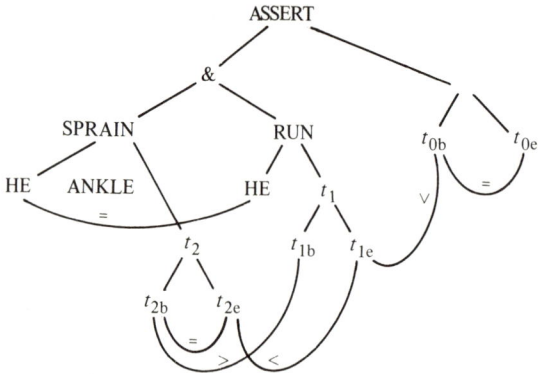

The mechanisms for expressing time and tense are already incorporated in the program mentioned above.

In the example above, a number of arguments and selectors are missing. In general, one can avoid untidy networks by including only the necessary details for the purpose at hand, confident that the others can be added as necessary. This is the approach we have followed in describing the semantics of our example in the text.

Note also that the primitives used in the examples given herein may not be truly primitive. It is, in fact, advantageous to be able to go upward and downward within the levels of primitiveness in experimental semantics work. Thompson has recognized this in his REL system (1974). It should be clear, for instance, that the abstract inchoative predicate BECOME is not primitive. If we adopt the analysis of McCawley (1968a) for "kill," the following would represent deeper and deeper levels of semantics (the

---

* Including the extensive treatment of time in Bruce (1972).

performative verb being omitted):

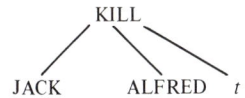

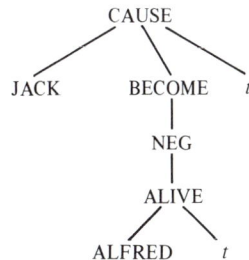

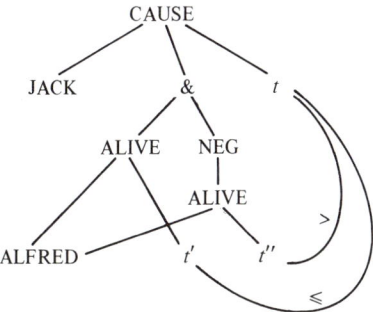

Modals are adverbials semantically: they have a time argument and one other argument, which is a predicate. Thus "he must come" is (using the conventional necessity symbol □) something like:

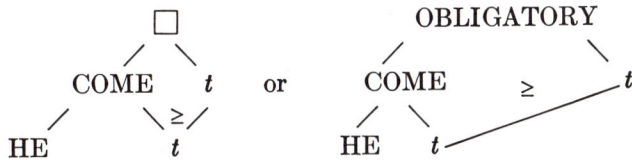

Other notions that may be needed in such a system (but are not yet part of it) include several "binding" operators, those that logically bind variables in the tree below them, quantifiers ∀ and ∃, the definite descriptor ι [this is also the definite formator of Leech (1969)], and perhaps a set operator ^ (Whitehead and Russell, 1925); although note that this is similar in its usefulness to ι. Robert Floyd has suggested that at some perhaps intermediate point, the abstraction operator λ is handy in expressing the structure of participles. Thus "Napoleon was beaten by Wellington"* would have some such structure as

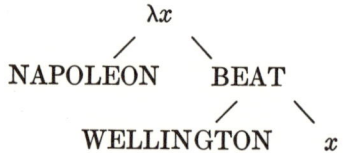

Compare the λ-converted form

```
          BEAT
         /    \
   WELLINGTON  NAPOLEON
```

"The beaten Napoleon was shipped off to the rock" would be (in non-primitive terms!)

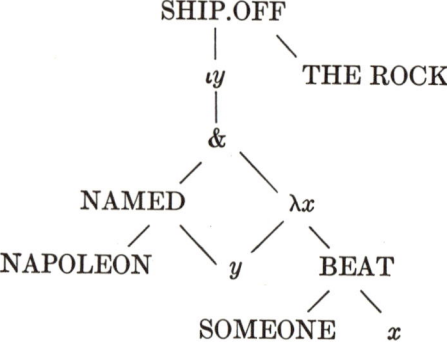

Thus (λx) (Wellington beat x) has the status of a predicate—in this case, an adjectival. "The beating of Napoleon by Wellington" would be expressed by

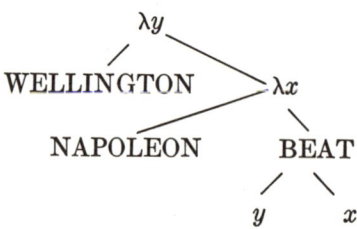

---

* Tenses and selectors are omitted in all the following examples.

The question of how many of these binding operations, if any, are necessary (or sufficient, or convenient) is currently under investigation.

In summary, then, the meaning representation used within PST is of a very general sort indeed. It appears that such a notation is a satisfactory one for expressing the base in generative semantic theory, and there is no reason to believe that it will not suffice for the expression of acquisitional phenomena as well. These considerations motivate (although they do not prove) its strong adequacy. One of the more important facets of the notation for the purposes of PST has been the fact that connected portions of the graph correspond naturally to the notion of "a subpart of the semantics."

REFERENCES

Anderson, J. R. (1974). "Language Acquisition by Computer and Child," Tech. Rep. No. 55. Human Performance Center, Ann Arbor, Michigan.

Anderson, J. R. (1975). Computer simulation of a language acquisition system. *In* "Information Processing and Cognition: The Loyola Symposium" (R. L. Solso, ed.). Lawrence Erlbaum, Washington, D.C.

Anderson, J. R., and Bower, G. H. (1973). "Human Associative Memory." Holt, New York.

Bach, E. (1968). Nouns and noun phrases. *In* "Universals of Linguistic Theory" (E. Bach and R. T. Harms, eds.), p. 90. Holt, New York.

Bach, E. (1974). "Syntactic Theory." Holt, New York.

Biermann, A. W., and Feldman, J. A. (1972). A survey of results in grammatical inference. *In* "Frontiers of Pattern Recognition" (S. Watanabe, ed.), p. 31. Academic Press, New York.

Bowerman, M. (1973). "Early Syntactic Development." Cambridge Univ. Press, London and New York.

Braine, M. D. S. (1963). On learning the grammatical order of words. *Psychol. Rev.* **70**, 332–48.

Brown, R. (1973). "A First Language: The Early Stages." Harvard Univ. Press, Cambridge, Massachusetts.

Bruce, B. (1972). A model for temporal references and its application in a question answering program. *Artif. Intell.* **3**, 1–25.

Chandrasekaran, B., and Reeker, L. H. (1974). Artificial intelligence—a case for agnosticism. *IEEE Trans. Syst., Man Cybernet.* **4**, 88–94.

Chomsky, N. (1957). "Syntactic Structures." Mouton, The Hague.

Chomsky, N. (1965). "Aspects of the Theory of Syntax." MIT Press, Cambridge, Massachusetts.

Clark, R. (1975). Some even simpler ways to learn to talk. *Int. Child Lang. Symp., 3rd, 1975* (to be published).

Culicover, P., and Wexler, K. (1973). "An Application of the Freezing Principle to the Dative in English," Social Science Working Paper No. 39. University of California, Irvine.

Dale, P. S. (1972). "Language Development: Structure and Function." Dryden, Hinsdale, Illinois.

Fillmore, C. J. (1971). Verbs of judging: An exercise in semantic description. *In* "Studies in Linguistic Semantics" (C. J. Fillmore and D. T. Langendoen, eds.), p. 273. Holt, New York.

Gold, E. M. (1967). Language identification in the limit. *Inf. Control* **10,** 447–474.

Gregg, L., and Simon, H. A. (1967). Process models and stochastic theories of simple concept formation. *J. Math. Psychol.* **4,** 246–276.

Hamburger, H., and Wexler, K. (1973). Identifiability of transformational grammars. *In* "Approaches to Natural Language" (J. Hintikka, J. Moravcik, and P. Suppes, eds.), p. 153. Reidel Publ., Dordrecht, Netherlands.

Harris, L. R. (1972). "A Model for Adaptive Problem Solving Applied to Language Acquisition." Cornell University, Ithaca, New York.

Hays, D. G. (1964). Dependency theory: A formalization and some observations. *Language* **40,** 511–525.

Jenkins, J. J., and Palermo, D. S. (1964). Mediation processes and the acquisition of linguistic structure. *Monogr. Society for Research in Child Development* **29,** 141–169.

Jesperson, O. (1922). "Language: Its Nature, Development and Origin." Allen & Unwin, London.

Jordan, S. R. (1972). "Learning to Use Contextual Patterns in Language Processing," Tech. Rep. No. 152. Computer Science Department, University of Wisconsin, Madison.

Katz, J. J., and Postal, P. M. (1964). "An Integrated Theory of Linguistic Description." MIT Press, Cambridge, Massachusetts.

Kelley, K. L. (1967). "Early Syntactic Acquisition," Rep. No. P-3719. Rand Corporation, Santa Monica, California.

Klein, S., and Kuppin, M. A. (1970). An interactive heuristic program for learning transformational grammars. *Comput. Stud. Hum. Verb. Behav.* **3,** 144–162.

Knuth, D. E. (1968). Semantics of context-free languages. *Math. Syst. Theory* **2,** 127–145.

Lakoff, G. (1970). "On Generative Semantics" (mimeogr.). University of Michigan, Ann Arbor.

Leech, G. N. (1969). "Towards a Semantic Description of English." Indiana Univ. Press, Bloomington.

Lucas, P., Lauer, P., and Stigleitner, H. (1968). "Methods and Notation for the Formal Definition of Programming Languages," Rep. No. TR25.087. IBM Vienna Laboratory, Vienna.

McCawley, J. D. (1968a). Lexical insertion in a transformational grammar without deep structure. *In* "Papers from the Fourth Regional Meeting of the Chicago Linguistic Society" (B. J. Darden, C.-J. N. Bailey, and A. Davison, eds.), p. 71. Department of Linguistics, University of Chicago, Chicago, Illinois.

McCawley, J. D. (1968b). Review of "Current Trends in Linguistics. Vol. 3. Theoretical Foundations." *Language* **44,** 556–593.

McMaster, I. (1975). "A Proposal for Computer Acquisition of Natural Language," Tech. Rep. No. TR75-3. Department of Computing Science, University of Alberta, Edmonton.

Osgood, C. E. (1963). On understanding and creating sentences. *Am. Psychol.* **18,** 735–51.

Peters, S. (1972). "Goals of Linguistic Theory." Prentice-Hall, Englewood Cliffs, New Jersey.

Piezer, D. B., and Olmstead, D. L. (1969). A theory of the child's learning of phonology. *Language* **17,** 60–96.

Postal, P. M. (1970). On the surface verb remind. *Linguistic Inquiry* **1,** 37–120.

Reeker, L. H. (1969). The generalization of syntactic specification. *Abstr., Meet. Handb., Annu. Meet., Linguistic Soc. Am.* p. 73.

Reeker, L. H. (1971). A problem solving theory of syntax acquisition. *J. Struct. Learn.* **2,** 1–10.

Reeker, L. H. (1974). The problem solving theory of syntactic acquisition. Doctoral Dissertation, Carnegie-Mellon University, Pittsburgh, Pennsylvania (unpublished).

Reeker, L. H. (1975). "An Examination of Innateness Arguments in Language Acquisition," Rep. No. TR-75-4, Department of Computer Science, University of Oregon, Eugene.

Reichenbach, H. (1947). "Elements of Symbolic Logic." Macmillan, New York.

Robinson, J. J. (1970). Dependency structures and transformational rules. *Language* **46,** 259–285.

Ross, J. R. (1970). On declarative sentences. *In* "Readings in English Transformational Grammar" (R. A. Jacobs and P. S. Rosenbaum, eds.), p. 273. Ginn, Boston, Massachusetts.

Schank, R. C. (1969). "A Conceptual Dependency Representation for a Computer-Oriented Semantics," A. I. Memo No. 172. Computer Science Department, Stanford University, Stanford, California.

Schank, R. C. (1973). Identification of conceptualizations underlying natural language. *In* "Computer Models of Thought and Language" (R. C. Schank and K. M. Colby, eds.), p. 187. Freeman, San Francisco, California.

Schwarcz, R. M. (1967). Steps towards a model of linguistic performance: A preliminary sketch. *Mech. Transl.* **10,** 39–52.

Siklóssy, L. (1972). Natural language learning by computer. *In* "Representation and Meaning: Experiments with Information Processing Systems" (H. A. Simon and L. Siklóssy, eds.), p. 288. Prentice-Hall, Englewood Cliffs, New Jersey.

Simmons, R. F. (1973). Semantic networks: Their computation and use for understanding english sentences. *In* "Computer Models of Thought and Language" (R. C. Schank and K. M. Colby, eds.), p. 63. Freeman, San Francisco, California.

Skinner, B. F. (1957). "Verbal Behavior." Appleton, New York.

Tarski, A. (1956). The concept of truth in formalized languages. "Logic, Semantics, Metamathematics" (transl. by J. H. Woodger). Oxford Univ. Press (Clarendon), London and New York (original paper presented in 1931).

Thompson, F. B. (1963). "The Semantic Interface in Man-Machine Communications," Rep. No. 63-TMP-35. General Electric, Santa Barbara, California.

Thompson, F. B., and Thompson, B. H. (1974). Practical natural language processing. *Adv. Comput.* **14,** 109–168.

Wexler, K., and Hamburger, H. (1973). On the insufficiency of surface data for the learning of transformational languages. *In* "Approaches to Natural Language" (J. Hintikka, J. Moravcik, and P. Suppes, eds.). Reidel Publ., Dordrecht, Netherlands.

Whitehead, A., and Russell, B. (1925). "Principia Mathematica." Cambridge Univ. Press, London and New York.

Winograd, T. (1973). A procedural model of understanding. *In* "Computer Models of Thought and Language" (R. C. Schank and K. M. Colby, eds.), p. 152. Freeman, San Francisco, California.

Woods, W. A. (1970). Transition network grammars for natural language analysis. *Commun. ACM* **13,** 591–606.

The Wide World of Computer-Based Education

DONALD BITZER

Computer-Based Education Research Laboratory
University of Illinois at Urbana-Champaign
Urbana, Illinois

1. Introduction 239
2. The PLATO System 243
3. System Configuration 254
4. Teaching Strategies 256
   4.1 Simulation 259
   4.2 Drill and Practice 262
5. Computational Applications 266
6. A Word about TUTOR 269
7. Evaluation 272
8. Cost of Services 276
9. Conclusion 281
   References 281

1. Introduction

Man has always striven to invent tools and machines to increase his productivity. While the industrial revolution has made material goods available to a large segment of the population, some service-oriented sectors of our economy still remain essentially labor intensive. One of these areas, education, spends over 60 billion dollars a year in the United States without significantly increasing its productivity.

The needs for help in the educational field are clear. The cost of education has increased rapidly, but the number of students who must be considered nonfunctional in our modern technological society has risen. Not only have the complexities of a modern society increased the demand for a better education, but they have also caused frequent retraining to meet the needs of the rapidly changing job opportunities. Our educational institutions, operating within the constraints of our present resources, cannot possibly meet the individualized educational needs of society for the broad range of applications from preschool through adult education. Resources to solve these unmet needs are not likely to be available through the traditional classroom approach.

Over the years, of course, some tools and machines have been introduced into our educational institutions. Many aids such as chalkboards, projectors, tape recorders, television equipment, and small teaching devices are used in many of our schools. However, textbooks, made possible by the invention of the printing press in the year 1440, are still regarded by most as the last great invention in education. The use of a digital computer for delivering education could change that opinion.

Having proved successful in aiding scientific research, computers were naturally appraised for other possible applications. Unlike many previous tools, which mainly increased productivity of material goods, the digital computer provided man with a tool that could increase productivity of the mind. However, the use of a computer for direct instruction is one of the most challenging applications of a computer, since it requires sophisticated interaction with the student at an economical price. The process of introducing the digital computer into the classroom has proven to be a long and difficult task.

Zinn (1967), who has since the early days of computer-based education recorded the development of the field, cites the early projects as developing simultaneously and independently under research psychologists and engineers. The concepts of how and what the computer should teach varied as widely as the background of the developers. Support for this research was eventually to come from many sources—the National Science Foundation, the Department of Defense, the United States Office of Education, various foundations, educational institutions, and some computer firms.

In a general sense, the use of the computer for scientific calculations is a computer-assisted instruction (CAI) role for the computer with the researcher being the recipient of the instruction. Dartmouth's later role in constructing a large, time-shared system utilized by faculty and students for research and design was an important step in this direction (Slesnick, 1969).

By 1960, several other projects were starting to emerge. Uttal (1962) at IBM connected several terminals to a computer using the system, among other things, for teaching stenotyping. The System Development Corp. connected several dozen terminals to a single computer (Coulson, 1962). These terminals consisted of a multiple-choice key input and a numerical display. Located at each terminal was a 35-mm filmstrip slide projector, which the student would manually turn to the slide number shown on his numerical display. The main purpose of this project was to collect better research data in the area of programmed instruction. Licklider (1962) at

Bolt, Beranak and Newman in Cambridge, Massachusetts, performed experiments in teaching language, math drills, and graphical responses as an aid in teaching analytical geometry. Bitzer and Braunfeld (see Kingery et al., 1967) at the University of Illinois began a project (the PLATO system) in which the terminal included a computer-generated graphic display and superimposed computer-selected slides. This system was used in the early stages for teaching computer topics, as well as math and language drills.

From these beginnings, CAI proliferated through the 1960s. It was difficult to pick up a Sunday newspaper without reading a story on a new CAI system that would solve the educational problems. Although such optimism was not warranted, many new and important developments did occur. Many educational institutions established centers for exploring CAI; Stanford University, Pennsylvania State University, Florida State University, The University of Michigan, The University of Texas, The University of California at Irvine, The U.S. Naval Academy at Annapolis, Coast Community College District, and Ohio State University are but a few institutions of higher learning that inititated CAI programs during this time.

Although much of the CAI work attempted to adapt the standard commercial computer equipment available, with the help of industry, several efforts were made to develop special computer and terminal equipment.

In connection with a project at Stanford University (Suppes, 1966) IBM developed a system especially for CAI applications (IBM 1500). Over a dozen of these systems were sold to a variety of educational institutions. The terminals consisted of an alphanumeric CRT display, a computer-controlled 35-mm slide projector, and a light pen, with a device to select prestored audio messages being added later. Although the system was capable of connecting 32 terminals, a typical system had between 12 and 16.

One of the first public school systems to get into CAI on their own was in Philadelphia, where a CAI center was established, headed by Sylvia Charp (1970). A special system was built for them (SAVI system) by Philco–Ford. Later, RCA installed a system of over 100 terminals for use in arithmetic drill and practice in some New York City primary schools. Devices invented specifically for use in CAI by the inventors at the University of Illinois PLATO Project were manufactured by Control Data Corp., Owens-Illinois Glass, and Magnavox Corp.

Some companies, sensing the impact that educational technology might soon have, formed new subsidiaries to work in this field—companies such as General Learning and Westinghouse Learning.

In addition to Philadelphia and New York, several other school districts were experimenting with CAI. School districts in Palo Alto, California, were working with Stanford University; McComb County, Mississippi, was participating in a fairly large-scale arithmetic drill and practice experiment; and the Waterford School District in Pontiac, Michigan, had its own special system developed. These are just a few of the activities in the United States. There were also CAI experiments taking place in Europe (CAI, 1970) and Japan (CAI, 1973).

Work today can be divided into three different areas: delivery systems, new system research and development, and component research for both hardware and software. Several of the systems developed in 1962 provided sufficient educational components to survive as delivery systems at their institutions. For example, Ohio State's CAI system is still being used for the delivery of medical education. Coast Community College District's CAI network is used for teaching in a variety of subjects, and the PLATO system at the University of Illinois has expanded to teach over one million student contact hours of instruction per year in more than 100 different subject areas.

Although other projects may have ceased, the influence of their efforts is still seen today, particularly in the drill and practice areas. For example, many school districts have acquired Hewlett Packard or Digital Equipment Corp. minicomputers and have connected as many as 32 terminals for teaching arithmetic skills. The Chicago School District in cooperation with UNIVAC has implanted approximately 800 alphanumeric CRT terminals for teaching math and reading skills in over 50 elementary schools.

Under National Science Foundation support, two extensive experiments in CAI have been undertaken—the TICCET system at the Mitre Corp., and expansion of the PLATO system at the University of Illinois. The results of these experiments will be evaluated by Educational Testing Services, Princeton, New Jersey.

The TICCET system is a medium-size system, which when fully loaded has 128 terminals connected to it. The terminals consist of modified Sony color television sets. Each terminal requires two television channels to connect it to the central computer system where the memory to support the displays is located. One channel is used to transmit the details of the picture composed of characters, either alphanumeric or specially designed to fit together to form a picture. The other channel is used to carry the color information. Together the process produces a quality picture, a necessity for instructional purposes. Authoring of material for the system is done on a separate system at a time when the system is not being used for instruction. For this experiment, materials in the areas of community college mathematics and English are being produced under the direction of C. Victor Bundersen (1974) at Brigham Young University. The material is being tested at two community colleges—Phoenix College, Phoenix, Arizona, and Northern Virginia Community College, Alexandria. Two small computers are used to support each system: one to echo the key inputs from the student and the other to determine the appropriate response to the student's input.

New research areas are also being explored in CAI. Voice recognition would be desirable in order to have a more natural medium for communication at the terminal. Research in the area of voice synthesis as well as recognition is presently being carried out at MIT, Bolt, Beranak and Newman, Stanford University, and the University of Illinois, among others. Development of new inexpensive terminal displays, large memories for library information retrieval, and many other interactive terminal devices is being explored. However, the development of inexpensive hardware is only one aspect of implementing CAI. Development of software that will understand and process student responses is also extremely important. Much is expected from the work in artificial intelligence at MIT, Stanford, Bolt, Beranak and Newman, Carnegie Mellon, and others. Presentation of lesson material and development of evaluation strategies will also be crucial to the further development and implementation of CAI on a broad scale. The computer industry will have to cooperate with educational institutions in order to make a significant impact.

To give a better idea of how a computer is used in the instructional process, a detailed description of a computer-based education system will be given and illustrated with various instructional examples. Although many types of systems are in use today, the PLATO system, which represents an advanced state of the art, will be discussed here. This system also represents the longest continuous work in the field.

2. The PLATO System

Beginning in early 1960 as a single terminal (Fig. 1) connected to ILLIAC I, PLATO evolved over the past 15 years to its present configuration. The present system utilizes a large central computer (Control Data Corp. Cyber 73-2), and as of June, 1975, over 900 terminals were connected to this system. There are presently 146 different sites distributed from the East to the West Coast and from Canada to Florida. A site may consist of from one to many terminals separated geographically from other sets of terminals. Figure 2 shows a classroom site located in the Foreign Language Building at the University of Illinois. During the calendar year 1975, over 1,000,000 student contact hours of instruction were delivered. Over 4000 lessons, representing approximately 3500 hours of instructional

FIG. 1. The PLATO terminal consisted of a small keyset and an ordinary television receiver. The television picture was refreshed from a storage tube memory. The terminal was connected to the ILLIAC I.

material in over 100 subject areas, are presently available. Approximately 275 courses using PLATO material were taught at as many as 40 different institutions (CERL, 1975). The data in Fig. 3 collected over a one-year period, illustrate for a few of the major subject areas the approximate number of students receiving instruction, the number of student contact hours, the number of instructors involved in using the lessons, and the number of lessons available. These data do not reflect time spent in authoring material in these areas or time spent by students in noncourse material.

As the system grew from a single terminal to the present size, some basic principles guided its development. Since these principles are crucial to understanding how and why the system operates as it does, they are discussed in some detail.

(1) The system should allow teachers of lesson material to function as authors of the material without becoming computer experts.

At the present time, there are over 1000 teachers authoring lesson materials in over 100 different subject areas. These subject areas include mathematics, music, medicine, political science, library science, accounting,

COMPUTER-BASED EDUCATION

FIG. 2. The Foreign Language Laboratory has one of the 25 PLATO sites on the University of Illinois campus. This site consists of 80 terminals.

speech, English, and many foreign languages. The teachers produce approximately 150 hours of new lesson material each week.

(2) The hardware and software development should be concurrent, each influencing the other and both being influenced by the needs of the students and teachers.

To provide for user input, the system has an easily accessible note file that allows users to make comments. These comments are reviewed each day and action on suggestions is often initiated before the next day. This approach has resulted in an extremely user-oriented system where an excellent hardware and software staff worked closely together to solve the users' problems. Because software to operate 1000 graphic terminals did not exist, an entirely new PLATO system software and TUTOR authoring language had to be developed. New hardware developments such as new display devices, communication devices, and memory devices were also developed as needed.

(3) Education should be viewed in a broad sense. The PLATO system should be able to handle any interaction taking place between student and terminal, whether it be use of the terminal as a computational tool or use for direct instruction.

Subject area (number of hours of available material)		Universities	Community colleges	Elementary and secondary schools	Governmental and others	Total
	Institutions	42	6	12	51	111
	Terminals	565	120	103	164	952
Accountancy (70)	S	675–700	1197			
	SCH	21,000	5478.3			
	T		9			
Biology (80)	S	150	1506			
	SCH	2500	8804.6			
	T	3	22			
Chemistry (50)	S	1890+	1308		30	
	SCH	30,958	6439.2			
	T		22			
Computer science (200)	S	800		20		
	SCH	25,600		2500		
	T	10		1		
English (100)	S	20	2633			
	SCH	900	8020.8			
	T	2	35			
Foreign language (900)	S	350		20		
	SCH	10,300		300		
	T			2		
Mathematics (100)	S	15	1592			
	SCH	200	5989.2			
	T		19			
Medicine (150)	S	200			30	
	SCH	10,000				
	T					
Veterinary medicine (440)	S	320				
	SCH	10,248				
	T					
Vocational training (250)	S		61		775	
	SCH		160		15,040	
	T		1			
Elementary math (125)	S			300		
	SCH			16,000		
	T			12		
Elementary reading (35)	S			405		
	SCH			6075		
	T					
Other (1000)	S	2500	200			
	SCH	10,000	300			
	T		10			

FIG. 3. The data shown here illustrate PLATO usage in a few major subject areas for a one-year period. Note: in column two, S is number of students, SCH is student contact hours, and T is number of teachers.

As a result of this general approach, important uses developed that were not anticipated. These included control of on-line experiments with automatic processing of the experimental data, vehicular simulations, and sophisticated model building for engineering design.

(4) Interterminal communication is essential, permitting students and teachers at one terminal to communicate through the central computer with students and teachers at other terminals.

Even if the system were not as widely distributed geographically as it is today, capability for intercommunication between terminals would be important. In the conventional classroom there are times when the teacher peers over the student's shoulder or must look at his work in order to provide assistance. In computer-based education there are times also when the only way a teacher who is geographically separated from his student can help that student is by actually looking at the student's screen. The PLATO system's ability to display on one screen what is on another, while simultaneously allowing written communication at the bottom of the screen, allows detailed communication between students and teachers, authors and authors, and teachers and consultants. This same capability has allowed the development of worldwide, on-line conferencing as well as interactive games.

(5) A school or other user must be able to experiment with the capabilities of the large system without having to invest in an entire system.

Users who ordinarily cannot consider computer-based education as an alternative because of prohibitively high initial capital investment are able to use and evaluate computer-based education for themselves. Many of the present remote sites began by using a single terminal, and as interest and applications increased, they acquired more terminals.

(6) Terminals must be able to communicate over a variety of media, including ordinary telephone lines, in order to provide availability to the largest number of people in the most economical manner.

Since the one form of private communication that reaches into most homes today is the telephone, the present capability of running as many as eight graphic terminals over a single ordinary telephone line is important. Because of this capability, on-line demonstrations of the system can be given anywhere in the world. However, the communication system is flexible enough so that when large numbers of users are within a 30-mile radius of a center, data are transmitted to the terminals in the picture field of an ITFS television channel and the key set data for many users returned on a single phone line.

(7) The system should use "key-by-key" interaction. Each key as it is pressed is sent to the computer for processing. This processing includes loading the necessary programs and student data, performing the calculations, generating the output, and transmitting it to the student's screen within approximately one-tenth of a second.

Key-by-key processing was necessary because less than 50% of the keys pressed by students could have been handled by key echoing. The remaining keys required the central computer to determine what response should be displayed on the student screen at that instant.

(8) Whenever possible, concepts rather than answers should be stored in the computer.

An attempt is made to have PLATO recognize and critique students' responses independently of how they are formulated. This is accomplished by storing models in the computer rather than storing all possible answers to questions. The computer processes the student's answer and formulates a response, which is calculated from the stored model.

As instructional experience was acquired, it became clear that the capability of the student terminal was a crucial element in the teaching function.

The terminal, which is used by the students as their means of communicating with the computer, must be extremely flexible in order to adapt to student needs in a variety of subject areas. Computer buffs may tolerate great inconveniences for gaining access to a computer, but to the majority of students, mastery of the lesson material is of primary concern and they expect the terminal and computer to assist them in this endeavor with a minimum of bother.

The terminal used in the present PLATO IV system (Fig. 4) resulted from user requirements that it be capable of superimposing computer graphics and slide images, speaking to the student, and detecting where the student touches the display.

Providing a reliable, inexpensive, point-by-point graphic terminal was a challenge that brought about the invention of the plasma display panel. The plasma display panel used in the PLATO terminals looks like a piece of window glass approximately $8\frac{1}{2}$ inches square (Agajanian, 1974; Johnson et al., 1971). The display is constructed of two flat panels of glass as shown in Fig. 5. On the inner surface of each of these panels of glass are deposited narrow, transparent, electrically conducting lines spaced 60 lines to the inch. A very thin layer of dielectric coating is deposited over these lines. The two panels, oriented with their lines perpendicular to each other, are separated by a few thousandths of an inch and sealed together at the

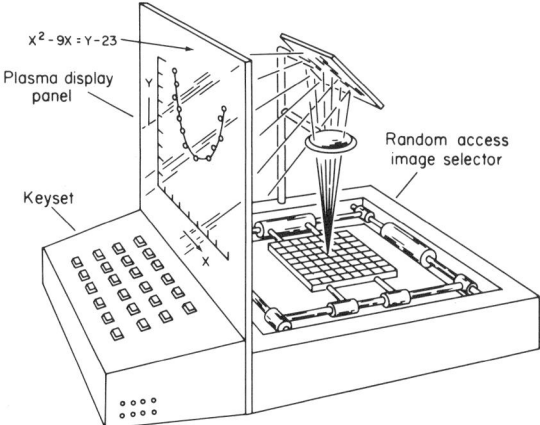

Fig. 4. The PLATO IV terminal uses a gas matrix display panel. This display panel not only permits computer displays to be drawn on the screen, but because it is constructed of flat transparent glass, slide images can be projected from the rear on the graphic display.

edges. The space between the panels is evacuated and filled with a gas mixture.

Because the electrode lines are separated from the gas by the dielectric layer, the operating characteristics of the plasma panel discharge are quite different from the normal dc discharge where the electrodes touch the gas (Fig. 6). If a dc voltage were applied to the plasma panel, only a single, short electric discharge and flash of light would appear instead of the

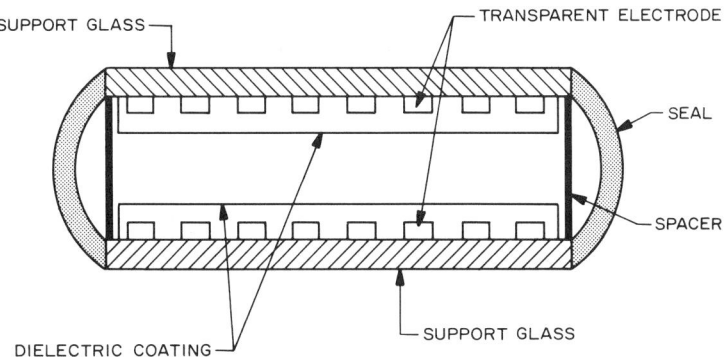

Fig. 5. In theory, the construction of the plasma panel is relatively simple, requiring only the deposition of metal electrodes and a dielectric over glass. However, in practice, the uniform deposition of material over large surface areas is a sophisticated process.

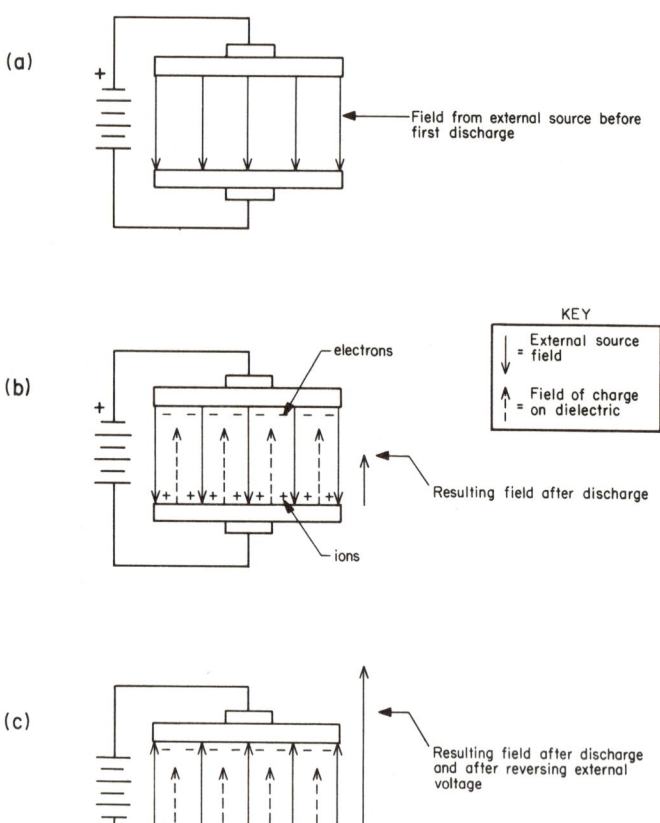

Fig. 6. The inherent memory characteristics of the plasma panel are caused by the electric charge deposited on the glass surfaces during and after the discharge. This sequence of diagrams illustrates how this charge, combined with an alternating external voltage, provides for the bistable region of operation.

steady glow as seen in dc discharges. The pulse discharge occurs because the electrons and ions produced during the discharge are insulated from the electrodes by the dielectric. The electric field at a point inside the panel is composed not only of the field caused by the external voltage, but also by the field created by the charge deposited on the dielectric surfaces. During the discharge, the electrical charges move to the dielectric surface in a manner that opposes the field from the external voltage, causing the discharge to cease.

Instead of applying a dc voltage across the electrodes, a rectangular-shaped voltage that alternates approximately 100,000 times per second is applied. The electric charge, which was transferred to the dielectric surface during the discharge, remains until another discharge occurs. However, the electric field from the external voltage is reversed when the voltage is reversed. The enhanced electric field causes another discharge, which is again extinguished by the movement of charge to the dielectric surfaces. This process is repeated each time the external voltage is reversed. These repeated short discharges, each lasting for a few tenths of a microsecond, produce what appears visually to be a continuous bright glow.

The charge deposited on the dielectric surfaces above and below a given spot also produces the inherent memory of the plasma panel. The external voltage, called the sustainer voltage, is applied simultaneously across all of the electrodes. The amplitude of the sustainer voltage is less than that required to cause a discharge. However, when combined with the field from the charges on the dielectric surface, it will produce the continuous succession of discharges. To turn a point "on" requires initiation of the first discharge for charging the dielectric surface. This is accomplished by applying a sufficiently large voltage across a single line on each of the surfaces. Since the lines on one surface are perpendicular to the lines on the other surface, only the point in the display where the lines pass over each other is selected. A similar technique is used to discharge the dielectric surface to "turn off" a selected point. Any of 512×512 discrete points can be selected this way and once a point is lighted, it stays lit until turned off. By lighting points sequentially, pictures can be drawn on the screen and remain there without flickering. This inherent memory of the panel eliminates the need for adjustments necessary with cathode ray tubes or TV sets. It also means that the flicker-free images, which are bright, sharp, and have high contrast, are easily readable for long periods of time in lighted rooms. Because of these features, which make the panel so readable, panels of various sizes and shapes have now been employed in a variety of other computer display systems.

The transparency of the panel is also important. For teaching in areas such as the medical sciences, chemistry, and biology, there is a need to display Kodachrome quality pictures such as tissue bisections, culture growth, chemical reactions, and X rays, and to superimpose these computer-generated graphics. The image selector, invented specifically to fill this need, projects images on the back of the plasma panel, which because of its transparency allows the slide to be clearly viewed from the front (Bitzer et al., 1970). An example from a children's reading lesson is shown in Fig. 7. The image selector is computer controlled and can select within

Fig. 7. The picture shown here is a superimposed image consisting of computer-generated writing on the plasma panel and a rear-projected slide. This material is used in an elementary reading program where the students interact and control the way a story is presented to them. If the student cannot read a word, he can touch it with his finger, and the computer will speak the word.

0.2 sec any of the 256 images on the 4 × 4 in. microfiche image sheet. The 256 images on the microfiche are arranged in 16 rows by 16 columns. The image selector moves the microfiche into position by controlling pneumatically driven pistons. A set of four pistons are connected end-to-end to move the fiche to the specified row and another set of four to move the fiche to the correct column. The stroke lengths of a set of pistons are 1, 2, 4, and 8 units. Thus, a combination of these stroke lengths can provide any of the 16 different positions needed. The computer sends an 8-bit code to the terminal, 4 bits of which are used to determine which pistons to extend for selecting the row and the remaining 4 bits to select the column.

In many instances it is important that the computer know where the panel has been touched by the student. Because the panel is flat and square, a touch system consisting of light-emitting diodes and diode detectors can be arranged on the front edges of the panel in a 16 × 16 matrix (Ebeling et al., 1972). When the student touches the front of the panel, a pair of light beams are interrupted and the location is transmitted to the computer. Thus, a student or user can respond by touching a word or picture on the screen. This capability is especially important when working with young children or others who might find using the typewriter keyboard difficult or cumbersome.

The terminal also permits authors to generate their own set of 126 characters in addition to the set of 126 always available in the terminal. These special characters, such as the Cyrillic alphabet used to teach Slavic languages and pictures of animals used to teach reading, are automatically transmitted to and stored in the terminal at the beginning of the lesson in which they are used.

In addition, there are many cases where the terminal must speak to the student. This speech capability has been used as an aid in teaching reading to children, in teaching foreign languages, and for playing special sounds such as heart beats. Because of these uses, the speech must be of high quality. The present audio device operates under computer control and can select from as many as 4096 messages or 22 min of audio, whichever is smaller (Johnson et al., 1971). These messages are stored on a thin, flexible, circular, magnetic disk and any message is retrievable within 0.3 sec. These 14-in. diameter magnetic disks are interchangeable and can be used to record messages as well as used to play back previously stored messages. The 4096 messages are located on 128 different tracks with each track divided into 32 sectors. The audio information is stored on the disk in analog form in the same way that information is stored on a tape recorder. The starting position of a message is given by choosing a track and sector. During record or playback, the disk moves at a rate of 11 sec per revolution, and the tape head switches smoothly from track to track for messages that are longer than 11 sec. However, when a new message is selected, the lightweight disk is rotated to the correct sector position at a high speed while the magnetic tape head moves to the correct track position. As with the image selector, the selection mechanisms are pneumatically driven pistons.

Finally, each terminal has an additional input–output connector for attaching any other devices. Data are transmitted to and from the devices through the terminal. This capability permits users to explore their creativity in both the software and hardware areas, and thus has been used to attach and control experimental laboratory apparatus.

3. System Configuration

The operation of hundreds of graphics terminals simultaneously at distances from the computer of a few hundred feet to hundreds of miles necessitates a highly efficient and unique system architecture, as shown in Fig. 8.

The PLATO system is based on a Control Data Corp. Cyber 73-2 computer with a high-speed central memory (CM) of 65,000 60-bit words and two central processing units (CPU) each capable of approximately one million instructions per second. Central memory is directly tied to 10 peripheral processing units (PPU), which act as minicomputers to handle input and output to the terminals and for controlling external devices such as printers, tapes, and disks. The heart of the system is the Control Data Corp. extended core storage (ECS) unit, a random-access electronic swapping memory that has direct ties to CM and to the PPU. The PLATO system presently has two million 60-bit words of extended core storage. Disk drives, accessed via the PPUs, furnish permanent storage of programs and data.

When a lesson is requested by a student or author, it is transferred from disk to the ECS unit, where it remains while in use. Programs and data in ECS are then swapped in and out of CM for processing by the CPUs, thus

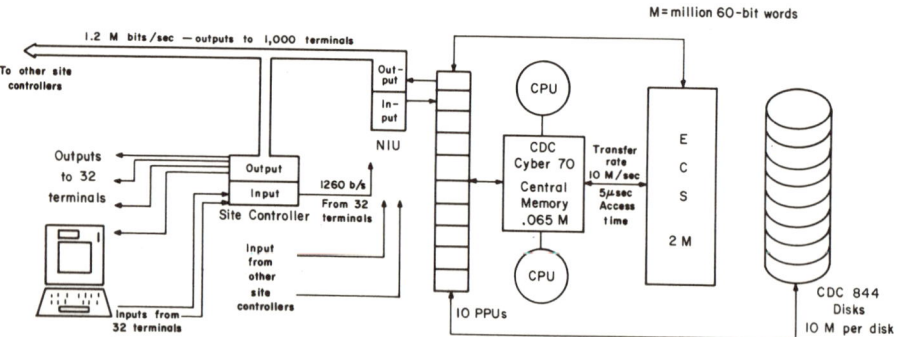

FIG. 8. In order to run hundreds of graphic terminals simultaneously, the computer system must be constructed in a way to provide rapid data transfer during the interactions of the users. The system configuration shown here provides for data transfer rates of 600 million bits per second.

eliminating any swapping of interactive jobs between CM and electromechanical disks or drum memory. The ECS unit has an access time of less than 5 μsec and a transfer rate of 600 million bits per second, or a transfer rate one hundred times greater and an access time one thousand times shorter than those for disks or drums. It is this enormous quantitative advantage of ECS over disk or drum memory that makes possible fractional-second response times to hundreds of terminals (the average response time is 125 msec). At the same time, ECS holds an economic advantage over high-speed CM.

A second element of the PLATO system architecture is the communications network interfacing the terminals at the computer. The major components of the communications system are a network interface unit (NIU) consisting of an input controller, an output controller, and a digital television transmitter (DTX), and a site controller, consisting of a digital television receiver (DTR) and a line concentrator. The computer delivers the output data packages for the terminals to the NIU, which multiplexes the data for 1008 terminals onto a standard TV channel. The TV-formatted data are then transmitted via microwave or cable to the 32 site controllers sharing the TV channel. Each site controller recovers from the TV channel all of the data destined for the 32 terminals serviced by that site controller and transmits the data to each terminal via a 1260-bit/sec telephone line. Present equipment permits the transmission of data at this rate to four terminals over a single ordinary telephone circuit. New equipment, currently under development, will allow transmission of data to eight terminals. Terminal to computer communication is exclusively via telephone line. A keypress from any terminal travels to the site controller over the connecting 1260-bit/sec circuit. At the site controller, a line concentrator multiplexes the data inputs from all 32 terminals onto a single telephone line for transmission to the NIU. The NIU receives the inputs from the 32 site controllers and delivers them to the computer for processing.

The NIU and the two PPUs dedicated to its services form the primary interface between the terminals and the computer. One PPU is dedicated to transmitting the data output packages from all the terminals from ECS into the NIU's output controller. The output controller is basically a parallel to serial converter consisting of two memories, each capable of storing one output package for each of the 1008 terminals served by the NIU. The contents of either of the memories in the controller are loaded or read in 1/60 sec. One memory is loaded by the computer during the 1/60 sec that the other is being read into the DTX. Each terminal is thus sent a 20-bit data output package 60 times each second, or 1200 bits/sec of information. If no new information is required, a terminal will receive an output of all zero bits.

The DTX encodes the data into a form compatible with the requirements of standard commercial TV equipment, including horizontal and vertical synchronization and blanking pulses. One bit of data for each of 84 terminals can be packed onto a single horizontal picture line. Twelve such lines can thus deliver one bit of information to 1008 terminals. The remaining horizontal lines deliver subsequent bits to each of the 1008 terminals to comprise 20-bit output packages. The data are transmitted serially so that two adjacent bits for any single terminal are separated by 1007 bits for the other terminals on the network. This data format has two advantages: the site controller need only forward data through to the terminal; it does not have to store data arriving at a high rate and forward it at a low rate to the terminal. Thus, the design and operation of the site controller is simplified. Second, a short burst of noise on the television channel disturbs one bit for several terminals rather than several bits for one terminal. This allows a simple parity bit check by the terminal to detect most transmission errors.

A second PPU channels input from the NIU to the computer for processing. Inputs from the 32 site controllers are routed to the input controller. The input controller constantly scans all incoming lines for data. When it detects data, it transfers them to the PPU, which forwards it to ECS and the CPUs for processing, and then resumes its scan.

4. Teaching Strategies

No matter how flexible the terminal or how sophisticated the computer processing, the quality of instruction is still greatly dependent on the caliber of the lesson material. The old computer adage "garbage in equals garbage out" is also true for computer-based education. Criteria for judging the material should include more than examination of the lesson content alone, because the way in which the computer is used is also important. Simply to copy a well-written book into a computer for sequential viewing by the student is likely to be a waste of computer resources and would probably not teach any better than just giving the book to the student in printed form.

However, the system's degree of flexibility, including its capability to respond to students' constructed responses, does not place a practical limit to the types of teaching strategies that can be employed.

Whenever possible, the objective is to permit the students to be creative in their answers and still be capable of processing the student's answer. Processing the student's answer should result not only in telling him whether he is right or wrong, but if wrong, how his answer is incorrect. In many instances there are a large if not infinite number of answers to a question, such as with an algebraic response to an engineering problem. Therefore, an attempt is made to store concepts in the computer rather than a list of answers, allowing students to have different correct answers to the same question. Figure 9 illustrates how these different answers can be judged correct by computer computation to determine that the student's algebraic response is equivalent to that of the teacher. In addition to mathematics, this concept-storing approach is utilized in many other areas such as chemistry, biology, geometry (Fig. 10), and even in the determination of the content of constructed sentences in grammar courses. In the teaching of computer programming, this approach allows a complete computer program to be accepted as the student's response.

Strategies for presentation of lesson material are often categorized into drill and practice, simulation, tutorial, inquiry, and dialogue. In practice, a mixture of these strategies is usually employed for teaching most subjects. For example, simulations utilized to introduce new concepts are much more effective when accompanied by some tutorial material to provide explana-

```
If the acceleration is constant, the average
velocity v̄ can be written as a simple function
of the initial velocity vᵢ and the final velocity
v_f. Write an expression involving vᵢ and v_f:

v̄ = ⟩ (vᵢ²-v_f²)sin3Ø°/(vᵢ-v_f)  ok

  Fine.  A simpler form is  (vᵢ+v_f)/2  .
```


Press BACK to return to index.

FIG. 9. This figure shows a student's unanticipated answer to a question posed in a beginning physics course. Although this answer was not the same as that supplied by the author, the computer judged the response to be equivalent to that of the author and therefore correct.

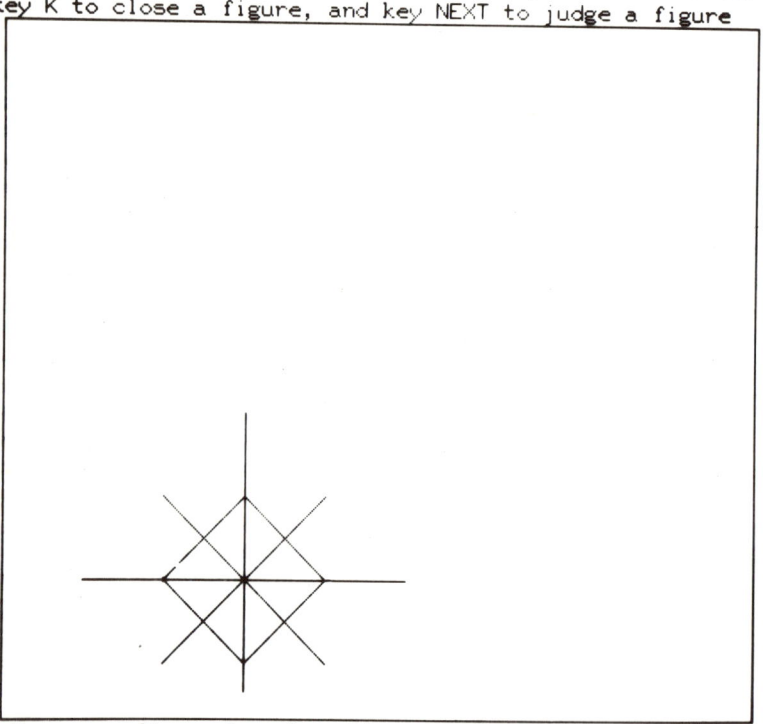

Fig. 10. In an elementary geometry program, the computer permits the free construction of polygons to meet specified conditions. Since the computer can analyze the student's responses, it can then inform him not only if his answer is right or wrong, but also how it is incorrect.

tion and some drill and practice material in order to assure the students' understanding and mastery of the material. Although it is impossible here to show much lesson content or to go into much depth, it is useful to give several examples illustrating how some different teaching strategies have been implemented. Computer-based education is a highly interactive process that is difficult to describe verbally. The best understanding of this process is gained by being a student at a terminal. However, since this is not possible, a large number of pictures from the student screen will be used to aid in the description of the various processes.

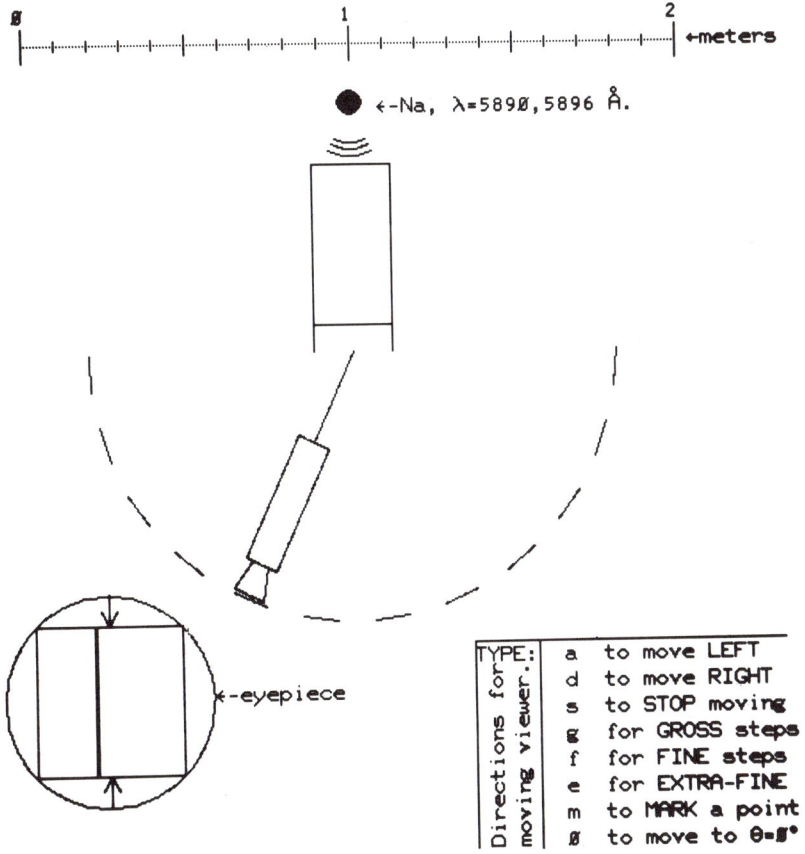

Fig. 11. This experiment uses a simulated spectroscope. It allows the student to choose a variety of light sources and change the angle of the viewing scope in order to determine the spectrum of a substance.

4.1 Simulation

Figures 11–13 show examples of simulated experiments used by students in physics (Bennett, 1972) and biology (Hyatt et al., 1972). The modern physics experiments were simulated on PLATO by Carol D. Bennett at the University of Illinois. In each case, a mathematical model stored in the computer is used to predict the outcome (experimental results) based on the input (student-controlled variables). Often the laboratory equipment is drawn on the terminal and the components move on the screen as the student manipulates the controls through his keyset. Simulated laboratory

(Temperature=21.8°C, Frequency=1800 Hz)

Part 1) Speed of sound from lengths of resonating pipes

a) Move the microphone to a position of high meter reading.
b) Move the plunger and mark points of maximum reading.
c) Press -LAB- to compute the speed of sound.

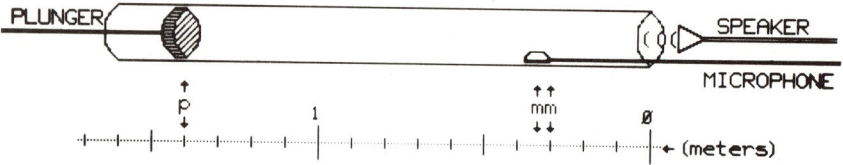

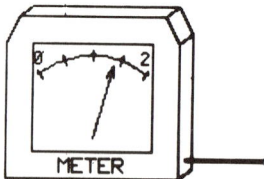

Key	Function
m	select microphone
p	select plunger
→	move m or p right
←	move m or p left
s	stop moving m or p
↑	mark a point with ↑

FIG. 12. This simulated physics experiment is used for measuring characteristics of the transmission of sound waves in air. The student uses the keyboard to adjust the apparatus and the computer generates and displays the resulting sound intensity levels on the meter.

experiments have several definite advantages:

(1) They give students experience in conducting experiments where either the actual laboratory equipment would be unavailable or too expensive and where the outcome of the experiment might be dangerous.

(2) They separate the cognitive skills from the manipulative skills associated with an experiment. For example, in qualitative organic chemistry, the student can master the theoretical procedures for identifying unknown compounds before going to a real laboratory, where he must also be concerned with the careful handling of the physical apparatus.

Fig. 13. This simulated biology laboratory allows the students to conduct their own genetic experiments with fruit flies. A model stored in the computer uses the genes of the parents to calculate the genes of the offspring. Using parents chosen by the student, the computer generates and displays detailed drawings of the resulting offspring.

(3) They permit students to perform a large number of experiments in a short period of time.

In some simulated experiments, such as the one shown in Fig. 14, the computer graphs the results of the experiment. The purpose of the exercise shown in this example is to allow the student to explore the effect of pH on a reaction that forms acetone oxime and a mixture of acetone and hydroxylamine (Smith and Ghesquiere, 1974). As the student varies the pH of the solution, the computer calculates the reaction rates and plots the results on the student's screen.

As the computer generates the experimental data, it also keeps a record of what experiments have been attempted. When the student indicates that he has completed his experimentation, the computer provides a critique of how well the experiment was conducted. In the case shown in Fig. 15, the

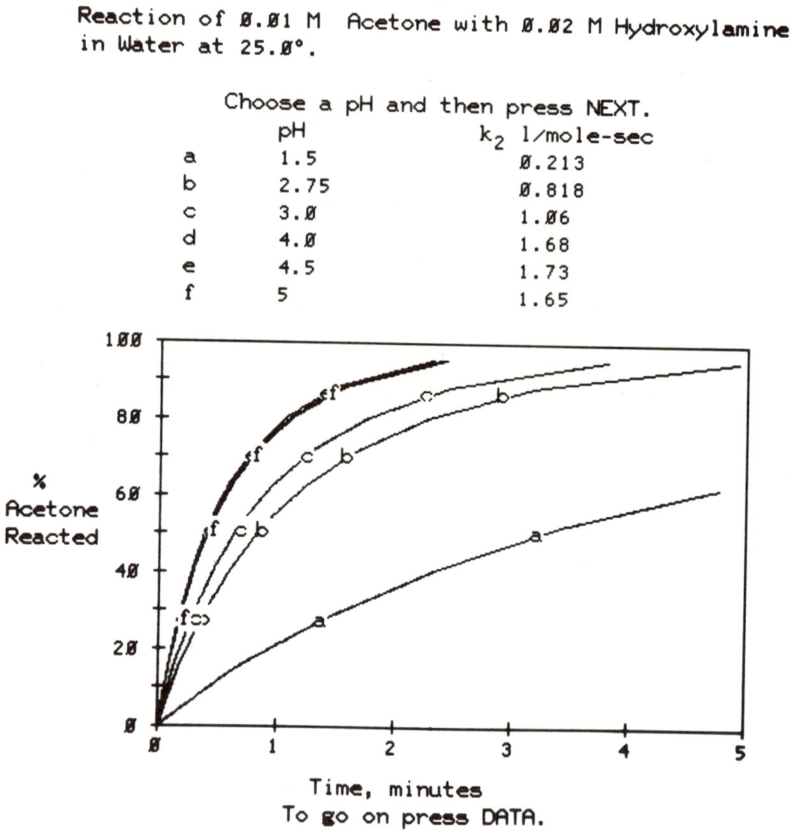

Reaction of 0.01 M Acetone with 0.02 M Hydroxylamine in Water at 25.0°.

Choose a pH and then press NEXT.

	pH	k_2 1/mole-sec
a	1.5	0.213
b	2.75	0.818
c	3.0	1.06
d	4.0	1.68
e	4.5	1.73
f	5	1.65

To go on press DATA.

FIG. 14. As the student chooses different pH values, the computer calculates the resulting reaction and plots the rate on the student's display. As shown in this illustration, many values can be plotted on the same display.

student is told that more data are needed in order to interpret the results of the experiment.

4.2 Drill and Practice

Often when a person thinks of drill and practice materials, he visualizes long sequences of addition problems or vocabulary words and associates such exercises with dull repetition, rote memory, low incentive, and few side benefits.

This need not be the case. Figures 16 (Hop Game), 17, 18 (Speedway),

Here is a summary of the experiment which you did on the effect of pH on the rate of formation of acetone oxime.

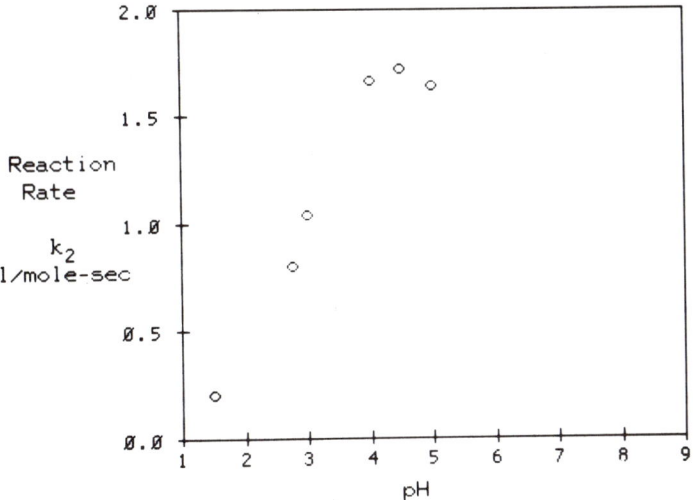

To interpret this plot of rate of oxime formation vs pH you need more data in the pH region of 5 to 7 Please press NEXT and do a few more experiments.

Fig. 15. When the student indicates to the computer that he is finished running the rate experiments, the computer displays a summary of the entire experiment and gives a critique.

and 19 (How the West Was Won)* show several examples of drill materials in elementary mathematics (Dugdale and Kibbey, 1975) and one in chemistry (Smith, 1971). Each of these examples exhibits more than just rote memory practice. First, motivation is provided by making a competitive game of the practice material. The student is competing against time, the computer, or another student. In addition to reinforcement by drilling, another objective of the material is practice in decision making and strategy development. The student must make decisions as to how to proceed in the game, and as he makes these decisions, he develops a strategy that helps determine the outcome of the game.

* These elementary mathematics materials were created by Bonnie Anderson Seiler, University of Illinois.

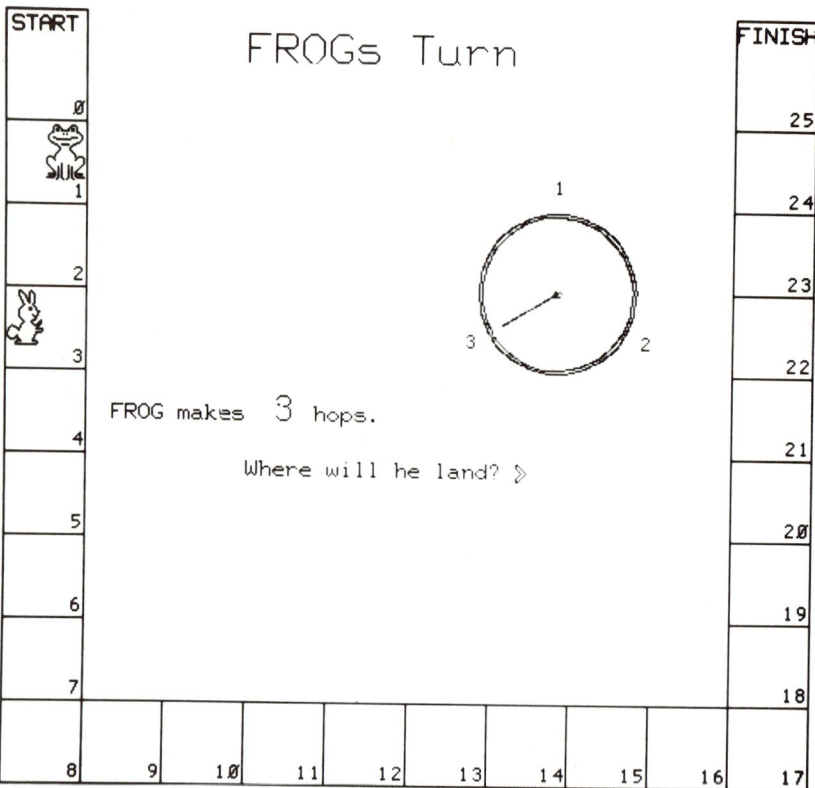

Fig. 16. The incentive of a competitive game is utilized for kindergarten children who are learning to count. The computer turns the spinner and the objective is to have the child correctly determine the new position for his animal on the game board. If his count is correct, the animal hops to the square that he has indicated, while an incorrect answer forfeits the turn.

To illustrate further, consider the elementary math game in Fig. 19. The computer draws the game board including towns in which it is both safe (cannot be sent back) and rewarding (extra ten moves) to land, and positions from which shortcuts can be taken. The object of the game is to be the first person to land exactly on the finish line. Turns are taken by having the computer randomly choose three single digit numbers shown on spinners. The players must combine these numbers by addition, subtraction, multiplication, or division to give a new number, which determines how far he will move. There are numerous ways of combining the numbers to give different results, and thus provide the student with different

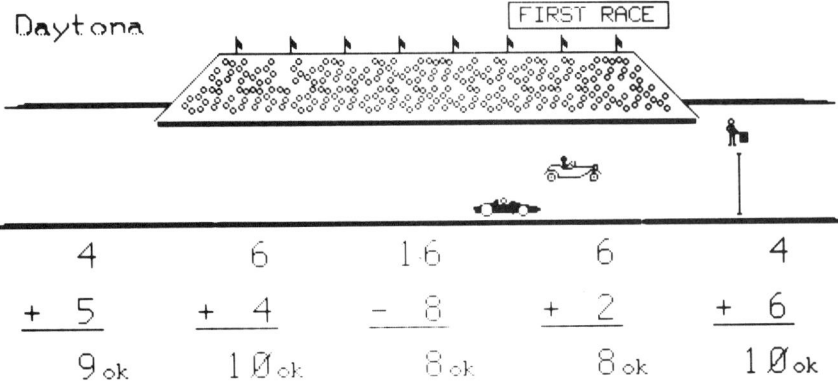

FIG. 17. In this racing game used for drill in elementary mathematics, the student is playing against himself. Since the opposing racer runs at the student's previous best performance, the student must improve on his past performance to win. At the end of each race, the student is given an analysis of the problems he missed, and these problems appear in the next race.

options, for instance, choosing to generate a smaller number if it allows him to take a shortcut or to land on the location of the other player and send that player back. The practice comes as the student generates (by addition, subtraction, multiplication, and division) many numbers in determining what he thinks is his best move. If he makes a mistake in evaluating the results, he loses his turn and thus is motivated to be accurate. This type of drill gives up some of the control needed to measure the type of difficulty a student is having, but it has many additional advantages, some of which have already been mentioned.

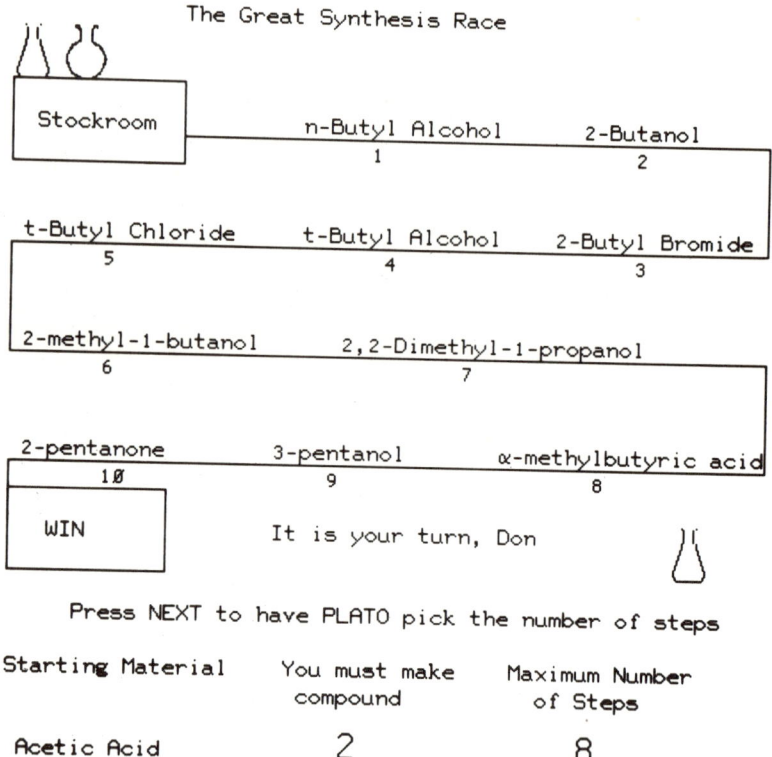

Fig. 18. In an organic chemistry course, the student can practice synthesizing different organic compounds from a variety of starting materials. The objective of the game is to reach the win box first. The student plays either against the computer or against another student, and the more complex the problem he solves, the faster his advancement toward the goal.

5. Computational Applications

The PLATO TUTOR (Sherwood, 1974; Tenczar, 1974) language facilitates the storing of algebraic and alphanumeric strings generated by the student. These strings can be compiled and run as computer language statements, making it possible to provide both instruction and programming capabilities in a variety of computer languages. Figure 20 shows a simple algebraic language that permits the student to write short programs and graph the results.* This type of language has been found useful in science

---

* The GRAFIT language was created by Bruce Sherwood at the University of Illinois.

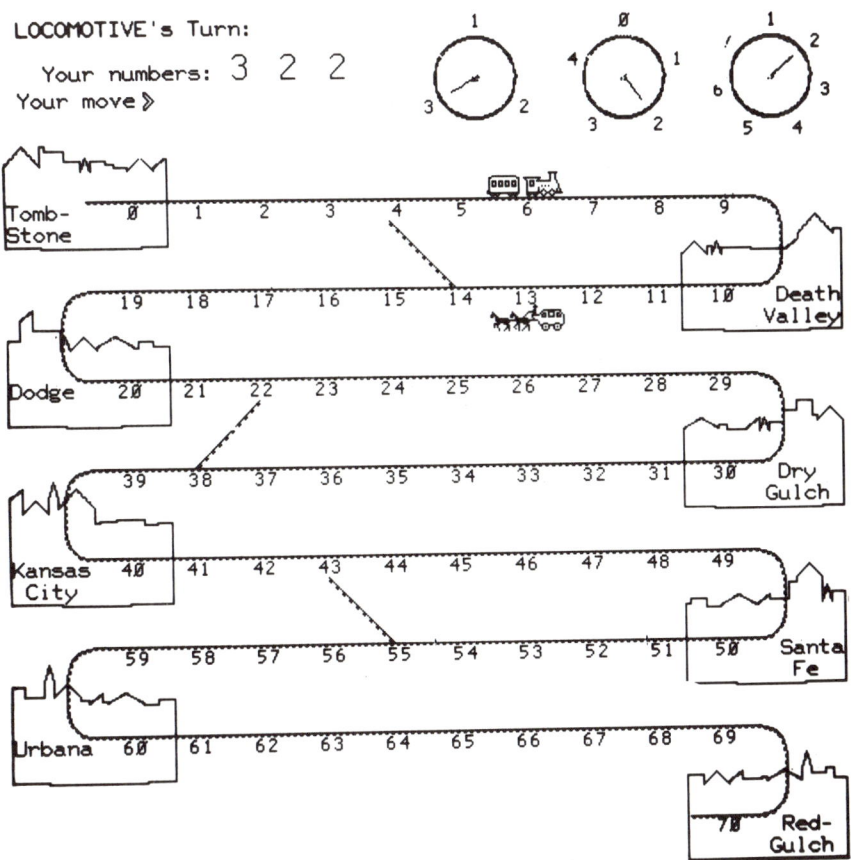

FIG. 19. The game of "How the West Was Won" is a race between two students or a student and the computer to reach the final city first. Since the numbers chosen by the computer can be combined in many different ways, the concept of developing a winning strategy is introduced.

courses such as physics, where the student uses the capability as an enrichment exercise after completing his regular lesson materials.

Common languages such as BASIC (Fig. 21) are also available in courses designed to teach computer languages and their applications.* Error

---

* This version of BASIC was implemented by Larry White and Axel Schreiner, University of Illinois.

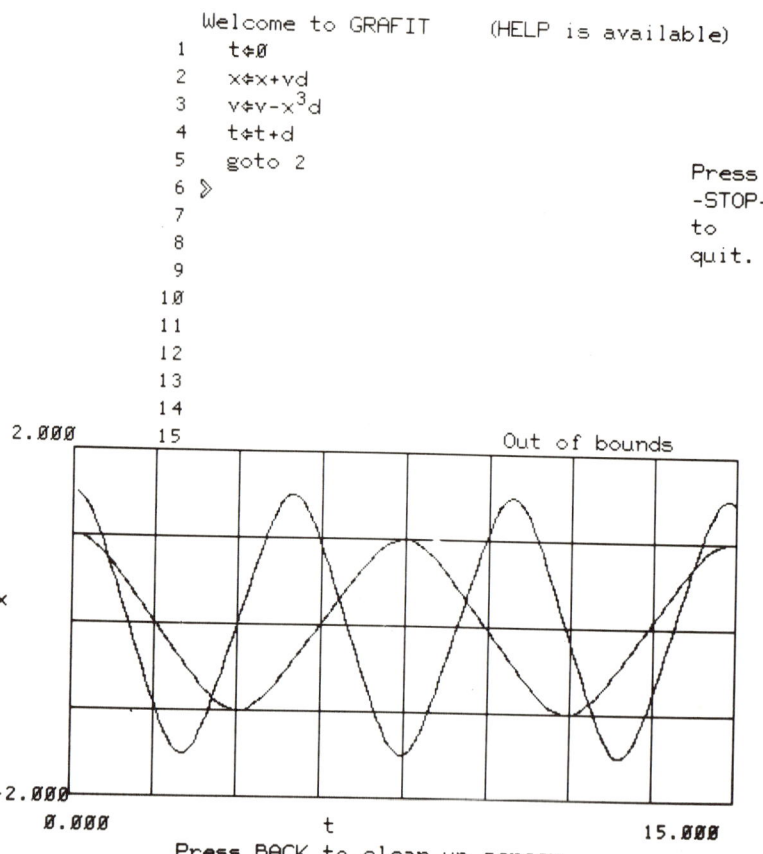

Fig. 20. GRAFIT is a simple algebraic programming language that permits a student to write short computer programs and plot the results on his display. Both the program and the parameters can be altered without disturbing the previous graph, thus allowing the plotting of superimposed curves.

analysis is available immediately, along with help indicating the type of error and hints on how to correct it.

Teaching a programming language is not limited to advanced students. A picture language (Fig. 22) is available for very young children.* In cases where the child has not yet learned to read, the instructions regarding the use of the picture commands in the language were given by the computer audio.

* The "PICTO" language was created by Paul Tenczar at the University of Illinois.

```
 4.6 MS/S           WITS VERSION 2.2          SPACE= 128
L
  10 PRINT 'TYPE IN A POSITIVE INTEGER'
  20 INPUT A
  25 LET C=INT(A)
  27 IF C<>A GOTO 10
  30 LET B=50
  40 PRINT B
  50 LET B=B-A
  60 IF B>=A+A GOTO 40
  70 PRINT'DO YOU WANT TO TRY AGAIN'
  80 INPUT Z
  90 IF Z=1 GOTO 10
>
```

-HELP- ON THE FILING SYSTEM, -SHIFT- -HELP- ON LANGUAGES

FIG. 21. The BASIC language shown here is but one of the many computer languages available to the students on an interactive basis.

6. A Word about TUTOR

The development of the TUTOR language, which made it possible for the classroom teachers to write these materials, was initiated and directed by Paul Tenczar at the Computer-Based Education Research Laboratory. As mentioned earlier, the development took place in a user environment where the language was continually adapted to the needs of the user. The TUTOR language statement appears as a command plus a tag field. At present, there are over 160 different TUTOR commands in the language. These commands fall into several categories: display, control, calculation, and judging.

2↑ 8← 5[🚶° 3→ 🚶 2[🚶° 🚶] ↓ 3←]

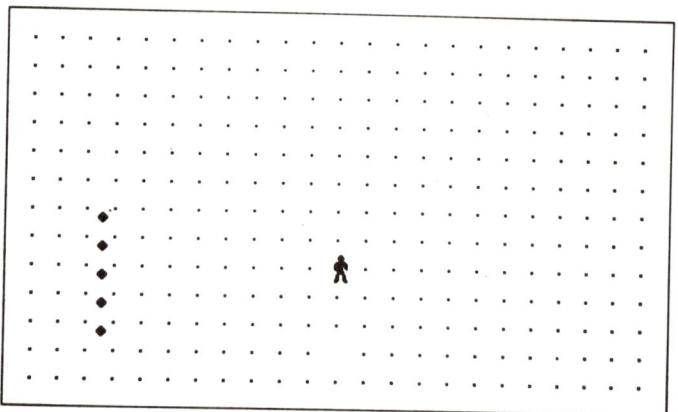

FIG. 22. The PICTO computer language is designed for use by elementary school children. The action of the man on the screen is controlled by the program. The language includes picture statements that allow the man to move in various directions, perform functions such as picking up and putting down objects, and perform repeated functions (those enclosed in brackets). As the program runs, the man moves on the screen with a cursor pointing to the statement then being executed by the program. The program shown contains a "nested DO loop," which causes the man to move in succession to each of the five balls. He picks each ball up, moves it three spaces to the right, puts it down, picks it up and down two or three more times, and then moves on to the next ball.

Examples of display commands are WRITE (to write on display), AT (where to write), SHOW (to display numbers), DRAW (to draw line figures), CIRCLE (to draw circle), and so forth. Some examples of control-type commands are JOIN (to join in another part of a lesson), JUMP (to go to another part of the lesson), and GOTO (looping instruction). The CALC command permits the author to write almost any computation statement in the tag field. Judging commands such as ANSWER, CONCEPT, or STORE permit the student's answer to be processed and responded to by the computer. The PLATO judging commands make it possible for the computer to process the student's

Item	%	Mean	sd
Computer-based education is nothing but an expensive gimmick.		4.339	0.343
Strongly agree	2.2		
Agree	2.4		
Uncertain	7.9		
Disagree	40.2		
Strongly disagree	47.4		
Computer-based education dehumanizes the student.		3.977	0.383
Strongly agree	2.4		
Agree	8.0		
Uncertain	9.9		
Disagree	45.5		
Strongly disagree	34.2		
For this course, which one of the following do you see as the most important advantage of PLATO? (Choose only one.)		—	—
Learn more in the same amount of time	9.9		
Learn the same amount of material in less time	16.8		
Learn with less trouble	20.7		
Better understanding of the material	42.2		
None (PLATO has no particular advantage in this course)	10.4		
How would you advise a friend who has a choice between taking this same U. of I. course (including PLATO) or another U. of I. course which covered the same material but without PLATO?		3.384	0.354
Avoid PLATO U. of I. course like the plague	2.2		
Avoid PLATO U. of I. course if convenient	2.9		
Take PLATO U. of I course only if convenient (it makes no difference but is a new experience)	38.7		
Take PLATO U. of I. course if at all possible	47.2		
Fight tooth and nail to get into PLATO U. of I. course	19.0		

FIG. 23. The results of this student attitudinal questionnaire given in 1974 showed that the students think of PLATO as a valid teaching aid and not a gimmick. The majority of students desired to continue using PLATO in their following courses.

Suppose that next semester you had to give the course for which you have had the most PLATO experience. Would you use PLATO again?	Univ. of Illinois				Non-Univ. of Illinois			
	$\bar{x}$	sd	n	%	$\bar{x}$	sd	n	%
	4.735	0.511			4.625	0.744		
Never			0	0			0	0
Probably not			0	0			0	0
Not really sure			1	2.94			1	12.50
Probably would			7	20.59			1	12.50
Absolutely			26	76.47			6	75.00

FIG. 24. The results of this instructor attitudinal questionnaire given in 1974 indicate the desire of teachers to continue their use of PLATO.

answer for such things as misspelled words or an out-of-order word, as well as to extract concepts from the student-generated sentences.

The ability to store standard algebraic responses and compute their values for various parameters also makes the PLATO judging very powerful for analysis of students' mathematical responses. The tag field of the TUTOR language describes in more detail what the command should do. Almost all commands determine what will be done in the tag field on the conditional basis, that is, the values of a variable will determine which part of a tag field to use. For example, JOIN (command) exp, a, b, c, d will join in the lesson unit a if exp is negative, unit b if exp is zero, unit c if exp is one, and unit d if exp is two or more. exp can be either a variable or an arithmetic expression. This flexibility makes branching very easy at the instant of computation.

7. Evaluation

The importance of on-going and continuing evaluation cannot be overemphasized when a new medium such as computer-based education is employed in a wide variety of applications. Evaluation consists of many facets, and to plan for future implementation of computer-based education it is necessary to know more than whether the given lesson material teaches and at what cost. It is also important to ascertain the attitudes and acceptance of the students and teachers to such things as subject area, the medium of instruction, and any redefinition of their roles that may occur in

	Exam means (standard deviations)				F Statistic (df) experimental vs. control
	10 A.M. sections		11 A.M. sections		
	Experimental	Control	Experimental	Control	
Exam 1	80.8 (8.8) $N = 35$	84.1 (9.3) $N = 35$	80.2 (9.8) $N = 30$	80.6 (11.9) $N = 40$	1.06 (1, 72)
Exam 2	63.8 (13.5) $N = 35$	67.8 (14.9) $N = 35$	63.1 (15.1) $N = 30$	66.2 (12.3) $N = 40$	0.90 (1, 72)
Exam 3	88.5 (9.2) $N = 33$	89.6 (16.7) $N = 34$	86.6 (11.8) $N = 28$	86.4 (9.6) $N = 36$	0.25 (1, 69)
Final exam (comprehensive)	81.2 (10.6) $N = 34$	74.4 (12.6) $N = 33$	76.2 (12.7) $N = 28$	70.7 (13.5) $N = 39$	9.12** (1, 75)
Students missing from final	1 prior B	1 prior F	1 prior B 1 prior C	1 prior F	

** Significant at 0.01 level.

FIG. 25. This table, taken from an evaluative study by James McKeown using PLATO for teaching an elementary accounting course, shows that a significant difference was measured in the final comprehensive examination even though no significant difference was found on the performance of students in hour exams. The total student study time of the PLATO group was less than that of the control group. (Reproduced from "PLATO Instruction for Elementary Accounting," James McKeown, by permission of the author.)

utilizing the new technology. Perhaps it is because all of these things have not been considered that most innovations in education seldom last past the period of the supporting grant.

A proper evaluation strategy is as difficult to formulate and implement as the implementation of the new educational technology itself. It appears from data gathered in many CAI experiments involving drill and practice that when the lesson material is finally revised and validated, computer-based education can deliver instruction as well as or better than the conventional classroom and in less time (Jamison *et al.*, 1976). It still remains to be proven conclusively how well the computer teaches material that requires more sophisticated strategies, but the preliminary indications look promising. One of the most difficult aspects of such an evaluation is the separation of what the medium can do from what a given piece of lesson material might do depending on how well it is prepared.

Educational Testing Services at Princeton, New Jersey, is conducting extensive evaluation studies on the use of PLATO in a variety of educational settings. At the conclusion of the National Science Foundation

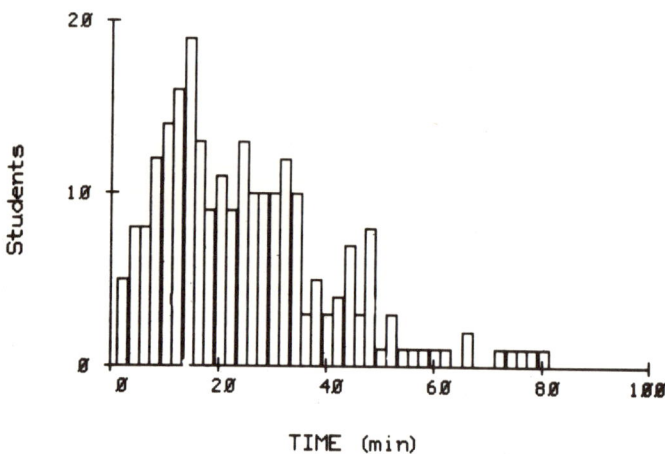

Fig. 26. These data indicate the wide variance in the time it takes different students to complete the same chemistry lesson. One advantage of using the computer for instruction is that such a time variance can be accommodated.

PLATO experiment in 1976, the results of these studies will be available. However, a number of evaluation studies concerning PLATO as a teaching medium have been conducted by the Computer-Based Education Research Laboratory and by instructors who use PLATO in their classes. In 1974, an attitudinal questionnaire was given both to students and instructors using PLATO. Some of the results of the attitudinal questionnaire given to 584 students from 23 separate courses (Siegel, 1974) are given in Fig. 23. The results of an attitudinal survey given to 34 University of Illinois instructors and eight non-University instructors who used PLATO (Siegel and Avner, 1974) is given in Fig. 24.

An example of an evaluation of PLATO instruction is one taken from an elementary accounting course (McKeowan, 1974). This particular evaluation was done with approximately 65 students in the PLATO group and 75 students in a normal classroom control group. The results of this evaluation are shown in Fig. 25. Although no significant difference was shown between the groups of students on the first three hourly examinations, the final examination showed approximately 5% better achievement for the PLATO

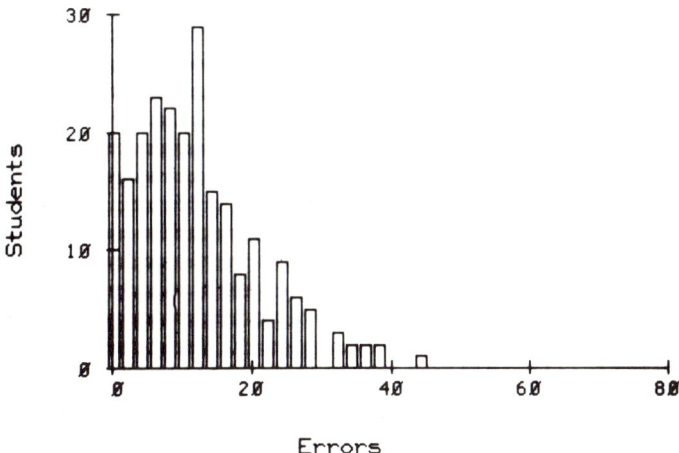

Fig. 27. The number of errors made by the students as they work through the lesson material is sometimes used by the author as an indication of whether his material and questions are at the appropriate level of difficulty.

group compared to the control group. This was accomplished with the PLATO group spending significantly less total study time.

PLATO has several aids to help students, teachers, and evaluators in gathering and processing relevant data. First, the author or teacher can specify what variable or computer–student transactions should be stored by the computer for later processing. This ability to specify different variables for different lessons is important since the meaning of input can have quite different interpretations in different lessons. For example, in two different lessons, the instructor may analyze a student's work by storing his correct responses. However, in one lesson, it may require storing a consistent set of steps describing a chemical process as his correct answer, whereas in the other lessons, it may require storing only a simple numerical answer.

Second, the stored information can be sorted, processed, and displayed in any manner specified by the teacher. The security of the system makes it possible for a student to see such things as his progress through the lesson material, test scores, and relative standing in the course, without being able to see the identified results of other students. Any teacher can examine the

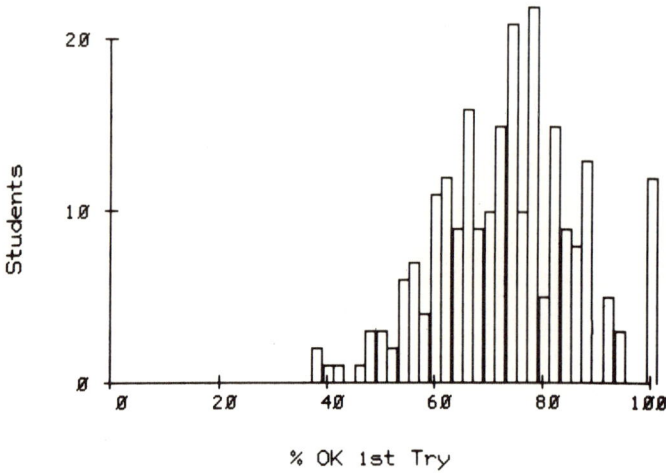

FIG. 28. The number of students who can answer a question correctly on the first try is a measurement that authors have found useful for revising their lesson material.

progress of individual students as well as all of his students and their standing relative to other classes in the course. Evaluators can view unidentified individual data as well as accumulated data from entire courses. Thus, an attempt is made to provide selectible, relevant data for those who have a right to see them, and protect the data from others who do not.

One example of how Stan Smith (Smith and Ghesquiere, 1974), a chemistry professor at the University of Illinois, processes and displays his accumulated student data is shown in Figs. 26–29. Other examples of how a physics professor displays his data are shown in Fig. 30 and 31 (Bennett, 1972).

8. Cost of Services

The cost of providing PLATO services depends on many factors such as the number of hours per day the system is used, the number of terminals connected to the system, the number of years the system will be used, and the proportion of the system which is purchased rather than rented.

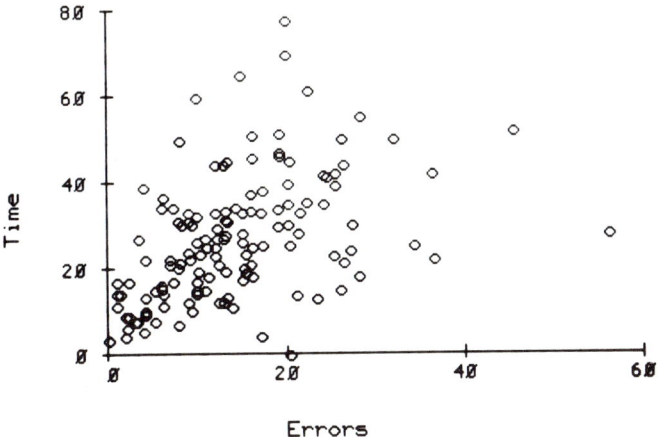

FIG. 29. Frequently it is important to compare data variables by cross correlation. This scatter diagram of the data shows that number of errors made by a student is not highly correlated to the time needed to complete the material.

Although the cost data provided here reflect the costs of a prototype 1000-terminal system using 1970 technology, the calculations are valuable for extrapolation of possible costs in the near future.

Costs for installing and operating a PLATO system can be placed into four different categories:

(1) Initial capital investments such as the cost of the central computer and terminals: these costs will be converted to an hourly rate by depreciating the capital investment over the life of the system. We will assume a fairly heavy use of eight hours per day, 300 days per year, and a five-year life which is already shortened to include interest cost. Therefore, the sum of all capital investments will be divided by 12,000 hours of use to determine the hourly cost.

(2) Capital costs that must be paid for by a subset of the users, such as the cost of producing lesson material: we will assume that each lesson will be paid for by 5000 users over its useful lifetime.

(3) Operational costs such as the management or maintenance of equipment.

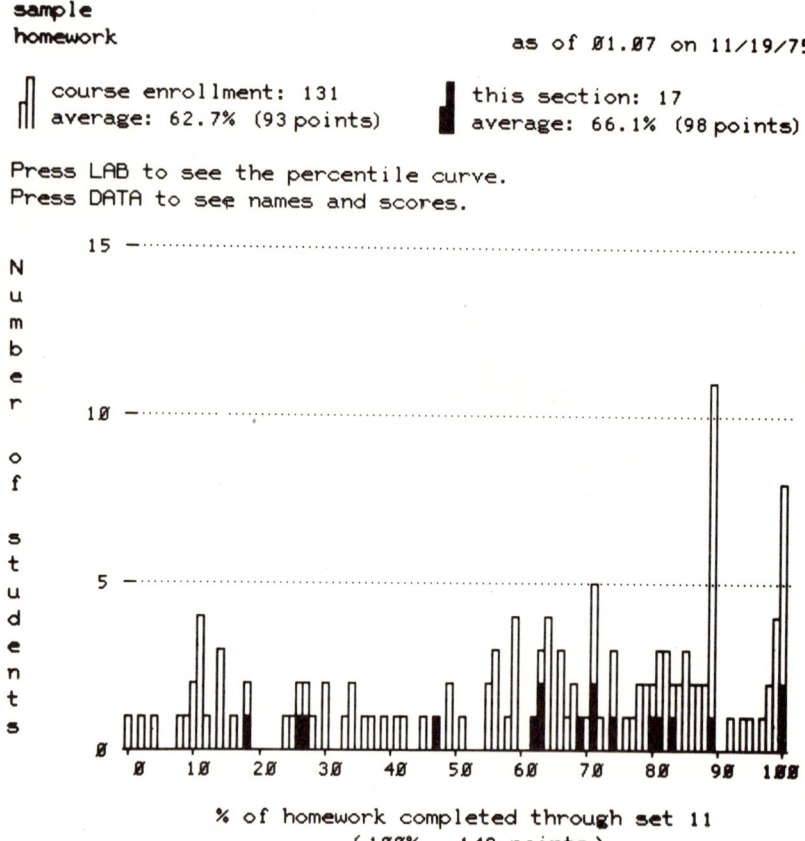

Fig. 30. In an elementary physics course taught partially by PLATO, the students do their homework on the system. The system is programmed (B. Sherwood, C. Bennett, and D. Kane) to record and process the progress of the students.

(4) Communications costs which vary by a factor of over 200 depending on the distance of the user from the center: because of the large variance in communication costs, they will be calculated separately (see Table I).

The present cost for a 1000-terminal system with the users located within a 20-mile radius is less than $1.20 per hour if the entire system is purchased. However, this cost may be increased in several ways: if, for example, the terminals are all located at a great distance from the center; if the terminals are unavailable for use much of the time; or if the entire

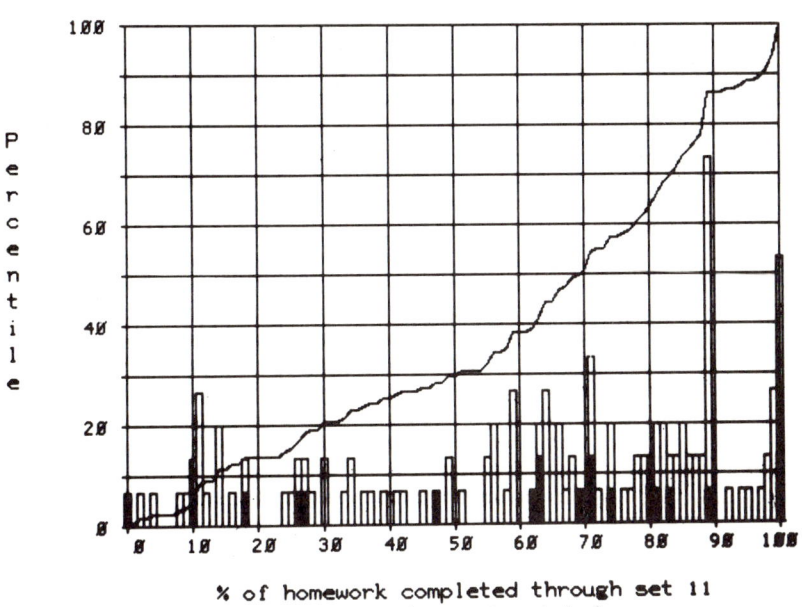

Fig. 31. In addition to the sorting and displaying of homework scores in this elementary physics course, the computer integrates the scores to simplify the identification of score percentiles.

service including computer and terminals is rented. In these instances, the costs are likely to be a factor of two or more greater. Nevertheless, it is likely that the cost of hardware, including the computer and terminals, will drop by a factor of three over the next five years, and that the operation costs and lesson material costs will be significantly less when there are many large systems in operation. Consequently, a target cost of about $.35 per hour by 1980 is not an unreasonable expectation. Thus, in view of rising educational costs, computer-based education is likely to be an attractive alternative to expanding educational needs.

TABLE I
CALCULATION OF COST PER HOUR OF INSTRUCTION

Initial capital investments

    Central computer system $3,000,000.00
    1000 terminals at $5000 each   5,000,000.00
    Purchase of software   100,000.00

                          Initial capital $8,100,000.00

    per user hour

$$\frac{\$8.1 \text{ million}}{12{,}000 \text{ hr} \times 1000 \text{ terminals}} = \$0.67$$

Operating costs

    Terminal maintenance   400.00 per year
    per user hour

$$\frac{\$400 \text{ per year}}{2400 \text{ hour per year}} = \$0.17$$

    System maintenance   150,000.00
    Managerial cost   150,000.00

                                       $300,000.00

    per user hour

$$\frac{\$300{,}000/\text{yr}}{2400 \text{ hr/yr}} \times 100 \text{ terminals} = \$0.13$$

Lesson material

    Lesson material $300 to $1000 per
      hour of material
    per user hour

$$\frac{\$1000 \text{ per hour}}{5000 \text{ students}} = \$0.20$$

Costs excluding communications   = $1.17 per hour

Communications costs

    By microwave within 20 mile radius   =   .005 per hour
    Up to several terminals on a
      telephone line at 1000-mile
      distance   =   1.00 per hour

9. Conclusion

When one considers the future potential uses of computer-based education, the number of terminals and applications involved in computer-based education today is but a proverbial drop in the bucket. Plans are already being made to develop large educational systems, which may have as many as a million interconnected computer graphic terminals by the early 1980s. These terminals would be located in homes as well as in educational institutions and industries. Graphic terminals contained in a small briefcase will be available for people to carry with them wherever they go and will be used over regular telephone lines.

Future services will extend far past the educational, computational, and game-playing services provided today. Electronic mail delivery services, inexpensive, international communication services, large library search and retrieval services, and automatic shopping services are only a few of the potential applications that should be available in the near future.

As advances in technology make such services available at low cost, one must also give attention to the social impact and changes brought about by the new medium. Certainly if such wide-scale computer services become commonly available, then will touch the lives of nearly all people and many such as students, workers, and homemakers will redefine their roles in light of their new activities. Over the next few years, careful studies should be conducted to help determine the sociological and psychological impact of the technology to avoid a technological success precipitating a sociological failure.

REFERENCES

Agajanian, A. H. (1974). A bibliography of plasma display panels. *Proc. Soc. Inf. Display* **15**, No. 4, 170–175.

Alpert, D., and Bitzer, D. L. (1970). Advances in computer-based education. *Science* **167**, 1582–1590.

Bennett, C. D. (1972). Computer-based education lessons for undergraduate quantum mechanics. *Proc. 1972, Conf. Comput. Undergrad. Curricula, 1972* pp. 369–374.

Bitzer, D. L., Johnson, R. L., and Skaperdas, D. (1970). "A Digitally Addressable Random-Access Image Selector and Random-Access Audio System," CERL Rep. X-13. University of Illinois Press, Urbana.

Bunderson, C. V. (1974). Team production of learner controlled courseware: A progress report. *Int. J. Man-Mach. Stud.* **6**, 479–491.

CAI. (1973). CAI in Japan. *ACM Sigcue Bull.* **7**, No. 1, 19–22 (CIJE '74 EJ 084 573).

CAI. (1970). "Computers and Education: An International Bibliography on Computers in Education." Int. Fed. Inf. Process., Amsterdam. (A specific publication on occasion of the IFIP World Conference on Computer Education.)

CERL (1975). "Demonstration of the PLATO IV Computer-based Education System." Computer-based Education Research Laboratory Annual Report to the National Science Foundation, July 1, 1974—June 30, 1975. University of Illinois Press, Urbana, Illinois.

Charp, S. (1970). Computer technology in education: How to make it viable. In "IFIP World Conference on Computer Education 1970" (B. Scheepmaker and K. L. Zinn, eds.), Part I, pp. 35–39. Int. Fed. Inf. Process., Amsterdam.

Coulson, J. E. (1962). A computer-based laboratory for research and development in education. In "Programmed Learning and Computer-Based Instruction" (J .E. Coulson, ed.), pp. 191–204. Wiley, New York.

Dugdale, S., and Kibbey, D. (1975). "The Fractions Curriculum—PLATO Elementary School Mathematics Project." Computer-based Education Research Laboratory, University of Illinois, Urbana.

Ebeling, F. A., Goldhor, R. S., and Johnson, R. J. (1972). "A Scanned Infrared Light Beam Touch Entry System," Soc. Inf. Display, 1972 Int. Symp., p. 134. Lewis Winner, New York.

Hyatt, G. W., Eades, D. C., and Tenczar, P. (1972). Computer-based education in biology. *BioScience* **22**, 401.

Jamison, D., Fletcher, J. D., Suppes, P., and Atkinson, R. C. (1976). Cost and performance of computer-assisted instruction for education of disadvantaged children. In "Education as an Industry" (J. Froomkin, D. Jamison, and R. Radner, eds.). Nat. Bur. Econ. Res. (to be published).

Johnson, R. L., Bitzer, D. L., and Slottow, H. G. (1971). The device characteristic of the plasma display element. *IEEE Trans. Electron Devices* **18**, 642.

Kingery, R. A., Berg, R. D., and Schillinger, E. H. (1967). A computer in the classroom. "Men and Ideas in Engineering: Twelve Histories from Illinois," pp. 147–164. Univ. of Illinois Press, Urbana.

Licklider, J. C. R. (1962). Preliminary experiment in computer-aided teaching. "Programmed Learning and Computer-Based Instruction" (J. E. Coulson, ed.), pp. 217–239. Wiley, New York.

McKeown, J. C. (1974). "PLATO Instruction for Elementary Accounting," CERL Rep. X-42. Univ. of Illinois Press, Urbana.

Ruth, G., and Anderson, N. (1959). "The IBM Research Teaching Machine Project—Automatic Teaching," pp. 117–130. Wiley, New York.

Sherwood, B. A. (1974). "The TUTOR Language." Computer-based Education Research Laboratory, University of Illinois, Urbana.

Siegel, M. A. (1974). "PLATO Evaluation Report, PLATO Student Attitude Survey, Urbana." Computer-based Education Research Laboratory, University of Illinois, Urbana.

Siegel, M. A., and Avner, R. A. (1974). "PLATO Evaluation Report, PLATO Instructor Survey, Urbana." Computer-based Education Research Laboratory, University of Illinois, Urbana.

Slesnick, W. E. (1969). "Educational Uses of the Computer at Dartmouth College" (Intern. Memo.). Kiewit Computation Center, Dartmouth College, Hanover, New Hampshire.

Smith, S. G. (1971). Computer-aided teaching of organic synthesis. *J. Chem. Educ.* **48**, 727–729.

Smith, S. G., and Ghesquiere, J. R. (1974). Computer-based teaching of organic chemistry. *Comput. Chem. Instrum.* **4**, 51–81.

Stifle, J. (1972). The PLATO IV student terminal. *Proc. Soc. Inf. Display* **13**, 35.

Suppes, P. (1966). The uses of computers in education. *Sci. Am.* **215,** No. 3, 206–233.
Tenczar, P. (1974). "TUTOR Graphic Capabilities," Soc. Inf. Display, 1974 Int. Symp., pp. 70–71. Lewis Winner, New York.
Uttal, W. R. (1962). On conversational interaction. *In* "Programmed Learning and Computer-Based Instruction" (J. E. Coulson, ed.), pp. 171–190. Wiley, New York.
Watson, P. G. (1972). "Using the Computer in Education: A Briefing for School Decision Makers." Educational Technology Publications, Englewood Cliffs, New Jersey.
Zinn, K. L. (1967). Computer assistance for instruction: A review of systems and projects. *In* "The Computer in American Education" (D. D. Bushnell and D. W. Allen, eds.), pp. 77–107. Wiley, New York.

Author Index

Numbers in italics refer to the pages on which the complete references are listed.

A

Abell, V., *117*
Abrams, P., 5, *59*
Adam, A., 8, *59*
Agajanian, A. H., 248, *281*
Alpert, D., *281*
Amarel, S., 16, *59*
Amdahl, G. M., 161, *176*
Anderson, J. R., 194, 195, *235*
Anderson, N., *282*
Atkinson, R. C., 273, *282*
Avner, R. A., 274, *282*

B

Bach, E., 226, 230, *235*
Baer, J. L., 131, 161, *176*
Balzer, R. M., 2, 47, 48, 49, 55, *59*
Barnes, G., 158, *176*
Barstow, D., 47, 48, 49, 50, 52, 55, *61*
Barzdin, J., 17, *59*
Batcher, K. E., 158, 171, *176*
Bauer, M., 23, *59*
Baum, R. I., 19, 23, *59*
Beatty, J. C., 131, *176*
Beneš, V. E., 171, *176*
Bennett, C. D., 259, 276, *281*
Berg, R. D., 241, *282*
Bernstein, A., 144, 148, *176*
Biermann, A. W., 17, 19, 23, 29, *59*, 188, *235*
Bingham, H. W., 141, 142, *177*
Bishop, P., 52, *61*
Bitzer, D. L., 241, 248, 251, 253, *281*, *282*
Bledsoe, W. W., 40, *60*
Blue, J. L., 80, *117*
Blum, L., 17, *59*
Blum, M., 17, *59*
Bobrow, D. G., 4, 40, *59*
Bower, G. H., 194, *235*
Bowerman, M., 190, *235*

Boyer, R. S., 27, 40, *59*
Braine, M. D. S., 191, *235*
Brent, R. P., 132, 133, 137, 138, 139, 175, *177*, *179*
Brown, R., 158, *176*, 188, 190, *235*
Bruce, B., 232, *235*
Buchanan, J. R., 31, 37, *59*, *60*
Buchholz, W., 163, *177*
Budnik, P., 149, 159, 161, 167, *177*, *178*
Bunderson, C. V., 242, *281*
Burger, J. F., 40, *63*
Burnett, G. J., 169, *177*

C

Carr, H. M., 158, *179*
Casaletto, J., 79, *117*
Chandrasekaran, B., 191, *235*
Chang, C.-L., 31, 32, 33, *60*, *61*
Chang, D., 170, *177*
Charniak, E., 4, 6, *63*
Charp, S., 241, *282*
Chen, S. C., 126, 137, 138, 139, 140, 146, 148, 149, 155, 157, 159, 161, 163, 174, 175, 176, *177*, *179*
Chomsky, N., 185, 186, 187, *235*
Clark, R., 199, *235*
Coffman, E. G., Jr., 83, *117*, 169, *177*
Coles, L. S., 40, *60*
Coulson, J. E., 240, *282*
Culicover, P., 190, *235*

D

Dahl, O.-J., 40, *60*
Dale, P. S., 190, *235*
Davis, E. W., Jr., 143, 149, 159, 161, 164, 175, *177*, *178*
de Boor, C., 79, 80, *117*
Denning, P. J., 83, *117*
Derksen, J. A., 4, 8, *62*
Dershowitz, N., 31, *60*

Dijkska, E. W., 40, *60*
Dugdale, S., 263, *282*
Duran, J. W., 31, *60*

E

Eades, D. C., 259, *282*
Earley, J., 4, 8, *60*
Ebeling, F. A., 253, *282*
Einarsson, B., 80, *117*
Elschlager, R., 47, 48, 49, 52, 55, *61*
Elspas, B., 40, *60*
Estrin, G., 131, 141, 161, *176*, *177*, *178*

F

Feldman, J. A., 2, 8, 9, 10, 11, 17, *59*, *60*, 188, *235*
Fikes, R. E., *60*
Fillmore, C. J., 230, 231, *236*
Fisher, D. A., 141, 142, 144, *177*
Fletcher, J. D., 273, *282*
Floyd, R. W., 40, *60*
Flynn, M., 127, 161, 162, *177*
Freivald, R. V., 17, *59*

G

Gentleman, M. W., 80, *117*
Gerhart, S. L., 40, *60*
Gerritsen, R., 40, *60*
Ghesquiere, J. R., 261, 263, 276, *282*
Ginzberg, M. J., 12, 48, *62*
Gold, E. M., 17, *60*, 188, *236*
Goldberg, P. C., 12, 14, 15, 47, *60*
Goldhor, R. S., 253, *282*
Goldstein, I. P., 48, *60*
Goldstein, P. C., 48, *60*
Good, D. I., 40, *60*
Green, C. C., 25, 28, 31, 33, 47, 48, 50, 52, 55, *60*, *61*, *62*
Gregg, L., 207, *236*
Gries, D., 10, 11, *60*, *61*

H

Halliday, M. A. K., 41, *61*
Hamburger, H., 189, *236*, *237*
Hammer, M. M., 12, *61*
Han, J., 149, 159, 161, *178*

Hardy, S., 4, 25, 28, *61*
Harris, L. R., 195, *236*
Hart, J. F., 116, *117*
Hays, D. G., 229, *236*
Heidorn, G. E., 40, 46, 47, 48, *61*
Hellerman, H., 169, *177*
Henisz, B., *237*
Hewitt, C. E., 47, 48, 52, *61*
Hintz, R. G., 158, *177*
Hoare, C. A. R., 40, *60*, *61*
Hollaar, L. A., 175, *177*
Hopcroft, J. E., 17, *61*
Horning, J. J., 11, *62*
Howe, W. G., 12, 15, *61*
Hu, T. C., 142, *178*
Hyatt, G. W., 259, *282*

I

Iverson, K. E., 4, *61*

J

Jamison, D., 273, *282*
Jenkins, J. J., 191, *236*
Jesperson, O., 190, *236*
Johnson, R. L., 248, 251, 253, *281*, *282*
Jordan, S. R., 195, *236*

K

Kaganove, J. J., 80, 116, *117*
Kahaner, D. K., 79, *117*
Kato, M., 158, *176*
Katz, J. J., 186, *236*
Kelley, K. L., 192, *236*
Kibbey, D., 263, *282*
Kingery, R. A., 241, *282*
Klein, S., 222, *236*
Knuth, D. E., 11, *61*, 138, *178*, 227, *236*
Kraska, P. W., 132, 149, 159, 161, *178*
Krishnaswamy, R., 19, 23, 29, *59*
Krogh, F. T., 80, *117*
Krumland, R., 12, 48, *62*
Kruskal, V. J., 15, *61*
Kuck, D. J., 126, 132, 133, 137, 138, 139, 147, 148, 149, 155, 157, 158, 159, 163, 166, 167, 170, 171, 173, 174, 175, *176*, *176*, *177*, *178*, *179*

AUTHOR INDEX

Kung, H. T., 148, *177*
Kuppin, M. A., 222, *236*

L

Lakoff, G., 186, *236*
Lamport, L., 146, *178*
Lauer, P., 230, *236*
Lawrie, D., 149, 159, 161, 168, 170, 171, *178*
Leavenworth, B. M., 2, 4, *61*
Lee, R. C. T., 31, 32, 33, *60*, *61*, *63*
Leech, G. N., 233, *236*
Lenat, D. B., 47, 48, 49, 50, 51, 52, 53, 55, *61*, *62*
Leondes, C., *178*
Levitt, K. N., 40, *60*
Licklider, J. C. R., 240, *282*
London, R. L., 40, *60*, *62*
Lorentz, G. G., 116, *117*
Low, J. R., 9, *60*, *62*
Lucas, P., 230, *236*
Luckham, D. C., 31, 37, *60*
Lyness, J. N., 80, 116, *117*

M

McCawley, J. D., 186, 191, 232, *236*
McCune, B. P., 47, 48, 49, 52, 55, *61*
McDermott, D. V., 4, *63*
McKeeman, W. M., 11, *62*
McKeown, J. C., 274, *282*
McMaster, I., 196, *236*
Manna, Z., 31, 33, 35, 36, 48, 56, *60*, *62*
Mark, B., 12, 48, *62*
Martin, D., 141, *178*
Martin, W. A., 12, 48, *62*
Maruyama, K., 132, 133, *178*
Mikelsons, M., 15, *62*
Minsky, M., 52, 55, *62*, 161, 162, *178*
Moore, J. S., 27, 40, *59*
Morgenstern, M., 12, 48, *62*
Morris, J. B., 8, *62*
Muller, D. E., 132, *178*
Muraoka, Y., 132, 133, 146, 148, 149, 159, 174, *178*

N

Niamir, B., 12, 48, *62*
Nilsson, N. J., 31, 37, *60*, *62*

O

Olmstead, D. L., 191, *236*
Opferman, D. C., 171, *178*
Osgood, C. E., 191, *236*

P

Palermo, D. S., 191, *236*
Patterson, T. N. L., 80, *117*
Pavlidis, T., 117, *117*
Pease, M. C., 171, *179*
Perlis, A. J., 2, *62*
Peters, S., 190, *236*
Petry, F. E., 19, 23, *59*, *62*
Picket, M., 79, *117*
Piessen, R., 80, *117*
Piezer, D. B., 191, *236*
Postal, P. M., 186, *236*, *237*
Preparata, F. P., 132, *178*

R

Rabin, M. O., *118*
Raphael, B., 4, 31, *59*, *61*
Ravi, C. V., 169, 170, *179*
Reeker, L. H., 187, 190, 191, 196, 198, 217, 224, 228, *235*, *237*
Reichenbach, H., 193, *237*
Reigel, E. W., 142, *177*
Rice, J. R., 78, 79, 115, *117*, *118*
Robinson, J., 31, *62*
Robinson, J. J., 229, *237*
Ross, J. R., 230, *237*
Rovner, P., 8, *60*
Rubinoff, M., *178*
Rulifson, J. F., 4, 8, *62*
Russell, B., 233, *237*
Russell, E. C., 141, *179*
Ruth, G., *282*

S

Sameh, A. H., 133, 137, 139, 148, 155, 175, *177*, *179*
Sammet, J. E., 2, 4, *61*
Samuel, A., 47, *62*
Schank, R. C., 184, 229, *237*
Schillinger, E. H., 241, *282*

Schwarcz, R. M., 40, *63*, 196, *237*
Schwartz, J. T., 4, 8, 9, *62*
Semon, W. L., 141, 142, *177*
Senzig, D., 161, *179*
Shank, R., 40, *62*
Shaw, D. E., 25, 28, 47, 48, 49, 52, 55, *61, 62*
Sherwood, B. A., 266, *282*
Siegel, M. A., 274, *282*
Siklóssy, L., 27, 48, *62, 63*, 193, *237*
Simmons, R. F., 40, *63, 237*
Simon, H. A., 48, *63*, 207, *236*
Skaperdas, D., 251, *281*
Skinner, B. F., 191, *237*
Slagle, J. R., 31, *63*
Slesnick, W. E., 240, *282*
Slotnick, D., 158, *176*
Slottow, H. G., 248, 253, *282*
Smith, B., 47, 48, 52, *61*
Smith, S. G., 261, 263, 276, *282*
Snowdon, R. A., 169, *177*
Snyder, M. V., 80, *117*
Solomonoff, R., 17, *63*
Srinivasan, C. V., 48, *63*
Steiger, R., 52, *61*
Steinberg, L. I., 47, 48, 49, 52, 55, *61*
Stellhorn, W. H., 175, *179*
Stifle, J., *282*
Stokes, R., 158, *176*
Strebendt, R. E., 149, 159, 161, 175, *178, 179*
Stigleitner, H., 230, *236*
Summers, P., *63*
Summers, P. D., 25, 27, *63*
Sunguroff, A., 12, 48, *62*
Suppes, P., 241, 273, *282*
Sussman, G. J., 4, 6, 47, 48, 55, *63*
Swanson, R. C., 168, *179*

Swartout, W. R., 25, 28, *62*
Swinehart, D., 9, *60*

T

Tarski, A., 226, *237*
Tate, D. P., 158, *177*
Taylor, R., 9, *60*
Tenczar, P., 259, 266, *282*
Thompson, F. B., 195, 232, *237*
Towle, R., 133, 144, 146, 148, 149, 155, 159, 161, 163, *177, 178, 179*
Tsao-Wu, N. T., 171, *178*
Turn, R., 141, *177*

U

Ullman, J. D., 17, *61*
Uttal, W. R., 240, *283*

W

Waksman, A., 40, *60*
Waldinger, R. J., 4, 8, 31, 32, 33, 35, 36, 40, 47, 48, 49, 52, 55, 56, *60, 61, 62, 63*
Watson, P. G., *283*
Watson, W. J., 158, *179*
Wexler, K., 189, 190, *235, 236, 237*
Whitehead, A., 233, *237*
Wiedmann, C., 6, *63*
Wilkes, M., 83, *118*
Winograd, S., 133, *179*
Winograd, T., 4, 6, 40, 48, *63*, 196, *237*
Wladawsky, I., 12, 15, *61*
Woods, W. A., 40, *63*, 194, *237*
Wortman, D. B., 11, *62*

Z

Zinn, K. L., 240, *283*

Subject Index

A

Acrylic dependence graph, in parallel processing of ordinary programs, 145
Algorithm, scheduling, 84–85
Algorithm program, vs. heuristic, 47
Algorithm selection problem, 65–117
  abstract models in, 67-77, 82–84
  algorithm space in, 67
  approximation forms in, 101
  approximation theory machinery in, 91–117
  artificial intelligence in, 66–67
  avoidable error in, 108–109
  best features of algorithm in, 71–72
  "best model" definitions in, 73–75
  "best" scheduler in, 85–90
  characterization question in, 113–115
  concrete application of, 77–82
  existence question in, 109–112
  feature space in, 83
  game-playing problem in, 69–70
  (general) optimization theory and, 115
  mathematical theory questions in, 109–115
  model with variable performance criteria in, 75–77
  open questions about, 115–117
  operating systems in, 66
  operating system schedulers in, 82–90
  performance measure in, 67, 83
  problem space in, 67–68, 78
  quadratic algorithms in, 77–82
  quadrature in, 66
  scheduling algorithm in, 84–85
  and selection based on features in, 70–73
  systematic evaluation in, 81–82
  uniqueness question in, 112–113
Algorithm space, in algorithm selection problem, 78
Algorithm synthesis, heuristic knowledge-based, 46–57

Alignment networks, in parallel processing of ordinary programs, 170–174
Anderson's language acquisition system, 194–195
APL language, 4–6
Approximation forms, in algorithm selection problem, 91–95, 101–106
Approximation theory
  see also Algorithm selection problem
  in algorithm selection problem, 91–117
  approximation forms in, 101–106
  characteristic question in, 112–115
  classification of problems in, 95–96
  complexity in, 98–100
  degree of convergence in, 96–97
  discrete forms in, 101–102
  general nonlinear forms in, 106–107
  linear forms in, 102–105
  mathematical theory questions in, 109–115
  norms and approximation forms in, 91–95, 101–106
  piecewise linear forms in, 105–106
  robustness in, 100
  tree and algorithm forms in, 108
  uniqueness question in, 112–113
Arithmetic expression, defined, 128–129
Arithmetic-expression tree-height reduction, 128–137
  see also Parallel processing of ordinary programs
ASC machine, 158, 174
Assembly language programming, 2
  see also Language; Language acquisition; Machine language
Assignment statement, in parallel processing, 142
Automatic backtracking, 4
Automatic programming
  see also Autoprogrammer; Program synthesis
  actors, beings, and frames in, 50–53

289

approaches to, 1–59
computations in, 20–23
data structures in, 52
examples in, 16–29
extensions to, 3–16
four major phases of, 48
Heidorn system in, 48–50
heuristic knowledge-based algorithm synthesis in, 46–57
mechanisms available for, 58
model verification in, 48
problem acquisition in, 48
process transformation in, 48
program synthesis in, 18–20
research in, 58
Summers system in, 25
translation of natural language commands in, 40–46
Autoprogrammer
see also Automatic programming
"continue" feature in, 24
other features of, 24–29
partial program in, 24

B

Backtracking, automatic, 4
BAS, see Blocking assignment statements
BASIC language, 266, 269
Batcher sorting network, 171
BDL language system, 12–15
Beneš network, 171
"Block" in PLANNER code, 42
Block of assignment statements, in parallel processing of ordinary programs, 142
Brigham Young University, 242
Burroughs ILLIAC machines, 158, 165, 170, 243
Business Definition Language, 12–15

C

CACM FORTRAN algorithms, 158
CAI, see Computer-assisted instruction
Carnegie Mellon Institute, 243
CDC 6500 system, scheduling algorithm on, 84
CDC 6600 machine, 158, 174
CDC 7600 machine, 158
CDC STAR machine, 158, 174
Central processing units, in PLATO system, 254

Characterization question, in algorithm selection problem, 113–115
Checkers, as heuristic process, 47
Chicago School District, 242
CLAP program, 196
Clause resolution, in program synthesis, 32
COBOL programs, in parallel processing analysis, 175
Coding tasks, repetitious, 15
Column sweep algorithm, in parallel processing of ordinary programs, 136–137
Competitive game, in computer-based education, 264–265
Compiler uniformity, 123–127
Comprehensive Language Acquisition Program, 196
Computational inefficiency, in programming, 15
Computer-assisted instruction, 240, 242, 273
see also Computer-based education
Computer-based education, 239–281
drill and practice in, 262–266
evaluation of, 272–276
languages used in, 266–272
simulation in, 259–262
system configuration in, 254–256
teaching strategies in, 256–266
Computer-Based Education Research Laboratory, 274
Computer design, applications in relation to, 120
Computer language, see Language; Machine language
Computer programming, see Programming; Program synthesis
CONNIVER language, 4
Constant-coefficient recurrences, in parallel processing, 139–140
Control Data Corp., 241, 254–256
STAR processor of, 158
Control successor, in parallel processing of ordinary programs, 152
Control units, for high-speed computers, 163

D

Data dependence graph, in parallel processing of ordinary programs, 144
Data flow language, 14

Defense Department, U.S., 240
DO-loops
  absence of in APL language, 6
  in FORTRAN program, 160–162
  in standard programming languages, 4–5
Drill and practice, in computer-based education, 262–266

E

Education, computer-based, *see* Computer-based education
Educational Testing Services, 273
EISPACK array, 159
Example program, in program synthesis, 20–23
Execution order, in parallel processing, 143
Existence question, in algorithm selection problem, 109–112

F

Feature space, in algorithm model, 83
FOR-loop, in standard programming languages, 4
FORTRAN program
  see also Parallel processing of ordinary programs
  in algorithm approximation program, 98
  comprehensive analyzer of, 159
  DO-loops in, 159–160
  fast execution of, 122–123
  IFs in loops of, 151–158, 176
  logic design and compiler uniformity in, 123–127
  machine considerations in, 158–174
  speed limits in, 122
  theoretical speedups in, 174
FORTRAN program analyzer, 149

G

Generalizations, in language acquisition, 216–223
General Learning Corp., 241
Goodyear Aerospace STARAN IV, 158
GPSS blocks, 159
GPSS language, 49
GPSS simulation program, 48–50
GRAFIT language, 268

Grammar representation, in language acquisition, 224–235
Grammars
  context-free, 183, 224–225
  context-sensitive, 183
  transformational, 185–186
Grammatical inference, 187–190
  and language identifiability in limit, 188
Grammatical theory
  in language acquisition, 182–184
  meaning representation in, 183

H

Hardware, design of, 120–121
Heidorn system, in queuing problems, 48–50
Heuristic program, vs. algorithmic, 47
Heuristics, in program synthesis, 27–28
Hexadecimal coding, 3
Higher level languages, 4–10
  advantages of, 15–16
  development of, 4
  program writing with, 9–10
  sets in, 8
High-speed computers
  control units for, 163
  multioperational capability in, 158

I

IBM assembly language, addition in, 3
IBM STRETCH, 165
IBM 360 series, 121
IBM 360/91, 158
IBM 370 machine language program, 2–3
Identifiability in the limit, 188
IF block, in parallel processing, 143, 152–158
IG, *see* Initial grammar
ILLIAC I, 243
ILLIAC II, 165
ILLIAC IV, 158, 170
Illinois, University of, 243
Immediate control successor, in parallel processing of ordinary programs, 152
Index set, in parallel processing, 143
Induction rule, in program synthesis, 34
Inductive argument, in looping program, 35–36

Initial grammar, in problem-solving theory, 197–198
Innateness, in language acquisition, 186–187
Input-output characteristics, in program synthesis, 29–40
International Business Machines Corp., 12, 240
  see also IBM 360 series, etc.

K

Kelley's language acquisition system, 192–193
Knowledge, representation of, 54
Knowledge about knowledge, development of, 53–57

L

Language(s)
  data flow vs. control flow, 14
  higher level, see Higher level languages
  manipulative, 11
  adjectives and adverbial phrases in, 232–235
  Anderson's system in, 194–195
  computational modes in, 191–196
  computational study of, 181–235
  CLAP system in, 196
Language acquisition
  comparison and difference reduction in, 201–203
  difference reduction in, 201–203
  example of, 207–216
  generalization and transformations in, 222–223
  grammar representation in, 224–235
  grammatical inference in, 187–190
  grammatical theories in, 182–184
  innateness in, 186–187
  internalization and, 206–207
  Kelley's system in, 192–193
  METQA system in, 195
  modeling of, 191–196
  noncomputational models in, 191
  reduced-sentence matching in, 200–201
  reduction process in, 199–200
  REPLACE operation in, 211
  robot system in, 195
  semantic dependency notation in, 228–235
  semantic mapping in, 226–228
  sentence-acquiring systems in, 189
  Siklóssy's system in, 193–194
  structural learning and generalization in, 184–185
  surface representation in, 224–226
Language-learning phenomena, 190
LHS (left-hand side or output) variable, in parallel processing of ordinary programs, 143, 149
Linear dependence, in parallel processing of ordinary programs, 144
Linear recurrences, in numerical programs, 134–136
Linear recurrence systems, 139–140
Linguistic transformations, 185
LISP machine language, 175–176
LISP programs
  "insane heuristic" in, 27
  synthesis of, 18, 25–29
Loop distribution, in parallel processing of ordinary programs, 148–149
Loop Distribution Algorithm, 150
Loop index, in parallel processing, 143
Looping constructions, in program synthesis, 33
Looping program, inductive argument and, 36
Loop speedup hierarchy, in parallel processing of ordinary programs, 146–148
Lower node condition, in semantic dependency notation, 230

M

Machine language
  see also Language; Language acquisition
  vs. assembly language programming, 2
  in computer-based education, 266–272
  hand coding in, 1–2
  higher level, see Higher level languages
Magnavox Corp., 241
Manipulative language, grammar for, 11
Massachusetts Institute of Technology, 243
Meaning, semantics and, 204
Meaning representation, in grammatical theory, 183

SUBJECT INDEX

METQA language acquisition system, 195
MIMD (multiple-instruction, multiple-data) operation, 127, 133
Mnemonic operation codes, 3

N

National Science Foundation, 240, 242, 273
Natural language commands
 generating PLANNER code in, 42–46
 syntactic analysis in, 41–42
 translation of, 40–46
New sentence, semantics for, 203–206
Nonlinear forms, in approximation theory, 106–107
Northern Virginia Community College, 243
Numerical programs
 arithmetic expressions and linear recurrences in, 127
 recurrence relations in, 134–136

O

Office of Education, U.S., 240
Ohio State University, 242
Operating system schedulers
 in algorithm selection problem, 82–90
 algorithm space in, 83
Optimization theory, algorithm selection problem and, 115
Ordinary programs, parallel processing of, see Parallel processing of ordinary programs
Owens-Illinois Glass Company, 241

P

Parallel processing of ordinary programs, 119–176
 see also FORTRAN program
 acyclic dependence graph in, 145
 alignment networks in, 170–174
 arithmetic-expression tree-height reduction in, 128–137
 array access in, 165–168
 column sweep algorithm in, 136–137
 constant coefficient recurrences in, 139–141
 control units in, 163–164

 FORTRAN program and, 122–127
 IFs in loops of, 152–158
 logic design and computer uniformity in, 123–127
 loop distribution in, 148–149
 loop speedup hierarchy in, 146–148
 machine details in, 173
 overall machine organization in, 164–165
 parallel memory access in, 165
 parallel random access in, 168–170
 product form recurrence method in, 137–138
 program analysis in, 141–158
 skewed storage in, 167–169
 speed limits in, 122–123
 theoretical fundamentals in, 127–141
 tree height reduction in, 133–137
 wave front method in, 145–146
 whole programs in, 141
Parallel random access, in parallel processing of ordinary programs, 168–170
Phoenix College, 243
PICTO computer language, 270
Piecewise linear forms, in approximation theory, 105–106
PLANNER CODE, in natural language commands, 42–46
PLANNER language, 4, 6–8
PLATO system, 241–254
 communications network in, 255
 cost of, 276–280
 evaluation of, 272–276
 simulation in, 259–262
 student and teacher aids in, 275–276
 subject area of, 246
 system configuration in, 254–256
 teaching strategies in, 256–266
 terminal system in, 251–254
PLATO IV system, 248–249
PLATO TUTOR language, 266–272
POPCORN language, 4
Problem reduction methods
 Buchanan-Luckham system in, 39
 in program synthesis, 37–40
Problem-solving theory, 196–223
 analogy in, 211, 216
 basic features of, 196–197
 exemplary grammar and system in, 197–198
 generalization process in, 216

initial grammar in, 197–198
reduction process in, 199–200
semantic structure in, 205
surface grammars in, 219
Processing, major phases of, 48
  see also Automatic processing
Processors, types of, 158–159
Program creation, mechanisms for, 58
Program generators, special purpose, 10–15
Program graph, in pseudo-FORTRAN program, 151
Programming
  automatic, see Automatic programming
  knowledge modules and, 52
  machine language in, 2
  modularity in, 51
  overcontrol in, 2
Programs, ordinary, see Parallel processing of ordinary programs
Program synthesis
  of branching and looping structures, 31–36
  clause resolution in, 32
  enumeration pruning and, 29
  example program in, 20–23
  from formal input-output specifications, 29–40
  heuristics in, 27–28
  induction rule in, 34–35
  in LISP programs, 25–29
  method in, 18–20
  problem reduction in, 37–40
  resolution theorem proving and, 31–32
  uniform or algorithmic approach in, 46
Program synthesizer
  function of, 17–18
  task of, 20
PROTOSYSTEM I, 12
pseudo-FORTRAN program, 150
PST, see Problem-solving theory
Purdue University Computing Center, 82–85

Q

Quadratic algorithms
  see also Algorithm selection problem
  previous evaluation work on, 79–80
  selection of, 77–82
Queuing problem, in Heidorn system, 48–50

R

RCA Corp., 241
Recurrence method, in parallel processing of ordinary programs, 137
Recurrence relations, examples of, 134–136
Recurrences, constant-coefficient, 139–140
Reduced sentence, matching of, 200–201
Reduction process, in language acquisition, 199–200
REPLACE operation, in language acquisition, 211
Resolution theorem proving, in program synthesis, 31–32
RHS (right-hand side or input) variable, in parallel processing of ordinary programs, 143, 149

S

SAVI system, 241
Scheduling algorithm
  "best," 85–90
  in CDC 6500 system, 84
Semantic dependency notation
  adjectives and adverbs in, 232
  in language acquisition, 228–235
Semantic mapping, in language acquisition, 226–228
Semantics
  meaning of, 204
  for new sentence, 203
Sentence-acquiring systems, 189
SETL language, 4
Sets, in higher level languages, 8
Shuffles, in parallel processing of ordinary programs, 171
Siklóssy's language acquisition system, 193–194
SIMD (single-instruction, multiple-data) operation, 127–133
Skewed storage, in parallel processing of ordinary programs, 167–169
SNOBOL machine language, 175
Software, design of, 120–121
Special purpose program generators, 10–16
  grammars and, 11
Stanford University, 243
STARAN IV processor, 158
STAR machine, 158
STRETCH machine, 165

Structural learning and generalization, in language acquisition, 184–185
Summers system, in LISP program synthesis, 25
Surface productions, interpretive rules for, 204
Surface structure, semantics and, 204
Sweeping scheme, in parallel processing, 138
Symbolic addresses, 3
Syntactic analysis, in natural language commands, 41–42
System design procedure, improvements in, 121
System Development Corp., 240

T

Teaching strategies, in computer-based education, 256–266
Terminal symbols, in grammar representation, 225
Texas Instruments ASC machine, 158, 174
Theorem proving, in program synthesis, 31–32
THFIND statement, in PLANNER code, 44
THGOAL statement, in PLANNER language, 6, 43
TICCET system, 242
Transformational grammars, 185–186
Tree-height reduction, in parallel processing of ordinary programs, 128–133
Turing machine computation, in algorithm selection problem, 98
TUTOR language, 245, 266–272

U

Uniqueness question, in algorithm selection problem, 112–113
Unshuffles, in parallel processing of ordinary programs, 171

V

VAS, *see* Vocabulary Acquisition System
VERS2 language, 4
Vocabulary Acquisition System, 196

W

Westinghouse Learning, Inc., 241

Contents of Previous Volumes

Volume 1

General-Purpose Programming for Business Applications
    CALVIN C. GOTLIEB
Numerical Weather Prediction
    NORMAN A. PHILLIPS
The Present Status of Automatic Translation of Languages
    YEHOSHUA BAR-HILLEL
Programming Computers to Play Games
    ARTHUR L. SAMUEL
Machine Recognition of Spoken Words
    RICHARD FATEHCHAND
Binary Arithmetic
    GEORGE W. REITWIESNER

Volume 2

A Survey of Numerical Methods for Parabolic Differential Equations
    JIM DOUGLAS, JR.
Advances in Orthonormalizing Computation
    PHILIP J. DAVIS AND PHILIP RABINOWITZ
Microelectronics Using Electron-Beam-Activated Machining Techniques
    KENNETH R. SHOULDERS
Recent Developments in Linear Programming
    SAUL I. GLASS
The Theory of Automata, a Survey
    ROBERT MCNAUGHTON

Volume 3

The Computation of Satellite Orbit Trajectories
    SAMUEL D. CONTE
Multiprogramming
    E. F. CODD
Recent Developments of Nonlinear Programming
    PHILIP WOLFE
Alternating Direction Implicit Methods
    GARRET BIRKHOFF, RICHARD S. VARGA, AND DAVID YOUNG
Combined Analog-Digital Techniques in Simulation
    HAROLD F. SKRAMSTAD
Information Technology and the Law
    REED C. LAWLOR

Volume 4

The Formulation of Data Processing Problems for Computers
    WILLIAM C. MCGEE
All-Magnetic Circuit Techniques
    DAVID R. BENNION AND HEWITT D. CRANE
Computer Education
    HOWARD E. TOMPKINS

Digital Fluid Logic Elements
    H. H. Glaettli
Multiple Computer Systems
    William A. Curtin

Volume 5

The Role of Computers in Election Night Broadcasting
    Jack Moshman
Some Results of Research on Automatic Programming in Eastern Europe
    Wladyslaw Turksi
A Discussion of Artificial Intelligence and Self-Organization
    Gordon Pask
Automatic Optical Design
    Orestes N. Stavroudis
Computing Problems and Methods in X-Ray Crystallography
    Charles L. Coulter
Digital Computers in Nuclear Reactor Design
    Elizabeth Cuthill
An Introduction to Procedure-Oriented Languages
    Harry D. Huskey

Volume 6

Information Retrieval
    Claude E. Walston
Speculations Concerning the First Ultraintelligent Machine
    Irving John Good
Digital Training Devices
    Charles R. Wickman
Number Systems and Arithmetic
    Harvey L. Garder
Considerations on Man versus Machine for Space Probing
    P. L. Bargellini
Data Collection and Reduction for Nuclear Particle Trace Detectors
    Herbert Gelernter

Volume 7

Highly Parallel Information Processing Systems
    John C. Murtha
Programming Language Processors
    Ruth M. Davis
The Man-Machine Combination for Computer-Assisted Copy Editing
    Wayne A. Danielson
Computer-Aided Typesetting
    William R. Bozman
Programming Languages for Computational Linguistics
    Arnold C. Satterthwait
Computer Driven Displays and Their Use in Man/Machine Interaction
    Andries van Dam

Volume 8

Time-Shared Computer Systems
 THOMAS N. PYKE, JR.
Formula Manipulation by Computer
 JEAN E. SAMMET
Standards for Computers and Information Processing
 T. B. STEEL, JR.
Syntactic Analysis of Natural Language
 NAOMI SAGER
Programming Languages and Computers: A Unified Metatheory
 R. NARASIMHAN
Incremental Computation
 LIONELLO A. LOMBARDI

Volume 9

What Next in Computer Technology?
 W. J. POPPELBAUM
Advances in Simulation
 JOHN MCLEOD
Symbol Manipulation Languages
 PAUL W. ABRAHAMS
Legal Information Retrieval
 AVIEZRI S. FRAENKEL
Large Scale Integration—an Appraisal
 L. M. SPANDORFER
Aerospace Computers
 A. S. BUCHMAN
The Distributed Processor Organization
 L. J. KOCZELA

Volume 10

Humanism, Technology, and Language
 CHARLES DECARLO
Three Computer Cultures: Computer Technology, Computer Mathematics, and Computer Science
 PETER WEGNER
Mathematics in 1984—The Impact of Computers
 BRYAN THWAITES
Computing from the Communication Point of View
 E. E. DAVID, JR.
Computer-Man Communication: Using Computer Graphics in the Instructional Process
 FREDERICK P. BROOKS, JR.
Computers and Publishing: Writing, Editing, and Printing
 ANDRIES VAN DAM AND DAVID E. RICE
A Unified Approach to Pattern Analysis
 ULF GRENANDER
Use of Computers in Biomedical Pattern Recognition
 ROBERT S. LEDLEY

Numerical Methods of Stress Analysis
  WILLIAM PRAGER
Spline Approximation and Computer-Aided Design
  J. H. AHLBERG
Logic per Track Devices
  D. L. SLOTNICK

Volume 11

Automatic Translation of Languages Since 1960: A Linguist's View
  HARRY H. JOSSELSON
Classification, Relevance, and Information Retrieval
  D. M. JACKSON
Approaches to the Machine Recognition of Conversational Speech
  KLAUS W. OTTEN
Man-Machine Interaction Using Speech
  DAVID R. HILL
Balanced Magnetic Circuits for Logic and Memory Devices
  R. B. KIEBURTZ AND E. E. NEWHALL
Command and Control: Technology and Social Impact
  ANTHONY DEBONS

Volume 12

Information Security in a Multi-User Computer Environment
  JAMES P. ANDERSON
Managers, Deterministic Models, and Computers
  G. M. FERRERO DIROCCAFERRERA
Uses of the Computer in Music Composition and Research
  HARRY B. LINCOLN
File Organization Techniques
  DAVID C. ROBERTS
Systems Programming Languages
  R. D. BERGERON, J. D. GANNON, D. P. SHECTER, F. W. TOMPA, AND A. VAN DAM
Parametric and Nonparametric Recognition by Computer: An Application to Leukocyte Image Processing
  JUDITH M. S. PREWITT

Volume 13

Programmed Control of Asynchronous Program Interrupts
  RICHARD L. WEXELBLAT
Poetry Generation and Analysis
  JAMES JOYCE
Mapping and Computers
  PATRICIA FULTON
Practical Natural Language Processing: The REL System as Prototype
  FREDERICK B. THOMPSON AND BOZENA HENISZ THOMPSON
Artificial Intelligence—The Past Decade
  B. CHANDRASEKARAN

Volume 14

On the Structure of Feasible Computations
   J. HARTMANIS AND J. SIMON
A Look at Programming and Programming Systems
   T. E. CHEATHAM, JR., AND JUDY A. TOWNELY
Parsing of General Context-Free Languages
   SUSAN L. GRAHAM AND MICHAEL A. HARRISON
Statistical Processors
   W. J. POPPELBAUM
Information Secure Systems
   DAVID K. HSIAO AND RICHARD I. BAUM

QA
76
A3
v.15

NOV 24 1976